*Green criminologists from all over the world have contributed to an outstanding piece of work that raises awareness of the importance of reducing environmental harm. In addition to scholars and students, the book should be read closely by policy makers who set priorities in the sustainable development of the world.*

Gorazd Meško, Professor of Criminology, Faculty of Criminal Justice and Security, University of Maribor, Slovenia.

*Rather than a specialist branch of what was once described as the 'infelicitous science', green criminology seems to gather the most felicitous moments in the history of the discipline: a focus on conducts that are harmful but are not regarded as criminal, the identification of powerful offenders, attention to interactions, including those between us and non-human animals. This book proves that criminology has still a tremendous repository of imagination to draw from.*

Vincenzo Ruggiero, Professor of Sociology, Middlesex University, London

Greening Criminology in the 21st Century *is a splendid addition to the rapidly expanding literature on green criminology. Its cutting-edge chapters are uniformly well-written and a pleasure to read. For green scholars and activists this book is a must read.*

Piers Beirne, Professor of Criminology and Legal Studies, University of Southern Maine.

# Greening Criminology in the 21st Century

In the 21st century, environmental harm is an ever-present reality of our globalised world. Over the last 20 years, criminologists, working alongside a range of other disciplines from the social and physical sciences, have made great strides in their understanding of how different institutions in society – and criminal justice systems in particular – respond – or fail to respond – to the harm imposed on ecosystems and their human and non-human components. Such research has crystallised into the rapidly evolving field of green criminology. This pioneering volume, with contributions from leading experts along with young scholars, represents the state of the art in criminologists' pursuit of understanding in the environmental sphere while at the same time challenging academics, lawmakers and policy developers to explore new directions in the study of environmental harm.

**Matthew Hall** graduated with a PhD from the University of Sheffield in 2007, having previously graduated from Sheffield's MA in International Criminology programme. He became a Lecturer in Law and Criminal Justice in 2008 and a Senior Lecturer in 2011, both at the University of Sheffield School of Law. In 2014, Matthew was appointed Professor of Law and Criminal Justice and Director of Research at the University of Lincoln School of Law. He has been interviewed on behalf of the European Commission as an expert contributor in the field of victimology to assist the development of a new directive on victims' rights and has also advised the South African Department of Justice and Constitutional Development concerning a review of South Africa's Victim Empowerment Scheme. More recently, Matthew has pioneered research on environmental victimisation and the application of environmental justice principles in the criminal justice system at the national and international levels.

**Jennifer Maher** is a Senior Lecturer at the Centre for Criminology at the University of South Wales. She completed her PhD in Criminology at the University of Glamorgan in 2007. She is currently involved in a FP7 (European Commission) project which is focused on the impact of environmental crime in Europe. She is specifically looking at the illegal trade in wildlife. Jennifer has previously undertaken funded projects which have looked at animal abuse and status dogs. She has published internationally in peer-reviewed journals and has co-edited a special journal issue on animal abuse in *Crime, Law and Social Change*. In July 2013, she hosted the third ESRC-funded seminar on wildlife crime and animal abuse.

**Angus Nurse** graduated from Birmingham City University in 2009 with a PhD in Wildlife Crime and the Enforcement of Wildlife, having previously completed his MSc in Criminal

Justice Studies at the University of Leicester. He is currently Associate Professor in Environmental Justice at Middlesex University's School of Law, where he teaches and researches criminology and law with research specialisms in environmental crime; animal law and its enforcement; alternative dispute resolution (particularly ombudsmans' schemes); and human rights and access to justice. He was a Lecturer in Criminology and Criminal Investigation at Birmingham City University from October 2011 to May 2013 and was a Research Fellow at the University of Lincoln's Law School from January 2008 to October 2011, researching civil justice systems, criminal justice and human rights. Prior to this, Angus was an Investigator for the Commission for Local Administration for England (the Local Government Ombudsman) from February 2000 to January 2008 and worked in the Investigations Section and Legal Compliance units at the Royal Society for the Protection of Birds from 1990 to 2000.

**Gary Potter** received his PhD from the University of Sheffield in 2007, where he also completed an MA in International Criminology (2001) and a BA in Law and Criminology (1999). He is currently a Senior Lecturer in Criminology at Lancaster University Law School. As well as researching and publishing in the field of green criminology, he writes about drug markets and cannabis cultivation. His recent books include *Weed, Need and Greed: A Study of Domestic Cannabis Cultivation* (2010, Free Association Books) and the edited collections *Change and Continuity: Researching Evolving Drug Landscapes in Europe* (2014, Pabst) and *Wide Weed: Global Trends in Cannabis Cultivation and Its Control* (2011, Ashgate, co-edited with Tom Decorte and Martin Bouchard). He hosted the two-day Green Criminology Conference in July 2014, which marked the culmination of the ESRC-funded seminar series at which the chapters in this book were initially presented.

**Nigel South** is a Professor in the Department of Sociology and Director of the Centre for Criminology, the Human Rights Centre, and the Essex Sustainability Institute at the University of Essex, England. He is a visiting Adjunct Professor in the School of Justice at Queensland University of Technology, Brisbane; a Fellow of the Academy of Social Sciences; a Fellow of the Royal Society of Arts, London; and in 2013, he received a Lifetime Achievement Award from the American Society of Criminology's Division on Critical Criminology. He has published widely on green criminology, drug use, health and crime, inequalities and citizenship, and theoretical and comparative criminology and currently serves as the European Editor for *Critical Criminology* and on the Editorial Boards of *Deviant Behavior* and the *International Journal for Crime, Justice and Social Democracy*. With Avi Brisman, he is co-editor of the *Routledge International Handbook of Green Criminology* (2013) and co-author of *Green Cultural Criminology: Constructions of Environmental Harm, Consumerism and Resistance to Ecocide* (2014).

**Tanya Wyatt** completed her PhD in Criminology at the University of Kent in 2009 after having worked as a law enforcement officer in the United States for nearly five years and finishing her MA in Criminology at Eastern Michigan University. She joined Northumbria University in 2010 and is now a Reader in Criminology. Tanya was the Principal Investigator on the ESRC Green Criminology Research Seminar Series at which the chapters in this collection were presented.

**Green Criminology**

Series Editors:

Michael J. Lynch
*University of South Florida, USA*

Paul B. Stretesky
*University of Northumbria, UK*

Now two decades old, green criminology – the study of environmental harm, crime, law, regulation, victimization, and justice – has increasing relevance to contemporary problems at local, national and international levels. This series comes at a time when societies and governments worldwide seek new ways to alleviate and deal with the consequences of various environmental harms as they relate to humans, non-human animals, plant species, and the ecosystem and its components. Green criminology offers a unique theoretical perspective on how human behavior causes and exacerbates environmental conditions that threaten the planet's viability. Volumes in the series consider such topics and controversies as corporate environmental crime, the complicity of international financial institutions, state-sponsored environmental destruction, and the role of non-governmental organizations in addressing environmental harms. Titles also examine the intersections among green criminology, other branches of criminology, and other areas of law, such as human rights and national security. The series is international in scope, investigating environmental crime in specific countries as well as comparatively and globally. In sum, by bringing together a diverse body of research on all aspects of this subject, the series makes a significant contribution to our understanding of the dynamics between the natural world and the quite imperfect human world and sets the stage for future study in this growing area of concern.

Titles in the series include:

**Governance of the Illegal Trade in E-Waste and Tropical Timber**
Case studies on transnational environmental crime
*Lieselot Bisschop*

**Environmental Crime and Social Conflict**
Contemporary and emerging issues
*Edited by Avi Brisman, Nigel South and Rob White*

**Environmental Crime and Its Victims**
Perspectives within Green criminology
*Edited by Toine Spapens, Rob White and Marieke Kluin*

# Greening Criminology in the 21st Century

## Contemporary Debates and Future Directions in the Study of Environmental Harm

**Edited by**
**Matthew Hall, Jennifer Maher, Angus Nurse, Gary Potter, Nigel South, Tanya Wyatt**

Routledge
Taylor & Francis Group
LONDON AND NEW YORK

First published 2017
by Routledge
2 Park Square, Milton Park, Abingdon, Oxfordshire OX14 4RN
711 Third Avenue, New York, NY 10017

*Routledge is an imprint of the Taylor & Francis Group, an informa business*

First issued in paperback 2018



*British Library Cataloguing in Publication Data*
A catalogue record for this book is available from the British Library

*Library of Congress Cataloging in Publication Data*
Names: Hall, Matthew (Criminologist), editor.
Title: Greening criminology in the 21st century : contemporary debates and future directions in the study of environmental harm / [edited by] Matthew Hall, Jennifer Maher, Angus Nurse, Gary Potter, Nigel South and Tanya Wyatt.
Description: Abingdon, Oxon ; New York, NY : Routledge, 2017.
Identifiers: LCCN 2016022815 | ISBN 9781472467560 (hardback) | ISBN 9781317124511 (adobe reader) | ISBN 9781317124504 (epub) | ISBN 9781317124498 (mobipocket)
Subjects: LCSH: Offenses against the environment. | Criminology—Environmental aspects.
Classification: LCC HV6401 .G746 2017 | DDC 364.1/45—dc23
LC record available at https://lccn.loc.gov/2016022815

ISBN: 978-1-4724-6756-0 (hbk)
ISBN: 978-0-367-02405-5 (pbk)

Typeset in Galliard
by Apex CoVantage, LLC

# Contents

# Notes on contributors

**Julie Ayling** is a Research Fellow at the Regulatory Institutions Network of the Australian National University College of Asia and the Pacific, Australia.

**Kimberly L. Barrett** is an Assistant Professor in the Sociology, Anthropology & Criminology Department of Eastern Michigan University, Ypsilanti, MI, USA.

**Avi Brisman** is an Associate Professor in the School of Justice Studies at Eastern Kentucky University, Richmond, KY, USA.

**Joseph F. Donnermeyer** is Professor Emeritus of the School of Environmental and Social Resources at The Ohio State University, Columbus, OH, USA.

**Matthew Hall** graduated with a PhD from the University of Sheffield in 2007, having previously graduated from Sheffield's MA in International Criminology programme. He became a Lecturer in Law and Criminal Justice in 2008 and a Senior Lecturer in 2011, both at the University of Sheffield School of Law. In 2014, Matthew was appointed Professor of Law and Criminal Justice and Director of Research at the University of Lincoln School of Law. He has been interviewed on behalf of the European Commission as an expert contributor in the field of victimology to assist the development of a new directive on victims' rights and has also advised the South African Department of Justice and Constitutional Development concerning a review of South Africa's Victim Empowerment Scheme. More recently, Matthew has pioneered research on environmental victimisation and the application of environmental justice principles in the criminal justice system at the national and international levels.

**Hope Johnson** is a PhD Candidate at Queensland University of Technology, Australia.

**Michael A. Long** is a Senior Lecturer of Social Sciences in the Department of Social Sciences and Languages at Northumbria University, UK.

**Michael J. Lynch** is a Professor of Criminology in the School of Global Sustainability at the University of South Florida, Tampa, FL, USA.

**Jennifer Maher** is a Senior Lecturer at the Centre for Criminology at the University of South Wales. She completed her PhD in Criminology at the University of Glamorgan in 2007. She is currently involved in a FP7 (European Commission) project which is focused on the impact of environmental crime in Europe. She is specifically looking at the illegal trade in wildlife. Jennifer has previously undertaken funded projects which have looked at animal abuse and status dogs. She has published internationally in peer-reviewed journals and has co-edited a special journal issue on animal abuse in *Crime, Law* *and Social Change*. In July 2013, she hosted the third ESRC-funded seminar on wildlife crime and animal abuse.

**Angus Nurse** graduated from Birmingham City University in 2009 with a PhD in Wildlife Crime and the Enforcement of Wildlife, having previously completed his MSc in Criminal Justice Studies at the University of Leicester. He is currently Associate Professor in Environmental Justice at Middlesex University's School of Law, where he teaches and researches criminology and law with research specialisms in environmental crime; animal law and its enforcement; alternative dispute resolution (particularly ombudsmans' schemes); and human rights and access to justice. He was a Lecturer in Criminology and Criminal Investigation at Birmingham City University from October 2011 to May 2013 and was a Research Fellow at the University of Lincoln's Law School from January 2008 to October 2011, researching civil justice systems, criminal justice and human rights. Prior to this, Angus was an Investigator for the Commission for Local Administration for England (the Local Government Ombudsman) from February 2000 to January 2008 and worked in the Investigations Section and Legal Compliance units at the Royal Society for the Protection of Birds from 1990 to 2000.

**Tara O'Connor Shelley** is an Associate Professor and Director of the Criminal Justice Leadership and Public Policy Institute in the School of Criminology and Criminal Justice and Strategic Studies at Tarleton State University. Dr. Shelley received her PhD in Criminology and Criminal Justice from Florida State University and her MS in Justice, Law and Society from American University.

**Tara Opsal** is an Assistant Professor of Sociology in the Department of Sociology at Colorado State University, Fort Collins, CO, USA.

**Grant Pink** is an Adjunct Research Fellow in the School of Law at the University of New England, Australia.

**Gary Potter** received his PhD from the University of Sheffield in 2007, where he also completed the MA in International Criminology (2001) and a BA in Law and Criminology (1999). He is currently a Senior Lecturer in Criminology at Lancaster University Law School. As well as researching and publishing in the field of green criminology, he writes about drug markets and cannabis cultivation. His recent books include *Weed, Need and Greed: A Study of Domestic Cannabis Cultivation* (2010, Free Association Books) and the edited collections *Change and Continuity: Researching Evolving Drug Landscapes in Europe* (2014, Pabst) and *Wide Weed: Global Trends in Cannabis Cultivation and Its Control* (2011, Ashgate, co-edited with Tom Decorte and Martin Bouchard). He hosted the two-day Green Criminology Conference in July 2014, which marked the culmination of the ESRC-funded seminar series at which the chapters in this book were initially presented.

**Malayna Raftopoulos** is an Assistant Professor in Latin American Studies at Aalborg University, Denmark.

**Damien Short** is a Reader in the School of Advanced Study at the University of London, UK.

**Ragnhild Sollund** is a Professor in the Department of Criminology and Sociology of Law at the University of Oslo, Norway.

**Nigel South** is a Professor in the Department of Sociology and Director of the Centre for Criminology, the Human Rights Centre, and the Essex Sustainability Institute at the University of Essex, England. He is a visiting Adjunct Professor in the School of Justice at Queensland University of Technology, Brisbane; a Fellow of the Academy of Social Sciences; a Fellow of the Royal Society of Arts, London; and in 2013, he received a Lifetime Achievement Award from the American Society of Criminology's Division on Critical Criminology. He has published widely on green criminology, drug use, health and crime, inequalities and citizenship, and theoretical and comparative criminology and currently serves as the European Editor for *Critical Criminology* and on the editorial boards of *Deviant Behavior* and the *International Journal for Crime, Justice and Social Democracy*. With Avi Brisman, he is co-editor of the *Routledge International Handbook of Green Criminology* (2013) and co-author of *Green Cultural Criminology: Constructions of Environmental Harm, Consumerism and Resistance to Ecocide* (2014).

**Reece Walters** is a Professor in the School of Justice at Queensland University of Technology, Australia.

**Rob White** is a Professor of Criminology at the University of Tasmania, Australia.

**Dominic A. Wood** is Head of the School of Law, Criminal Justice and Computing at Canterbury Christ Church University, UK.

**Tanya Wyatt** completed her PhD in Criminology at the University of Kent in 2009 after having worked as a law enforcement officer in the United States for nearly five years and finishing her MA in Criminology at Eastern Michigan University. She joined Northumbria University in 2010 and is now a Reader in Criminology. Tanya was the Principal Investigator on the ESRC Green Criminology Research Seminar Series at which the chapters in this collection were presented.

# Introduction

## Green criminology in the 21st century

*Matthew Hall, Jennifer Maher, Angus Nurse, Gary Potter, Nigel South and Tanya Wyatt*

The term 'green criminology' was first introduced by Lynch in 1990, although the history of criminologists concerning themselves with specific environmental and animal-related crimes goes back further than this. For example, Pecar (1981) put forward an even earlier statement about new, environmentally damaging forms of criminality in Slovenia and the role of criminology and sciences related to this (Eman et al., 2009: 584), but with no English-language translation, Pecar's article made no international impact. Furthermore, although Lynch set out the scope and aims of a green criminology in a way that can still stand as a 'manifesto' statement, the article's place of publication meant that it did not reach a wide audience at the time (although once 'rediscovered', it proved to be highly influential). Potter (2013) has reviewed arguments that might be put in order to 'justify' a green criminology, and this is a useful exercise. But in an important sense, a green criminology is justified because it was inevitable and necessary. It reflected scientific interests and political challenges of the moment, carried forward the momentum of critical non-conformist criminology, and offered a point of contact and convergence. So, no particular contribution was required as the 'first' or 'unique' catalyst for the development of a green or eco-criminology, for this was already under way in many places, for similar reasons, with teachers, researchers and writers expressing parallel concerns and proposing a similar project for criminology (see, for example, Clifford, 1998; Edwards et al., 1996; Halsey and White, 1998; Koser Wilson, 1999; Lynch and Stretesky, 2001, 2003; Pecar, 1981; Sollund, 2008; South, 1998; Walters, 2004, 2006; White, 2008).

Nevertheless, until very recently, such issues were not generally considered to be within the remit of mainstream criminology, and what green criminological work there was tended towards the piecemeal publication of papers by some dedicated researchers, along with the odd special edition or edited collection, the occasional panel at generalist criminological conferences, and a few specialist under- and post-graduate courses taught at a select few institutions in Europe and the United States. But as environmental problems have become more pressing for – and more widely acknowledged by – society at large, so green criminology has become more firmly established: with the criminal law increasingly used to regulate environmentally harmful activities, so a mainstream, administrative criminology has had to acknowledge such crimes as within its remit, while an extra-legal, harm-based perspective on the environment fits firmly within the traditions of critical and radical criminologies (see, for example, Potter, 2014) and, more recently, the burgeoning field of cultural criminology (Brisman and South, 2014). It is clear that criminology, whether widely or narrowly defined, both can and should provide insightful analysis to the environmental challenges facing the world today.

We are pleased to recognise that this is happening. While there is still a long way to go before environmental crimes are as firmly embedded within the parent discipline as, say, corporate or state crimes (both of which were also initially dismissed by the criminological establishment as being beyond the remit of criminology; see Katz, 2010), green criminology has firmly come of age. There are, of course, other important terminologies and approaches to the same issues and problems. 'Conservation criminology' (Gibbs et al., 2010) aims to support evidence-based practice in addressing environmental crimes and risks, integrating criminology, criminal justice, environmental and species conservation, natural resource management, and risk and decision science. Walters (2010) suggests that the term 'eco-crime' could encapsulate 'existing legal definitions of environmental crime, as well as sociological analyses of those environmental harms not necessarily specified by law' (308), while White (2010: 6) proposes an 'eco-global criminology . . . informed by ecological considerations and by a critical analysis that is worldwide in its scale and perspective . . . that expresses a concern that there be an inclusive definition of harm' – a criminology that is multi-disciplinary. Finally, and most obviously, the term 'environmental criminology' might be used, and White (2008) has argued that the name should be reclaimed from what is more properly considered 'place-based criminology'. This would reflect the way that the word 'environment' is employed in everyday discussion and contemporary media but suffers the drawback of possible confusion with its longer established usage to describe relationships between the incidence of crime and the spatial features of the built and urban environment.

More and more universities feature green criminology within their degree programmes, and an increasing number of general criminology textbooks include chapters or sections on environmental crime. Large conferences such as those held by the American, European and British societies of criminology now have green criminology strands, as standard and dedicated green criminology conferences and seminars now feature regularly on the academic calendar, attracting delegates from around the world. Indeed, the genesis of this book was the Green Criminology Conference held at London South Bank University in July 2014, which represented the culmination of an Economic and Social Research Council (ESRC)–funded seminar series held at institutions throughout the UK in 2013 and 2014. The editors would like to express their sincere thanks to the ESRC for its funding of this endeavour.

More significantly (and essential in enabling the aforementioned developments), research and publication in green criminology, environmental crime and conservation criminology have boomed in the last ten years, with a number of specialist books (including two current dedicated green criminology book series from Palgrave and Ashgate) and countless papers focusing on substantive topics as diverse as deforestation, animal poaching and the illegal trade in wildlife, toxic emissions, and waste disposal. In the body of work as a whole, green criminologists have sought not only to document a wide variety of specific incidences of environmental crime but also to begin to generalise – to analyse environmental harm as a whole. Further, scholarly work in this area has gone some way to establish a theoretical base for green criminology that had previously been acknowledged in its absence (South, 1998). Work from Stretesky and colleagues (2014) on the 'treadmill of production' has sought to demonstrate how the workings of modern capitalism are essentially environmentally harmful – even ecocidal; work by Agnew (2013) has sought to explain everyday environmental harm in terms of established criminological theory and also to argue that environmental harm is essentially criminogenic – not just in the sense that environmental harm can be seen as crime but also as a cause of (more everyday concepts of) crime (see also Hall and Farrell, 2012; Potter, 2014).

In addition to substantive and theoretical developments, we have also seen rapid and significant advances in methodological approaches to developing (a) green criminology. In most circumstances, arguments are strengthened by evidence, and green criminologists have employed a range of methods and orientations appropriate to the gathering of empirical data, including the use of surveys, observation, experiments (although this is uncommon) and existing sources (Brisman and South, in press; White and Heckenberg, 2014). Lynch and Stretesky (2014) have argued that by 'drawing on the scientific knowledge base of green sciences' (68) – i.e. natural sciences concerned with environmental matters – it is possible to improve the examination of green crime and justice issues, and this is 'important because it illustrates the extent to which green criminology can be linked to scientific values and principles' (68). Of course, not all questions and issues lend themselves to scientific research design, and in cases where environmental crimes or harms are hidden, the research task may require ethnographic and qualitative methods, although here, too, challenges arise with the tasks of interpretation, analysis and representation. Immersion in any research field brings numerous well-known methodological and ethical dilemmas, and the green field of research is no different – indeed, because of the diverse interests and conflicting views involved, it can be a particularly sensitive area to work in. For example, ethical questions and hence methodological problems might arise when research is designed to support the needs of one group (whether human or non-human) but has negative implications for another group or species. As Hall (this volume) remarks, 'the "correct" methods to use in different situations for green criminology may reflect the principles of pragmatism' (33), and it is interesting to note that although green criminology is still a new and developing area, this point is also recognised in wider criminological discussion.

It is against this background of history, conceptualisation and method with regard to green criminology that we present the current collection – primarily consisting of papers from the aforementioned conference held in London in 2014. These contributions represent a diverse range of issues which serve to illustrate the wide scope and shifting contours of the green criminological project; for the purposes of this volume, these have been split into three broad parts.

In Part I of this volume, we present discussions of the nature and scope of green criminology as it presently stands. In the opening chapter, Rob White discusses how business and government responses continue to sustain rather than address ecocide ('extensive damage, destruction to or loss of ecosystems of a given territory' [11]) in the context of a dominant neo-liberal ideology which commodifies nature as opposed to protecting it. As the author surmises,

> the reason why we are not addressing the ecocide stemming from climate change – even though it is to the advantage of all that we work together in our common interest – is that specific class interests intrude upon the process whereby planetary well-being might be prioritised.
>
> (this volume: 22)

White argues that much environmental degradation occurs with the consent of those who benefit in the short term (but will inevitably suffer in the longer term) and calls for a significant change in social attitudes, requiring multiple actions across multiple domains if governments are to be prompted to act.

Matthew Hall's chapter focuses on methodological questions in green criminology. Ultimately he concludes that there is a real case for the utilisation of both positivist and interpretist perspectives in the area, even though, as a matter of methodological theory, they are grounded in very different epistemological and ontological positions. Nevertheless, Hall argues that traditional research strategies associated with criminology (whether qualitative or quantitative) are arguably not well suited to gathering information about non-human impacts and effects, or even to linking such effects back to human suffering. As such, it is submitted that green criminologists are better off acknowledging their 'green' or 'eco-centric' credentials from the outset, building these into a reflexive and robust research exercise which genuinely reflects that perspective. This, Hall argues, is the real contribution a *green* criminology can make over and above more traditional 'criminologies of the environment' (27).

In his chapter, Dominic A. Wood discusses the extent to which the individual has a place within a green criminology, arguing that the individual has always enjoyed a privileged place within other liberally framed criminal justice contexts. Nevertheless, for Wood, ecological discourse challenges the logic of liberal individualism by extending, expanding and broadening the scope of the various considerations that establish liberal judicial norms. In so doing, the significance and importance of the individual are undermined the more we take seriously the consideration of non-human species, ecosystems, the rights of indigenous and traditional human societies, and future generations. The solution, Wood argues, is to focus on the concept of the individual. In short, this allows us to develop a framework through which it is possible to overcome the need to sacrifice either human or environmental well-being by emphasising the *interconnectedness* of human and ecological concerns rather than seeking to prioritise one or the other.

In her chapter, Julie Ayling discusses the challenges of responding to transnational environmental crime in an effort to broaden the dialogue beyond the traditional policing context, arguing that this 'is an area crying out for lateral thinking about how to deal with the dire problem of conduct that is causing environmental degradation, habitat destruction, and species extinction on a life-threatening scale' (64). The author highlights the challenges posed by transnational environmental crime (TEC), including the existence of adaptive and resilient criminal networks along with the profitability and – indeed – growing demand for TEC products. These challenges call for what she calls 'meta-smart regulatory networks' to plan, guide and build capacity for innovative regulation to take place at local levels.

Part II of this volume turns to a number of case studies of specific examples of environmental harms addressed by researchers within the field. Ragnhild Sollund explores the victimization of non-human animals through a case study of illegal predator theriocides in Norway (wolves, bears, lynxes and wolverines). Core to her argument is that state sanctioning and licensing of legally organised hunts and culls of such animals by the state serve to legitimate illegal predator theriocides. In addition, Sollund argues, when illegal killings are prosecuted, penalties are often very lenient. For the author, this reflects the continued 'othering' of non-human animals within Norway and a 'failure to recognise that non-human animals are our fellow beings, rather than the ultimate other, merely objects or nature, and as our fellow beings they should be entitled to compassion and concern rather than alienation and disregard' (95).

In their chapter, Tara O'Connor Shelley and Tara Opsal offer another analysis of environmental victimization concerning experiences with harm that have resulted from energy development and extraction in the state of Colorado in the United States. The study documents a wide range of concerns, revealing that this type of environmental victimization is complex as well as contextual. Energy-related harms were not isolated and one-time occurrences; rather, they tend to be persistent and patterned. In addition, many of the problems uncovered represent 'quality of life' concerns which to the specific victims were seen as quite harmful. Respondents often reported significant stress, anxiety, depression and economic loss from repeated instances of surface damage to their property followed by tense (sometimes hostile) interactions with the industry as they sought relief for such damages. The authors further point to the probable existence of a significant 'dark figure' of energy crime and harm.

In the following chapter, Angus Nurse offers an assessment of the use by non-governmental organizations (NGOs) of 'extreme' activism and allegedly illegal means to pursue a legitimate environmental protection goal. Through a green criminological examination of a recent US case involving the Sea Shepherd Conservation Society and the ongoing debate about the legitimacy of Japanese whaling, the chapter examines how branding activists as eco-terrorists arguably undermines their legitimacy and marginalises social acceptance of their cause. It also examines the justifications for extreme actions, such as the alleged use of violence and the extent to which such actions may not achieve NGO or activist objectives.

In Chapter 8, Hope Johnson, Nigel South and Reece Walters examine the unsustainable and exploitative use of water as an eco-crime. In particular, the authors focus on the commodification and privatisation of water by global business interests. They go further to argue that this has 'enabled corporate monopolies and corrupt states to exploit a fundamental human right [to water] and has created new forms of criminality' (133). Addressing this worrying trend, it is argued, will involve working towards legal and governance frameworks that acknowledge water as a public good – that is, as part of the commons. This would involve user self-governance approaches that are informed by the human right to water.

In his chapter, Joseph F. Donnermeyer examines the often-overlooked issue of crimes and harms committed by those who grow food and raise livestock. The author reviews a wide variety of literature linking farming to offending of various kinds. This includes entrepreneurial offending associated with the farming activity itself as well the prevalence of child abuse, domestic violence, animal abuse and human trafficking amongst farmers. The author explores the extent to which such criminogenic tendencies can be associated with 'the farming lifestyle' and the normative and social structures of rural and remote communities. In addition, the author examines how the normative and social structures of rural and remote communities may well create a social-psychological climate of support for farmers who engage in illegal behaviours, especially those related to violation of wildlife and environmental rules.

In Part III, this volume moves on to discussions detailing the wider agenda and future directions for a green criminology. Here, Malayna Raftopoulos and Damien Short discuss the prospects for Human Rights Impact Assessments as an alternative to standard environmental impact assessment models. They focus on the example of the REDD+ framework from the United Nations (UN) that sets out to create a system that provides forest users with economic incentives to reduce net emissions of greenhouse gases through enhanced forest management and improved forest carbon stocks. The authors note how in recent years REDD+ has taken centre stage in international climate change discussions. How REDD+ works in practice is proving to be highly controversial, raising complex and emotive issues of national sovereignty, human rights and corruption. With the world's tropical forests home to some of the poorest and most politically marginalised communities in the world, their management not only has economic and environmental consequences but also has considerable social implications. Therefore, the authors argue, policies such as REDD+ will have profound consequences for the rights and welfare of indigenous peoples and forest dwellers whose livelihoods, culture and way of life rely on forests. In particular, concerns have been raised regarding the possible harmful impacts of the REDD+ initiative's activities at a local level on the protection and promotion of indigenous and forest peoples' human rights and the initiative's potential to act as a form of neo-colonialism, further transferring forest resources out of the hands of forest communities.

In Grant Pink's chapter, the author examines the important role that regulatory professionals play in the effective implementation and enforcement of environmental law. Key to his findings is the observation that, increasingly, public servants in environmental regulatory agencies are being obliged to work alongside more highly trained mainstream law enforcement agencies such as police agencies and customs and border agencies. In particular, this has required such agencies to adopt far more adversarial procedures than they are used to. Pink calls for further training amongst public servants to adequately address this new reality in the environmental regulatory sphere.

In Chapter 12, Michael J. Lynch, Michael A. Long, Kimberly L. Barrett and Paul B. Stretesky discuss how secondary ecological disorganisation results from wildlife harms. They argue that the secondary ecological harms caused by wildlife destruction have received relatively little attention, even from green criminologists. Drawing on a number of case studies, the authors demonstrate how species richness impacts ecosystem viability and illustrate that wildlife harm can have detrimental secondary ecological impacts. For the authors, species richness or its absence is itself a function of damage to wildlife promoted by the continual expansion of global capitalism and the ecological disorganisation that capitalism produces through ecological additions (pollution) and ecological withdrawals (e.g. mining, deforestation, changing land use patterns, etc.).

In Chapter 13, Avi Brisman and Nigel South put forward a proposal for a *green cultural criminology*, which brings together green criminology and cultural criminology, and identify points of overlap. In particular, the authors draw on work by Hayward (1998) to argue that the erosion of 'life stages' and their replacement by a 'generational mulch', which conflates adolescence and adulthood, render our present culture less able to take responsibility for intergenerational equity and environmental sustainability. As a result, they argue, all generations – now and in the future – may suffer, largely because the present generation feels unable to threaten economic growth by taking the necessary steps to curb environmental harm.

What is clear from this collection is that green criminology has matured into a healthy and vibrant field over the last 25 years. It is an area in which the exact contours and limits of study are still being debated and defined, which we argue is much to its benefit. That said, a number of pervasive themes are emerging. These include analysis of the circumstances, predicates and social/political context of environmental crimes, and broader environmental harms (including the handling of natural disasters and other risks). Green criminologists are also clearly concerned with the impacts of such harms on human and animal life and on the environment itself, as well as the level of social, political and legal censures attributed to these harms. It is also clear that *regulatory* measures are as significant in green criminology as formal criminal justice per se, as well as mechanisms of restitution and redress in the wake of environmentally destructive activities and omissions. Judging by the extent to which this volume has prompted still further areas of inquiry – whether these are along cultural lines, the othering of non-human animals or methodological innovations in the field – it is clear that green criminology can only grow in importance and reach as environmental harm becomes an ever more pressing issue in the social, legal and scientific fields.

## References

Agnew, R. (2013) 'The ordinary acts that contribute to ecocide: A criminological analysis'. In N. South and A. Brisman (eds.) *The Routledge International Handbook of Green Criminology*, Abingdon, England: Routledge, pp. 58–72.

Brisman, A. and South, N. (2014) *Green Cultural Criminology: Constructions of Environmental Harm, Consumerism, and Resistance to Ecocide*, London: Routledge.

Brisman, A. and South, N. (in press) 'Methodological approaches and ethical challenges in green criminology'. In M. Cowburn, L. Gelsthorpe and A. Wahidin (eds.) *Research Ethics in Criminology and Criminal Justice: Dilemmas, Problems and Issues*, London: Routledge.

Clifford, M. (1998) *Environmental Crime: Enforcement, Policy, and Social Responsibility*, London: Jones & Bartlett Learning International.

Edwards, S., Edwards, T. and Fields, C. (eds.) (1996) *Environmental Crime and Criminality: Theoretical and Practical Issues*, New York: Garland.

Eman, K., Meško, G. and Fields, G. (2009) 'Crime against the environment: Green criminology and research challenges in Slovenia', *VARSTVOSLOVJE, Journal of Criminal Justice and Social Change*, **59**(3): 341–358.

Gibbs, C., Gore, M. and Rivers, L. (2010) 'Introducing conservation criminology: Towards interdisciplinary scholarship on environmental crimes and risks', *British Journal of Criminology*, **50**(1): 124–144.

Hall, M. and Farrell, S. (2012) 'The criminogenic consequences of climate change: Blurring the boundaries between offenders and victims'. In N. South and A. Brisman (eds.) *The Routledge International Handbook of Green Criminology*, Abingdon, England: Routledge, pp. 26–58.

Halsey, M. and White, R. (1998) 'Crime, ecophilosophy and environmental harm', *Theoretical Criminology*, **2**(3): 345–372.

Hayward, T. (1998) *Political Theory and Ecological Values*, Cambridge: Polity Press.

Katz, R. (2010) 'The corporate crimes of Dow Chemical and the failure to regulate environmental pollution', *Critical Criminology*, **18**: 295–306.

Lynch, M. and Stretesky, P. (2001) 'Toxic crimes: Examining corporate victimization of the general public employing medical and epidemiological evidence', *Critical Criminology*, **10**: 153–172.

Lynch, M. and Stretesky, P. (2003) 'The meaning of green: Towards a clarification of the term green and its meaning for the development of a green criminology', *Theoretical Criminology*, 7: 217–238.

Lynch, M. and Stretesky, P. (2014) *Exploring Green Criminology: Toward a Green Criminological Approach*, Farnham, England: Ashgate.

Pecar, J. (1981) 'Ekoloska kriminalitera in kriminologija', *Revija za kriminologijo in kriminologijo*, **34**(1): 33–45.

Potter, G. (2013) 'Justifying "green" criminology: Values and "taking sides" in an ecologically informed social science'. In M. Cowburn, M. Duggan, A. Robinson and P. Senior (eds.) *The Value(s) of Criminology and Criminal Justice*, London: Policy Press, pp. 125–142.

Potter, G. (2014) 'The criminogenic effects of environmental harm: Bringing a "green" perspective to mainstream criminology'. In T. Spapens, R. White and M. Kluin (eds.) *Environmental Crime and Its Victims: Perspectives within Green Criminology*, Farnham, England: Ashgate, pp. 7–22.

Sollund, R. (2008) 'Causes for speciesism: Difference, distance and denial'. In R. Sollund (ed.) *Global Harms: Ecological Crime and Speciesism*, New York: Nova Science Publishers, pp. 109–131.

South, N. (1998) 'A green field for criminology: A proposal for a perspective', *Theoretical Criminology*, **2**(2): 211–233.

Stretesky, P., Long, M. and Lynch, M. (2014) *The Treadmill of Crime: Political Economy and Green Criminology*, Abingdon, England: Routledge.

Walters, R. (2004) 'Criminology and genetically modified food', *British Journal of Criminology*, **44**(2): 151–167.

Walters, R. (2006) 'Crime, bio-agriculture and the exploitation of hunger', *British Journal of Criminology*, **46**(1): 26–45.

Walters, R. (2010) 'Toxic atmospheres: Air pollution and the politics of regulation', *Critical Criminology*, **18**(4): 307–323.

White, R. (2008) *Crimes against Nature: Environmental Criminology and Ecological Justice*, Cullompton, England: Willan.

White, R. (2010) *Global Environmental Harm: Criminological Perspectives*, Cullompton, England: Willan.

White, R. and Heckenberg, D. (2014) *Green Criminology: An Introduction to the Study of Environmental Harm*, London: Routledge.

Wilson, N.K. (1999) 'Eco-critical criminology – An introduction', *Criminal Justice Policy Review*, **10**(2): 155–160.

# Part I

# Examining green criminology

# 1 Carbon economics and transnational resistance to ecocide

*Rob White*

## Introduction

The concept of 'ecocide' refers to extensive damage, destruction or loss of the ecosystems of a given territory and includes both natural (for example, pest infestation of an ecosystem) and anthropocentric (that is, as a result of human activity) causes for the harm. From a legal and criminological perspective, it is argued that if such harms occur as a result of human agency, then these acts or omissions should be defined as a crime against humanity (Higgins, 2010, 2012). The reason why detailed descriptions, definitions and histories of ecocide are once again emerging – and why the efficacy of the concept is currently being debated in various forums at the international level – is due to the sheer scale of environmental degradation now occurring worldwide. The concept of ecocide has been around since at least the 1970s (Gray, 1996; Teclaff, 1994) and for a time was under consideration for inclusion in the Rome Statute as a 'crime against humanity' (Higgins et al., 2013). But the impetus for ecocide to be officially recognised as a bona fide crime at the present time has been heightened by the current inadequacy of government responses, individually and collectively, to global warming.

Climate change is rapidly and radically altering the very basis of world ecology, yet until very recently little action has been taken by states or corporations to rein in the worst contributors to the problem. Carbon emissions are not decreasing, and 'dirty industries' such as coal and oil continue to flourish (although recent pronouncements by world leaders such as President Obama of the United States indicate that such industries have now been placed on notice to either change their methods or pay a premium for their continued pollution; see The White House, 2015). Meanwhile, the widespread destruction of natural amenities (such as forests, lakes, rivers, oceans, mountaintops and marshlands), systematic pollution of the environment (air, land and water), and rampant exploitation of plant and animal species (via destruction of habitats, illegal and legal trade, and the introduction and mass use of genetically modified organisms) are not only bad in their own right – destroying ecosystems and leading to species extinction – but also simultaneously contribute to present and looming climate chaos. This is ecocide on a planetary scale.

This chapter provides a critical examination of the causes of ecocide in the contemporary era, the reasons why business and government responses have sustained rather than addressed environmental calamity, and the need for counter-hegemonic challenges to the neo-liberal movement. It begins by outlining the varied ways in which ecocide is being accomplished, especially through global warming, and then explores the commodification of nature and the privileging of corporate interests, in large measure fostered by neo-liberal policies and practices. It then turns to the question of global solidarity and the pursuit of social and ecological justice and the need for a platform of transformative politics in a period demanding revolutionary change if ecocide is to be averted. Environmental harm requires urgent action, as the scale, pace and specific nature of the harm mean that everyone is affected by it, especially in the light of climate change. It is therefore vital that action be taken *now* to ensure that ecocide is robustly addressed. At the centre of our efforts must be the reduction of carbon emissions.

## Climate change, carbon and commodities

Climate change is the most important international issue facing humanity today. Global warming is transforming the bio-physical world in ways that are radically and rapidly reshaping social and ecological futures. The Intergovernmental Panel on Climate Change (IPCC) (2013) reports that:

- 'Warming of the climate system is unequivocal, and since the 1950s, many of the observed changes are unprecedented over decades to millennia. The atmosphere and ocean have warmed, the amounts of snow and ice have diminished, [the] sea level has risen, and the concentrations of greenhouse gases have increased' (4).
- 'Each of the last three decades has been successively warmer at the Earth's surface than any preceding decade since 1850' (5).
- 'Ocean warming dominates the increase in energy stored in the climate system, accounting for more than 90% of the energy accumulated between 1971 and 2010' (8).
- 'Over the last two decades, the Greenland and Antarctic ice sheets have been losing mass, glaciers have continued to shrink almost worldwide, and Arctic sea ice and Northern Hemisphere spring snow cover have continued to decrease in extent' (9).
- 'The rate of sea level rise since the mid-19th century has been larger than the mean rate during the previous two millennia' (11).

Climate change has been associated with the advent of varying types of natural disasters, which are projected to increase in intensity and frequency in the foreseeable future. These include such phenomena as floods, cyclones and extreme heat spells.

Bio-physical changes have been and will continue to be accompanied by various crime threats. But the destruction of the environment in ways that differentially, unequally and universally affect humans, ecosystems and non-human species can also be conceptualised criminologically as a specific type of crime – namely, ecocide. A key feature of this crime is that it occurs in the context of foreknowledge and intent. That is, ecocide arising from global warming, while marked by uncertainty in regards to specific rates and types of ecological change, is nonetheless founded upon generalised scientific knowledge that profound change is unavoidable unless carbon emissions – the key source of global warming – are not radically reduced *now*.

Ecocide describes an attempt to criminalise human activities that destroy and diminish the well-being and health of ecosystems and species within these, including humans. Climate change and the gross exploitation of natural resources are leading to the general demise of the ecological status quo – hence increasing the need for just such a crime. From an eco-justice perspective, ecocide involves transgressions that violate the principles and central constituent elements of environmental justice, ecological justice and species justice. At the core of the problem are carbon emissions. As pointed out by the IPCC (2013):

- 'The atmospheric concentrations of carbon dioxide, methane and nitrous oxide have increased to levels unprecedented in at least the last 800,000 years' (11).

- 'Carbon dioxide concentrations have increased by 40% since pre-industrial times, primarily from fossil fuel emissions and secondarily from net land use change emissions' (11).
- 'Continued emissions of greenhouse gases will cause further warming and changes in all components of the climate system. Limiting climate change will require substantial and sustained reductions of greenhouse gas emissions' (19).

If carbon emissions are at the forefront of the causes of global warming and subsequent climate chaos, then the obvious question is: why continue to emit such dangerous, planet-altering substances into the atmosphere? To explain this requires an understanding of the relationship between nature and commodification.

In the capitalist mode of production (which dominates on a world scale), goods and services are produced for exchange on the market. These goods and services are 'commodities' in that they are produced not for their immediate use value but for their exchange value (i.e. the monetary equivalent they fetch on the market). Although these commodities possess qualitatively distinct use values (e.g. shoes, sandwiches, sun cream), they also express quantitatively distinct exchange values (i.e. dollar value). As Marx (1954: 45) points out: 'As use-values, commodities are, above all, of different qualities, but as exchange-values they are merely different quantities.' What counts for business, therefore, is the exchange value of the commodity, for this is where the realisation of profit occurs.

Profit comes from the process of production itself. The total value of a commodity is made up of the expenditure of capital in the production of a good or service, plus a surplus value which is added. Labour power possesses the exceptional quality of being able to produce more value than is necessary to reproduce it. Simply stated, labour is the only thing in the production process which can be exploited (as distinct from machinery and raw materials, which constitute 'fixed' or constant capital). The total value of a commodity is greater than the elements which combine to produce it (i.e. constant capital and 'variable' capital as represented in the wages paid for the use of workers' labour power). The source of surplus value therefore lies in the surplus labour power which is expended by the worker, for which he or she is not paid. The product of this surplus labour ultimately translates into profit for the capitalist (Mandel, 1968; Onimode, 1985).

The sphere of production worldwide is dominated by the production of commodities, the advance of technology and bio-technologies, and the exploitation of labour in the service of mass production of goods and services that, in turn, demand a high turnover rate. Extensive and intensive forms of consumption are essential to the realisation of surplus value – that is, profit depends upon a critical mass of buyers purchasing the mass-produced commodities. Economic efficiency is measured by how quickly and cheaply commodities can be produced, channelled to markets and consumed. It is a process that is inherently exploitative of both humans and nature (Pepper, 1993) and that has a huge impact on the wider environment, humans and non-human animals (for example, in the form of pollution and toxicity levels in air, water and land). These same processes pose major threats to biodiversity and the shrinking of the number of plant and animal species generally.

Expansion of material consumption is built into the logic and dynamics of capitalism (Foster, 2002), a tendency that is reinforced and facilitated by neo-liberal ideologies and policies. Commodification refers to the transformation of use value into exchange value, as more and more aspects of social life and environment are commercialised and 'worth' is gauged by how much something, including basic necessities such as water, sells for on the commodity markets. The monopolisation of control over production (and thereby consumption) by corporate conglomerates has ensured that private interests dominate over public interests in the use and re-use of natural resources.

*Table 1.1* Productive and Unproductive Labour and Consumption

| *Politics of Labour* | *Politics of Consumption* |
|---|---|
| 'Productive labour'<br>(based upon profit, private ownership of means of production and extraction of surplus value) | 'Productive consumption'<br>(based upon profit and exchange value of commodities that are capitalistically produced) |
| Versus | Versus |
| 'Unproductive labour'<br>(based upon need and ownership of own means of production and collective ownership of resources) | 'Unproductive consumption'<br>(based upon need and satisfied via self-sufficiency, state provision and/or cooperatives) |

The capitalist accumulation process is one driven by the fundamental imperative to continually extend the horizons of productive labour (the source of surplus value) and productive consumption (related to the realisation – and further creation – of surplus value) (see Table 1.1). In simple terms, this means that capital is constantly seeking new areas for investment and consumption in order to maintain and increase profit rates. Thus, every aspect of human existence is subject to transformation insofar as capital seeks to create new forms of consumption (e.g. fads, fashions) and seeks the transformation of existing use values into exchange values through commodification of all types of human activity and human requirements (e.g. water, food, entertainment, recreation).

Increasing the production of surplus value by labour – the source of profit – demands constant changes to the ways in which labour is exploited and in the things which can be transformed from simple use values (i.e. objects of need) into exchange values (i.e. commodities). The first can be achieved via changes in the organisation of work, by manipulation of the conditions within specific workplaces and by transforming previously unproductive or non-capitalist forms of activity into sites of productive labour (e.g. family farming and subsistence farming into agribusiness). The second can be achieved by not only subsuming previously non-capitalist activities into capitalist forms of production but also by expanding capitalist commodity consumption into new spheres of activity. The exploitation of human beings and the exploitation of the natural world are inextricably bound up in this process.

The four elements – water, air, earth (land) and sun (energy) – are thus ever more subject to conversion into something that produces value for private interests. Effectively, consumption has been put at the service of production in the sense that consumer decisions and practices are embedded in what is actually produced and how it is produced. Yet it is via consumption practices, and the cultural contexts for constantly growing and changing forms of consumption, that production realises its value.

'Consumerism' is the name given to a process in which certain habits of consumption are generated by the pursuit of profit. The process involves the transformation of the production of goods and services according to the dictates of exchange rather than simply immediate use. It involves the incorporation of certain kinds of consumption, over time, into the unconscious routines of everyday life. For instance, it has been observed that the 'reproduction of the commodity of labour-power is increasingly achieved by means of capitalistically produced commodities and capitalistically organized and supplied services' (Mandel, 1975: 391). This takes the form of pre-cooked meals, ready-made clothes, electrical household appliances and so on, goods which previously would have been produced by family members as immediate use values (and to which contemporary community farms and local self-help environmental groups are, in part, responding and objecting to). Importantly, consumerism is driven by private interests rather than communal or state concerns. It is based upon private investments by individuals or private companies in production, in distribution services, in entertainment and shopping complexes, in food outlets and restaurants, in leisure pursuits, and in financial services (Bocock, 1993).

Systemic imperatives to expand require that natural resources be subjected to varying processes of commodification – that is, the transformation of existing or potential use values into exchange values (for example, clean drinking water becomes something to be bought and sold amongst consumers rather than being a right for citizens). One consequence of commodification is that the distribution of goods and services using market mechanisms is privileged rather than, for instance, being based upon communal and ecological assessments of need. In this context – and somewhat perversely – scarcity makes the natural commodity (for example, clean drinking water) even more valuable to the owner. Scarcity thus equates to high profit levels.

Commodity production and consumption take place within the context of a global political system that is hierarchical and uneven. In the area of energy, the oil and gas companies have long dominated and have held major sway in terms of government policies regarding carbon emissions as well as renewable energy sources. Who controls energy supplies (as evident in several wars in the Gulf region of the Middle East as well as Russian exploits in Eastern Europe) also dominates politically and economically. Energy provision grants profit and power.

Present institutional arrangements benefit some while disadvantaging others. For instance, Stretesky and Lynch (2009) argue that on the basis of analysis of carbon emissions and consumer imports to the United States, it is US consumer demand that is fuelling harmful production practices in other exporting countries. They examined the relationship between per capita carbon dioxide emissions and exports for 169 countries. The data suggest that consumption practices in the United States are partially responsible for elevated per capital carbon dioxide emissions in other nations and that carbon dioxide trends in other nations are in part driven by US demands for goods. US consumers, however, are unaware of how their consumption stimulates rising global carbon emissions because of the disconnection or dissociation between the two phenomena.

It is 'the market' which has skewed production and its harmful emissions to the Third World for the sake of First World consumers. Simultaneously, it is the market which is now being seen as the solution to global environmental problems such as climate change. Resolution of the problems arising from commodification involves commodification of the solutions – for instance, in the form of carbon emission trading. Given the vested interests involved in protecting and maintaining existing interstate inequalities, as well as those associated with particular industries (such as oil and coal), the critiques of carbon emission trading schemes, in practice, could be anticipated in advance. For example, as much as anything, carbon emission trading favours the polluter and the practice of polluting (Shiva, 2008). Likewise, the European Union's Emission Trading Scheme has been criticised because it sets lax national emission targets, encourages and grants the right to pollute, and encourages the export of the problem from rich to poor countries. The cap on carbon dioxide emissions was so lenient that the price on carbon dioxide drastically decreased, thus eliminating the main incentive to reduce emissions (see Baer and Singer, 2009).

Critiques of carbon off-setting make similar points and ask similar questions. For instance, it is hard to calculate how much carbon dioxide is being absorbed in tree planting projects and how quickly it will be absorbed from the atmosphere (Baer and Singer, 2009). More generally, it is difficult to know what is actually being planted if the off-set is half-way around the world in a poor country, especially if accounting, data measurement and communications systems in these countries are poor or non-existent. Ultimately, carbon off-setting has also been criticised for not encouraging a change in consumption practices since it implies that the problem is being off-set by the measure. It is also associated with various forms of carbon colonisation which involve displacing local peoples off their lands as part of carbon credit schemes. Poor regulation of carbon emissions and reliance upon bio-fuels and other new technologies are similarly contributing to global warming, as well as transferring problems to poorer countries and adding additional forms of toxic pollution into the equation.

One impact of unsustainable environmental practices is that these put more pressure on companies to seek out new resources (natural and human) to exploit as existing reserves dwindle due to over-exploitation and contamination from already-produced waste. Under capitalism, there are constant pressures to increase productive force and thus a tendency towards cyclical crises of over-production and under-consumption. What makes both labour and consumption 'productive' from the point of view of capitalism is whether such activity directly contributes to a profit-making process. To make and/or to consume something yourself (whether at the individual, cooperative or societal level) and to so do on the basis of need (rather than for profit or artificially manufactured desire) is the exception. Rather, goods and services tend to be produced in the context of privately owned and managed businesses for the purpose of generating profits for the private shareholders. Similarly, consumption tends to be based upon capitalistically produced goods and services (that is, goods and services sold in a buyer-seller nexus) rather than homemade goods and services (for example, vegetables from your own garden or hand-sewn shirts). Small alternative forms of non-capitalist production and consumption exist (for example, community gardens, local exchange trading systems [LETS] and small-scale residential cooperatives), but the general pattern is dominated by profit-making exchanges.

Periodic economic crises lead to system transformations towards ever more commodification of basic necessities – food, water, air and energy. For example, what was once 'free', such as water from a tap, is now sold in bottles. Living outside the polluted areas of a city carries with it premium housing costs for the privilege of breathing (relatively) fresh air. For the past thirty years, this commodification of nature has occurred within a particular political economic context. Neo-liberalism describes a broad political and economic orientation that places greatest emphasis on the individual, responsibility for one's own actions and accountability for the consequences of these actions within the institutional framework of strong private property rights and unfettered commodity markets.

Neo-liberalism ostensibly favours market forces over state intervention, and it views inequality as a natural outcome of competition between individuals. At an abstract level, each person is seen to be personally responsible for his or her own welfare and life choices. In practice, economic power tends to already be monopolised and concentrated in ways that foreclose any possibility of fair or free competition. The main policy and practical trends associated with neo-liberalism include reduced trade protection, user pays, privatisation and deregulation (Harvey, 2005). As White (2015) states:

> Institutionally the policies and ethics of neo-liberalism are reflected in reliance upon the market for the allocation of goods and services, the shrinking of the welfare state, assertion of the role of the state as 'night watchman' (albeit with little government oversight

> for those at the top), and an emphasis on strong law and order and defence of private property (that includes strict control over those at the bottom).
>
> (219)

Historical analysis demonstrates empirically that social inequality is intrinsic to the capitalist system (Piketty, 2014). This has been exacerbated and further entrenched over the past three decades of aggressive neo-liberalisation, involving the collusion of international corporate elites working in conjunction with high-level political leaders in the United States and other hegemonic nation-states (Beder, 2006). Neo-liberal 'free trade' policies are linked to the commodification of a wider range of services and products which were formerly state owned and operated ostensibly for public benefit. For example, education, water and power are being sold by governments to private concerns as profit-making enterprises. This is yet another instance in which the consumption relations of ordinary citizens are being transformed in ways that reduce the possibility of democratic participation in decision making. It is also an example of control being exercised by the state over how resources are managed and consumed.

## Protecting their own

Neo-liberalism as a practice, policy and ideal is basically built upon a falsehood. Powerful sectional interests already substantially own and control the bulk of the world's resources (including natural, financial and technical capital). There is no 'free market' as such. Land, water, food and energy are under the control of a small and shrinking number of private firms, and the community outside is both growing and increasingly powerless in the face of this concentrated ownership. One consequence of this concentration of power is that the carbon-emitting industries have continued to exercise considerable economic and political clout, especially in ostensibly resource-dependent economies such as Canada and Australia.

Exploitation of natural resources is big business, and big business ensures that its interests (that is, private interests) are protected across many different spheres of activity. This is evident, for example, in ongoing natural resource developments in which oil and coal industries – the 'dirty' industries – are privileged still; where coal-seam fracking is allowed to pose a threat to prime agricultural land; in the advent of deep-drill oil exploration and exploitation and, similarly, mega-mines and open-cut mining; and also in the continued resistance by powerful businesses to global agreements on carbon emission reductions and use of carbon taxes.

Given that the largest private corporations are economically more powerful than many nation-states, and given that they own and control great expanses of the world's land, water and food resources, individually and collectively they are a formidable force. On occasion, as well, they may combine their collective muscle to influence world opinion or global efforts to curtail their activities. For example, analysis of how big business has responded to global warming reveals a multi-pronged strategy to deter or defer action on climate change (Bulkeley and Newell, 2010). Some of these include:

- Challenging the science behind climate change
- Creating business-funded environmental non-governmental organisations (NGOs)
- Emphasising the economic costs of tackling climate change
- Using double-edged diplomacy to create stalemates in international negotiations
- Using domestic politics (particularly in the United States) to stall international progress
- Influencing climate change negotiations through direct lobbying

In a similar vein, work done on the politics of climate change in the United States has demonstrated close connections between business and the government, culminating in a form of state-corporate contrarianism (Brisman, 2013; Kramer and Michalowski, 2012, 2013). The essential stumbling blocks to any type of progressive or concrete response to climate change include denying that global warming is caused by human activity; blocking efforts to mitigate greenhouse gas emissions; excluding progressive, ecologically just adaptations to climate change from the political arena; and responding to the social conflicts that arise from climate change by transforming societies into fortress states that exclude the rest of the world (Kramer and Michalowski, 2012).

Climate change is also dealt with by focusing on the economic potentials of 'dirty industry' development and the employment and financial costs of their demise rather than their impacts on global warming. This is highlighted, for example, in the active governmental and political defence of the Alberta Tar Sands project, one of the most polluting and carbon-charged developments in the world (Klare, 2012). This massive industrial project involves the collusion of both provincial and federal governments with big oil companies. The project is based upon efforts to extract and refine naturally created tar-bearing sand into exportable and consumable oil. One result of the project is a wide range of different types of harm to the ecosystem, animals and humans. For instance, it has been pointed out that tar sands oil production is the single largest contributor to the increase of global warming pollution in Canada. It is associated with the destruction of vast swaths of boreal forest, it contributes greatly to air pollution, and it is having negative health impacts on aquatic life and animals. It is also affecting the health of humans who live nearby (Klare, 2012; Smandych and Kueneman, 2010). Placed within the larger global context of climate change, the scale and impact of this project also fit neatly with the concept of ecocide.

So, too, do recent Australian government decisions. For example, the then–Environment Minister Greg Hunt proclaimed that he takes climate change seriously. Nonetheless, in 2014 he approved a Queensland coal mining project – Australia's largest ever – subject to 'the absolute strictest of conditions'. Left out of these 'conditions' was any mention of the mine's impact on atmospheric carbon levels. As one commentator pointed out:

> When Carmichael coal is exported to India and burned, it will release 100 million tonnes of carbon dioxide each year for the mine's lifetime of more than half a century. This is about one-fifth of Australia's annual total from all sources, way beyond any single enterprise in our history.
>
> (Boyer, 2014: 13)

As this incident further illustrates, not only is there state-corporate collusion in perpetrating harm, but responsibility for such harm is frequently externalised as well. This externalisation occurs both directly ('we are selling the coal to India') and indirectly ('no one country can do it alone'). Economy yet again trumps ecology and is defended by those whose ostensible task is to protect the environment.

Meanwhile, the former Prime Minister of Australia, Tony Abbott, extolled the virtues of coal not so long ago. As he put it:

> 'Coal is good for humanity, coal is good for prosperity, coal is an essential part of our economic future, here in Australia, and right around the world.'
>
> 'Coal is essential for the prosperity of the world.'

> 'Energy is what sustains our prosperity, and coal is the world's principal energy source and it will be for many decades to come.'
>
> '. . . we think that coal has a big future as well as a big past'.
>
> (Abbott, quoted in Massola et al., 2014)

These statements were made just a few weeks before the IPCC released its 2014 report. According to the IPCC (2014: 5; emphasis added):

> Total anthropogenic greenhouse gas emissions have continued to increase over 1970 to 2010 with larger absolute increases between 2000 and 2010, despite a growing number of climate change mitigation policies. . . . *Increased use of coal* has *reversed* the long-standing trend of gradual decarbonization (i.e., reducing the carbon intensity of energy) of the world's energy supply.

Political judgement in this case is thus decidedly skewed in favour of dirty industry and away from the science that tells us that coal is, in fact, bad for humanity. Indeed, there is a close intersection of global warming, government action or inaction, and corporate behaviour (Kramer, 2013; Lynch et al., 2010) and how these contribute to the overall problem of climate change. In this instance, the state is itself implicated as a perpetrator of harm. Government subsidies for coal-fired power stations and government approval of dams that destroy large swaths of rainforest constitute substantial crimes against nature. In light of the existing scientific evidence on global warming, continued encouragement of such activities represents intentional harm that is immoral and destructive of collective public interest whilst at the same time benefiting private industrial interests.

Given the stakes involved, we might well ask: should the impending destruction of ecosystems, and the human (and other species) collateral damage associated with this, be thought of as a form of ecocide? If so, then it is state leaders and government bureaucrats, as well as corporate heads and key shareholders, who should ultimately be held responsible for this crime.

## Beyond the carbon agenda

Pressure from below by grassroots groups and global activists could moderate and/or change the actions of these powerful industries. However, the moral and material universe within which these trends occur is one that is generally supportive of this sort of natural resource exploitation. In other words, the ravaging of nature generally takes place with the *consent* of its beneficiaries, among whom are the general populaces of advanced industrialised countries (Agnew, 2013; White, 2014).

There are certain key elements to the proposition that 'ordinary acts' contribute to ecocide: 'These ordinary acts have several characteristics: they are widely and regularly performed by individuals as part of their routine activities; they are generally viewed as acceptable, even desirable; and they collectively have a substantial impact on environmental problems' (Agnew, 2013: 58). For example, livestock grazing that supports meat consumption is a major cause of deforestation, water pollution and climate change – accounting for 18 percent of greenhouse gas emissions. For many in the West, their contribution to ecocide takes the form of living in large, climate-controlled homes; using gas-based cars; having high meat consumption; and continually purchasing consumer products (Agnew, 2013).

Nonetheless, there are limits to this exploitation and enjoyment of natural resources, as evidenced by the increasing scarcity of both non-renewables (e.g. oil and minerals) and renewables (e.g. fresh water, forests, fertile soils). Sustainable use occurs when the underlying stock is not depleted in quantity or degraded in quality, but this is rarely the case today. Scarcity can arise from the depletion or degradation of the resource (supply), the increased demand for it (demand), and the unequal distribution and/or resource capture (structural scarcity) (Homer-Dixon, 1999). As Homer-Dixon (1999: 47) comments, these three factors are inter-related: 'Deforestation increases the scarcity of forest resources, water pollution increases the scarcity of clean water, and climate change increases the scarcity of the regular patterns of rainfall and temperature on which farmers rely.' These observations point to a series of systemic contradictions putting pressure on existing global political economic arrangements.

First, the treadmill of production embodies a tension or 'metabolic rift' between economy and ecology. Productivist and consumerist ideologies and practices ensure continued economic growth at the expense of ecological limits (Brisman and South, 2014; Stretesky et al., 2014). These limits are now being reached, and global warming is exacerbating the situation.

Second, harm is perpetrated via a series of feedback loops that are, in turn, generated in the first place as politically and economically 'safe' responses to climate change. This occurs because 'non-reformist reforms' preferred by powerful government and business interests (such as proposals for deep earth repositories for carbon storage) override those which would actually address the key ecological problems underlying climate change (such as keeping the coal in the ground). The result is that not enough is being done to combat global warming.

Third, effective responses need to address deep-seated inequalities and trends within the treadmill of production that go to the heart of ownership, control and exploitation of resources, and human relationships with nature. Adequate responses to climate change demand a transformation of the basic concepts of ownership and the relationships underpinning these. The public interest and accountability for harm need to take precedence over sectional interests and existing private controls over resources that affect us all.

Without widescale change, climate change will continue to accelerate, with disastrous consequences for all. The super-exploitation of natural resources, through both legal and illegal means, and the continued reliance upon energy sources that we know contribute to global warming are instances of ecocide. There is foreknowledge of the harm, and we know who the perpetrators are. While we are all implicated in the wrongs contributing to climate change (particularly in regards to consumption in the affluent West), some are more culpable than others – it is the capitalist system and transnational corporations that are at the heart of present trends (Tombs and Whyte, 2015).

Responses to climate change ecocide must be built upon solid foundations and involve many diverse sets of actors. Fundamentally, the fight for climate justice must involve the assertion of democratic control over land, air, water and energy. A good starting point, therefore, is to identify the present 'owners'. This involves finding out who the key players are in specific industry areas. For example, in the case of energy and oil, a short list of names serves to identify who dominates the industry. Just a handful of global oil corporations produce oil that contributes to a significant proportion of the world's carbon emissions (Bruno et al., 1999). These companies are responsible for more greenhouse gases than most countries. But several of these companies have also been involved in prominent events involving considerable harm to the environment – such as the Exxon Valdez oil spill off the coast of Alaska and the BP oil spill in the Gulf of Mexico, not to mention the continuing civil strife and social unrest associated with Shell's operations in Nigeria.

A pressing task is to identify the major corporations underpinning and dominating specific industries (such as waste, water, food, oil and nuclear) and to undertake a sustained analysis of how specific companies operate. Such analysis would have to consider a wide range of activities – including mergers and takeovers within the specific industry, the corporation's relationship to local communities and to specific national/regional governments, and the social conflicts associated with its core business (such as disputes over land use). An integral part of this analysis would involve identifying those environmental harms that may well be perfectly legal (at the moment) but are ecologically disastrous. Tracking illegal, criminal and harmful activity over time also means examining the background of key decision makers and the changing forms and guises of contemporary transnational corporations. In addition, it means investigating the links between corporate directors and between business and government leaders (see Beder, 2006).

The pursuit of climate justice will necessarily involve pushing the boundaries of the status quo. Demands such as the communal appropriation of 'private property' are central to this. It is 'people power' that will ensure that the decisions being made about land, air, water and energy are distributed more fairly. The essence of the struggle is to transform as well as challenge, to democratise through resistance and to change institutions as well as criticise them. Pushing the pause button on climate change inevitably demands diverse forms of participatory resistance and the realisation that it was the militancy of the women's liberation movement, the civil rights movement and the anti-slavery movement that enabled some to claim their freedom and legitimate place in society. Radical action is urgently required given the rapid ticking of the climate change clock.

Progress towards significant social change demands multiple actions across multiple domains. History teaches us that momentum for revolutionary transformation must incorporate many different interest groups (in alliance formally or in a united front), pursuing the struggle from within existing state and civil institutions as well as fighting against the powerful elite. The matrix of an action plan against climate change could therefore include activities and responses that involve the law and legal change, environmental law enforcement activities, courts and adjudication processes, and direct social action (for elaboration, see White and Kramer, 2015). The strategic message is that intervention counts and that it counts along many different frontiers of engagement. The politics of this surrounds what it is that we are actually fighting for.

It is also important to acknowledge that global action frequently finds purchase at the local level. There is scope for action by everyone regardless of where they live. Consider, for example, the 'divest' movement. This refers to efforts by activists to get mainstream institutions to stop investing in fossil fuels – in other words, to divest from putting funds into the 'dirty industries' of late capitalism (Redpath, 2015). This is now a global movement and includes such figures as the actor Leonardo DiCaprio and institutions such as the World Council of Churches, the British Medical Association and Norway's sovereign fund. The ironies of divestment are particularly apparent in the case of universities. For example, the University of Tasmania (UTAS) puts millions of dollars into climate science and leads the world in Antarctic studies, the results of which confirm the veracity of claims that it is anthropocentric causes which are escalating global warming. Simultaneously, according to student activists who recently occupied the Vice Chancellor's offices in protest against the investment portfolio of the university, UTAS still has $300 million invested in the fossil fuel industry (Redpath, 2015).

Universities in Australia are currently facing considerable budgetary pressures as the federal government continues to cut funding to the higher education sector. In such circumstances, some universities are reluctant to divest from areas that previously have provided significant financial returns. Revealing the paradoxes of university investment, however, also reveals the dilemmas and decisions we all face in confronting climate change. It is here that science meets politics.

> Decades of research (much produced by UTAS scientists) tells us that burning fossil fuels harms people, the climate and ecosystems on a vast scale. Tasmanian, Australian and international scientists, financiers and analysts agree that in order to limit global warming to 2C we will have to leave most (80 per cent) fossil fuels in the ground. This is no longer a scientific question. It's a question of leadership, values and good governance.
>
> (Redpath, 2015: 37)

In this statement, the student activist basically summarises the gist of the problem. Tackling the carbon economy at its roots requires political intervention at the grassroots. The intention is to hit the companies where it hurts. For this, everyone can have a role to play. Corporate power and state collusion are mirrored in this example of institutional collaboration, and both need to be met with community resistance. There are lessons here for all.

## Conclusion

This chapter has provided a discussion of the nature and dynamics of the carbon economy by explaining the central importance of the commodity in contemporary global society. The commodification of nature translates into the degradation and destruction of natural resources and the ongoing mass production of carbon emissions. These emissions are largely responsible for global warming. Yet, these emissions continue with little restraint even given recent government pronouncements to the contrary. This is because economy still dominates ecology at the level of business-state relations and in terms of consumerist practice among many of the world's populations.

Yet climate change is a global catastrophe. Our common human interests (as well as those associated with ecological and species justice) need to take priority over any other kind of interests if we, as a species, are to survive. However, while everyone on the planet has a common interest in the survival of the human race, the specific class interests of transnational corporations and the 'dirty industries', propped up by nation-states and governments at all levels, mean that they and their state sponsors are not willing to implement or enact strategies and policies that would, in fact, further universal human interests. In other words, the reason why we are not addressing the ecocide stemming from climate change – even though it is to the advantage of all that we work together in our common interest – is that specific class interests intrude upon the process whereby planetary well-being might be prioritised (see Anthanasiou, 1996).

This is the context in which resistance to ecocide must be built. It is only by transforming this context that we simultaneously open the door to a radically different type of future. Exposing key decisions about land, air, water and energy to public scrutiny and expanding the democratic impulse are vital to this task.

## References

Agnew, R. (2013) 'The ordinary acts that contribute to ecocide: A criminological analysis'. In N. South and A. Brisman (eds.) *Routledge International Handbook of Green Criminology*, London: Routledge, pp. 58–72.

Athanasiou, T. (1996) *Divided Planet: The Ecology of Rich and Poor*, Boston: Little, Brown.
Baer, H. and Singer, M. (2009) *Global Warming and the Political Economy of Health: Emerging Crises and Systemic Solutions*, Walnut Creek, CA: Left Coast Press.
Beder, S. (2006) *Suiting Themselves: How Corporations Drive the Global Agenda*, London: Earthscan.
Bocock, R. (1993) *Consumption*, London: Routledge.
Boyer, P. (2014) 'Keeping up appearances is really a complicated business', *The Mercury*, 12 August, pp. 12–13.
Brisman, A. (2013) 'The violence of silence: Some reflections on access to information, public participation in decision-making, and access to justice in matters concerning the environment', *Crime, Law and Social Change*, **59**(3): 291–303.
Brisman, A. and South, N. (2014) *Green Cultural Criminology: Constructions of Environmental Harm, Consumerism, and Resistance to Ecocide*, London: Routledge.
Bruno, K., Karliner, J. and Brotsky, C. (1999) *Greenhouse Gangsters vs. Climate Justice*, San Francisco: Transnational Resource and Action Center.
Bulkeley, H. and Newell, P. (2010) *Governing Climate Change*, London: Routledge.
Foster, J. (2002) *Ecology against Capitalism*, New York: Monthly Review Press.
Gray, M. (1996) 'The international crime of ecocide', *California Western International Law Journal*, **26**: 215–271.
Harvey, D. (2005) *A Brief History of Neoliberalism*, Oxford: Oxford University Press.
Higgins, P. (2010) *Eradicating Ecocide: Laws and Governance to Prevent the Destruction of Our Planet*, London: Shepheard-Walwyn.
Higgins, P. (2012) *Earth is Our Business: Changing the Rules of the Game*, London: Shepheard-Walwyn.
Higgins, P., Short, D. and South, N. (2013) 'Protecting the planet: A proposal for a law of ecocide', *Crime Law and Social Change*, **59**(3): 251–266.
Homer-Dixon, T. (1999) *Environment, Scarcity, and Violence*, Princeton: Princeton University Press.
Intergovernmental Panel on Climate Change (2013) *Working Group I Contribution to the IPCC Fifth Assessment Report Climate Change 2013: The Physical Science Basis: Summary for Policymakers*, 27 September 2013.
Intergovernmental Panel on Climate Change (2014) *Climate Change 2014 Synthesis Report, Approved Summary for Policymakers*, 1 November 2014.
Klare, M. (2012) *The Race for What's Left: The Global Scramble for the World's Last Resources*, New York: Henry Holt.
Kramer, R. (2013) 'Carbon in the atmosphere and power in America: Climate change as state-corporate crime', *Journal of Crime & Justice*, **36**(2): 153–170.
Kramer, R. and Michalowski, R. (2012) 'Is global warming a state-corporate crime?' In R. White (ed.) *Climate Change from a Criminological Perspective*, New York: Springer, pp. 71–88.
Lynch, M., Burns, R. and Stretesky, P. (2010) 'Global warming and state-corporate crime: The politicalization of global warming under the Bush administration', *Crime, Law and Social Change*, **54**: 213–239.
Mandel, E. (1968) *Marxist Economic Theory*, London: Merlin Press.
Mandel, E. (1975) *Late Capitalism*, London: Verso.
Marx, K. (1954) *Capital*, Moscow: Progress Publishers.
Massola, J., Ker, P. and Cox, L. (2014) 'Coal is "good for humanity", says Tony Abbott at mine opening', *The Sydney Morning Herald*, 13 October. Retrieved from http://www.smh.com.au/federal-politics/political-news/coal-is-good-for-humanity-says-tony-abbott-at-mine-opening-20141013-115bgs.html.
Onimode, B. (1985) *An Introduction to Marxist Political Economy*, London: Zed Books.
Pepper, D. (1993) *Eco-Socialism: From Deep Ecology to Social Justice*, New York: Routledge.
Piketty, T. (2014) *Capital in the Twenty-First Century*, Cambridge, MA: Belknap Press.
Redpath, J. (2015) 'UTAS must lead by example and drop fossil fuels', *The Mercury*, 17 October. Retrieved from http://www.themercury.com.au/news/opinion/talking-point-utas-

must-lead-by-example-and-drop-fossil-fuels/news-story/ed9eb34d5930862c3df2366c00605962.
Shiva, V. (2008) *Soil Not Oil: Environmental Justice in an Age of Climate Crisis*, Brooklyn: South End Press.
Smandych, R. and Kueneman, R. (2010) 'The Canadian-Alberta tar sands: A case study of state-corporate environmental crime'. In R. White (ed.) *Global Environmental Harm: Criminological Perspectives*, Cullompton, England: Willan, pp. 87–109.
Stretesky, P., Long, M. and Lynch, M. (2014) *The Treadmill of Crime: Political Economy and Green Criminology*, London: Routledge.
Stretesky, P. and Lynch, M. (2009) 'A cross-national study of the association between per capita carbon dioxide emissions and exports to the United States', *Social Science Research*, **38**: 239–250.
Teclaff, M. (1994) 'Beyond restoration: The case of ecocide', *Natural Resources Journal*, **Fall**: 933–956.
Tombs, S. and Whyte, D. (2015) *The Corporate Criminal: Why Corporations Must Be Abolished*, London: Routledge.
White, R. (2014) 'Environmental insecurity and fortress mentality', *International Affairs*, **90**(4): 835–851.
White, R. (2015) 'Climate change, ecocide and crimes of the powerful'. In G. Barak (ed.) *The Routledge International Handbook of the Crimes of the Powerful*, London: Routledge, pp. 211–222.
White, R. and Kramer, R. (2015) 'Critical criminology and the struggle against climate change ecocide', *Critical Criminology*, **23**: 383–399.
The White House (2015) *Climate change and President Obama's action plan.* Retrieved from http://www.whitehouse.gov/climate-change.

# 2 Doing 'green criminology'

## Methodologies, research strategies and values (or lack thereof?)

*Matthew Hall*

### Introduction

The development of green criminology has proceeded apace over the last 20 years, with a substantial increase in the number of commentators identifying themselves as working, researching and writing within the field. Evidence of this growth is to be found in the expanding volume of specialist texts, papers and conferences dedicated to the analysis of environmental crime and wider conceptions of environmental harm through a criminological lens. As our understanding of both the causes and the consequences of environmental change develop over the course of the 21st century, the challenges to be met by this still relatively new field can only increase. This being the case, now seems to be an opportune moment to focus reflexively on what it means to 'do' green criminological research from a methodological perspective, and such will be the key purpose of the present chapter.

This discussion must be prefaced with a clear statement that my goal here is neither to propose nor impose a 'standard' model of green criminological enquiry. Green criminology has developed as a loose umbrella term which has undoubtedly served as a useful focal point for those interested in environmental crime, harms and risks. Indeed, White (2013) has commented that 'there is no green criminology *theory* as such' (22; italics in the original) and that 'those who are doing green criminology define it in ways that best suit their own conception of what it is they are doing' (17). Certainly, green criminologists are (like other criminologists) drawn from an array of subject disciplines with different methodological paradigms and epistemological leanings. Given the widely recognised benefits of multidisciplinary research (see McAdam, 2012), such plurality in approach is to be positively encouraged as the specialism gains maturity. That said, in a major contribution to this literature, Stretesky et al. (2014) have criticised the slow pace of theoretical development in the field, arguing that 'this lack of clarity about the scope, purpose, and theoretical orientation of green criminology proves difficult when it comes to identifying the kinds of crimes and harms that ought to be included as legitimate subject matter within the discipline' (122). The point is well made, and although commentators must remain wary of the academic tendency to 'force social phenomena into false chronologies' (Kearon and Godfrey, 2007: 30), the proposition that greater certainty as to what it means to 'do' green criminology would be beneficial at this stage of the field's development will underlie the following discussion.

The goal of this chapter is to focus attention specifically on the formation of research strategies in green criminology. The chapter will examine how such strategies might be informed by ontological and epistemological positioning and in particular will highlight the implication of such positioning for the generally eco-centric perspective adopted by many commentators in the area. Such an exercise has yet to be carried out holistically in the green field and, as such, this chapter will contribute to the evolution of the robust methodological rigor that is the hallmark of a mature and established field of study. The goal here is *not* to develop a new theoretical model for green criminology per se, although – as a discussion of method*ology* rather than restricting itself to *method* – this piece will also critique a number of the main conceptual approaches to green criminological enquiry pursuant to its foremost objectives. Greater clarity on the methodological questions raised by green criminology can only result in a more focused and productive debate, which in turn has a greater likelihood of exerting real influence over the range of ecological problems identified by green criminologists and, perhaps more significantly, over the social, political and economic institutions underpinning those problems.

The question of what kind(s) of data we might need to examine environmental harm *as criminologists* is a complex one. Suppose we take, as an example, the question of how regulatory or criminalising regimes in Brazil impact illegal logging activities in the rainforest (see van Solinge, 2014). Clearly, criminologists keen on a more qualitative strategy might seek to gather opinions and perspectives from those (humans) involved in the commitment, detection, regulation and prosecution of such activities and their aftermath. Such data could then be used for the purposes of a bottom-up analysis of the issues and an assessment of the law 'in action'. Further context might also be provided through interviews with experts on the ecology and fauna of the region, as well as with environmentalists, non-governmental organisations (NGOs), government officials and so on. As an alternative, or in conjunction with this, the more positivistic-inclined criminologist might gather large amounts of quantitative[1] data concerning the measurable impacts of logging in order to derive numerical estimates of the number of trees removed and animal life displaced, as well as the impacts of subsequent desertification in the region on plant life (see Chatham House, 2015). Such data could also be combined with enforcement figures to arrive at an estimate of how regulatory/criminal justice mechanisms had impacted these numbers.

In this chapter, the methodological precepts and implications of both of the aforementioned broadly outlined research strategies will be examined in some detail. The chapter also focuses attention on the methodological implications of the less anthropocentric approach to research that is often championed by those identifying as green criminologists. As such, the chapter will examine the place of 'values' in green criminological research and the subsequent impacts on questions of 'objectivity' within the field.

## Asking 'green' questions?

In order to examine how green criminology might develop and the methodological positions it will require to set about meeting the challenges put to it in the 21st century, it seems useful to begin by mapping out the kinds of questions green criminologists are asking and, with these, the likely parameters of the field. Various authors have set out typologies or 'road maps' for the development of the area (see Carrabine et al., 2004; South, 1998; White,

1 Throughout this chapter, I will generally base my discussion upon the common understanding of 'quantitative' research strategies as being heavily influenced by positivism, objectivism and a deductive approach to the relationship between theory and research. Similarly, for present purposes, I will take 'qualitative' strategies as being largely informed by interpretivism, constructivism and an inductive approach to theory. It should be recognised, however, that this conventional picture in fact betrays innumerable combinations of points on the continua between various epistemological and ontological viewpoints approached in various studies by any given researcher or in any given research project (see Robson, 2011).

2007). Producing anything like a definitive list of green criminological issues is not possible given the pace of change in our understanding of environmental issues and, in any case, this seems manifestly undesirable for the continued growth of the field. We can, however, derive from this prevailing literature several major themes, including the circumstances, predicates and social/political context of environmental crimes and broader environmental harms; the handling of natural disasters and the management of environmental risks; the impacts of such harms on human and animal life and on the ecosystem itself; the social, political and legal censures attributed to these harms (their form, goals and enforcement); the broader regulation of environmentally destructive acts and omissions; the mechanisms of restitution and redress in the wake of environmentally destructive activities/omissions; and the limits of the law in addressing environmental harm.

Incomplete as it may be, most criminologists – especially those pursuing more critical criminologies – will find much that is familiar in the previous list. Indeed, remove the references to 'environment' and 'animal life' and, with little further adaptation, one might easily substitute these for a host of other issues which have concerned criminologists for decades. This raises the important question of whether 'green criminology' goes further than the straightforward application of established criminological theory and method to the relatively 'new' business of environmental crime and (from the more critical criminological perspective) environmental harms. In offering an answer to this question, I want to distinguish green criminology from what I will call 'criminologies of the environment', arguing that the former implies different underlying theoretical positions, different assumptions and different ways of thinking about the nature of justice. Indeed, on this last point, the green criminological literature has seen the swift development of numerous conceptualisations of 'environmental', 'ecological' and 'species' justice (see White, 2013). Like green criminology itself, there is little agreement as to what precisely constitutes 'justice' in this context, although the broad term 'eco-justice' has been used to encapsulate all these differing ideas under one label (White, 2013). As summarised by Benton (2007):

> If anything, the green challenge requires us to give still more attention to the question of justice, as well as providing new work for the concept and principles of justice to do. (29)

Ultimately, we will see how such differences between orthodox and green criminological approaches to justice constitute the need to adapt and develop methodological precepts and, with these, our research methods themselves. To illustrate this distinction between 'criminologies of the environment' and 'green criminology', I will take Hall and Farrell's (2012) discussion of the criminological consequences of climate change. Drawing on the literature concerning the causes of (non-environmental) crimes, the authors set out in that paper to make a case that climate change is itself criminogenic. To this end, the authors noted how reductions in crop yields, rises in the price of food, and threats to supplies of food and water (often referred to in the literature as food and/or water 'security'; United Nations Food and Agriculture Organization, 2010) may lead to increased violent behaviour and food riots in the parts of the world most affected (Ivanic and Martin, 2008). Other crimes may follow, such as adulteration of foodstuffs by producers and consumers turning to illegal food markets which themselves may be associated with wider offending activities. Furthermore, the *displacement* of peoples prompted by the desertification of farmland has been particularly apparent in recent years in parts of Africa. Several studies have demonstrated that displaced peoples not only find themselves turning to crime to survive but are also susceptible to people trafficking (Jasparro and Taylor, 2008). Trafficking of all kinds itself tends to be linked with and facilitate other crimes such as smuggling, drug distribution and prostitution in receiving countries (Lee, 2009).

Hall and Farrell's (2012) analysis is intended to develop an understanding of how environmental issues and crime are linked. The paper is not, however, concerned with the environment or with ecological harms per se. In fact, the authors' discussion in this piece was largely anthropocentric, focusing on the ultimate implications of these criminogenic effects for *human* populations. No criticism is implied by this observation, nor is it disputed that this contribution offers much of interest to green criminologists. What that discussion lacks, however, is the more *eco-centric* perspective taken by many of the commentators now identifying themselves as green criminologists (to be discussed in more detail in the last section of this chapter). This being the case, in conceptualising what it is to 'do' green criminology at a methodological level, it may indeed be beneficial to draw distinctions between various 'criminologies of the environment' – such as 'the criminology of climate change', as in Hall and Farrell's discussion or the 'criminology of pollution' – and a truly *green* criminology. The latter, it is argued, implies wider conceptions of harm and risks which encompass non-human victimisation and the victimisation of an ecosystem as a whole.

In addition to being less anthropocentric, a *green* criminology is often regarded (for example, as conceived by Lynch, 1990) as one principally concerned with the political, social and economic relationships in society that breed ecological damage (see South, 2014). It is therefore much more of a *radical* criminology than an orthodox one. Such an approach to the field was developed by Lynch and Stretesky (2007) and, most recently, Stretesky et al. (2014) have refined this discussion still further by adapting Schnaiberg's 'treadmill of production' to explain environmental crimes and harms (see also Johnson et al.; Stretesky et al., this volume). Their resulting 'treadmill of crime' theoretical model grounds environmental crimes, environmental harms and ecological destruction in general within the contemporary capitalistic imperative to increase production. It is the unimpeded pursuit of such production, the authors argue, that leads to green 'crimes', defined here as incorporating harms that are not officially criminalised. Such crimes can be grouped into those prompting ecological withdrawals (extracting raw materials and resources from the environment) and those resulting in ecological additions ('pollution' in its various forms). For Stretesky et al. (2014), the boundaries of green criminology therefore lie in restricting the field to acts and omissions that cause or have the potential to cause significant harm to ecological systems *for the purposes of increasing or supporting economic production*. In short form, under *this* construction, green criminologists examine areas where economic production is prioritised over ecological production; for these authors, green criminology is *not* a blanket study of all forms of harm that may be related to the environment, nor is it a form of eco-zemiology (Tombs and Whyte, 2007). This in fact illustrates an ongoing debate in the literature in which both White (2013) and South et al. (2013) advocate an understanding of green criminology which functions far more as an umbrella concept for wider categories of harm. Returning to the example of Hall and Farrell's (2012) paper, we can see how under a treadmill of crime understanding this study again fails to qualify as green criminology. Whilst that paper does link economic and political factors to criminal activity, the focus is not on how economic production breeds *ecological* harm, but rather how it ultimately breeds further, more orthodox, criminal harm.

The treadmill of crime understanding of green criminology explicitly focuses on the structural factors leading to 'public' environmental crimes and harms. Work by Robert Agnew (2013) has, as an alternative, focused much more on what he calls 'ordinary acts' that contribute to ecocide which are 'widely and regularly performed by individuals as part of their routine activities; they are generally viewed as acceptable, even desirable, and they collectively have a substantial impact on environmental problems' (59). Agnew sees the tendency of green criminologists to underplay or simply ignore such 'ordinary harms' as understandable given the 'tremendous damage caused to the environment by states, corporations and organised crime groups' (69). Nevertheless, for Agnew, ordinary harms and the headline-grabbing 'public' disaster events may in fact be inter-related, with one driving the other. This is because 'the harmful behaviour of individuals is a function of larger social forces' (69). Thus, these ordinary harms – which do not necessarily derive from economic production, at least directly – must also be a key focus for green criminology. Agnew goes on to demonstrate that such ordinary, private harms perpetrated mainly by individuals against the environment can be subject to persuasive explanation by many standard criminological perspectives, including strain theory, social control and rational choice perspectives. In summation, the author notes:

> Taken together, the crime theories point to multiple reasons why ordinary harms are so common (and environmentally responsible behaviours are uncommon).
>
> (Agnew, 2013: 69)

Of course, the differences in approaches taken by Agnew (2013) and Stretesky et al. (2014) reflect far wider divergences within criminology as a whole, essentially between the radical/structural and the orthodox/individual explanations of crime. One way to unite both perspectives under the 'green' label may be to simply define green criminology by its less anthropocentric, more eco-centric stance on crime and harm and the necessary consideration of 'eco-justice'. This is arguably still a more bounded concept than 'every harm related to the environment' (as decried by Stretesky et al., 2014: 54) because the latter conception might still prioritise the ultimate impact of such harm *on humans.* In any case, the purpose of this chapter is not to reconcile a single theoretical position for green criminology out of these debates. Rather, having now established broadly what green criminology 'is' (or might be), the remainder of this discussion will instead examine the methodological implications of both conceptions of green criminology coupled with a particular focus on those implications deriving from a less anthropocentric stance on social harm. This will be achieved through an analysis of research strategy as a marriage of ontological positioning on the nature of the subject under study and epistemological views on the best means of acquiring 'real' knowledge of that subject.

## Ontological positioning in green criminology

The extent to which the subject matter of green criminology combines 'objective' realities with socially constructed phenomena is closely related to the debates already discussed concerning a structural or more individualistic focus for the field. Critical criminologists have long argued that crime is a product of the social world in the sense that it has no reality separate from human society (Hulsman, 1986). Such an approach acknowledges that social phenomena are being constantly revised. From the perspective of legal theory, this social constructivist view sees law as 'an aspect or field of social experience, not some mysterious force working on it'. Law and social ordering are therefore 'mutually constituting' (Cotterell, 2006: 25). This has important implications for the conceptualisation of green criminology under the treadmill of crime because the treadmill model prioritises an understanding of how laws and regulations are produced *by* and operate *within* their socio-political contexts in a way that ranks economic production above ecological additions and withdrawals.

Social constructivism is equally applicable to a more individualistic conception of environmental crime. This is because societal views of what counts as 'real' harm or 'real' crime may in practice have a much larger impact on the 'everyday' crimes perpetrated by individuals, and discussed by Agnew (2013), than any official regulatory or criminalising regimes. Commentators such as Tyler (1990) have long argued this to be the case in relation to crimes beyond the environmental sphere. So, whether people drop litter – for example – may be more determined by whether they believe it is 'wrong' or 'acceptable' to do so than any specific laws (or other regulations) on littering (see Groombridge, 2013). Seen in this light, littering as an ecological addition becomes more about the social construction of the 'problem' and any 'harms' that derive from it than the classification of this activity as an official crime (or not).

Of course, determining the extent to which people do in fact refrain from littering for fear of punishment at the hands of formal criminal justice actors and regulators might be a key question for both an orthodox criminology of the environment *and*, in considering the resulting impact on the ecosystem itself, for green criminologists. In any case, a constructivist perspective also incorporates the radical criminological view in that it fundamentally problematises which forms of harm do and do not become labelled as 'criminal'. This in turn incorporates within our methodological reasoning the reality of environmental *harm* as well as officially acknowledged and labelled environmental *crime*.

An understanding of environmental crime as being (in part) socially constructed is arguably corroborated by the fast-paced changes witnessed in the criminalisation and wider social censure of environmentally harmful practices in recent decades. Certainly, the slow development of environmental law and regulation at a national and international level can be viewed as the result of changes in attitudes towards the environment and the use we humans make of it. A related example might be the expansion of animal rights laws, even in parts of the world traditionally lacking such regulations (see Park and Singer, 2012). Such laws reflect greater social censure of animal abuse in many jurisdictions in line with conceptions of animal rights and the notion of species justice. We might also consider here the growing discontent amongst some parts of society (especially following the 2008 financial crisis) with the prioritisation of business interests, the development of notions of corporate/social responsibility and the rejection of unsustainable growth as legitimate goals for corporations or states (Blowfield and Murray, 2011).

Of course, in spite of such social movements, the treadmill of crime predicts that a pro-production agenda will continue to win out over ecological concerns due to the power differentials in our political economic system. Nevertheless, the fact that this system must concede *any* ground to ecological production is evidence that such harms are being construed in a different light by persuasive segments of society. This remains true even when such 'concessions' ultimately serve the interests of production in other ways. Although this may be 'greenwashing' at a macro-level, economic powers at least do, it seems, feel the need to greenwash (Laufer, 2003).

In sum, the social constructivist perspective provides the ontological context in which the treadmill of crime operates and helps explain the pressures put on social and economic institutions in their pursuance of production. These in turn influence – and help green criminologists to understand – the degree to which ecological values and notions of eco-justice are entirely sidelined, partly acknowledged or imperfectly addressed. Social constructivism, it is submitted, therefore has a central (if not exclusive) place in a green criminological research strategy aimed at uncovering the political, economic and social context of ecological harm as envisioned by Stretesky et al. (2014) and also in the more individualistic approach taken by Agnew (2013).

Nevertheless, it is at this point that we must also consider more objectivist components of the green criminological project. Stretesky et al. (2014), as noted, see environmental crime in terms of ecological additions and withdrawals. In principle, these are empirically measureable phenomena. Mares (2010), in a forerunner to Stretesky et al.'s (2014) analysis, presented a conceptual framework for understanding the criminalisation of environmentally destructive acts which shares this trait. For him, the harm caused by polluting activities is ultimately reflected by a reduction in the 'carrying capacity' of the planet (that is, its ability to sustain a given amount of human, plant and animal life). In this sense, any person, corporation or state which allows, facilitates, or engages in actions that undermine the future means of existence for life on Earth carries a degree of responsibility for reducing its carrying capacity and therefore engages in a crime against the planet. As the author continues, the notion of carrying capacity is a fundamental omission from the majority of modern legal systems but, again, in principle if not entirely in practice, it would constitute an objectively verifiable 'number'.

We can compare social constructivism with a more objectivist stance to explaining ecological harm and its regulation by considering a discrete example from the UK: that of fox hunting. The banning of hunting with dogs (in particular the hunting and killing of foxes with packs of specially bred and trained hounds) was introduced in Scotland in the 2002 Protection of Wild Mammals (Scotland) Act and in England and Wales under Hunting Act 2004. From a constructivist perspective, one might understand this legal move as originating with a shift in normative attitudes concerning the rights and wrongs of hunting (killing, causing prolonged distress to foxes, etc.). Such changes have arguably led to shifts in the social and political climate, leading to a position where economic production (in the form of the dominant commercial interests behind hunting and farming) made this apparent concession to ecological production (the proliferation of foxes and the avoidance of harm to them). Pursuant to this approach, a green criminologist wishing to understand this example of ecological criminalisation might therefore examine the role of prominent social actors and institutions with a stake in the ban and the resulting policy networks that helped facilitate this social/legal change (see Nurse, 2013).

The previous factors notwithstanding, a green criminologist might equally seek to examine the issue of fox hunting and its criminalisation through a more objectivist lens. This might involve marshalling empirical evidence in an attempt to demonstrate how fox populations had reduced as a result of hunting practices in the UK and, similarly, deriving an objective 'number' of foxes below which the population became at risk. Indeed, this is essentially the system used by the International Union for Conservation of Nature (IUCN) to place animals in different categories of endangerment and resulting protection (in most countries) on its 'Red List'. It is thus on the basis of objective, quantified harm that the criminal law might be prompted to act. Notably, however, in the case of red foxes (the target of most hunts), the IUCN classifies the animal as being of 'least concern' owing to its abundant population across Europe, North America and Japan. Indeed, the categorising (construction) of the red fox as a copious 'pest' to farmers by pro-hunting lobbyists remains for many a key argument in favour of the practice. These pro-hunting arguments are often backed by more objectivist contentions about numbers of game birds, livestock and wild animals killed by foxes (see Burns, 2000).

The difference between the (apparent lack of) objective evidence for significant 'harm' to red foxes (at least in terms of population decline) versus the increased social construction of fox hunting as a harmful activity demonstrates how the different sides of this ontological debate result in different perceptions of an issue. In this case, to 'understand' the criminalisation of fox hunting in the UK, it seems that one must look to the wider socio-political factors beyond the 'maths' of fox populations (see Nurse, 2013). Furthermore, many contend that the process and impact of this particular legal change cannot be understood in isolation from the political and class context in which it is heavily situated, itself tied up with cultural and economic divides between urban and rural populations within the UK (see Anderson, 2006). Indeed, at the time of writing, the Conservative majority government is proposing a relaxation of the fox hunting prohibition. Many anti-hunting activists and commentators see this as a wholly predictable outcome of the renewed political influence of a capitalist elite, driven by the economic interest of farmers concerned about their livestock (economic production) (League Against Cruel Sports, 2015).

Whilst the weight of the aforementioned observations might well swing in favour of a less objectivist strategy for understanding ecological harm in the case of fox hunting, the risk of taking an exclusively constructivist research strategy here is that green criminologists thereby become so embroiled in an anthropocentric, political dialogue that they risk losing the eco-centric perspective, which I have argued is at the core of the whole endeavour. Social constructivism is, after all, by its nature concerned with ***human*** perspectives on a given environmental issue. In the case of fox hunting, then, we might conclude that whilst prevailing social attitudes ultimately led to a ban in the UK, more objectively, and perhaps from an eco-justice perspective, this may not have been the most 'pressing' example of environmental harm which might instead have been considered by reformists and legislators at the time. Nurse (2013) has commented in detail on the human biases that tend to impact the specific animals and environments left to bear the brunt of environmental harms versus those which are deemed more 'worthy' of protection:

> Informal rules, embedded in specific practices and nuances might dictate, for example, that in some inner-city police areas most animal harm (except possibly wildlife crime and the trade in endangered species) is seen as being a low priority for police investigation whereas in rural areas (such as Scotland where rarer birds such as the golden eagle and the osprey are seen as being part of Scotland's heritage, or those parts of the United States where California condors or bald eagles hold special cultural significance) considerable police and criminal justice resources may be directed at those offenders who seek to exploit wildlife resources.
>
> (201)

From this, we can draw the conclusion that, from an anthropocentric perspective, not all animals are equally without worth to all humans, although notably the worth they do have is once again based entirely on human prejudices and social/cultural labelling.

It follows from the previous discussion that to retain its (more) eco-centric credentials, it is vital that green criminology focus not only on environmental harms which have become problematic in the eyes of society at large but also on more objectivist representations of such harm which have escaped public condemnation. Many examples of more objectivist sources of data for use by green criminologists might be given. For example, the EU's Emissions Trading System (ETS) – the largest greenhouse gas emissions trading system in the world – is premised on the notion of precisely counting carbon emissions and placing a respective numerical (and economic) value on these. For their part, Stretesky et al. (2014) draw on national and international figures concerning car use, oil production, carbon emissions and timber production to illustrate environmental crime (both ecological additions and withdrawals).

In addition to the aforementioned topics, and perhaps contrary to Agnew's (2013) line of thought, we might also look to large-scale environmental harms such as the effects of the 2010 BP oil spill (Flournoy et al., 2010) and the sinking of the Maldives (Davis, 2005). These are not socially constructed, normative problems, but (from an eco-centric perspective) they can be measured in tons of fish and other marine life killed per year and, in the latter case, changes in the depth and temperature of the ocean. In sum, whilst traditional notions of crime as a social construct have an important place in understanding the criminalisation of environmental harm, approaching such harm as an objective reality separate from human interpretation is also key in many cases to reducing anthropocentric (and, indeed, political) bias.

## Epistemological positioning in green criminology

In terms of epistemology, the previous discussion implies that green criminologists must embrace mixed-methods approaches which combine both qualitative and quantitative strategies of data collection/analysis and essentially discount an unduly rigid focus on what purists might see as the epistemological and ontological inconsistencies this implies. Johnson and Onwuegbuzie (2004), for example, argue strongly in favour of such methods. Campbell et al. (2011) also highlight the utility of mixed-methods approaches in examining 'complex phenomena in real-world settings' (377). In this sense, the 'correct' methods to use in different situations for green criminology may reflect the principles of pragmatism (see Robson, 2011). It is interesting to note here that whilst green criminology is still a new and developing area, this methodological direction in fact reflects more recent ideas seen in wider criminology as well (see Fielding, 2010).

In any case, it is submitted that the data sources employed by green criminologists need to reflect the *dynamic* nature of environmental harm. Thus, from an interpretivist epistemological position, green criminologists are concerned with *understanding* a *process* whereby environmentally destructive activities come to be thought of as criminal, harmful or perhaps 'deviant' (and vice versa), rather than trying to *explain* a fixed social phenomenon (Bryman, 2012). The current moves *away* from fox hunting restrictions in the UK are a case in point. It follows that documentary analysis of (criminal and other) legal instruments and policy discussions related to the environment, being *static* representations, can only take us so far. That said, the previous discussion does point in the direction of other qualitative strategies that tap into the lived experience of environmental degradation (from both anthropocentric and eco-centric perspectives). This might imply surveys, interviewing and focus groups carried out in affected communities, ideally employing a longitudinal element. The notion of environmental harm *as a process* also suggests the use of narrative analysis, focused on how people make sense of their experiences through narrative accounts (Maines, 1993) to reflect this temporal component.

The previous factors notwithstanding, traditional qualitative approaches by themselves are likely to provide only human perceptions of harm and human narratives, as we have seen. A key question for commentators in the field is therefore how research strategies like those outlined previously can be adapted to reflect a more eco-centric perspective, giving a voice to the environment itself and to non-human animals. On this point, there have been numerous texts (grounded in both philosophy and physical science) arguing that it might be possible for humans to derive only a very limited understanding of what it is like to be an animal (Daston and Mitman, 2005; Nagel, 1974) or a plant (Chamovitz, 2013; Stone, 2010). As criminologists, it is clear that these non-human aspects of the ecosystem cannot be interviewed or put in a focus group. One might argue that incorporating the work of or interviewing 'experts' in various forms of environmental degradation, animal rights and so on might to some extent stand as proxy but, by definition, this remains the ***human*** view.

At first glance, positivist approaches might therefore seem more encouraging in this regard, providing as they do direct information on the non-human environment. Nevertheless, many commentators now agree that the gathering of quantitative data, even in the physical sciences, and in relation to environmental harm in particular, is far from objective or value free (Herrick, 2004). Indeed, it is on such an understanding that international environmental law adopts the so-called precautionary principle whereby the absence of scientific certainty does not negate a state's duty to proactively minimise environmental risk (Kriebel et al., 2001). This is because the application of such quantitative strategies will always be heavily influenced by the biases of the researchers carrying out the studies at both the data collection and data analysis stages. These data are therefore 'produced' rather than 'collected'. Indeed, ultimately, such quantitative approaches are themselves the product of a long and socially/politically driven process of scholars refining their means of counting, analysing and presenting a given subject from the perspective of human beings. For example, the commonly accepted 5% threshold for statistical confidence in empirical results is acknowledged by most statisticians as being entirely arbitrary – another human construction in which we accept that 1 in 20 of the 'facts' produced are in fact wrong. It is for such reasons that arguments between the most positivist-inclined researchers still continue over the exact causes (and, in some cases, the very existence) of climate change (see Weber, 2010).

Data derived from the most quantitative research strategies do not therefore shed the subjectivities of the human-driven research exercise simply by reason of being more positivistic. In any case, if green criminologists are also to examine the workings of justice and regulatory systems, along with the impacts of environmental harms themselves, criminal justice and regulation scholars have long recognised that the bare figures coming out of these mechanisms only ever tell part of the story. Thus, one cannot understand, say, the real workings of a system like that put in place to prevent illegal logging in Brazil without *also* looking at the social and political context of that system, as well as the occupational cultures and working practices of both the regulators and the regulated (whether such regulation is voluntary or involuntary).

Of course, the previous epistemological discussion is still to some extent confined within traditional conventions of research design, whether the approach be qualitative or quantitative or both. In fact, however, green criminology is likely to go further – towards challenging traditional ways in which data are collected and analysed at a more fundamental level. Williams (2013) has recently commented on the diversification of data sources in the study and enforcement of environmental law and regulation, largely as a result of developments in technology. One example is the use of satellite imagery to chart the growth in waste dumps. Purdy (2010) has argued that high-quality satellite imagery has already become a vital component of the successful enforcement of environmental law. Such images have also been employed to monitor the tipping of waste into the sea off the South Korean coast (Son et al., 2011), and the technology has already been used to achieve prosecutions by the Environment Agency in the UK (Brosnan, 2013). In another example, unmanned drones are now being employed to monitor air quality in India (Think India Foundation, 2011) and poaching in parts of Africa (BBC, 2014). With scholarly commentary and more activist-inspired critique often overlapping in the green domain, we will see in the following how green criminology is also likely to challenge established notions of *who* collects our data as well as *how* those data are collected.

The last point brings us to the question of subjectivity and values within green criminological discourse (see Potter, 2013). Accepting that both of these are likely to exert a significant influence over research in the field represents a further departure from the positivism that dominated much of mainstream criminology during the 20th century. That such values inevitably influence the research exercise in all areas is nevertheless becoming more widely accepted (House and Howe, 1999). In many instances, this shadow of subjectivism is still often presented in the literature as a 'necessary evil' and something we would prefer not to be present, chiefly because this inevitably constitutes a form of bias (Bailey, 1994). In the case of environmental harms, however, it may be argued that the views and values the researchers bring with them are – when appropriately acknowledged, and when steps are taken to ensure that the research remains robust – in fact very valuable. This chapter will therefore conclude by turning to look at the place of 'values' in green criminology.

## Eco-centrism and 'green' values

It has been argued previously in this chapter that the distinguishing feature of green criminology (as opposed to criminologies of the environment) is an eco-centric (or at least a less anthropocentric) approach. It is therefore worth dwelling on the implications of this from a methodological standpoint. At its most basic level, eco-centrism considers non-human animals and the environment itself alongside human beings and often deprioritises the human perspective as being no more significant than that of any other aspect of the ecosystem as a whole. In other words, it is a perspective in which human beings (and, in particular, 'harm' to humans, broadly defined) enjoy no special place or prioritisation within the wider natural world. We have seen throughout this discussion how this is a disarmingly simple proposition for a social science traditionally dominated by anthropocentric bias. In fact, such ideas permeate deeply into many of the assumptions social scientists of all kinds employ when carrying out their research. More than this, however, eco-centrism is, to a large extent, a normative position in which value judgements are inevitably being made about the relative worth of the human and non-human environment. Consequently, it needs to be acknowledged that the eco-centric *values* of many of those involved in the green criminological enterprise have inevitably impacted – and will continue to impact – the nature of that research exercise and its outputs. Indeed, it is likely that this form of subjectivity will have an even greater influence on the direction of the field than the alignment of its practitioners with different ontological and epistemological positions. With environmentalism sometimes being labelled as a 'religion' (Maintenay, 2013), this is scarcely avoidable.

An orthodox critique would see the previous facts as representing serious flaws in the conduct of green criminological research, as they clearly introduce bias. An alternative view is that it can in fact enhance the practice of research for green criminologists to acknowledge and proceed with a reflexive awareness of their own values and the influence of these on their practice. This reasoning has previously been argued to apply to feminist study: Mies (1993) goes so far as to argue that 'value-free research' is not only impossible but also manifestly undesirable in this area. Her argument is thus that feminist work should be written *for women* by researchers who are indeed 'consciously partial'. This perspective has bridged feminist and environmental issues in the eco-feminist literature, where a normative (i.e. value-based) standpoint is frequently defended. Indeed, feminist contributors to the animal rights field have criticised within that literature the dismissal of purportedly 'unmasculine' traits of sentimentality and emotional attachment to animals. This 'effectively equates "sentimental" and "emotional" with "irrational" and all three traits with "less than male" and "female"' (Beirne, 2007: 71). In contrast, it is argued that from a feminist perspective, such traits are perfectly acceptable as moral justifications for the recognition of animal rights (Beirne, 2007).

A research approach that admits and even promotes the acceptance of eco-centric values as a contributor to the research exercise does not, it is submitted, necessarily equate with a sacrifice in quality. On this point, Johnson and Onwuegbuzie (2004) argue:

> We agree with qualitative researchers that value stances are often needed in research; however, it also is important that research is more than simply one researcher's highly idiosyncratic opinions written into a report. Fortunately, many strategies are recognized and regularly used in qualitative research (such as member checking, triangulation, negative case sampling, pattern matching, external audits) to help overcome this potential problem and produce high-quality and rigorous qualitative research.
>
> (17)

Thus, certainly in terms of qualitative research strategies, there are many options available to counter the more negative implications of allowing values to permeate our research. Nor must a criminologist wholly subscribe to the argument that non-humans have intrinsic worth, or any of the more so-called deep green perspectives (concerning animal rights, animal abuse and so on) (Gibbs et al., 2010), to appreciate the value of incorporating impacts of harm on the (non-human) environment into his or her research, if only for the more instrumental purposes of establishing *how* those effects might also impact humans, crime and the law. On this point, Potter (2013) has argued that the study of environmental harms is vital regardless of one's eco-philosophical position, if only because all such harms eventually result in social harm. That said, acknowledging such value positions when they do exist may be the real lesser of two evils – the greater of which would be an outright loss of the eco-centric perspective which, as argued previously, is a core contribution of the whole green criminology project.

Of course, it will be recognised that the aforementioned approach to methodology might generate a closer relationship (and perhaps overlap) between 'activists' and 'researchers' in the green criminological field. In fact, this juxtaposition is by no means alien to other areas of criminological debate. In particular, those working in the sub-field of victimology have long had to grapple with this issue: noted victimologist Jan Van Dijk pointed out as long ago as 1997 that victimologists tended to resist being labelled 'as either researcher or activist' and that 'most of [them] are happy to wear both hats' (3). Munro (2012) provides a concise review of arguments for and against the greater cooperation and interaction between academics (specifically social movement scholars) and social activists in many areas but within the animal rights sphere in particular. Despite the numerous practical and theoretical hurdles, Munro's conclusion is that

> their [social movement scholars] academic 'tool kit' might prove to be more useful than the philosopher's more abstract concepts and reasoning; this would certainly be the case in the everyday practice of activism where strategy and tactics are of paramount importance. . . . It is surely logical that social movement theories and concepts are enhanced by a scholar's engagement with activists whose 'practical knowledge' provides empirical credibility for what otherwise is often perceived as esoteric, abstract theory.
>
> (2012: 515)

Methodologically, this closer synergy between value-laden activism and academic debate is already present in the environmental crime literature – both in relation to the regulation of environmental harm and in terms of the collecting of more quantitative data on the subject. In the former case, we might look to the example of the League Against Cruel Sports in the UK, which has turned its attention since 2004 to supporting prosecutions of those who defy or otherwise circumvent the fox hunting ban. In terms of its successes, the League maintains:

> Through our investigations and legal team we have worked closely with the police and CPS to ensure those who illegally hunt animals for sport are brought to justice. To date there has been at least one conviction every two weeks since the ban began in 2005.
>
> (League Against Cruel Sports, 2014)

The emergence of a charity as a key investigator and enforcer of national criminal law is clearly significant for both green and more orthodox criminologists (albeit in the UK, the Royal Society for the Prevention of Cruelty to Animals has a long history of assuming this role). What is also significant from a research perspective is that a portion of the data and evidence collected by the League (including photographs and filming of alleged illegal hunting activities) is done through covert operations. Such operations challenge traditional notions of informed consent employed in most mainstream research ethics statements. The League's strategy also relies on recruiting the public to gather information about illegal hunting activities, calling on their website for the public to 'be our eyes and ears in the countryside' (League Against Cruel Sports, 2014). In a similar vein, O'Rourke and Macey (2003) report how communities in the United States are forming 'bucket brigades' using inexpensive homemade equipment (buckets) to assist authorities in monitoring air omissions near industrial facilities. This last case is particularly significant not just because the data are being collected through new (positivist) methods, but because they are being collected *by* members of the public rather than by professional researchers or environmental enforcement officers. In the UK, we might also draw on the example of the now-annual crowd-sourced 'Big Garden Birdwatch' research project from the Royal Society for the Protection of Birds (RSPB, 2015). Indeed, it will often be the case that those interested in collecting such data – frequently for the express purposes of providing evidence at criminal or regulatory proceedings – are in fact representatives of the activist community. In a broader sense, this move towards gathering large amounts of information from multiple, diverse sources may see green criminology moving further in the direction of so-called 'big data', whereby very large data sets are amassed from multiple (often online) repositories (Boyd and Crawford, 2011). Such examples lend weight to the contention made at the end of the last section that green criminology could well challenge certain methodological conventions in truly fundamental ways.

## Conclusions

Green criminology is in the process of solidifying itself as a serious and long-term project dedicated to the analysis of environmental harm and the response of society to it. We have seen in this paper that the exact focus of that project is still in flux; however, it seems inevitable that a simple and wholesale alignment to any single orthodox methodological position is unlikely to be suitable or result in the long-term growth of the field. From the researcher's perspective, much of this chapter has emphasised a constructivist viewpoint whereby environmental harm and crime are seen as heavily influenced by social, political and economic forces. Equally, however, we have seen that objectivist approaches and positivistic data may constitute a key means by which a more eco-centric perspective can be injected into the exercise. So, whilst we cannot ascertain the opinion of, for example, birds whose flight patterns are affected by wind farms (Drewitt and Langston, 2006; Marris and Fairless, 2007), we can derive statistical estimates of how many birds are affected and to what extent. Of course, ultimately, such statistics are generated by human 'experts', and thus we must be wary of any claim that they in fact present an objective reality, much less an eco-centric one. Ultimately, we have seen that there is a real case for both positivist and interpretivist perspectives in green criminology, even though, as a matter of methodological theory, they are grounded in very different epistemological and ontological positions.

The aforementioned factors notwithstanding, we have seen throughout the course of this discussion that traditional research strategies associated with criminology (whether qualitative or quantitative) are arguably not well suited to gathering information about non-human impacts and effects, or even to linking such effects back to human suffering. Fundamentally, up until very recently, criminology has been an almost exclusively anthropocentric discipline: it has focused on human needs, expectations and harms. Yet to proceed further down the route of eco-centrism is to invite criticism that the research of green criminologists is overly swayed by normative standpoints on the rights and wrongs of ecological production versus economic production. Meeting such criticism partly relies on the marshalling of more positivist data to support the claims made by green criminologists concerning the (more) objective ecological harms vested by unfettered production. Nevertheless, even such quantifying data are increasingly derived from less orthodox, more public (perhaps activist) sources as the field expands. As such, it is submitted that green criminologists are better off acknowledging their 'green' credentials from the outset, building these into a reflexive and robust research exercise and reaping the very real advantages of doing so in the form of a green criminology which genuinely makes contributions over and above an orthodox and anthropocentric criminology of the environment.

## References

Agnew, R. (2013) 'The ordinary acts that contribute to ecocide: A criminological analysis'. In N. South and A. Brisman (eds.) *The Routledge International Handbook of Green Criminology*, Abingdon, England: Routledge, pp. 58–72.

Anderson, A. (2006) 'Spinning the rural agenda: The countryside alliance, fox hunting and social policy', *Social Policy & Administration*, **40**(6): 722–738.

Bailey, K. (1994) *Methods of Social Research*, 4th edition, New York: Free Press.

Beirne, P. (2007) 'Animal rights, animal abuse and green criminology'. In P. Beirne and N. South (eds.) *Issues in Green Criminology: Confronting Harms against Environments, Humanity and Other Animals*, Cullompton, England: Willan, pp. 55–86.

Benton, T. (2007) 'Ecology, community and justice: The meaning of green'. In P. Beirne and N. South (eds.) *Issues in Green Criminology: Confronting Harms against Environments, Humanity and Other Animals*, Cullompton, England: Willan, pp. 3–31.

Blowfield, M. and Murray, A. (2011) *Corporate Responsibility*, Oxford: Oxford University Press.

Boyd, D. and Crawford, K. (2011) 'Six provocations for big data', Presented at *A Decade in Internet Time: Symposium on the Dynamics of the Internet and Society*, September 2011. Retrieved from http://papers.ssrn.com/sol3/papers.cfm?abstract_id=1926431.

British Broadcasting Corporation (BBC) (2014) *Can drones help tackle Africa's wildlife poaching crisis?* Retrieved from http://www.bbc.co.uk/news/business-28132521.

Brosnan, A. (2013) 'Prosecuting environmental crime', Paper presented at the ICOSS Climate Change, Law and Victimisation Seminar, University of Sheffield, 30 October 2013.

Bryman, A. (2012) *Social Research Methods*, 4th edition, Oxford: Oxford University Press.

Burns, L. (2000) *Final report of the committee of inquiry into hunting with dogs in England and Wales*. Retrieved from http://webarchive.nationalarchives.gov.uk/20100512151544/http:/www.huntinginquiry.gov.uk/mainsections/huntingreport.htm.

Campbell, R., Patterson, D. and Bybee, D. (2011) 'Using mixed methods to evaluate a community intervention for sexual assault survivors: A methodological tale', *Violence against Women*, **17**(3): 376–388.

Carrabine, E., Cox, P., Lee, M., Plummer, K. and South, N. (2004) *Criminology: A Sociological Introduction*, Abingdon, England: Routledge.

Chamovitz, D. (2013) *What a Plant Knows*, London: Oneworld Publications.

Chatham House, The Royal Institute of International Affairs (2015) *Illegal logging and related trade: Indicators of the global response*. Retrieved from http://indicators.chathamhouse.org/background-methodology.

Cotterell, R. (2006) *Law, Culture and Society: Legal Ideas in the Mirror of Society*, Aldershot, England: Ashgate.

Daston, L. and Mitman, G. (2005) *Thinking with Animals: New Perspectives on Anthropomorphism*, New York: Columbia University Press.

Davis, J.-D. (2005) *State Responsibility for Global Climate Change: The Case of the Maldives*, Medford, OR: Tufts Fletcher School.

Drewitt, A. and Langston, R. (2006) 'Assessing the impacts of wind farms on birds', *IBIS International Journal of Avian Science*, **148**(S1): 29–42.

Fielding, N. (2010) 'Mixed methods research in the real world', *International Journal of Social Research Methodology*, **13**(2): 127–138.

Flournoy, A., Andreen, W., Bratspies, R., Doremus, H., Flatt, V., Glicksman, R. and Mintz, J. (2010) *Regulatory blowout: How regulatory failures made the BP disaster possible, and how the system can be fixed to avoid a recurrence*, Centre for Progressive Reform White Paper No. 1007, Washington, DC: Centre for Progressive Reform.

Gibbs, C., Gore, M., McGarrell, E. and Rivers, L. (2010) 'Introducing conservation criminology: Towards interdisciplinary scholarship on environmental crimes and risks', *British Journal of Criminology*, **50**(1): 124–144.

Groombridge, N. (2013) 'Matter all over the place: Litter, criminology and criminal justice'. In N. South and A. Brisman (eds.) *Routledge International Handbook of Green Criminology*, Abingdon, England: Routledge, pp. 394–409.

Hall, M. and Farrell, S. (2012) 'The criminogenic consequences of climate change: Blurring the boundaries between offenders and victims'. In N. South and A. Brisman (eds.) *The Routledge International Handbook of Green Criminology*, Abingdon, England: Routledge, pp. 26–58.

Herrick, C. (2004) 'Objectivity versus narrative coherence: Science, environmental policy, and the US Data Quality Act', *Environmental Science & Policy*, 7(5): 419–433.

House, E. and Howe, K. (1999) *Values in Evaluation and Social Research*, Thousand Oaks, CA: Sage.

Hulsman, L. (1986) 'Critical criminology and the concept of crime'. In H. Bianchi and R. van Swaaningen (eds.) *Abolitionism: Towards a Non-Repressive Approach to Crime*, Amsterdam: Free University Press, pp. 63–80.

Ivanic, M. and Martin, W. (2008) *Implications of higher global food prices for poverty in low-income countries*, World Bank Policy Research Working Paper No. 4594, Washington, DC: The World Bank.

Jasparro, C. and Taylor, J. (2008) 'Climate change and regional vulnerability to transnational security threats in Southeast Asia', *Geopolitics*, **13**(2): 232–256.

Johnson, B. and Onwuegbuzie, A. (2004) 'Mixed methods research: A research paradigm whose time has come', *Educational Researcher*, **33**(7): 14–26.

Kearon, T. and Godfrey, B. (2007) 'Setting the scene: A question of history'. In S. Walklate (ed.) *Handbook of Victims and Victimology*, Cullompton, England: Willan, pp. 17–36.

Kriebel, D., Tickner, J., Epstein, P., Lemons, J., Levins, R., Loechler, E. and Stoto, M. (2001) 'The precautionary principle in environmental science', *Environmental Health Perspectives*, **109**(9): 871–892.
Laufer, W. (2003) 'Social accountability and corporate greenwashing', *Journal of Business Ethics*, **43**(3): 253–261.
League Against Cruel Sports (2014) *Who we are*. Retrieved from http://www.league.org.uk/who-we-are.
League Against Cruel Sports (2015) 'Today's hunting act proposals show government is deceiving the public', Press Release, 9 July 2015. Retrieved from http://www.league.org.uk/news-and-opinion/press-releases/2015/july-15/todays-hunting-act-proposals-show-government-is-deceiving-the-public.
Lee, T.-P. (2009) *A welfare approach to mitigating environmental injustice: Exploring needs of pollution victims*. Retrieved from http://www.welfareacademy.org/pubs/international/epckdi/2.pdf.
Lynch, M. (1990) 'The greening of criminology', *Critical Criminologist*, **2**: 1–5.
Lynch, M. and Stretesky, P. (2007) 'Green criminology in the United States'. In P. Beirne and N. South (eds.) *Issues in Green Criminology: Confronting Harms against Environments, Humanity and Other Animals*, Cullompton, England: Willan, pp. 248–269.
Maines, D. (1993) 'Narrative's moment and sociology's phenomena: Toward a narrative sociology', *Sociological Quarterly*, **34**: 17–38.
Maintenay, A. (2013) 'Environmentalism as religion: A fruitful concept? A roundtable discussion', *Studies in Religion/Sciences Religieuses*, **42**: 291–292.
Mares, D. (2010) 'Criminalizing ecological harm: Crimes against carrying capacity and the criminalization of eco-sinners', *Critical Criminology*, **18**: 279–293.
Marris, E. and Fairless, D. (2007) 'Wind farms' deadly reputation hard to shift', *Nature*, **447**: 126.
McAdam, J. (2012) *Climate Change and Displacement: Multidisciplinary Perspectives*, Oxford: Hart.
Mies, M. (1993) 'Towards a methodology for feminist research'. In M. Hammersley (ed.) *Social Research: Philosophy, Politics and Practice*, Thousand Oaks, CA: Sage, pp. 64–82.
Munro, L. (2012) 'Teaching & learning guide for: The animal rights movement in theory and practice: A review of the sociological literature', *Sociology Compass*, **6**(6): 511–518.
Nagel, T. (1974) 'What is it like to be a bat?' *The Philosophical Review*, **83**: 435–450.
Nurse, A. (2013) *Animal Harm: Perspective on Why People Harm and Kill Animals*, Farnham, England: Ashgate.
O'Rourke, D. and Macey, G. (2003) 'Community environmental policing: Assessing new strategies of public participation in environmental regulation', *Journal of Policy Analysis and Management*, **22**(3): 383–414.
Park, M. and Singer, S. (2012) 'The globalization of animal welfare: More food does not require more suffering', *Foreign Affairs*, **91**(2): 1–4.
Potter, G. (2013) 'Justifying "green" criminology: Values and "taking sides" in an ecologically informed social science'. In M. Cowburn, M. Duggan, A. Robinson and P. Senior (eds.) *Values in Criminology and Criminal Justice*, Bristol, England: Policy Press, pp. 125–142.
Purdy, R. (2010) 'Using earth observation technologies for better regulatory compliance and enforcement of environmental laws', *Journal of Environmental Law*, **22**(1): 59–87.
Robson, C. (2011) *Real World Research: A Resource for Users of Social Research Methods in Applied Settings*, Chichester, England: Wiley.
RSPB (2015) *Big garden birdwatch*. Retrieved from https://www.rspb.org.uk/discoverandenjoynature/discoverandlearn/birdwatch/?utm_medium=website.
Son, S., Menghua, W. and Shon, J.-K. (2011) 'Satellite observations of optical and biological properties in the Korean dump site of the Yellow Sea', *Remote Sensing of Environment*, **115**(2): 562–572.

South, N. (1998) 'A green field for criminology: A proposal for a perspective', *Theoretical Criminology*, **2**(2): 211–233.
South, N. (2014) 'Green criminology: Reflections, connections, horizons', *International Journal for Crime, Justice and Social Democracy*, **3**(2): 6–20.
South, N., Brisman, A. and Beirne, P. (2013) 'A guide to green criminology'. In N. South and A. Brisman (eds.) *The Routledge International Handbook of Green Criminology*, London: Routledge, pp. 27–42.
Stone, C. (2010) *Should Trees Have Standing?* New York: Oxford University Press.
Stretesky, P., Long, M. and Lynch, M. (2014) *The Treadmill of Crime: Political Economy and Green Criminology*, Abingdon, England: Routledge.
Think India Foundation (2011) *Now, a UAV to monitor air quality*. Retrieved from http://www.thinkindia.net.in/2011/09/now-a-uav-to-monitor-air-quality.html.
Tombs, S. and Whyte, D. (2007) 'Researching white collar and corporate crime in an era of neo-liberalism'. In H. Pontell and G. Geis (eds.) *International Handbook of White Collar and Corporate Crime*, New York: Springer, pp. 125–147.
Tyler, T. (1990) *Why People Obey the Law*, New Haven, CT: Yale University Press.
United Nations Food and Agriculture Organization (2010) *Special Programme for Food Security*. Retrieved from www.fao.org/spfs.
van Solinge, T. B. (2014) 'Researching illegal logging and deforestation', *Journal of Crime, Criminal Law and Criminal Justice*, **3**(2): 35–48.
Weber, E. (2010) 'What shapes perceptions of climate change?' *Wiley Interdisciplinary Reviews: Climate Change*, **1**(3): 332–342.
White, R. (2007) 'Green criminology and the pursuit of social and ecological justice'. In P. Beirne and N. South (eds.) *Issues in Green Criminology: Confronting Harms against Environments, Humanity and Other Animals*, Cullompton, England: Willan, pp. 32–54.
White, R. (2013) 'The conceptual contours of green criminology'. In R. Walters, D. Westerhuisand and T. Wyatt (eds.) *Emerging Issues in Green Criminology: Exploring Power, Justice and Harm*, Basingstoke, England: Palgrave Macmillan, pp. 17–33.
Williams, C. (2013) 'Research methodologies in examining climate change law and victimisation'. Paper presented at the ICOSS Climate Change, Law and Victimisation Seminar, University of Sheffield, 30 October 2013.

# 3 Can the individual survive the greening of criminology?

*Dominic A. Wood*

## Introduction

The emergence of green criminology as a theme within academia has given rise to important areas of criminological research across a diverse range of topics (Beirne and South, 2007; Brisman and South, 2013; Lynch and Stretesky, 2003; South, 1998; Walters, 2006; White, 2003, 2008, 2010). Indeed, so diverse and interdisciplinary is this range that it is not obvious what connects such an apparently disparate array of issues (Hall, 2014; White, 2013). Moreover, the meaning of 'green' is contested within political science and philosophy (Dobson and Eckersley, 2006; Doherty and de Geus, 1996; Dryzeck, 2005; Eckersley, 1992), and the very purpose of criminology is itself increasingly called into question.[1] Green criminology is therefore born into a highly contested academic world in which competing green and criminological perspectives produce rich, philosophical and normative debates.

The purpose of this chapter is to contribute to these debates by considering the extent to which the concept of the individual can retain a significant place within a greened criminology. Criminology is traditionally framed within liberal democratic criminal justice contexts, shaped in particular by liberal individual concerns.[2] The idealised individual is at the heart of traditional criminal justice debates and is used as the measure between competing perspectives. Irrespective of where we position ourselves in such debates, it is imperative that we pay due consideration to the individual if we are to remain within a broadly liberal democratic perspective.

Criminology has, in this respect, been shaped by, and framed within, liberal democratic tensions that can be articulated as liberal dilemmas – for example, through the enduring question of how we protect society sufficiently without unnecessarily undermining civil liberties. However, the magnitude and urgency of environmental concerns are such that they give rise to what we might call 'green dilemmas', with extremities that far surpass the parameters of liberal dilemmas. To put it bluntly, green dilemmas do not simply address objectionable voices and opinions that pose threats, nor even acts of terrorism that threaten the lives of innocents. Rather, green dilemmas are concerned with things that may threaten human existence. Clearly, the more we accept this dystopian vision, the less importance we

1 At the 2013 British Society of Criminology Annual Conference at the University of Wolverhampton, the theme of the conference was 'criminology on trial'. Professor Steve Tombs criticised criminology for perpetuating an exaggerated and disproportionate focus on crime at the expense of other, more serious and substantive social ills.

2 The philosophical underpinnings of Rawls (1971) have been dominant across liberal democratic institutions.

attach to the individual. So whilst the individual is at the heart of liberal dilemmas, this is not the case with green dilemmas. Environmental issues diminish individual concerns because of the extent to which they present significant, urgent, long-lasting and even irreversible challenges. It is difficult to take environmental problems seriously without becoming dismissive of liberal concerns, or at the very least qualifying the extent to which they should feature prominently within meaningful solutions (Eckersley, 2006; Sagoff, 1988; Wissenburg, 2006). Therefore, the elevation of green values into criminological discourse has the potential to minimise concern for the individual and trivialise the underpinning ethical preoccupations that have been dominant within traditional criminology.

This chapter considers four aspects of green criminology that are highly problematic from the perspective of the liberal individual. First, the importance of values within green perspectives challenges the ideal of ethical neutrality that characterises traditional liberal concerns (Boyd, 2004). In this respect, green criminology contributes to an ongoing shift away from negative conceptions of liberty that favour individual freedom towards more positive expressions of liberty that champion particular values above the freedom of the individual (see Berlin, 1958; Gray, 2000). Second, within green criminology, too little attention has been paid to the conservative character of many green concepts, especially those that stress the importance of intergenerational over intragenerational matters. Intergenerational concerns limit the claims of the present generation relative to the additional weight given to future and past generations. The dominant voice within green criminology has favoured a social justice focus that prioritises intragenerational equity issues over intergenerational equity concerns (Beirne and South, 2007; Lynch and Stretesky, 2003; White, 2003, 2008). Whilst intragenerational equity allows for greater consideration of individuals, especially those most disadvantaged and/or discriminated against, it is intergenerational equity that better captures distinctively green sentiments (Dobson, 2000). The intergenerational aspect of green thought arguably has more in common with conservative thinking than radical left philosophies (Bramwell, 1994; Giddens, 1994; Gray, 1993; Scruton, 2006). Third, green thought has contributed to debates about liberal democracy that have, in different ways, challenged liberal individualism (Dobson, 2000; Dobson and Eckersley, 2006; Doherty and de Geus, 1996). On the one hand, the urgency with which environmental issues impose themselves on us has led some to adopt authoritarian responses against democracy (Ophuls, 1977), whilst at the other extreme, greens have argued for an extended democratic community to include non-human species and future generations (Dryzeck, 2005; Eckersley, 1992, 1998, 1999). Fourth, the explicitly anti-anthropocentric view that characterises green thinking (Dobson, 2000) is at odds with the language of liberal individualism. This includes, for example, the way in which liberalism is expressed through the concept of human rights. Beyond the obvious connection between anthropocentric perspectives and human rights, at least linguistically, the relationship between human rights and green concerns is contentious and complex (Boyle, 2012; Gearty, 2010).

In considering these four challenges to liberal individualism, I will conclude by suggesting ways in which green issues can be addressed within the pre-green understanding of environmental criminology presented by Bottoms and Wiles (2002) – what White (2008) suggests is better understood as 'place-based crime prevention' (7) – in a way that does not require the complete abandonment of traditional liberal concerns regarding the protection of individual rights and the human welfare components of a social justice criminological agenda. It is inevitable that the liberal prioritisation of the individual is unsustainable from a green perspective, but this does not necessarily equate to the rejection of anthropocentrism. It does, however, demand an expanded understanding of what it means to be human. We need to be more cognisant of the inter-relationship between humans and the non-human world and much more appreciative of how the non-human world shapes humanity in aesthetic, spiritual and emotional ways. Such an understanding allows for a better balance between the alleviation of the pain and suffering of the most deprived and disenfranchised human beings alive today and giving due consideration to other species and future generations.

## The importance of values within green perspectives

Values are important within green perspectives. As much as environmental concerns deal with very real, significant and substantive challenges to the future of human societies, green perspectives are, in many respects, also defined by the extent to which environmental problems are presented in moral terms (Hayward, 1998). This is expressed by Fiorino (2006: 38) when he says that environmental regulation is guided from a perspective that presents pollution 'as a moral transgression, not a problem to be solved'. Foster (2000: 10) likewise says that, to a large extent, the 'ecological question is reduced . . . to one of values'. Even from the perspective of a prominent environmental scientist such as E. O. Wilson, environmental problems are discussed as being 'innately ethical' (Wilson, 1992: 298), while the physicist Capra (1997: 9) argues that in responding to environmental challenges, we need 'not only an expansion of our perceptions and ways of thinking, but also of our values'. In his seminal book *Small Is Beautiful*, Schumacher (1973: 80) discusses the problems facing society in terms of 'our central convictions' being in 'disorder', and this is reinforced by Orr (1992: 4) when he refers to ecological problems as a consequence of 'a crisis of spirit and spiritual resources'. This aspect of green thought expresses what Dickson (2000) refers to as the *ethicist conception of environmental problems*. This refers to the fact that environmental problems are presented as a consequence of 'ethically inappropriate attitudes' and/or that encouraging people to adopt 'ethically appropriate attitudes' is seen as an important step towards resolving environmental matters (Dickson, 2000: 128).

This focus on values is a key feature within green criminology, even if it is not always an explicit aim or motivation. It is most evident in the green criminology that has evolved from a morally informed criticism of criminology (Lynch, 1990; Schwendinger and Schwendinger, 1970). The failure of criminology to address inequalities in the administration of justice leads to concerns about the extent to which criminology fails to protect the vulnerable and/or support the prosecution of socially and economically powerful offenders (Tombs, 2007). Green perspectives have been incorporated into social justice–inspired models of criminology and, as such, offer an alternative intellectual framework that calls into question many of the assumptions that underpin criminology (South, 1998). This *greening* of criminology involves explicitly reconstituting the principles and normative conventions that shape our understanding of criminology and indeed more broadly our understanding of rights and justice (Benton, 1998, 2007, 2008; White and Graham, 2015).

However, green criminology includes the criminologist applying his or her trade to issues that are designated as green, in which there is a continuation of existing and established criminological theories being extended to emerging criminological problems that have a green flavour. Green criminology of this kind is determined by the focus rather than the nature of the criminological enquiry and is likely to be motivated by time-honoured criminological concerns, which do not necessarily begin from an explicit moral position. However, even when the focus on green issues is driven by a scientifically objective, empirical, positivist criminological approach, it nonetheless invariably leads to a greater awareness of the normative considerations that call into question established criminological assumptions.

The consideration of green issues, in other words, has a profound influence on the generation and elevation of deeply moral questions. No matter what the starting point is, at the point of arrival, green criminology has a strong, explicit focus on values that is at odds with traditional, *exclusively* empirical criminological enquiry. No matter how much a green criminology perspective draws upon an empirical evidential base to support its claim, its *necessarily* normative base comes through in an explicit and overt way (e.g. see White, 2010, edited collection).

From a traditional liberal democratically framed criminological perspective, such a focus on values is highly challenging because of the extent to which it potentially extends the permissibility of authorities to intervene in society. It represents a shift from a negative conception of liberty, which seeks to curb state authority over individuals, towards a positive conception of liberty, which seeks to influence the nature of the authority over individuals (see Berlin, 1958; Gray, 2000). An immediate concern from a traditional, liberally framed criminal justice perspective is that it raises the potential dangers of over-policing and over-regulating behaviour in the pursuit of what is deemed to constitute acceptable green behaviour.

The focus on values also removes the option of pragmatic responses to issues by demanding some form of moral retribution beyond practical resolutions. The green moral challenge is part of a much wider retreat from a liberal favouring of ethical neutrality (Boyd, 2004). MacIntyre (1985) argues that liberalism was never actually ethically neutral but rather, as Bellamy (2000) suggests, favoured the valuing of the individual over other, more communal and/or societal concerns. In particular, green criminology develops the view that liberalism – and, even more so, neo-liberalism – has been guilty of supporting the individual rights of the most powerful at the expense of the vast majority, whose suffering at the hands of the powerful is largely ignored. Nonetheless, the liberal insight is that the more explicit we are about the kind of values that we think are important, the more willing we are to ensure that these values are championed across society, and the more willing we are to override the concerns of individuals who do not agree with, or accept, these values. This is a move away from the kind of thinking associated with the nineteenth-century liberal John Stuart Mill, who was at pains to champion the rights of individuals to be non-conformist (Mill, 1849). The explicit focus on green values, with an imperative to comply with ecological principles, significantly reduces tolerance towards the non-conformity of individuals.

## The conservative characteristic of green thought: intergenerational versus intragenerational priorities within green criminology

A second point to address is the perception that a green perspective is necessarily supportive of the kind of left-wing ideas associated with human emancipation. The literature addressing the greening of criminology has tended to focus on environmental concerns as they relate to existing matters of social justice (Lynch and Stretesky, 2003; South, 1998; Walters, 2006; White, 2003). Environmental issues have undoubtedly provided an opportunity to re-invigorate critical criminological perspectives that emphasise the harm caused by people in positions of power (Walters, 2006) and the extent to which this is too often ignored in criminological debate. Walters (2007), for example, uses concern over radioactive waste to demonstrate how large companies and governments are implicit in creating environmental harm. South (2007) likewise addresses ways in which corporate and commercial interests lead to an ecologically destructive exploitation of natural resources. This approach is expressed explicitly by Beirne and South (2007: xiv) when they present green criminology 'as a welcome addition to existing critical, democratic and left-oriented perspectives on crime and social harm'.

The focus on the inequalities of harm distribution within criminology is easily applied to environmental harms that are disproportionately inflicted on the poor – for example, in relation to the racial and class bias of subjection to toxic waste (Schwendinger et al., 2002). Indeed, the linking of environmental issues and corresponding notions of environmental justice to existing injustices and discrimination is a valid and worthy enterprise, but it is unclear as to whether this constitutes a greening of criminology. The social justice focus within green criminology emphasises intragenerational equity issues that do not necessarily address what is different about ecological thought. Although it is acknowledged within the green criminology literature that any discussion about greening criminology needs to engage with broader arguments about green understandings of nature, the debate invariably focuses on ways in which environmental issues disproportionately impact those already discriminated against. The intergenerational equity issues, which are arguably more characteristic of a green perspective, play second fiddle here to the intragenerational equity issues, which are the cornerstone of traditional left-oriented perspectives.

Framing the greening discussion around existing social justice concerns ignores the conservative values underpinning many green ideas (see Gray, 1993; Scruton, 2006) – especially the green focus on intergenerational equity, precaution and the limits to growth. Indeed, the highly normative characteristic of green thinking highlights the fact that many green values have conservative antecedents (Bramwell, 1994). This needs to be stressed for two reasons. First, it runs counter to an assumption within much of the literature on green criminology that sees environmental concerns fitting neatly within traditional social justice concerns. Second, and perhaps more importantly, it ignores potentially illiberal consequences of aspects of green thinking, such as those expressed by Ophuls (1977). The roots of environmentalism are complex and can be traced back to almost any political tradition, including anarchist and socialist movements. But we can also establish trajectories back to conservative and even far-right ideologies (Bramwell, 1989, 1994; Dobson and Eckersly, 2006; Pepper, 1984, 1996). Indeed, Bramwell (1994) refers to the perception that 'prior to the late 1970s, Greenness was seen as an incipiently sinister conservative or even Fascist idea in German thought' (94). Without wishing to suggest that this is the case today, there are some uncomfortable components of a green perspective for liberal-minded individuals that arise from the green focus on limits and the need to give more priority to future generations when considering the needs of those alive today.

The relationship between green thinking and conservative values has been noted by a number of influential commentators (Giddens, 1994; Gray, 1993; Scruton, 2006). Giddens (1994: 11) states, for example, that there are 'rather obvious affinities between ecological thinking . . . and philosophic conservatism' in drawing a parallel between green ideas and the arguments developed by Edmund Burke at the end of the eighteenth century. Similarly, Scruton (2006) and Gray (1993) argue that ecological and conservative perspectives coincide on many points. One idea that Gray (1993: 136–137) expands upon is the 'multi-generational perspective' that has its roots in Burke. Scruton (2006), likewise, makes much of this connection between Burke's understanding of intergenerational equity and the contemporary ecological variant. Dobson (2000) challenges this green connection to Burke by highlighting important differences between ecological and conservative ideas and the historical contexts in which they arise. In particular, he notes that ecological perspectives are more concerned with future generations as opposed to the conservative emphasis on the past. But Scruton (2006) sees in Burke an inherent connection between reverence for past generations and consideration of future ones. He argues that it is only when we truly appreciate what we have inherited from our forebears will we be willing to make sacrifices for those who will follow us. He says that when we forget the dead, we also 'remove the unborn' from the agenda (Scruton, 2006: 17).

Despite the philosophical connections between conservative and green ideas, there has nonetheless undoubtedly tended to be hostility between their respective advocates. However, both Gray (1993) and Scruton (2006) explain this hostility in contextual terms. They argue that conservatives have objected to what they see as the excesses of particular radical green groups rather than underlying green philosophical sentiments and, similarly, that greens have tended to be hostile towards a particular variant of conservatism, one associated with the right's adherence to neo-liberal, free market ideas from the mid-1970s onwards. Both Gray (1993) and Scruton (2006) stress that this understanding of conservatism is misleading, and in identifying the commonalities between conservative and ecological perspectives, they challenge the view that the process of 'greening' should be associated exclusively, if at all, with left or liberal traditions.

At the very least, appreciating the philosophically conservative characteristics of green ideas, such as precaution, natural limits and intergenerational equity, requires us to go beyond simply assuming a synergy between red and green perspectives if we are to fully understand the implications of a greened criminology. For Scruton (2006), the problem with what he sees as left-minded greens is that they fail to appreciate what motivates humans to behave in ecologically bad ways and, more importantly, what it would take to get them to change lifestyles to ones that are more conducive to realising a greener world. He contrasts here the global aspirations of socialist traditions with the localism of conservative thinking. Scruton (2006: 18) argues that social justice–inspired green thinking is imbued with a degree of 'self-righteousness' that is unlikely to convince people to make sacrifices. Conservative appeals, on the other hand, to locality, territory, tradition and family, are considered by Scruton (2006) to be much more likely to produce the required levels of concern that will lead to changes in behaviour for the sake of those we hold most dear. He suggests that when it comes to motivating individuals to adapt and change, we need to consider 'that human beings are creatures of limited and local affections' (Scruton, 2006: 19). Importantly for the purposes of this chapter, we should note that the conservative language emphasises individual sacrifice over liberty and presents more of a communal and familial focus to the debate.

The criminological implications arising from this conservative understanding of green thought are clearly problematic from the perspective of the liberal individual. For example, the regulatory framework established through the precautionary principle is illustrative of a trend within criminology that emphasises prevention over cure, a focus on 'pre-crime' (Zedner, 2009) and a more intrusive form of control (Garland, 2001), all of which trivialise the importance of the individual. The precautionary principle originated in West Germany in 1976 as the 'Vorsorgeprinzip' (Boehmer-Christiansen, 1994). Warren (1993) notes that it was first endorsed by the UK government at the Second International Conference on the Protection of the North Sea in 1987 (MacGarvin, 1994). This endorsement was later formalised as UK government policy in the 1990 white paper *This Common Inheritance* (Jordan, 1998). The Rio Earth Summit in 1992 was also an important vehicle for ensuring that the precautionary principle was widely adopted and practised (O'Riordan and Cameron, 1994). The precautionary principle establishes a shift in decisions about environmental matters that is self-evidently against the potential polluter (Wynne, 1994). For those familiar with the Dr Seuss (1971) children's classic *The Lorax*, the precautionary principle would have made it much more difficult for the Once-ler to chop down all of the Truffula Trees and would have conversely given much more weight to the Lorax's voice: 'I speak for the trees, for the trees have no tongues' (Dr Seuss, 1971: 10). It might be the case that ongoing developments around the world, especially recently in relation to fracking, suggest that the precautionary principle is no longer being taken as seriously as was intended; however, this is indicative of what Gray (1993) and Scruton (2006) see as the free market, neo-liberal perversion of conservatism rather than conservative values per se.

## Greens, liberalism, democracy and authoritarianism

The conservative underpinning of many green concepts is important when considering the relationship between green and liberal perspectives (Eckersley, 1996; Sagoff, 1988; Vincent, 1998; Wissenburg, 2006). It is also important in considering the potential for authoritarian conclusions to be drawn by greens frustrated by the time democratic processes can take in addressing urgent, pressing, irreversible levels of ecological degradation. Eckersley (1996: 212) notes the logic of liberal democracy when she says that individuals 'must be "free" to make ecologically bad decisions'. A conflict arises here from the possibility that citizens do not recognise the importance of ecological imperatives and, should this occur, either democracy or the environment will be sacrificed. As Saward (1996: 92) argues, from a democratic perspective, 'greens have little comeback if a majority does not want green outcomes'.

One issue that illustrates this problem is human population growth. This, more than any other issue, sits uncomfortably for those wishing to pursue a social justice, democratically informed agenda – even more so for those concerned primarily with traditional liberal rights. Population control is contentious for many greens, but it is hard to completely escape the Malthusian[3] logic of the kind associated with Ehrlich (1968) when considering the human-led destruction of the planet. The Malthusian perspective is expressed most starkly by Brown and Kane's (1995) publication *Full House*. Any emphasis on the growing number of humans and the impact this is having on the planet undermines social justice arguments favouring intragenerational equity. The Malthusian logic favours intergenerational thinking over intragenerational concerns, and the redistribution of wealth, equality and justice between generations takes precedence over such a redistribution within the existing generation. The shadow of Malthus clearly informs a potentially authoritarian dimension within green perspectives.

The logic of the authoritarian conclusions is derived from the doomsday scenarios that have been a constant feature in green thought since at least the early 1970s when a survivalist agenda was established (e.g. Goldsmith et al., 1972; Meadows et al., 1972). Clearly, the survival of the planet would appear to be of far greater significance than the need for democratic procedures. Saward (1996: 92) suggests that the authoritarian impulses arise to the extent that environmental values are understood as being 'external' to democratic concerns, giving rise to 'ecological imperatives' that are seen to take precedence over democracy. This authoritarian impulse is demonstrated most clearly in the work of Olphus (1977), who supports 'the need for external coercion' where the self-restraint of individuals is not

3 Malthus (1798) argued that the geometric growth of the human population would always outstrip the arithmetic growth in the productivity of the land, meaning that growth in human numbers would produce an increasingly impoverished life.

forthcoming (cited in Eckersley, 1992: 15). As Dobson (2000: 117) asks rhetorically: 'If getting the right thing done is more important than how it gets done, why should greens not endorse authoritarian means to green ends?' The urgency of environmental issues has the potential to undermine democratic processes. Although democracy might be seen as the best process for eventually producing the 'right' answer, this might be too late, ecologically speaking. It is easy to see why authoritarianism could be seen as a necessary last resort and could be achieved by installing a benevolent green Leviathan to rule in an absolute, but ecologically sound, manner. The Hobbesian logic of this view is that an authoritarian society is better than having no society at all.

This is not to suggest that authoritarianism is the choice of greens who would, by and large, prefer people to recognise the need for environmental self-restraint and to adopt an ecological lifestyle democratically, as both Dobson (2000) and Eckersley (1999) stress. Indeed, the sensibilities of today are increasingly communitarian and democratic, and a green perspective adds to these by defining the democratic community in ecological, rather than simply human, terms (Dobson, 2000; Eckersley, 1992, 1998, 1999, 2006; Schlosberg, 2005). A green perspective builds upon existing ideas of social justice that emphasise the common good over the rights of individuals by extending what we mean by the common good to include all species and/or future generations. As such, greens have stressed the need to extend, increase and re-invigorate democracy in order to truly achieve a greened society. Eckersley (1992) refers favourably to Bookchin's brand of 'social ecology', which is premised upon the belief that ecologism should increase human freedom rather than act as a restraint upon it (Bookchin, 1995). Likewise, Paehlke (1993: 46) calls for an 'enhanced political democracy' to replace the representative, constitutional form that guarantees its citizens certain liberties but hardly involves them at all in the political process. Porritt (1984: 166) also questions the representative aspect of democracy, saying that the 'representative element of the system has insidiously undermined the element of participation'. In a similar vein, Connelly and Smith's (1999: 61) reference to 'deliberative democracy' is used to promote an extension of democratic participation which emerges from an interaction between 'ecological thinking and other streams of emancipatory thought'.

Importantly, though, from a liberal perspective, the more we extend and expand what constitutes the community, and the more we emphasise democratic virtues over liberal ones, the more we diminish the significance of the individual as a primary concern. Green thinking does not need to be authoritarian for it to be illiberal. Whilst green thinking arguably implies an extension to the democratic community to include non-human considerations and intergenerational concerns, it might also imply a correspondingly diminished importance of the individual voices of human beings alive today.

## The green rejection of anthropocentrism

Perhaps the aspect of green thinking that poses the greatest challenge to liberal individualism is its attack on anthropocentricism. For Dobson (2000), it is an eco-centric perspective that characterises green thought, and he argues that it is important to establish a much clearer distinction between environmentalism and ecologism in defining a green perspective. He suggests that this requires establishing a qualitative break between the two on the grounds that the former is anthropocentric and the latter is eco-centric. With this in mind, Dobson (2000) challenges the distinction made by Naess (1973) between shallow and light green and between deep and dark green, where the difference between these perspectives is a matter of degree. Dobson (2000) argues instead that only ecologism can be classified as green ideology because eco-centrism is its defining feature. He argues that this, more than anything else, sets it apart from environmentalism, which remains rooted within an anthropocentric world view. Dobson (2000: 2) is adamant that the difference is qualitative, arguing that 'environmentalism and ecologism need to be kept apart because they differ not only in degree but also in kind'.

Within green thought, eco-centric and bio-centric perspectives are presented as alternatives to anthropocentricism. Central to these alternative perspectives is the argument that we need to go beyond seeing only human life as having 'moral status' (Attfield, 2003; Dryzek, 2005; Schlosberg, 2005). The critique of anthropocentric valuing is illustrated by Dryzek's (2005: 183–184) reference to the founding principles of deep ecology. These are that individuals need to conceptualise themselves within the context of a larger organic entity and support the bio-centric view that there is equality between species and that no single species, including humanity, should be regarded as having more value than other species. In this respect, 'biocentric equality' presents itself as the opposite of 'anthropocentric arrogance' (Dryzek, 2005: 184).

The eminent philosopher Mary Midgley considers how anthropocentricism has evolved and developed over time, in particular noting the extent to which Christian and other religious accounts of an anthropocentric perspective were extended through Enlightenment thinkers such as Kant and Marx in a fairly robust and violent fashion (Midgley, 1994: 104–105). She also notes the changing fortunes of anthropocentrism over the twentieth century from an 'exaggerated, euphoric idea of human standing' towards 'a despairing nihilism' that results in seeing human beings as pollution (Midgley, 1994: 105).

For Midgley (1994), it makes no sense to speak of anthropocentricism in cosmological terms because we are increasingly coming to understand that, in physical terms, there is no centre. But, she argues, there is an inevitability of a human – indeed, individual – self-centredness within the context of the lives we live in order for our lives to have meaning. If we do not 'see our own self as in some sense the centre of the world' (Midgley, 1994: 103), then it is difficult to conceive of how or why we could be motivated to care about environmental concerns. The point here is that even if we are willing to sacrifice ourselves wholly to the pursuit of a greener world, in doing so we assume a degree of self-importance to the extent to which we believe that our actions have importance and influence. The issue for Midgely (1994) here is an enduring argument that in order to love others, we must first love ourselves. From this perspective, the problems in the world stem not from too much self-love per se but rather from not loving ourselves and/or others enough.

Here, Midgley (1994) approaches the concept of anthropocentricism by considering the way it is used today to denote a chauvinistic approach to non-human species. She notes that there is a tendency for us as individuals and as groups to give meaning to our lives by establishing artificial boundaries between ourselves and others. The anthropicist is, in this respect, the person, or group of people, that draws boundaries in a chauvinist manner between humans and non-human species. For Midgely (1994), the important point here is not to attack the self-centredness of the anthropocentric perspective but rather to challenge the extent to which self-centredness becomes narrow, exclusionary and chauvinistic. She says:

> We need, then, to recognize that people do right, not wrong, to have a particular regard for their own kin and their own species . . . because the measures needed today to save the human race are, by and large, the same measures that are needed to save the rest of the biosphere.
>
> (Midgley, 1994: 111)

The second part of this quotation is supported by Morrow (2011: 1) when she speaks of the 'shared predicament . . . between ourselves and the environment'. In this regard, we are perhaps better off thinking about the sentiment of an eco-centric perspective as an extension of anthropocentricism rather than a qualitative break. This avoids an unhelpful binary opposition between eco-centric and anthropocentric views of the kind suggested by Dobson (2000). This approach provides greater understanding of what it means to be human in a way that embeds ecological considerations. This concords more with the view that the origins of eco-centrism in Aldo Leopold's *Land Ethic* build upon and extend anthropocentric morality rather than opposing it (Dussault, 2013, 2014; Frierson, 2007).

There are important reasons for resisting the outright rejection of anthropocentricism. First, it can mask an underlying misanthropy. Dryzek (2005: 184) illustrates this with reference to an article written under the pseudonym Miss Ann Thropy in the *Earth First!* journal. The article, published in 1987, 'welcomed famine and disease (such as AIDS) as useful checks on human numbers' (cited in Dryzek, 2005: 184). Murray Bookchin, regarded as the founder of social ecology, also noted the growing misanthropy within ecological debates and turned much of his attention to challenging this tendency (Bookchin, 1995).

Second, there is a danger that even if non-anthropocentric views do not graduate towards misanthropy, there is still the possibility of undermining human efforts at averting ecological catastrophes. More thought needs to be given to how anthropocentricism can be developed in a manner that makes it capable of addressing ecological concerns (Cooper, 1992; O'Neill, 1993). Hayward (1998) raises important concerns about the rejection of anthropocentrism, which he sees as an unnecessary and unhelpful line of argument to pursue. He suggests that the real problem ecologists need to address is not that we suffer from being too human centred but rather that we lack care and compassion towards the non-human world. He argues that most examples that are provided of anthropocentrism are in fact committed by people who have no respect for others, whether they are human or non-human, and not by people who are overly human centred. He prefers to use the term 'speciesism' to refer to unacceptable practices that show a lack of compassion towards the non-human world in a way that mirrors the aforementioned arguments presented by Midgley (1994). Importantly, we should note that even where the environment is being valued instrumentally from a human-centred perspective, it should not be equated exclusively with an economic or market valuation. An instrumental valuation of the environment could also reflect aesthetic, religious or survival considerations. How we value the non-human world and the extent to which this valuation is of an intrinsic or instrumental kind[4] is an important consideration for criminologists to make sense of ecological perspectives and how they might inform a green conception of criminology.

O'Neill's (1993) identification of three different ways in which we might refer to something having intrinsic value is instructive here. His first use of 'intrinsic value' relates to how it is applied in opposition to instrumental value. By defining a value as intrinsic, in this sense we are saying that it represents a desired end in relation to other values that are a means towards this end. The distinction here between intrinsic and instrumental is hierarchical, with intrinsic values being of a more fundamental character. O'Neill (1993) demonstrates that intrinsic value, in this first sense, is required to avoid a problem that emerges if we only have instrumental value. Instrumental values need to be measured against something constant. An ecological concern can operate as an intrinsic value in this sense, informing the

4 See Lockwood's (1999) discussion of this in relation to valuing biodiversity.

instrumental measures required within any given environmental context. Such an understanding of intrinsic value does not require the rejection of anthropocentricism. We can establish ecological values as the guiding principles within a human-centred framework.

O'Neill's (1993) second use of 'intrinsic value' is concerned not with means and ends, or indeed any relationship between what is being valued and another entity. Instead, we are defining something as having intrinsic value if it can be established that it has value in and of itself. This understanding of intrinsic value can be applied to non-human entities without considering any relational properties they might have to human welfare or, indeed, to other non-human species. However, this perspective is also problematic from an ecological viewpoint in that it is not clear why one species, or indeed a particular ecological scenario, is favoured over alternatives. Lovelock (1989) makes this point when he says that the notion of an ideal ecological balance has no meaning in ecological terms beyond human valuation. There are, he argues, different ecological possibilities that can be more or less suitable to particular species and/or ecosystems. How do we establish that a stable climate is better than one that fluctuates widely? Likewise, why is a particular climate favoured over alternatives? It is easy to answer both of these questions from an anthropocentric perspective in which we wish to preserve human life, but it is not so easy to respond from an eco-centric position.

The third use of intrinsic value identified by O'Neill (1993) concerns the relationship between the person valuing and what is being valued. For something to be said to have intrinsic value in this third sense, we say that its value is independent of being valued. Here, the value is said to be objective rather than defined by the subjectivity of the person valuing. The importance of this third use is the ontological assumption that an entity can be said to have value even if there was no one to value it. This can be illustrated by Haldane's (1997) discussion about the aesthetic valuing of nature in terms of 'aesthetic object' and 'aesthetic attitude'. He argues that the former is found in the writings of Aquinas and Aristotle and is popular within green literature, whereas the latter concords with Enlightenment thinking. The significance of this difference is that the 'aesthetic object' understanding is premised on the notion that there is something inherently beautiful about the things we perceive to be aesthetically pleasing. In this sense, an aesthetic view is explained as the realisation or recognition of this beauty, which exists whether we see it or not. The counter 'aesthetic attitude' view is that aesthetic value is deposited into forms by an attitude – i.e. an object becomes aesthetic because it is perceived to be so. This third use of intrinsic value provides the most significant challenge to anthropocentricism, but in a way that is not particularly helpful from a green perspective. For example, photographs of planets within our solar system could be seen to have the kind of objective beauty associated with an aesthetic valuing of non-human aspects of our biosphere and ecosystems on Earth, despite the fact that they are devoid of life.

A further point noted by O'Neill (1993) concerns a common error in confusing these different uses of intrinsic value, in particular relating to the source of value and the object of value. O'Neill (1993) demonstrates that there is no logical connection between these two aspects and, in particular, that there is nothing inconsistent about establishing the view that only humans are the source of value, but that the non-human world can nonetheless be the primary object of value.

## Is there a place for human rights within a greened criminology?

As Midgley (1994) notes, the chauvinism of anthropocentricism is expressed to some extent in the defining of rights in a way that is exclusive to human beings 'who can speak in lawcourts, and . . . who have, in a recognized human sense, duties' (111). She notes that this was not the intention of those fighting for rights in previous centuries, where the articulation of the rights of man was intended to include all human beings rather than to exclude non-human species (notwithstanding the gendered language).[5] From a green perspective, however, human rights are self-evidently anthropocentric in conception, articulation and manifestation, and this presents a challenge for green criminology. On face value at least, it is hard to see how human rights fit within a green perspective.

The reason this is such a challenge within green criminology is partly because of the extent to which human rights are so well established and embedded within the intellectual and institutional fabric of contemporary Western society. Indeed, many individuals involved in establishing and propagating green criminology are also committed to ensuring that human rights are protected and enshrined universally the world over. Green criminology, in this respect, has built on the growing importance of human rights within criminological discourse, following the lead set by Schwendinger and Schwendinger (1970). There has been a concerted effort within criminology to replace its focus on 'crime' with an emphasis on the 'protection of human rights' (Hayle et al., 2009: 11). This is notwithstanding the enduring question about the universality of human rights (Agnew, 2011) and the difficulty of ensuring that human rights can be applied consistently across the world (Hogg, 2002).

Importantly, however, the proliferation of human rights has become increasingly informed by democratic as opposed to liberal concerns. There has, in this respect, been a response to the perceived shortcomings of a liberal individual–inspired, human rights–based criminology reflected in what Hopkins Burke (2009: 333) refers to as a 'new liberalism' that balances 'respect for the rights and *responsibilities* of both individuals and *communities*' (emphasis added). Human rights thus become more indicative of democratic values, such as transparency and a rejection of deference, rather than championing liberal values of privacy and its associated privileges. As such, the relationship between human rights and green thought is not straightforward (Boyle, 2012). At times, human rights can be drawn upon to pursue environmental issues (Morrow, 2010; Weston and Bollier, 2013), but as Hall (2014) notes, there is a lack of consistency in how this can happen, and indeed there is a lack of clarity in how the law more broadly can be used to address environmental harms. In other respects, the institutionalisation of human rights perpetuates existing power relations, and this is illustrated by Lindroth (2014) in relation to the role that indigenous rights play within the framework of a neo-liberal form of governance. This means that the use of human rights by green campaigners is selective and tactical (Gearty, 2010). Furthermore, it would be wrong to think of human rights as being an expression of liberal individualism, and again with reference to Dr Seuss (1971), human rights have come to mean something different from the Once-ler's right to keep on 'biggering': 'I have my rights, sir, and I'm telling *you*, I intend to go on doing just what I do!' Human rights are increasingly articulated in ways that would stress the Once-ler's duties and responsibilities towards preserving the trees protected by the Lorax.

## Concluding remarks

A question that this chapter has raised, and sought to address, is the extent to which the individual has a place within a greened criminology. The imperative nature of ecological

5 Mary Wollstonecraft's (1790) *A Vindication of the Rights of Men* was offered in support of Thomas Paine against Edmund Burke, but clearly she felt the need to redress any gender assumptions in her later 1792 publication, *A Vindication of the Rights of Woman*.

concerns exacerbates existing tensions within liberalism to the extent that it is difficult to see how the individual can retain the kind of privileged position that it has enjoyed within liberally framed criminal justice contexts. A green perspective implies that urgent and dramatic action is required to avert ecological catastrophe, whereas the logic of individual rights challenges majority perceptions of what is necessary and expedient, focusing instead on minority voices, including non-conformist views. Ecological discourse challenges the logic of liberal individualism by extending, expanding and broadening the scope of the various considerations that establish liberal judicial norms. In so doing, the significance and importance of the individual are undermined the more we take seriously consideration of non-human species, ecosystems, the rights of indigenous and traditional human societies and future generations. In the face of ecological problems that require urgent and dramatic action, liberal democratic ideals and principles that privilege minority groups and non-conformists are perhaps a luxury that cannot be afforded from a green criminological perspective.

However, Dobson's (2000) insistence on seeing a qualitative distinction between eco-centric and anthropocentric perspectives does not seem to be particularly useful. Rather, approaching eco-centric perspectives more as an extension of anthropocentrism allows for greater recognition of attempts to use criminology as a mechanism of achieving a more humane, compassionate and considerate society. This makes the tension between intergenerational and intragenerational equity concerns more manageable. It also allows for a social justice agenda, which prioritises the well-being of humans most adversely affected by environmental degradation, to co-exist alongside green considerations that relate more to non-humans and future generations.

As noted in the introduction, green criminology has been defined as being distinct from the notion of environmental criminology that focused on the spatial dimensions of crime (White, 2008). However, in so doing, we have perhaps missed an opportunity to consider green criminology in terms of being an extension of the pre-green environmental criminology. As Bottoms and Wiles (2002: 649) note, the scope of (pre-green) environmental criminological attention has become increasingly fluid, particularly within the 'late modernity' context. There has been a shift away from fixed understandings of how place informs criminality towards recognising the more spatially dynamic characteristics of the environmental influences that inform criminal behaviour and forms of crime control.

In understanding what constitutes environmental influences today, it would be impossible for environmental criminologists not to consider our relationship to the non-human world and future generations. This provides us with the opportunity for green anthropocentricism in a way that redefines what it means to be human. By focusing on the interrelationships between humans, non-human species and ecosystems and by emphasising the human qualities of compassion and consideration of others, we can begin to construct a green criminology that challenges the chauvinistic and destructive mindlessness of the narrow, market-driven understanding of human well-being. We replace the liberal individual with a greened individual. This enables green criminology to build upon social justice initiatives that favour a more rounded, sophisticated and environmentally aware understanding of humanity.

## References

Agnew, R. (2011) *Toward a Unified Criminology: Integrating Assumptions about Crime, People and Society*, New York: New York University Press.

Attfield, R. (2003) *Environmental Ethics*, Cambridge: Polity.

Beirne, P. and South, N. (eds.) (2007) *Issues in Green Criminology*, Cullompton, England: Willan.
Bellamy, R. (2000) *Rethinking Liberalism*, London: Pinter.
Benton, T. (1998) 'Rights and justice on a shared planet: More rights or new relations?' *Theoretical Criminology*, **2**(2): 149–175.
Benton, T. (2007) 'Ecology, community and justice: The meaning of green'. In P. Beirne and N. South (eds.) *Issues in Green Criminology*, Cullompton, England: Willan, pp. 3–31.
Benton, T. (2008) 'Environmental values and human purposes', *Environmental Values*, **17**(2): 201–220.
Berlin, I. (1958) 'Two concepts of liberty'. Reprinted in I. Berlin (1990) *Four Essays on Liberty*, Oxford: Oxford University Press, pp. 118–172.
Boehmer-Christiansen, S. (1994) 'The precautionary principle in Germany – Enabling government'. In T. O'Riordan and J. Cameron (eds.) *Interpreting the Precautionary Principle*, London: Earthscan, pp. 31–60.
Bookchin, M. (1995) *Re-Enchanting Humanity*, London: Cassell.
Bottoms, A. and Wiles, P. (2002) 'Environmental criminology'. In M. Maguire, R. Morgan and R. Reiner (eds.) *The Oxford Handbook of Criminology*, 3rd edition, Oxford: Oxford University Press, pp. 620–656.
Boyd, R. (2004) *Uncivil Society: The Perils of Pluralism and the Making of Modern Liberalism*, Lanham, MD: Lexington.
Boyle, A. (2012) 'Human rights and the environment: Where next?' *European Journal of International Law*, **23**(3): 613–642.
Bramwell, A. (1989) *Ecology in the 20th Century: A History*, New Haven, CT: Yale University.
Bramwell, A. (1994) *The Fading of the Greens: The Decline of Environmental Politics in the West*, New Haven, CT: Yale University.
Brisman, A. and South, N. (2013) 'A green-cultural criminology: An exploratory outline', *Crime Media Culture*, **9**(2): 115–135.
Brown, L. and Kane, H. (1995) *Full House: Reassessing the Earth's Population Carrying Capacity (Worldwatch Environmental Alert Series)*, London: Earthscan.
Capra, F. (1997) *The Web of Life: A New Synthesis of Mind and Matter*, London: Flamingo.
Connelly, J. and Smith, G. (1999) *Politics and the Environment: From Theory to Practice*, London: Routledge.
Cooper, D. (1992) 'The idea of environment'. In D. Cooper and J. Palmer (eds.) *The Environment in Question: Ethics and Global Issues*, London: Routledge, pp. 165–180.
Dickson, B. (2000) 'The ethicist conception of environmental problems', *Environmental Values*, **9**(2): 127–152.
Dobson, A. (2000) *Green Political Thought*, 3rd edition, London: Routledge.
Dobson, A. and Eckersley, R. (2006) *Political Theory and the Ecological Challenge*, Cambridge: Cambridge University Press.
Doherty, B. and de Geus, M. (1996) *Democracy and Green Political Thought*, London: Routledge.
Dr Seuss (1971) *The Lorax*, London: HarperCollins.
Dryzek, J. (2005) *The Politics of the Earth: Environmental Discourses*, 2nd edition, Oxford: Oxford University Press.
Dussault, A. (2013) 'In search of ecocentric sentiments', *Environmental Ethics*, **35**(4): 419–437.
Dussault, A. (2014) 'Ecocentrism and appeals to nature's goodness: Must they be fallacious?', PhilPapers, *Philosophical Research Online*. Retrieved from http://philpapers.org/rec/DUSEAA.
Eckersley, R. (1992) *Environmentalism and Political Theory: Toward an Ecocentric Approach*, London: UCL Press.
Eckersley, R. (1996) 'Greening liberal democracy: The rights discourse revisited'. In B. Doherty and M. de Geus (eds.) *Democracy and Green Political Thought*, London: Routledge, pp. 212–236.
Eckersley, R. (1998) 'Beyond human racism', *Environmental Values*, 7(2): 165–182.

Eckersley, R. (1999) 'The discourse ethic and the problem of representing nature', *Environmental Politics*, **8**(2): 24–29.

Eckersley, R. (2006) 'Communitarianism'. In A. Dobson and R. Eckersley (eds.) *Political Theory and the Ecological Challenge*, Cambridge: Cambridge University Press, pp. 91–108.

Ehrlich, P. (1968) *The Population Bomb*, New York: Ballantine.

Fiorino, D. (2006) *The New Environmental Regulation*, Cambridge, MA: MIT Press.

Foster, J. (2000) *Marx's Ecology: Materialism and Nature*, New York: Monthly Review Press.

Frierson, P. (2007) 'Metastandards in the ethics of Adam Smith and Aldo Leopold', *Environmental Ethics*, **29**(2): 171–191.

Garland, D. (2001) *The Culture of Control*, Oxford: Oxford University Press.

Gearty, C. (2010) 'Do human rights help or hinder environmental protection?' *Journal of Human Rights and the Environment*, **1**(1): 7–22.

Giddens, A. (1994) *Beyond Left and Right: The Future of Radical Politics*, Cambridge: Polity.

Goldsmith, E., Allen, R., Allaby, M., Davoll, J. and Lawrence, S. (1972) *A Blueprint for Survival*, Harmondsworth: Penguin.

Gray, J. (1993) *Beyond the New Right: Markets, Government and the Common Environment*, London: Routledge.

Gray, J. (2000) *Two Faces of Liberalism*, Cambridge: Polity.

Haldane, J. (1997) '"Admiring the high mountains": The aesthetics of environment'. In T. Chappell (ed.) *The Philosophy of the Environment*, Edinburgh: Edinburgh University Press, pp. 78–88.

Hall, M. (2014) 'The roles and use of law in green criminology', *International Journal for Crime, Justice and Social Democracy*, **3**(2): 96–109.

Hayle, C., Hayward, K., Wahidin, A. and Wincup, E. (2009) *Criminology*, 2nd edition, Oxford: Oxford University Press.

Hayward, T. (1998) *Political Theory and Ecological Values*, Cambridge: Polity Press.

Hogg, R. (2002) 'Criminology beyond the nation state: Global conflicts, human rights and the "new world order"'. In K. Carrington and R. Hogg (eds.) *Critical Criminology: Issues, Debates, Challenges*, Cullompton, England: Willan, pp. 185–217.

Hopkins Burke, R. (2009) *An Introduction to Criminological Theory*, 3rd edition, London: Routledge.

Jordan, A. (1998) 'The impact on UK environmental administration'. In P. Lowe and S. Ward (eds.) *British Environmental Policy and Europe: Politics and Policy in Transition*, London: Routledge, pp. 173–194.

Lindroth, M. (2014) 'Indigenous rights as tactics of neoliberal governance: Practices of expertise in the United Nations', *Social and Legal Studies*, **23**(3): 341–360.

Lockwood, M. (1999) 'Humans valuing nature', *Environmental Values*, **8**(3): 381–401.

Lovelock, J. (1989) *The Ages of Gaia: A Biography of Our Living Earth*, Oxford: Oxford University Press.

Lynch, M. (1990) 'The greening of criminology: A perspective for the 1990s', *The Critical Criminologist*, **2**: 11–12.

Lynch, M. and Stretesky, P. (2003) 'The meaning of green: Contrasting criminological perspectives', *Theoretical Criminology*, 7(2): 217–238.

MacGarvin, M. (1994) 'Precaution, science and the sin of hubris'. In T. O'Riordan and J. Cameron (eds.) *Interpreting the Precautionary Principle*, London: Earthscan, pp. 69–101.

MacIntyre, A. (1985) *After Virtue*, 2nd edition, London: Duckworth.

Malthus, T. (1798, reprinted in 1993) *An Essay on the Principle of Population*, London: Oxford University Press.

Meadows, D., Meadows, D., Randers, J. and Behrens, W. (1972) *The Limits to Growth*, London: Pan.

Midgley, M. (1994) 'The end of anthropocentricism?' *Royal Institute of Philosophy Supplement*, **36**: 103–112.

Mill, J.S. (1849) 'On liberty', Reprinted in J.S. Mill (1973) *The Utilitarians*, New York: Anchor Press, pp. 473–600.

Morrow, K. (2010) 'Climate change and human rights: The defining dilemma of our times?' *Journal of Human Rights and the Environment*, **1**(2): 131–134.

Morrow, K. (2011) 'Ontological vulnerability: A viable alternative lens through which to view human/environmental relations', *Journal of Human Rights and the Environment*, **2**(1): 1–4.

Naess, A. (1973) 'The shallow and the deep, long-range ecology movement', *Inquiry*, **16**(1): 95–100.

O'Neill, J. (1993) *Ecology, Policy and Politics: Human Well-Being and the Natural World*, London: Routledge.

Ophuls, W. (1977) *Ecology and the Politics of Scarcity*, San Francisco: W.H. Freeman.

O'Riordan, T. and Cameron, J. (1994) *Interpreting the Precautionary Principle*, London: Earthscan.

Orr, D. (1992) *Ecological Literacy: Education and the Transition to a Postmodern World*, Albany: State University of New York.

Paehlke, R. (1993) 'Environmentalism: Values to politics to policy'. In J. Gilroy (ed.) *Environmental Risk, Environmental Values, and Political Choices: Beyond Efficiency Trade-Offs in Public Policy Analysis*, Oxford: Westview Press, pp. 44–58.

Pepper, D. (1984) *The Roots of Modern Environmentalism*, London: Croom Helm.

Pepper, D. (1996) *Modern Environmentalism: An Introduction*, London: Routledge.

Porritt, J. (1984) *Seeing Green*, Oxford: Blackwell.

Rawls, J. (1971) *A Theory of Justice*, Cambridge, MA: Belknap.

Sagoff, M. (1988) 'Can environmentalists be liberals?' In M. Sagoff (ed.), *The Economy of the Earth*, Cambridge: Cambridge University Press, pp. 146–170.

Saward, M. (1996) 'Must Democrats be environmentalists?' In B. Doherty and M. de Geus (eds.) *Democracy and Green Political Thought*, London: Routledge, pp. 79–96.

Schlosberg, D. (2005) 'Environmental and ecological justice: Theory and practice in the United States'. In J. Barry and R. Eckersley (eds.) *The State and the Global Ecological Crisis*, Cambridge, MA: MIT Press, pp. 97–116.

Schumacher, E. (1973) *Small is Beautiful*, London: Vintage Edition.

Schwendinger, H. and Schwendinger, J. (1970) 'Defenders of order or guardians of human rights?', *Issues in Criminology*, 7: 72–81.

Schwendinger, H., Schwendinger, J. and Lynch, M. (2002) 'Critical criminology in the United States: The Berkley School and theoretical trajectories'. In K. Carrington and R. Hogg (eds.) *Critical Criminology: Issues, Debates, Challenges*, Cullompton, England: Willan, pp. 41–72.

Scruton, R. (2006) 'Conservatism'. In A. Dobson and R. Eckersley (eds.) *Political Theory and the Ecological Challenge*, Cambridge: Cambridge University Press, pp. 7–19.

South, N. (1998) 'A green field for criminology? A proposal for a perspective', *Theoretical Criminology*, **2**(2): 211–233.

South, N. (2007) 'The "corporate colonization of nature": Bio-prospecting, bio-piracy and the development of green criminology'. In P. Beirne and N. South (eds.) *Issues in Green Criminology*, Cullompton, England: Willan, pp. 230–247.

Tombs, S. (2007) '"Violence", safety crimes and criminology', *British Journal of Criminology*, **47**(4): 531–550.

Vincent, A. (1998) 'Liberalism and the environment', *Environmental Values*, 7(4): 443–459.

Walters, R. (2006) 'Crime, bio-agriculture and the exploitation of hunger', *British Journal of Criminology*, **46**(1): 26–45.

Walters, R. (2007) 'Crime, regulation and radioactive waste in the United Kingdom'. In P. Beirne and N. South (eds.) *Issues in Green Criminology*, Cullompton, England: Willan, pp. 186–205.

Warren, L. (1993) 'The precautionary principle: Use with caution!' In K. Milton (ed.) *Environmentalism: The View from Anthropology*, London: Routledge, pp. 97–111.

Weston, B. and Bollier, D. (2013) 'Toward a recalibrated human right to a clean and healthy environment: Making the conceptual transition', *Journal of Human Rights and the Environment*, **4**(2): 116–142.
White, R. (2003) 'Environmental issues and the criminological imagination', *Theoretical Criminology*, 7(4): 483–506.
White, R. (2008) *Crimes against Nature: Environmental Criminology and Ecological Justice*, Cullompton, England: Willan.
White, R. (2010) *Global Environmental Harm: Criminological Perspectives.* Cullompton, England: Willan.
White, R. (2013) 'The conceptual contours of green criminology'. In R. Walters, D. Westerhuisand and T. Wyatt (eds.) *Emerging Issues in Green Criminology: Exploring Power, Justice and Harm*, Basingstoke, England: Palgrave Macmillan, pp. 17–33.
White, R. and Graham, H. (2015) 'Greening justice: Examining the interfaces of criminal, social and ecological justice', *British Journal of Criminology*, **55**(5): 845–865.
Wilson, E. (1992) *The Diversity of Life*, London: Penguin.
Wissenburg, M. (2006) 'Liberalism'. In A. Dobson and R. Eckersley (eds.) *Political Theory and the Ecological Challenge*, Cambridge: Cambridge University Press, pp. 20–34.
Wollstonecraft, M. (1790, reprinted in 2008) *A Vindication of the Rights of Men*, Oxford: Oxford University Press.
Wynne, B. (1994) 'Scientific knowledge and the global environment'. In M. Redclift and T. Benton (eds.) *Social Theory and the Global Environment*, London: Routledge, pp. 169–189.
Zedner, L. (2009) *Security*, Abingdon, England: Routledge.

# 4 Transnational environmental crime

## Meeting future challenges through networked regulatory innovations

*Julie Ayling*

### Introduction

It is easy to be gloomy about transnational environmental crime (TEC) and the prospects of effective responses being found and implemented soon. Each week brings more bad news of imminent extinctions due to wildlife poaching and environmental harms and injustices resulting from toxic waste dumping, ozone trafficking, water theft, deforestation and over-fishing. The demand for many illegal environmental products keeps growing, new types of crime and new markets are emerging and climate change is adding another layer of environmental destruction and human misery to the problems associated with TEC. Beyond the extent of these problems themselves, the political, strategic and operational challenges confronting states and the international community in dealing with TEC are immense. TEC is such a complex and multi-layered area that it confounds the making of generalisations. For example, as Wyatt (2013) shows, wildlife trafficking encompasses a range of crimes with different crime scripts (Cornish, 1994) that involve offenders with various (sometimes mixed) motivations and that have sundry victims, who suffer diverse outcomes of variable severity. There is nothing straightforward about TEC nor, therefore, about its remedies. There are no 'one-size-fits-all' solutions. Policing strategies, penalties and other responses need to be tailored to individual crimes and their particular circumstances.

As with other big transnational 'wicked' problems, to negotiate and coordinate international efforts to deal with TEC is politically and logistically demanding as well as time-consuming. Furthermore, the criminal networks involved in many TEC crimes are not static entities but are becoming increasingly sophisticated and adaptable (Interpol, 2015a). Slaughter's observation that '[n]etworked threats require a networked response' (2004: 160) means that law enforcement agencies have to develop their own networked responses, matching the sophistication and adaptability of criminal TEC networks and becoming 'learning organisations' (Kenney, 2007: 3–4). As the expression goes, it's a big ship to turn around. It will take time, dedication, good policies, good tools and, most importantly, good ideas.

This chapter aims to broaden the dialogue about good ideas for responding to TEC and to go beyond the traditional policing context. The chapter begins by highlighting some of the challenges ahead. The case is then made for additional, more responsive, flexible and inclusive (that is, 'smarter') regulatory approaches, focusing on regulatory pluralism in three areas: TEC-centred technological innovations; the creative reshaping of policies, prosecutions and penalties; and demand reduction measures. The chapter emphasises the need for meta-smart regulation networks in order to deal effectively with TEC's networked threats.

## The challenges

### *Putting TEC on the radar*

Green criminologists have written extensively about the 'invisibility' of TEC, its low priority for law enforcement agencies globally and the failure of states to afford it the attention it deserves (see, for example, Davies et al., 2014; Wright, 2011).

For some of these crimes, this perceptual problem is gradually abating. Wildlife trafficking has over the last few years been increasingly recognised as a significant problem, with mounting calls for action by international organizations such as the United Nations (UN) General Assembly, the European Parliament, the Asia-Pacific Economic Cooperation (APEC) forum, the G8 and Interpol, as well as individual states.[1] Reports such as the UN Environment Assembly's *The Environmental Crime Crisis – Threats to Sustainable Development from Illegal Exploitation and Trade in Wildlife and Forest Resources* (Nelleman et al., 2014), international conferences such as those held in London in February 2014 and in Kasane in March 2015, and other high-level international and regional forums are exploring the threats that wildlife trafficking poses to social and economic security at multiple levels.[2] Similarly, e-waste trafficking has become an important issue for the international community, attracting both academic attention (Bisschop, 2014; Gibbs et al., 2010) and contributions from organisations such as the International Labour Office (Lundgren, 2012), Interpol (through its Pollution Crime Working Group and Environmental Crime Compliance and Enforcement Committee) and the European Commission.[3]

The growing rhetoric of concern over TEC is beginning to trickle down into the priorities and resources states afford to combating these crimes. Money and effort are going into training and deployment of personnel and new technologies for crime prevention, detection and forensics. Bi-lateral and multi-lateral agreements designed to strengthen political will and law enforcement responses are being negotiated. Campaigns are under way to educate consumers about the horrendous consequences of demanding particular environmental products and services for the animals, ecologies and societies of source countries.

However, while TEC seems to be slowly becoming more visible on political agendas, many aspects of these crimes remain invisible or obscured. Knowledge about who is committing them and why, and how the perpetrators operate, remains patchy. Research into the practical responses that might prove most effective is limited. Theory building, too, still has a long way to go. Overcoming all of this is, by itself, an enormous challenge. Many of the data that need to be pieced together to improve our knowledge of these crimes is either 'dark' (not available, being hidden or difficult to observe and research) (Biderman and Reiss, 1967; Wyatt, 2013) or scattered among law enforcement agencies, regulatory agencies, international organisations and non-governmental organisations (NGOs) globally and

1 For a fuller history of the progressive recognition at the highest levels of wildlife crime as serious crime, see van Asch (2015).

2 Even so, there are instances of illegal activity that have remained virtually invisible – for example, the extensive illegal trade in ornamental plants which is rife in Southeast Asia but is only now coming to light (see NUS, 2015).

3 The European Commission has funded a consortium, known as Countering WEEE Illegal Trade (CWIT), to study the issue: see http://www.cwitproject.eu/. The consortium includes Compliance & Risks, the Cross-Border Research Association (CBRA), Interpol, the United Nations Interregional Crime and Justice Research Institute (UNICRI), United Nations University (UNU), WEEE Forum AISBL and Zanasi & Partners.

has yet to be collated and assessed. The late arrival of a political consciousness has meant that funding for research has lagged behind the need. Nevertheless, there is hope. Through the efforts of NGOs, international organisations and state agencies, knowledge about the operation of the criminal networks perpetrating these crimes is advancing. Increased interest from governments bodes well for the prospects of further knowledge production.

### *Adaptive and resilient criminal networks*

As states become savvier about TEC, offenders will need to become smarter about committing these crimes. TEC's high (and often increasing) profitability, together with the growing difficulties of evading law enforcement, indicates that a rise in the involvement of organised criminal groups is likely, particularly those with experience of other criminal markets and with well-established transnational trafficking corridors and trading contacts (Elliott, 2012). The October 2015 Interpol report showing environmental crimes and other types of serious crimes apparently converging bears out this contention (Interpol, 2015a).

A huge variety of network forms can perpetrate TEC – from close-knit kinship groups to far more loosely connected and fluid groups, some connected only online, to vertically integrated organised crime groups akin to legitimate businesses in their degree of organisation and operational know-how (Pires and Moreto, 2011; van Asch, 2015). Criminal networks towards the latter end of that spectrum are often resilient to law enforcement interventions (Ayling, 2009). Being learning organisations (as Kenney, 2007, demonstrates by reference to drug organisations in South America), they are able not only to bounce back from disruptive interventions but also to adapt their future operations to reduce the likelihood of detection and capture.

From where do they acquire this resilience? Resilience often has multiple sources (Ayling, 2009). It can stem from the way criminal networks are structured, allowing them to quickly replace members who are taken out by law enforcement action or to be flexible enough to change their modus operandi when needed. Resilience can also stem from the environments in which they operate, including where there is community support for the criminal activity or connivance by public officials, influential individuals or private organisations. Situations in which there is a general acceptance of corruption as unremarkable, a disconnection between rules and their implementation (shown in lax law enforcement and/or weak penalties), or a conflict between a society's norms and its laws (for example, a tradition of using legally protected wildlife for medicinal ingredients) all constitute environments conducive to resilience (Ayling, 2013b).

Furthermore, like global corporations, criminal networks are adept at taking advantage of the complexity of rules and of trading off the regulatory environment of one jurisdiction against another to identify places in which it is least problematic to do business (Ayling, 2013b). The rules for the wildlife trade, especially those that subject the same species to different trade regimes, provide an example of complexity. The existence of a legal trade (for example, in hunting trophies) alongside international rules that severely limit trade in the very same species has, for instance, enabled organised criminal groups to launder illegally taken wildlife products (Ayling, 2013b; Wyatt, 2013). Similarly, jurisdictional differences in laws and policies on water theft in adjacent countries that share water supplies enable water smugglers to avoid prosecution by crossing borders (Global Initiative, 2014).

The ability of criminal networks to adapt to their environments is a huge challenge for law enforcement agencies, as it requires them to also adapt and change – that is, to successfully 'co-evolve' (or in Kenney's, 2007, words, 'competitively adapt' [104]). Slaughter's

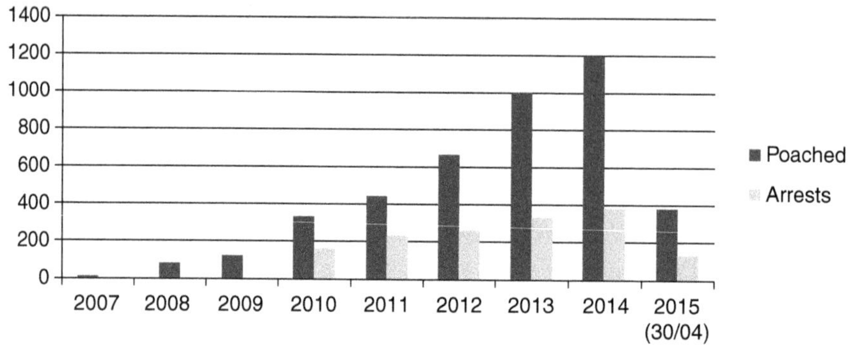


*Figure 4.1* Rhino Poaching and Arrests, South Africa, 2007–2015

(2004) call for a networked response to networked threats (160) has been answered with some moves to greater collaboration to counter TEC.[4] Still, for cumbersome bureaucracies such as police organisations and government environmental agencies, changing, adapting and networking are often difficult (Pink, 2013). It is one thing to keep up with and match the tools that organised crime groups use to perpetrate crime. It is quite another to envisage how criminal networks will adapt to law enforcement interventions or to changes in their own circumstances over time and to design strategies and structures, including international enforcement networks, that can prevent or at least respond to those adaptations in criminal operations. It requires a sustained and consistent forensic- and intelligence-led approach, and, for transnational crimes, nations must commit to systematic information sharing, requiring modifications to both the structures and cultures of policing.

It is apparent that in many areas of TEC, law enforcement is struggling to have a noticeable impact on crime. The rhino poaching statistics for South Africa illustrate this. As Figure 4.1 shows, in 2007, there were seven rhino poached in South Africa; in 2014, the figure was 1,215, an increase of more than 9200%. Arrests for poaching have increased since 2010 (when figures first became available), remaining fairly steady as a percentage of poaching incidents, but poaching has shown no sign of diminishing, despite big investments in law enforcement training and operations.

## *A growth industry – profitability, scale and evolution*

TEC is a growing problem primarily because it is not a losing proposition. Many TEC crimes are extremely profitable. Wildlife trafficking, for instance, according to the Secretary-General of the Convention on International Trade in Endangered Species of Wild Fauna and Flora (CITES), has become an 'industrial-scale' operation generating at least USD 20 billion each year (Carnie, 2015). Without effective interventions in TEC markets to make these crimes more difficult and to reduce demand, this problem of profitability will

4 For example, the International Consortium on Combating Wildlife Crime (ICCWC) involves five intergovernmental organisations – the CITES Secretariat, Interpol, the United Nations Office on Drugs and Crime (UNODC), the World Bank and the World Customs Organisation (WCO) – and 'seeks to ensure that perpetrators of serious wildlife crimes face a formidable and coordinated response' (Interpol, 2015b).

only worsen. As the supply of the trafficked products of TEC, such as endangered species, becomes restricted through the impact of the crimes themselves, together with that of climate change, urbanisation, deforestation and so on, their value escalates. For example, rhino horn and ivory are being stockpiled in large quantities in the expectation of future capital gains due to their increasing rarity. Economists studying this issue conclude that stockpiling creates an incentive for speculators to subsidise or support the extinction of the wild species so that they can earn monopoly rents (Mason et al., 2012). The trafficking of e-waste is another example of a highly profitable but low-risk TEC (Gibbs et al., 2010) where there seems to be little prospect of a reduction in the trade or its value.

To add to this parlous state of affairs, the detrimental impacts of climate change on natural resources such as water, foodstuffs and energy sources will inevitably result in the creation of new illicit markets (Hall and Farrall, 2013). New forms of taking and smuggling will undoubtedly emerge. Types of crime already in existence are similarly likely to become more sophisticated – frauds, money laundering and internet crimes relating to carbon trading schemes, for instance (Interpol Environmental Crime Programme, 2013). The rise of new technological tools such as the darknet and alternative currencies such as Bitcoin are already complicating the job of detecting TEC and catching perpetrators. Emerging technologies such as artificial intelligence systems and nanotechnologies will create further challenges.

### *The challenge of demand*

Alongside, or perhaps overlain by, the challenges posed by emergent criminal markets and new ways of criminally operating lies the problem of growing demand for TEC products and services. Increasingly at both national and international levels, there are calls to pay more attention to the demand end of TEC trades amidst mounting recognition that demand often drives supply and that curbing it is therefore just as essential as dealing with supply (Ayling, 2015).

There is a growing and progressively wealthier middle class in many developing countries. In 2014, China's share of the global middle class was one third (Credit Suisse Research Institute, 2014). China's urban middle-class population alone is already larger than the entire U.S. population. Even with the current slowdown in China's economy, the middle class is likely to continue to increase as the government implements plans to urbanize millions of rural dwellers. India's middle class is proportionally much smaller than China's but still substantial given its huge population. Household wealth there is projected to grow quickly if there are fundamental economic reforms (Credit Suisse Research Institute, 2014). By 2030, the global middle class is predicted to be in the realm of 4.9 billion people, two thirds of whom will hail from Asia. Sub-Saharan Africa, too, is experiencing a surge in its middle class numbers (Pezzini, 2012). In addition, there is a widespread movement from the lower middle class to the upper middle class (Barton et al., 2013).

The middle classes are 'a motor of consumption and domestic demand' (Pezzini, 2012). Class changes therefore bring with them an increase in discretionary spending. The newly wealthy become interested in buying luxuries. In 2012, the Chinese were the largest purchasers of luxury goods, with about 27% of worldwide luxury consumption, a figure then estimated to rise to 34% by 2015 (Atsmon et al., 2012). While the recent economic deceleration in China and other Asian countries may certainly have an impact on levels of luxury spending, status is likely to remain a significant driver of luxury consumption in those countries. This bodes ill for the demand for some of the rarer TEC products, such as rhino horn, ivory and rosewood, all items that are used in creating and maintaining status, or 'face' (Ayling, 2015; Milliken and Shaw, 2012).

The increased mobility that is frequently associated with a rise in wealth is also likely to open up more opportunities for illicit trades in the years ahead. Tourism is not the only culprit here. Investment opportunities in developing countries also result in an increase in foreign populations who bring their own cultures, traditions and links to 'home' with them. For instance, direct Chinese investment in Africa, mainly in oil and mineral extraction, finance, construction and manufacturing, is currently valued at more than USD 40 billion and is expanding (Pigato and Tang, 2015). How to tackle the changing dynamics of demand is part of the challenge of regulating TEC more smartly in the future.

### *Smarter regulation*

TEC, therefore, is an area crying out for lateral thinking about how to deal with the dire problem of conduct that is causing environmental degradation, habitat destruction and species extinction on a life-threatening scale. One of the most important strategies for dealing with environmental problems is regulation. By regulation, we mean not only conventional governmental 'command and control' but also more flexible and innovative forms of social intervention to achieve public goals. These interventions could be legal, political, economic, social or psychological. The benefit of applying a regulatory lens to the challenges posed by TEC is that it fosters a broader view of both the actors who might be engaged in addressing these challenges and the range of potentially effective strategies and ways of implementing them.

Ayres and Braithwaite's (1992) seminal work on responsive regulation (including the much-used regulatory pyramid), Gunningham and Grabosky's (1998) work on 'smart regulation' and other important works in the regulatory studies field (for example, those of Drahos, 2004; Grabosky, 1995) highlight the potential roles that private actors, such as business, community groups and individuals, can play as regulators and the ways in which the state can both facilitate and catalyse effective action by such actors. Those state actions can range from informal 'nudges' (Thaler and Sunstein, 2008) to formal legislative requirements, encompassing a whole range of mechanisms in between (Ayling, 2013b; Grabosky, 1995). *Smart Regulation* points to the importance of regulators (defined broadly) having a wide variety of regulatory tools in the policy toolbox and of those tools being used in a nuanced way, taking into account their complementarities and conflicts, their potential for effectiveness and their responsiveness to the particular context.

The following paragraphs explore both emerging instances of and other possibilities for regulating TEC in more innovative ways. Three areas have been selected: regulating through technology, broadening the options available in the criminal justice stable (policies, prosecutions and penalties) and exploring new demand reduction strategies. The plurality of both actors and strategies that could be enlisted in each area is emphasised, as is the need for meta-smart regulation networks to provide coordination of the regulatory efforts of these actors.

### ***Regulating through technology***

A key feature of the post-regulatory state is a shift towards bases for regulation that go beyond the state and its primary tool of regulation: the law (Scott, 2003). One of these bases is architecture (Lessig, 1999; Shearing and Stenning, 1985) or design (Murray and

Scott, 2002). Technology can be a key regulator, as Lessig (2000) has argued in relation to the architecture of cyberspace, where 'code is law'. Technology is certainly emerging as an actor in the regulation of TEC, particularly with respect to the taking and trafficking of wildlife (including timber and marine resources). Both private businesses and state bodies are creating and using new technologies to detect and track offenders and their potential targets, with the primary aim of preventing TEC from occurring.

Some interesting examples of regulation through technological means, involving both state and non-state actors,[5] include:

- An NGO injecting rhino horn with ectoparasiticides and indelible dye to devalue the horns on criminal markets and deter poaching and human consumption (Rhino Rescue Project, 2011–2015).
- Governments and private businesses using drones to track animals and poachers in public and private reserves in South Africa, Kenya and India (Bhaumik, 2013; Wall, 2014).
- A bio-tech company bio-engineering and 3D printing rhino horn replicas that are genetically and visually identical to real horns (Zak, 2015).
- Global Forest Watch, a partnership between international organisations, national agencies, NGOs and private businesses, using satellite imagery to map forest loss and providing an interactive online forum for sharing data and stories from the ground.[6]
- A start-up company using old smartphones to monitor forests for illegal logging by converting the phones into solar-powered listening stations to detect the noise of chainsaws and send alerts (via Global System for Mobile Communications [GSM]) to responsible authorities (Rainforest Connection, 2015).
- A partnership between technology firms launching an interactive web tool, Global Fishing Watch, which enables the tracking, using satellite technology, of individual fishing vessels, all vessels operating under a particular flag or fishing activity in any particular area (including protected zones).[7]
- Also in the fisheries area, the establishment of a central database in the United States to trace wild fish and crustaceans from harvest to port, with the aim of curbing illegal, unreported and unregulated fishing and seafood fraud (Fears, 2015). All federal, state and local authorities at ports must submit specified information for collation and sharing.

States are also harnessing the talents of citizens in pursuit of TEC solutions by providing them with 'nudges' in the form of incentives. The Wildlife Crime Tech Challenge was an initiative of the U.S. Agency for International Development (USAID) in partnership with the National Geographic Society, the Smithsonian Institution and TRAFFIC (the wildlife trade monitoring network). This was an online global competition to design innovative science and technology solutions for specific wildlife trafficking issues:[8] detecting transit routes, strengthening forensic evidence, reducing consumer demand and tackling corruption. These solutions did not need to be high-end technologies; they could even involve the redeployment of existing technologies. Entries were evaluated on the basis of potential

5 For further examples related to wildlife crime, see UNEP (2014).
6 See http://www.globalforestwatch.org/about/about-gfw.
7 See http://globalfishingwatch.org/. This technology is still at the prototype stage.
8 See http://wildlifecrimetech.org/index.

impact and capacity to scale. Cash prizes were offered, with accompanying recognition and technical and networking support to scale, test and market the product. Three hundred people and organisations from 52 countries applied for the challenge, and there were 16 winners, with 10 of those projects in the 'strengthening forensic evidence' category.[9]

All of the previous examples suggest that technology could play an important role in regulating TEC. However, there are some problems with this regulatory path. First, there is no guarantee of effectiveness with technological solutions, which is consistent with their experimental nature. Both drones as offender detectors in parks and reserves and the infusion of rhino horns with dyes and toxins, for example, have been criticised as being less than successful.[10] Second, there is currently no apparent ordering of these regulatory contributions into coordinated technological 'architecture(s)' which would be sufficiently nuanced to merit the label of 'smart regulation'. The challenge of coordination needs to be addressed by extensive collaborations, with participants forming influential nodes within meta-smart regulatory networks that explore innovative technological solutions for different forms of TEC and help bring them into being.

### *Broadening criminal justice regulation*

Currently, criminalisation and law enforcement are regarded as the primary weapons against TEC. Interpol, an international policing organisation, understandably promotes a law enforcement approach to deal with TEC through training, information and operations. In addition, states and international organisations are increasingly adopting the language of national security when talking about transnational environmental issues (see, for example, Eliasson, 2015). This has prompted scholars to raise concerns about the militarisation and securitisation of state responses (Duffy, 2014; Elliott, 2016). Despite this relentless emphasis on state coercion, it is clear that often this approach is not as effective as one would hope and ignores the broader social context in which criminal activity breeds and is supported. More imagination, a wider array of strategies and greater community involvement in crafting solutions are needed to deal with the adaptive and resilient criminal networks feeding off vulnerable populations and exploiting criminal opportunities, and to meet the challenge of evolving and emerging new criminal environmental markets.

### *Policies*

The increasing influence of organised crime in the environmental arena requires a response that combines law enforcement tools and other regulatory strategies and requires creative thinking. In addition to tapping into research that demonstrates how these crime groups operate in other contexts, authorities could seek to explore different jurisdictions' approaches to dealing with organised crime. There are some innovative models available for examination. For example, in Japan, authorities have criminalised collaborating or otherwise doing business with the Yakuza, alongside the normal offence provisions aimed at the

9 See https://wildlifecrimetech.org/winners.

10 For example, one NGO cites the potential for misuse of drones, the cost, technical issues and the need for a skilled operator as obstacles to their usefulness in detecting rhino horn poachers (Save the Rhino, 2015). A report by scientists has contested the effectiveness of rhino horn infusion to deal with the poaching threat (Ferreira et al., 2014).

Yakuza themselves, and have empowered citizens to take legal and community-based action against these groups (Rankin, 2012). At the regulatory frontier, the Dutch administrative approach seeks to guard against official facilitation of the activities of organised crime groups and their infiltration of legitimate businesses through a networked regulatory architecture designed to limit access by organised criminals to privileges such as licences, permits and subsidies (Huisman and Nelen, 2007).

At the same time, it is important to be alive to potential criminogenic consequences of new laws and policies, including those of a regulatory nature. Cannepele et al. (2013) have demonstrated this in their exposé of how the Mafia in Italy has exploited and distorted the regulatory regime for wind farming.

### *Prosecutions*

Usually when we talk about prosecutions, it is the role of the state that is the focus. However, *private prosecutorial mechanisms* play a part in some jurisdictions' environmental laws. In Australia and the United States, non-state actors have been given the right in environmental laws to take legal action to protect public environmental goods and force government action.[11] This kind of model potentially could be useful in dealing with domestic aspects of TEC and, as such, could be promoted in international forums.

However, Bucy (2002) found a low rate of uptake of these mechanisms by citizens in the United States, concluding that this was insufficient to have a significant impact on regulatory compliance. She argued that this failure of private enforcement to deliver real change in the environmental area as well as in other areas was, at least in part, due to the fact that it provides no incentives for those with real knowledge of offending behaviour (insiders) to disclose that information.

John Braithwaite suggests that Bucy's conclusions indicate a need to find ways to provide these incentives. In his book *Regulatory Capitalism: How It Works, Ideas for Making It Work Better* (2008), Braithwaite argues strongly in favour of *qui tam* actions.[12] *Qui tam* is used extensively in the United States in relation to false claims – that is, frauds against the government. Essentially, *qui tam* is a way to encourage whistleblowing by rewarding the whistleblower. Under the False Claims Act (31 USC §3729–3733), a whistleblower is entitled, for exposing wrongdoing and recovering funds for the government, to between 15% and 25% of the case proceeds, plus reasonable expenses and costs. Penalties are treble damages, so a great deal of money can be obtained by the complainant. The suit may be conducted by the government with the whistleblower's participation or taken by the whistleblower alone if the state is not interested. Typical environmental *qui tam* actions relate to companies billing the government for work not done (such as remediating sites of natural disasters), submitting false information such as certifications or logs and inflating bid prices for government contracts (Foster, 2000).

Braithwaite makes the point that providing for *qui tam* suits could be a good tool to address chronic under-enforcement of laws *because* they provide the very incentive to disclose insider knowledge that Bucy (2002) identifies as lacking in more general citizen suit

11 See, for example, in Australia, Section 475 of the Environment Protection and Biodiversity Conservation Act 1999.

12 *Qui tam* is short for *qui tam pro domino rege, quam pro se ipso in hoc parte sequitur*, meaning 'he who sues as much for the King as for himself' (Braithwaite, 2008: 66).

provisions. According to Braithwaite (2008), *qui tam* 'in effect networks whistle-blowers with law firms, state regulators and prosecutors, extending the intelligence, evidence-gathering and litigation capabilities in big, difficult cases' (82).

So could *qui tam* provisions be a tool for addressing TEC? Chronic under-enforcement of laws against TEC is certainly a problem in many jurisdictions. But the lack of state capacity in the policing, prosecutions and judicial arenas in many of those jurisdictions may militate against the efficacy of a *qui tam* scheme. However, Braithwaite (2008) argues that *qui tam* provisions can enhance the capacity of weak actors in developing countries to enroll stronger ones (such as northern NGOs and lawyers) to help them take on multi-nationals who are exploiting the vulnerabilities of those developing countries and that this networked response may compensate for the weak regulatory capacities of some developing countries. So, for example, an insider might whistleblow as to the role of a multi-national in toxic waste dumping in a developing country and be rewarded through *qui tam* action taken via networked partners based in developed countries.[13]

Private enforcement regimes can multiply the resources devoted to prosecutions, shift regulatory costs from the government to the private sector and signal that violations are considered serious and will almost certainly attract prosecution. By taking a bottom-up approach, private litigation can also influence state approaches, prodding public enforcement agencies to take note of and act against violations of laws and even potentially 'lead to experimentation with a multiplicity of policy responses to a problem' (Burbank et al., 2011: 39). However, private enforcement regimes may also have disadvantages; for example, they may interfere with the development of coherent state regulatory policies – given that 'privately prosecuted litigation is guided by private (often economic) interests that may be in conflict with the public interest' – and could potentially discourage voluntary compliance by regulatees (Burbank et al., 2011). Any scheme for private enforcement of laws to thwart certain types of TEC therefore needs to be well designed and take such potential risks into account.

### *Penalties*

The UN Convention against Transnational Organized Crime (UNTOC) defines serious crime as 'conduct constituting an offence punishable by at least four years' imprisonment or a more serious penalty'. Many jurisdictions do not treat all or some environmental crimes as 'serious' in terms of the penalties imposed. Even in areas with relatively high socio-economic status such as the EU, the levels of criminal sanctions applicable to wildlife trafficking and the criminal and administrative penalties for e-waste trafficking vary significantly (Huisman et al., 2015; International Fund for Animal Welfare, 2014). This is important not just because low or absent penalties signal to criminals that jurisdictions are open for business, but because identifying crimes as serious expands the range of strategies available to deal with them. For example, pursuant to UNTOC Article 12, state parties are required to adopt proceeds of crime confiscation provisions for serious transnational crimes.

Harmonisation of penalties across jurisdictions for transnational environmental crimes also requires greater attention. Rose and Tsamenyi (2013) argue for harmonisation of

13 *Qui tam* has clear application to white-collar environmental crimes. Whether *qui tam*, or some version of it, could be useful where the perpetrator of an environmental crime is less 'corporate' is an issue for further consideration.

national laws on crimes towards marine living resources, including the universal categorisation of those crimes as serious, so that international law enforcement cooperation mechanisms (information exchange, joint operations, mutual legal assistance, extradition, etc.) will be triggered and so that penalties are 'sufficiently severe to prevent, deter and punish' (Rose and Tsamenyi, 2013: 6). Similarly, the Countering Waste Electrical and Electronic Equipment (WEEE) Illegal Trade (CWIT) report has suggested harmonising penalties (whether criminal or administrative) across the EU as a way to 'limit the shift of illegal activities among countries, and . . . facilitate investigations, prosecution and sentencing and thus . . . create a true disincentive for offenders' (Huisman et al., 2015: 21).

Apart from the *level* and *distribution* of penalties for TEC, the *nature* of penalties might also be explored. An example of more creative thinking in this field is an idea for sanctioning of corporate wrongdoing that has been around for decades but has not gained a great deal of traction – that of *equity fines*. Fisse and Braithwaite (1984) discuss this idea in some detail. Equity fines replace normal fines. A court can order that a convicted public company must issue, to a state crime victim compensation scheme, a set number of new shares with an expected market value equal to the cash fine needed to deter the corporate wrongdoing (which could be more than the liquid assets of the corporation). This effective dilution of the value of the company's shares is borne by the shareholders, which in turn should animate them to hold senior management accountable. Equity fines, unlike cash fines, should also prevent companies from passing on the costs of their wrongdoing to their employees or their customers and improve their behaviour in the long run. Equity fines are an example of lateral thinking of the kind that is needed with respect to penalties for TEC. Consideration is needed about to whom it would be most appropriate for corporate TEC offenders to issue equity fine shares, as victimization can be complex when it comes to environmental crime (particularly of the transnational variety), and victims are not always human or readily named (Spapens and White, 2014). Dedicated conservation, animal welfare or environmental restitution funds might, in some circumstances, be appropriate. Given that multi-national companies are often among the ranks of TEC offenders, the need to coordinate across jurisdictions about penalties is also clear.

### *Regulating demand*

Demand reduction is potentially even more difficult to deal with than supply because a huge range of motivations drive consumption (Ayling, 2015). As yet, the scale of action to deal with demand is small compared with that designed to detect and prevent supply. It is essential to take a whole-of-society approach to this problem; both states and an array of non-state actors must be involved.

Demand reduction has so far mainly focused on consumer campaigns, conducted primarily by NGOs, and on legal prohibitions on consumption imposed by states. There is still scope for more action in both areas. States could require better product labelling as to the environmental impacts of purchase and disseminate information about TEC's effects on the state economy and on individuals, businesses and communities, including loss of revenues and opportunities for development. Reputable local businesses, inevitably affected, need to publicly support consumer campaigns or take a leadership role.

The effectiveness of legislative prohibitions on consumption of TEC products, like China's on the purchase and eating of endangered wildlife (Kaiman, 2014), depends heavily on the law-making state having both the political will and capacity for enforcement. Other states, international organisations and NGOs need to hold states accountable for enforcement and also assist with capacity building.

However, demand reduction clearly requires more than uncoordinated doses of consumer education and piecemeal enforcement of idiosyncratic laws. There is a range of other potential strategies between the dialogic strategies at the base of the regulatory pyramid (Ayres and Braithwaite, 1992) and 'big stick' strategies at its peak. In other areas of regulation, these 'in-between' strategies have included shaming; the provision of incentives; enforced self-regulation; monitoring, reporting and auditing requirements; and administrative and civil penalties of varying severity. While states are beginning to consider these more creative measures in detecting and preventing supply and are harnessing public and private actors to implement them (Ayling, 2013a), these strategies as demand reduction tools have as yet had little examination. The kinds of strategies that would be appropriate vary according to the commodity in question, the responsiveness of 'demanders' to attempts to regulate them and, of course, the availability and capacities of parties who could be enlisted to do so. A detailed discussion of all such potential strategies is not possible here, given the breadth of TEC, although they have been considered elsewhere for the illegal wildlife trade (see Ayling, 2015).

Examples of effective demand reduction through coordinated regulatory pluralism are currently hard to find. The Kimberley Process (KP) for 'conflict diamonds' is often lauded as a successful example of multi-stakeholder collaboration. It began with a tripartite process (states, industry and NGOs) that resulted in the establishment in 2003 of a certification scheme (KPCS) to exclude conflict (or 'blood') diamonds from trade – that is, rough diamonds used by rebel militias to fund wars against legitimate governments. And in fact the KPCS has resulted in a large fall in the proportion of diamonds traded that are conflict diamonds, from around 15% in the 1990s to less than 1% today (Bieri, 2010; Kimberley Process, 2016). Potential for an effective pluralistic scheme can also be seen in the case of 'conflict minerals'. Disclosure rules were established by the US Securities and Exchange Commission in 2012 (§1502 of the Dodd-Frank Wall Street Reform and Consumer Protection Act) requiring manufacturers to disclose annually whether their products contain gold or tin, tantalum or tungsten ('3T') from Congo or its neighbours (Meger, 2012). If they do, companies must explain their due diligence measures used to determine the minerals' source. The reputational consequences for companies of using conflict minerals have affected both demand and mineral prices. The number of 3T mines controlled by armed groups has reportedly decreased and an independent certification mechanism for 3T mines is emerging, involving UN officials and Congolese government, civil society and business (Enough Project, 2015).

But the implementation of each scheme has not been smooth sailing, and there are allegations that corruption is rife and that smuggling of both conflict diamonds and conflict minerals persists. NGOs who were key to the KPCS's establishment walked away from involvement in 2011, citing governmental abuses of the scheme and states' failure to heed calls for reform, especially concerning human rights issues at the mines (Ford, 2011; Nicolson, 2013). Similarly, the top-down design of the conflict mineral rules has meant that traditional artisanal miners in Congo have lacked support to comply with the conflict mineral requirements. As a result, Western companies have found it difficult to discriminate between legitimate and illegitimate producers, and a de facto boycott of Congo minerals has resulted, with devastating consequences for the legitimate industry and its dependents (Sheriff, 2015).

Both of these examples illustrate that networked regulatory innovations have great potential to reduce demand for criminally obtained or traded natural resources but also that, for long-term effectiveness, solutions need to be grounded in and responsive to what Duffy et al. (2016) term the 'structural context'. In other words, networked solutions need to engage with local economic, political and social conditions and history, address issues of social justice, and engage affected communities in the process of policy development.

## Conclusion

To deal successfully with the existing and emerging threats of the diverse landscape that constitutes TEC is a huge and complex challenge. A regulatory approach that recognises the importance of utilising the full range of actors and strategies available to tackle TEC is immensely important, but it is even more vital to recognise that those actors – be they states, international organisations, NGOs, business or communities – can only achieve a limited amount if they act alone. What is needed are meta-smart regulatory networks to plan, guide and build capacity for innovative regulation to take place at local levels, taking into account relevant structural contexts. The building of such networks among concerned and knowledgeable actors needs to accelerate if networked threats are to be met with networked responses within a time frame that has any chance of delivering effective, context-sensitive solutions in the urgent situations now facing the world, such as global biodiversity loss.

## References

Atsmon, Y., Ducarme, D., Magni, M. and Wu, C. (2012) 'Luxury without borders: China's new class of shoppers take on the world', *McKinsey Insights China*. Retrieved from https://solutions.mckinsey.com/insightschina/default/en-us/about/our_publications.aspx.

Ayling, J. (2009) 'Criminal organizations and resilience', *International Journal of Law, Crime and Justice*, **37**(4): 182–196.

Ayling, J. (2013a) 'Harnessing third parties for transnational environmental crime prevention', *Transnational Environmental Law*, **2**(2): 339–362.

Ayling, J. (2013b) 'What sustains wildlife crime? Rhino horn trading and the resilience of criminal networks', *Journal of International Wildlife Law and Policy*, **16**(1): 57–80 [reprinted in R. White (ed.) *Green Criminology, Vol. 3: Criminal Justice Responses to Environmental Crime*, London: Routledge, 2014, Chapter 54].

Ayling, J. (2015) *A regulatory approach to demand reduction in the illegal wildlife market*, RegNet Research Paper No. 2015/82. Retrieved from http://ssrn.com/abstract=2634303.

Ayres, I. and Braithwaite, J. (1992) *Responsive Regulation: Transcending the Deregulation Debate*, Oxford: Oxford University Press.

Barton, D., Chen, Y. and Jin, A. (2013) 'Mapping China's middle class', *McKinsey Quarterly*, June. Retrieved from http://www.mckinsey.com/insights/consumer_and_retail/mapping_chinas_middle_class.

Bhaumik, S. (2013) 'India deploys drones to save rhinos in Assam state', *BBC News*, 9 April. Retrieved from http://www.bbc.co.uk/news/world-asia-india-22075311.

Biderman, A. and Reiss, A. (1967) 'On exploring the "dark figure" of crime', *The Annals of the American Academy of Political and Social Science*, **374**(1): 1–15.

Bieri, F. (2010) *From Blood Diamonds to the Kimberley Process*, Farnham, England: Ashgate.

Bisschop, L. (2014) 'Illegal e-waste transports: Exploring their harmfulness, scale, social organization and governance'. In T. Spapens, R. White and M. Kluin (eds.) *Environmental Crime and Its Victims: Perspectives Within Green Criminology*, Farnham, England: Ashgate, pp. 171–184.

Braithwaite, J. (2008) *Regulatory Capitalism: How It Works, Ideas for Making It Work Better*, Cheltenham, England: Edward Elgar.

Bucy, P. (2002) 'Private justice', *Southern California Law Review*, **76**(1): 1–160.

Burbank, S., Farhang, S. and Kritzer, H. (2011) *Private enforcement of statutory and administrative law in the United States (and other common law countries)*, Public Law Research Paper

No. 11–08, Philadelphia: University of Pennsylvania Law School. Retrieved from http://papers.ssrn.com/sol3/papers.cfm?abstract_id=1781047.

Cannepele, S., Riccardi, M. and Standridge, P. (2013) 'Green energy and black economy: Mafia investments in the wind power sector in Italy', *Crime, Law and Social Change*, **59**: 319–339.

Carnie, T. (2015) 'Illegal wildlife trade now "industrial-scale"', *The Mercury*, 12 September. Retrieved from http://www.iol.co.za/scitech/science/environment/illegal-wildlife-trade-now-industrial-scale-1.1914682#.Vfwogpdr_ps.

Cornish, D. (1994) 'The procedural analysis of offending and its relevance to situational prevention'. In R. Clarke (ed.) *Crime Prevention Studies*, Vol. 3, Monsey, NY: Criminal Justice Press, pp. 151–196.

Credit Suisse Research Institute (2014) *Global Wealth Report 2014*. Zurich: Credit Suisse AG.

Davies, P., Francis, P. and Wyatt, T. (2014) 'Taking invisible crimes and social harms seriously'. In P. Davies, P. Francis and T. Wyatt (eds.) *Invisible Crimes and Social Harms*, Basingstoke, England: Palgrave Macmillan, pp. 1–25.

Drahos, P. (2004) 'Intellectual property and pharmaceutical markets: A nodal governance approach', *Temple Law Review*, 77: 401–424.

Duffy, R. (2014) 'Waging a war to save biodiversity: The rise of militarized conservation', *International Affairs*, **90**(4): 819–834.

Duffy, R., St. John, F., Büscher, D. and Brockington, D. (2016) 'Towards a new understanding of the links between poverty and illegal wildlife hunting', *Conservation Biology*, **30**(1): 14–22.

Eliasson, J. (2015) 'Wildlife crime deters sustainable development, threatens national security, Deputy Secretary-General warns at high-level general assembly meeting', 4 March. Retrieved from http://www.un.org/press/en/2015/dsgsm852.

Elliott, L. (2012) 'Fighting transnational environmental crime', *Journal of International Affairs*, **66**(1): 87–104.

Elliott, L. (2016) 'The securitization of TEC and the militarization of conservation'. In L. Elliott and W. Schaedla (eds.) *Handbook of Transnational Environmental Crime*, Cheltenham, England: Edward Elgar, pp. 68–87.

Enough Project (2015) *Progress and challenges on conflict minerals: Facts on Dodd-Frank 1502*. Retrieved from http://www.enoughproject.org/special-topics/progress-and-challenges-conflict-minerals-facts-dodd-frank-1502.

Fears, D. (2015) 'Federal officials plan to track every fish and crustacean shipped to U.S. ports', *Washington Post*, 15 March. Retrieved from https://www.washingtonpost.com/national/health-science/sea-hunt-officials-plan-to-track-seafood-bait-to-plate-to-end-fraud/2015/03/14/0ab191d8-c7fe-11e4-aa1a-86135599fb0f_story.html.

Ferreira, S., Hofmeyr, M., Pienaar, D. and Cooper, D. (2014) 'Chemical horn infusions: A poaching deterrent or an unnecessary deception?' *Pachyderm*, **55**: 54–61.

Fisse, B. and Braithwaite, J. (1984) 'Sanctions against corporations: Dissolving the monopoly of fines'. In R. Tomasic (ed.) *Business Regulation in Australia*, North Ryde, New South Wales, Australia: CCH Australia, pp. 129–145.

Ford, L. (2011) 'Global witness quits Kimberley process in protest at "diamond laundering"', *The Guardian*, 6 December. Retrieved from https://www.theguardian.com/global-development/2011/dec/05/kimberley-process-global-witness-withdraws.

Foster, L. (2000) 'Environment is new target for old fraud law', *BNA Toxics Law Reporter*, 14 September. Retrieved from http://www.phillipsandcohen.com/Articles-by-Attorneys/Environment-is-new-target-of-qui-tam-lawsuits.shtml.

Gibbs, C., McGarrell, E. and Axelrod, M. (2010) 'Transnational white-collar crime and risk: Lessons from the global trade in electronic waste', *Criminology and Public Policy*, **9**(3): 543–560.

Global Initiative (2014) *Water, water everywhere? Charting the growth of organized water theft*, 21 June. Retrieved from http://www.globalinitiative.net/analyzing-organized-crime-june-2014/.

Grabosky, P. (1995) 'Using non-governmental resources to foster regulatory compliance', *Governance: An International Journal of Policy and Administration*, **8**(4): 527–550.

Gunningham, N. and Grabosky, P. (1998) *Smart Regulation: Designing Environmental Policy*, Oxford: Oxford University Press.

Hall, M. and Farrall, S. (2013) 'The criminogenic consequences of climate change: Blurring the boundaries between offenders and victims'. In N. South and A. Brisman (eds.) *Routledge International Handbook of Green Criminology*, Abingdon, England: Routledge, pp. 120–133.

Huisman, J., Botezatu, I., Herreras, L., Liddane, M., Hintsa, J., Luda di Cortemiglia, V., . . . Bonzio, A. (2015) *Countering WEEE Illegal Trade (CWIT) Summary Report: Market Assessment, Legal Analysis, Crime Analysis and Recommendations Roadmap*, 30 August. Lyon, France: CWIT Consortium.

Huisman, W. and Nelen, H. (2007) 'Gotham unbound Dutch style: The administrative approach to organized crime in Amsterdam', *Crime, Law and Social Change*, **48**: 87–103.

International Fund for Animal Welfare (2014) 'IFAW submission: European commission communication on the EU approach against wildlife trafficking'. Retrieved from http://www.ifaw.org/sites/default/files/2014-IFAW-Consultation-on-EU-Internal-Security.pdf.

Interpol (2015a) *Environmental crime and its convergence with other serious crimes*, 2015/999/OEC/ENS/SLO, 30 October. Retrieved from http://www.interpol.int/Crime-areas/Environmental-crime/Resourcesinterpol.

Interpol (2015b) *International Consortium on Combating Wildlife Crime*. Retrieved from http://www.interpol.int/Crime-areas/Environmental-crime/International-Consortium-on-Combating-Wildlife-Crime.

Interpol Environmental Crime Programme (2013) *Guide to carbon trading crime*, June 2013. Lyon: Interpol. Retrieved from http://www.interpol.int/en/News-and-media/News/2013/PR090/.

Kaiman, J. (2014) 'China hopes to take rare animals off the menu with tough jail sentences', *The Guardian*, 25 April. Retrieved from http://www.theguardian.com/environment/2014/apr/25/china-rareanimal-products-eat-jail-sentences.

Kenney, M. (2007) *From Pablo to Osama: Trafficking and Terrorist Networks, Government Bureaucracies and Competitive Adaptation*, University Park, PA: Pennsylvania State University Press.

Kimberley Process (2016) *About*. Retrieved from http://www.kimberleyprocess.com/node/1122.

Lessig, L. (1999) *Code and Other Laws of Cyberspace*, New York: Basic Books.

Lessig, L. (2000) 'Code is law: On liberty in cyberspace', *Harvard Magazine*, 1 January. Retrieved from http://harvardmagazine.com/2000/01/code-is-law-html.

Lundgren, K. (2012) *The Global Impact of E-Waste: Addressing the Challenge*. Geneva: International Labour Office, Programme on Safety and Health at Work and the Environment (SafeWork), Sectoral Activities Department (SECTOR).

Mason, C., Bulte, E. and Horan, R. (2012) 'Banking on extinction', *Oxford Review of Economic Policy*, **28**(1): 180–192.

Meger, S. (2012) 'SEC takes on humanitarian role over Congo's "conflict" minerals', *The Conversation*, 31 August. Retrieved from https://theconversation.com/sec-takes-on-humanitarian-role-over-congos-conflict-minerals-9129.

Milliken, T. and Shaw, J. (2012) 'The South Africa-Viet Nam Rhino Horn Trade Nexus: A deadly combination of institutional lapses, corrupt wildlife industry professionals and Asian crime syndicates', *TRAFFIC Report*. Retrieved from http://www.traffic.org/speciesreports/traffic-speciesmammals66.pdf.

Murray, A. and Scott, C. (2002) 'Controlling the new media: Hybrid responses to new forms of power', *Modern Law Review*, **65**: 491–516.

National University of Singapore (NUS) (2015) 'Researchers uncover an "invisible" wildlife trade'. Retrieved from http://www.newswise.com/articles/nus-researchers-uncover-an-invisible-wildlife-trade.

Nellemann, C., Henriksen, R., Raxter, P., Ash, N. and Mrema, E. (eds.) (2014) *The Environmental Crime Crisis – Threats to Sustainable Development from Illegal Exploitation and Trade in Wildlife and Forest Resources: A UNEP Rapid Response Assessment*, Nairobi and Arendal: United Nations Environment Programme and GRID-Arendal.

Nicolson, G. (2013) 'Blood diamond trail leads to loopholes in Kimberley Process', *The Guardian*, 6 June. Retrieved from https://www.theguardian.com/world/2013/jun/05/blood-diamonds-kimberley-process.

Pezzini, M. (2012) *An emerging middle class: OECD Yearbook 2012*. Retrieved from http://www.oecdobserver.org/news/fullstory.php/aid/3681/An_emerging_middle_class.html.

Pigato, M. and Tang, W. (2015) *China and Africa: Expanding economic ties in an evolving global context*, Investing in Africa Forum. Retrieved from http://www.worldbank.org/content/dam/Worldbank/Event/Africa/Investing%20in%20Africa%20Forum/2015/investing-in-africa-forum-china-and-africa-expanding-economic-ties-in-an-evolving-global-context.pdf.

Pink, G. (2013) *Law enforcement responses to transnational environmental crime: Choices, challenges, and culture*, Transnational Environmental Crime Project Working Paper 4/2013, Canberra: Department of International Relations, Australian National University. Retrieved from http://ips.cap.anu.edu.au/ir/tec/publications.

Pires, S. and Moreto, W. (2011) 'Preventing wildlife crime: Solutions that can overcome the "Tragedy of the Commons"', *European Journal on Criminal Policy and Research*, **17**(2): 101–123.

Rainforest Connection (2015) *Rainforest Connection – phones turned to forest guardians*. Retrieved from https://www.kickstarter.com/projects/topherwhite/rainforest-connection-phones-turned-to-forest-guar/description.

Rankin, A. (2012) 'Recent trends in organized crime in Japan: Yakuza vs the police, & foreign crime gangs – Part 2', *The Asia-Pacific Journal*, **10**(7): 1.

Rhino Rescue Project (2011–2015) *How it works*. Retrieved from http://rhinorescueproject.org/how-it-works/.

Rose, G. and Tsamenyi, M. (2013) *Universalizing jurisdiction over marine living resources crimes*, Report for WWF International, October. Gland Switzerland: WWF. Retrieved from http://ips.cap.anu.edu.au/sites/default/files/IPS/IR/TEC/Rose,_G_Universalizing%20Jurisdiction_Marine%20Living_Crime.pdf.

Save the Rhino (2015) *The use of drones in rhino conservation*. Retrieved from https://www.savetherhino.org/rhino_info/thorny_issues/the_use_of_drones_in_rhino_conservation.

Scott, C. (2003) 'Regulation in the age of governance: The rise of the post-regulatory state'. In J. Jordana and D. Levi-Faur (eds.) *The Politics of Regulation: Institutions and Regulatory Reforms for the Age of Governance*, Cheltenham, England: Edward Elgar, pp. 145–174.

Shearing, C. and Stenning, P. (1985) 'From the panopticon to Disney World: The development of the discipline'. In A. Doob and E. Greenspan (eds.) *Perspectives in Criminal Law*, Toronto: Canada Law Book, pp. 300–304.

Sheriff, N. (2015) 'The losing battle against conflict minerals', *Aljazeera America*, 14 September. Retrieved from http://america.aljazeera.com/articles/2015/9/14/the-losing-battle-against-conflict-minerals.html.

Slaughter, A.-M. (2004) 'Disaggregated sovereignty: Towards the public accountability of global government networks', *Government and Opposition*, **39**(2): 159–190.

Spapens, T. and White, R. (2014) 'Introduction'. In T. Spapens, R. White and M. Kluin (eds.) *Environmental Crime and Its Victims: Perspectives Within Green Criminology*, Farnham, England: Ashgate, pp. i–v.

Thaler, R. and Sunstein, C. (2008) *Nudge: Improving Decisions about Health, Wealth, and Happiness*, New Haven, CT: Yale University Press.

United Nations Environment Programme (UNEP) (2014) *Emerging technologies: Smarter ways to fight wildlife crime*, June. Retrieved from http://na.unep.net/geas/getUNEPPageWithArticleIDScript.php?article_id=113.

van Asch, E. (2015) 'Countering transnational organized wildlife crime: Regional and sub-regional initiatives, global responses and the need for more effective coordination'. In M. Faure, P. De Smedt and A. Stas (eds.) *Environmental Enforcement Networks: Concepts, Implementation and Effectiveness*, Cheltenham, England: Edward Elgar, pp. 187–222.

Wall, M. (2014) 'Can drones help tackle Africa's wildlife poaching crisis?' *BBC News*, 21 July. Retrieved from http://www.bbc.co.uk/news/business-28132521.

Wright, G. (2011) 'Conceptualising and combating transnational environmental crime', *Trends in Organized Crime*, **14**: 332–346.

Wyatt, T. (2013) *Wildlife Trafficking: A Deconstruction of the Crime, the Victims, and the Offenders*, Basingstoke, England: Palgrave Macmillan.

Zak, A. (2015) 'Here's how and why this Seattle startup is bioengineering rhino horns', *Puget Sound Business Journal*, 28 January. Retrieved from http://www.bizjournals.com/seattle/blog/health-care-inc/2015/01/heres-how-and-why-this-seattle-startup-is.html?page=all.

# Part II

# Case studies in green criminology

# 5 The animal other

## Legal and illegal theriocide

*Ragnhild Sollund*

## Introduction

In this chapter, I discuss Norway's treatment of its predator species and legal and illegal harms[1] and theriocides committed against free-born, non-human animals. Theriocide is a relatively new concept. According to Piers Beirne (2014):

> Like the killing of one human by another, a theriocide may be socially acceptable or unacceptable, legal or illegal. It may be intentional or unintentional. It may involve active maltreatment or passive neglect. Theriocides may occur one-on-one, in small groups or in large-scale social institutions. The numerous and sometimes intersecting sites of theriocide include intensive rearing regimes; hunting; trafficking; vivisection; militarism; pollution; and climate change.
>
> (49)

I argue that the killing of predators and also the fatal treatment of victims of the wildlife trade, whether legal or illegal, are morally reprehensible. Using a threefold approach, I will discuss such treatment of animals and the ways in which this is punished or condoned by the legal system as a consequence of (1) othering, (2) objectification and (3) the perception that animals are equivalent to nature. I will further situate my discussion within green criminology; then, I will turn to penal cases involving animal theriocides before discussing these in relation to the aforementioned dimensions.

In addition, I will discuss whether the legality, instigation and acceptance of state policy harms and the lack of law enforcement of such crimes when theriocides are illegal may serve to legitimate theriocide of predators for offenders. I will evaluate whether the Bern[2] and CITES[3]

1 By harm, I mean destruction and infliction of pain or discomfort, whether psychological or physical, and whether this pain is inflicted purposely or as a means to an end – e.g. to kill or get rid of a non-human animal or to use the victim for a purpose (e.g. as a pet), as adornment or to produce derivatives from their bodies. Doing harm implies objectification and alienation (Sollund, 2008).

2 The Council of Europe (2014) describes the Bern Convention as

> a binding international legal instrument in the field of nature conservation, covering most of the natural heritage of the European continent and [extending] to some states of Africa. It is the only regional Convention of its kind worldwide, and aims to conserve wild flora and fauna and their natural habitats, as well as to promote European co-operation in this field.

3 CITES is an acronym for Convention in International Trade in Endangered Species of Wild Fauna and Flora.

Conventions (Norway is party to both), designated to protect 'wild'[4] animals, may in fact legitimate crimes against animals because of their anthropocentric biases. This will include a focus on the illegal 'wildlife' trade – herein limited to trade in animals. In both the legal and illegal wildlife trade, animals are trafficked dead or alive, regarded as exploitable commodities wanted for various reasons – as 'pets', medicinal products, food and collector items or for clothing, accessories or souvenirs (Schneider, 2012; Sollund and Maher, 2015; Wyatt, 2013).

1 Othering is a sociological process that entails creating social, though not necessarily physical, distance between oneself and another, one different from oneself, resulting in a lack of concern for those unlike oneself; it is a categorizing of beings, for example through anthropocentrism, androcentrism, racism and speciesism. In regards to racism, othering is expressed e.g. in the genocide of Jews in the Second World War (Smith, 2015; Cohen, 2001). A current example of othering motivated by xenophobia is the indifference in Europe to the repeated drowning of refugees[5] from northern Africa that prevailed for so long. Animals too are categorized and othered. This cannot be disconnected from anthropocentrism and speciesism through which othering is doxic and generally morally accepted (Ryder, 2010; Nibert, 2002; Sollund, 2012). When nonhuman animals are involved, justice perspectives like ecological justice and species justice are important in discussing why these individuals are treated as though they do not deserve moral consideration (see White, 2013).
2 Objectification of non-animals results in failing to recognize that they have intrinsic value and proper interests (Francione, 2010; Regan, 1999) and is also manifested in them being regarded as property (in the case of this chapter, the state's).
3 When non-human animals are regarded as 'nature', they are accorded the right of protection but only in so far as their species is threatened, and only while they are regarded as important in some way for humans such as being a necessary part of our ecosystems. They are not respected as individuals with interests, but only as more or less valuable 'specimens'.

(Sollund, 2015a: 148)

Trade in 'wildlife' is regulated by the CITES Convention, with 180 signatories. Threatened species are organized into three appendices. Species in danger of extinction are listed in Appendix I; trade of them is usually banned. Appendix II comprises threatened species that are monitored to prevent over-exploitation and whose 'trade must be controlled in order to avoid utilization incompatible with their survival' (CITES, 2013). Appendix III includes species that are threatened in a country that has requested assistance to control the trade of those species.

## Clarification of language

Some clarification of language will be helpful here. While I wish to avoid speciesist language, doing so presents multiple difficulties. Beirne (1999, 2007, 2009), Cazaux (1999), myself and others have discussed how words such as 'animal', 'wildlife', 'fisheries' and 'livestock'

4 The word 'wild' is an alienating word that implies the opposite of civilized, disregarding that non-human animals (as humans) are individuals with social bonds, communicative practices and often also culture (for example, see Newitz, 2013, for how crows and dolphins fabricate and use tools).
5 See, for example, http://time.com/3827557/migrant-boat-capsizing-mediterranean-europe/.

fail to represent 'other' animals with justice and as individuals with inherent value. Instead, these words serve to 'alienate' them. Jacques Derridá (2002) analyses how the use of the word 'animal' in and of itself is othering, producing and sustaining an abyss between humans and all the other individuals of 'animal' species. According to Derridá, 'animal' reflects the idea humans hold of animals – that is, that animals are other than human – rather than describing what animals are. What is it that animals have in common to the exclusion of humans? We could ask: in what way is a leopard gecko more similar to a dog than to a human? To address the fact that 'animal' is nothing but an othering word, Derridá suggests replacing it with the word 'animot' (2002: 416), a combination of 'animal' and 'word' to show that this is but a construct. Terms used by some authors, such as 'non-human animals' and 'animals other than humans', do not really resolve the 'animal word problem' because humans remain the measure, and such terms conceal the diversity among animal species of which the human species is only one. One could take up Derridá's suggestion; however, animals would then remain in the conceptual realm rather than as flesh-and-blood creatures who are the focus of this chapter.

Introducing theriocide as a concept, according to Beirne (2014), offers some kind of remedy to the animals who are killed and shows that theriocide may be as morally reproachable as homicide because 'both in life and death, animals also have the right to respectful treatment' (Beirne, 2014: 62).

In line with Beirne's (2014) definition – e.g. that theriocide may be legal or illegal, single, serial or in mass and perpetrated by one or many – the killing of wild non-human animals by the state is identified herein as organised state theriocide in that these acts are legal; require a high degree of organization, both by and for killers (for example, assessing the number of families and to which genetic breed offspring belong, where the killable victims are, distributing licences, etc.); and are systematic or deeply ingrained in cultural practices. Because theriocide also implies wilful intent, though the motivations behind such intent vary, these acts will also be referred to as killing. This is in direct contrast to the terminology used by the Norwegian authorities, who refer to the act of killing a wolverine mother and her pups as *hiuttak* – 'to take out from the den'. The term *uttak* is used for both the legal and illegal killing of all wildlife. This is an example of a euphemism concealing the character of the act when humans kill non-human animals (see also Beirne, 2014).

I use 'who' rather than 'it' or 'that' when referring to non-human animals to emphasise that they are individuals with interests rather than objects (Regan, 1999). In fact, I accept that non-human animals, just like human animals, are persons (Francione, 2008), with different personalities and interests.

Finally, for the sake of simplicity, I will continue to use certain anthropocentric terms: humans, non-human animals and predators for non-human predators,[6] even prey and livestock (for which I apologise).

## Situating non-human animal abuse in green criminology

The topic of this chapter may appear to be a non-topic for an orthodox criminologist or a lawyer. Why study legal animal killing when it is not a crime? However, within green

6 Humans are animals and very often predators, so the word combination 'human predators' could also have been applied (referring to individuals of the animal species humans, with the dietary practice of eating flesh).

criminology, to investigate such harms and label them crimes, even when these harms are not illegal or require a breach of specific conditions to be illegal, is not controversial (see Beirne, 2014; Beirne and South, 2007; Nurse, 2015; Walters, 2010; White, 2013; Wyatt, 2013). Stretesky et al. (2013) state that 'green crimes are acts that produce ecological damage whether or not that is recognized in law' (3). I concur in discarding legalistic definitions of crime and instead base my inquiry on notions of harm, inequality, social exclusion, suffering and pain (Beirne, 2007; South et al., 2013: 23). To totally discard legal definitions, however, would prevent one from seeing how the normative climate in society is reflected through legislation (and wording). General norms in society generally reflect legislation, and legislation at least is intended to affect general norms (Aubert, 1954), so rather than discarding the definitions, I find it important to highlight them. Changing legislation may give historical insight into precisely how norms alter over time within a society – e.g. Norway's Section 2 of the National Constitution, between 1814 and 1851, prohibited the entry of Jews and Jesuits (Ulvund, 2015), and the hostility towards Jews was also clear in media representations in the 1930s, thus reflecting the normative climate. This, in turn, may be seen as background for the lack of protection given to Norwegian Jews and the police's willingness to participate in deportations of Norwegian Jews during the Second World War, resulting that only 34 out of 772 Jews who were deported to the concentration camps survived the Holocaust (Johansen, 1984).

The ways in which legislation is enforced is also an indicator of the human-animal relationship and can regulate humans' relationship to non-human animals (Nurse, 2015). Analysis of enforcement (or lack of enforcement) can show the influence of general norms on legislation and vice versa and whether duties towards wildlife are respected.

A green criminology must embrace an inclusive victimology (Fitzgerald, 2010), accepting the same standards for acknowledging victimization, whether human or non-human animal. While environmental victimisation is usually discussed in relation to humans (Farmer et al., 2015; Hall, 2013; Natali, 2015), I include free-born, non-human animals in this concept because they are also dependent on their natural environment, and therefore they should also be considered environmental victims when their lives are harmed by ecological damage. They are thus victims of both eco-injustice and species injustice due to direct attacks on their personal well-being through theriocide or abduction or indirectly due to habitat loss or habitat destruction. For example, predators are environmental victims when they are displaced and treated like an enemy because humans and sheep are taking over their habitats. Environmental victims can be divided into five categories according to (1) the nature of wrongful acts, (2) the type of harm to victims, (3) the extent of damages suffered, (4) the scale or scope of harm and (5) the perpetrator-victim relationship (Skinnider, 2011: 31). This categorisation can include both human and non-human victims, although it is particularly useful and relevant for the understanding of non-human animal victims. Constructing a harm as a crime often serves to identify someone as a legitimate victim, thereby (mostly) making the harm reproachable. Because only humans have legal rights, non-human animals, who have no rights equivalent to human rights that can be breached, are not accorded victim status (Nurse, 2015).

I find violence against non-human animals to be a legitimate field of study in green criminology, and that violence per se, whether perpetuated against human or non-human animals, may on occasion be caused by the same mechanisms, such as social distance and denial (Christie, 1975; Cohen, 2001; Sollund, 2008) and the desirable effect of control and power (Sollund, 2001). The subjectification of non-human animals through which they are transformed into all kinds of products or are constructed as humans' enemies is, as proposed by

Derridá (2002), violence in the most morally neutral (non-speciesist) sense of the term, often entailing non-human animal genocide (394).

In analysing harm, I recognise the importance of governing, doxic ideologies (Adams, 1990; Gålmark, 2008; Nibert, 2002; Sollund, 2012). That is, '[r]ather than being an objective measure of harm, law is a social construction that registers the amount and kinds of harms that the social forces that make laws are willing to allow' (Stretesky et al., 2013: 110). Consequently, whether harm is a breach of law or not must not determine what a green criminologist studies. Green criminology is rooted in *critical* criminology, which focuses on revealing the power structures that form social ideologies and the subsequent harm this causes to the powerless (Hillyard et al., 1996; Sollund, 2015b; Stretesky et al., 2013). Non-human animals are powerless, 'voiceless' and more frequently subjected to this abuse of power than are humans. Furthermore, green criminology has taken a different path than a previous generation of criminologists who abstained from including non-human animal abuse in their field of study. As Beirne (2011) explains: 'For reasons of speciesism and anthropocentrism, including naked self-interest, denial, indifference and simple ignorance, animals' master status in criminology – and in law, religion and most other discourse – has traditionally been that of property' (353).

Green criminology invites us to study the inconsistencies in law regarding non-human animals – for example, why some non-human animal individuals and species are protected and not others (Beirne, 1999, 2009) and how and why only some offenders are punished. The fact that some abuse is criminalised while other equally or more harmful non-human animal abuse is not makes the discussion of how capitalism affects legislation in relation to one kind of abuse and not the other particularly relevant. The maceration of male chicks, for example, is legal because they have no economic potential, as they cannot lay eggs (Sollund, 2013b).

Other green criminologists take their point of departure for discussing non-human animal abuse from philosophy (Beirne, 1999; Cazaux, 1999; Sollund, 2008), particularly the works of Peter Singer and Tom Regan, the latter in my view being the most important for his emphasis on non-human animals as subjects of a life with intrinsic value. This perspective is highly compatible with ecological and species justice, which are central to green criminology and discussed by Rob White (2013). Non-human animals, whether victims of systemic animal abuse as in factory farming, abused in private households or as trafficking victims, or forced to slave on fields or in circuses, are all victims and treated counter to species and ecological justice. Therefore, abuse and the ways in which this abuse is supported, controlled or counteracted by legislation should be integrated as important into the field of green criminology. Essentially, I would like *all* criminology to be green, insofar as it should include the environment and non-human animals in its considerations and research.

While Stretesky et al. (2013) argue that only harms against non-human animals that can be linked to the treadmill of production should be legitimate fields of study in green criminology, I find it hard to see where the treadmill of production starts and where it stops; in which contexts, for example, are animals not regarded as commodities, property or means to an end and thereby exploitable resources? I therefore propose including all kinds of non-human animal abuse in green criminology for the following reasons:

1 In studying non-human animal abuse, the effects of power structures and the question of why some harms against non-human animals are criminalised but others are not are all studied.

2 Non-human animal abuse – like human abuse – has victims who must be acknowledged and the mechanisms behind their abuse studied in order to prevent further victimisation.
3 For reasons of justice – environmental, ecological and species – all non-human animal victims should be included, rather than some groups being selected based on artificial, categorical divisions. Categorical discrimination based on speciesism may serve to uphold the abuse against many because they are ignored or excluded.
4 Critically, green criminology has a particular responsibility to focus on victims who are made invisible in the more orthodox parts of the discipline. Non-human animals should be recognised as environmental victims.

With this as a background, my focus is on (1) the acts of abuse and theriocide which sometimes are legal while others are illegal; (2) how legal crimes against non-human animals legitimate, support and encourage illegal crimes; and (3) how legal and illegal crimes are tightly intertwined. The socio-legal approach taken here includes both a species justice and an environmental justice perspective, which does *not* exclude non-human species the way environmental justice is usually defined (see Sollund, 2013c; White, 2013).

To return to the concept of harm versus crime – precisely the fact that in some situations killing a non-human animal belonging to a critically endangered species is *legal*, while in other situations killing him or her using the same method and with the same outcome is *illegal* – merits the killing being defined as criminal, whether the killing is licensed, encouraged and condoned by the state or not. This is because these harms have the same outcome for the individual victim as well as for the destruction of the ecosystem. But whether a non-human animal belongs to an endangered species or not, harm is harm.

## Methodology

I have analysed 26 verdicts of illegal predator theriocides in Norway involving the illegal (e.g. untimely) killing of wolves, bears, lynxes and wolverines. General knowledge gained from this analysis will be applied to support my argument but will not be detailed here (but see Sollund, 2015c). Here, I will present two cases in brief before I present two cases concerning trafficking victims who were also ultimately killed by the Norwegian state. I will look at the motivation for the crimes, the way in which the perpetrators were punished (or not) and how these crimes can be seen in relation to other legal predator theriocides or state-committed theriocides. I will show how legal and illegal theriocide can be mutually supportive acts and how illegal theriocides can even be inspired by legal theriocides which are based on state policy. Although these cases represent different species, they still have some basic traits in common – e.g. human versus non-human animal conflicts of interest.

The trafficking research used for this chapter was carried out from 2010 to 2015 and includes data from Colombia,[7] Brazil and Norway. In relation to this project, I have accessed nearly a hundred penal CITES cases coded as '2510: Illegal importation of alien wildlife species' (Section 47 of the Wildlife Law) and roughly 700 cases coded as '5901: Illegal

7 Data from South America were collected by David Rodriguez Goyes, under the author's guidance, in the form of qualitative interviews with experts, veterinarians, police and others, in addition to some statistics from the police and court rulings, for which I am grateful. I am also grateful to Dyrevernfondet (the Norwegian Animal Protection Fund) for initial funding for the project.

importation/dealing with exotic species' (Section 30, No. 76, under the Animal Welfare Act) in STRASAK, the police crime statistics database. Further, I have statistics from Customs (CITES confiscations of products or live animals). A selected part of these data will be used to support the discussion.

## Legal and illegal theriocide crimes in Norway

Spring is a lovely season in Norway when nature blossoms after a long, dark winter. This is also the time of year when state-licensed killing of endangered predators – wolves, lynxes, wolverines and bears – is at its peak, as this is the season when sheep, who are vulnerable to attack, are let out to graze. This hunt takes place despite the general ban against hunting brown bears, wolverines, lynxes and wolves, which was first introduced in 1973 in southern Norway and then introduced in 1982 throughout the country. In reality, however, the predators have little protection. Take wolverines as an example. In 2013, there were approximately 350 adult wolverines in Norway, a decline from 395 in 2012. That year, between 1 January 2013 and 5 February 2014, 97 wolverines were shot. In 2014, the estimated population was 340 individuals, yet the hunting quota for that year was 142 (Rovviltportalen, 2015c).

Illegal theriocides in Norway usually concern predators who are protected under the Bern Convention, under the CITES Convention and under the Norwegian Wildlife Law, amongst others.[8] The predators in question are wolverines, lynxes, wolves, brown bears, polar bears (on Svalbard), golden eagles, sea eagles, fish eagles and, occasionally, hawks. Stortinget (the Norwegian Parliament) has decided on a set number of existing predators as a goal balancing Norway's obligations under the Bern Convention and the interests of farmers. As this goal is a minimum number to secure the species, licensed hunting and *hiuttak* are permitted. Through this 'regulation' of the wolverine population specifically, humans dig the mother and her pups out of their den and kill them. According to the Norwegian Environment Agency, the government pays particular attention to setting quotas as to whether the various species 'produce a *harvestable surplus*,[9] and whether they have *resource significance*' (Rovviltportalen, 2015a); author's translation and emphasis). In addition, the hunting traditions of the areas where the species are found and the harm the species does to livestock shall be given weight. Although I concentrate on wolverine and lynx cases as examples of predator theriocide in this chapter, the following will form a background for Norwegian cultural hunting practices, which I find important to understand current practices.

In Norway, there was a bounty on wolverines until 1974 (BrØseth et al., 2010), but in 2010 they were placed on the International Union for Conservation of Nature (IUCN) Red List as critically threatened in Norway.[10] Nevertheless, the wolverine population is controlled by Stortinget, and in 2014 the number of wolverine litters as set by Stortinget was reached (Rovviltportalen, 2015b). In order to maintain this number, hunting and *hiuttak* are allowed. The Norwegian Environment Agency's website states that of the

8 For Norwegian laws on hunting and catching wildlife, see Lovdata (29 May 1981).

9 This terminology indicates that animals are regarded as a crop, to be harvested and exploited as plants, and that there may even be a surplus of them.

10 See Artsdatabanken (2010) for the complete 2010 list. A new IUCN list was published in November 2015.

52 wolverine litters registered in the spring of 2014, 12 *hiuttak* were conducted by *Statens naturoppsyn*[11] (SNO, the government agency that tracks the status of predators). Between 15 February 2015 and 15 May 2015, 15 dens were attacked and 15 mothers and 31 pups were killed. In addition, 13 males and eight females were shot (Rovviltportalen, 2015b).

From 1845 to 1980, there was also a bounty on lynxes, and there were no hunting limits on these animals. Today, lynxes are also listed as critically threatened on the Norwegian Red List. Despite this, in 2015, the quota for killing lynxes was set at 87 individuals (Rovviltportalen, 2015c). The national goal for lynxes is to have 65 litters annually. This goal was not met in 2014, but the quota remained for 2015.

Despite Norway's obligations under the Bern Convention, wandering wolves are killed for preventative reasons (Lovdata, 2005) when they pass through zones that are not designated predator zones (Sollund, 2015c). In May 2015, a wandering young male wolf, observed not far from where sheep were soon to be released, was shot because there was concern that he would take sheep.

While most illegal theriocides of predators in Norway concern wolverines, lynxes, wolves and brown bears, nonendangered species are also hunted. According to Statistics Norway, 27,720 foxes were killed from 2011 to 2012, an increase of 47% from the year before (Nationen, 2013). Other non-human animals are killed on a large scale for meat, including deer, moose, reindeer, hares, badgers, beavers, squirrels, and a large number of bird species, including ptarmigan, grouse, hazel hen, woodcock, goose, duck and wading birds. A large number of birds, including thousands of crows, magpies, jays, ravens and seagulls, are killed for unknown reasons (SNL, 2009). The economic value of fur and meat from legal organised theriocide in Norway is about 1 billion Norwegian kroner (NOK) annually (SNL, 2009; about 100 million British pounds).

There were 456,000 registered hunters in 2012 and 2013 combined, or 9.2% of the entire Norwegian population (approximately 5,000,000). Just under 3% of Norwegian women hunt, and 19% of Norwegian men are listed in the Register of Hunters (Statistisk Sentralbyrå, 2015). Norway has a long tradition of hunting. Its foundation lies on a farming culture in which farmers hunted based on a harvesting principle (Bye, 2003). Living on what nature offered, non-human animals were regarded as important resources for humans to exploit; this idea is also central in Norwegian farming culture. However, an increasing number of hunters are coming from urban areas, suggesting that more hunters are now involved for recreational purposes (Presser and Williams, 2011).[12] Norwegian heroes are thus not only adventurers like Fridtjof Nansen, who crossed Greenland and went to the North Pole, but also archaeologist Helge Ingstad, who wrote a book about hunting for fur among the indigenous people of Arctic Canada (Ingstad, 1965).

The widespread and deeply ingrained cultural practices of legal organised theriocide in Norway, carried out for both pleasure and economic reasons, form the background for the illegal theriocides of the big predators – wolves, lynxes, wolverines and brown bears – in Norway. I present this background in more detail in the following section, although on this occasion, emphasis is placed on the lynx and wolverine (see Sollund, 2015c).

11 See http://www.naturoppsyn.no/.

12 How anybody can feel recreational value from killing or feel that theriocide connects them to nature goes beyond my comprehension but will not be further debated here.

## Legal and administrative framework for predator policy and its background

Norwegian hunting traditions and the cultural identity that goes along with them have been strongly supported by previous state policy. In 1845, a hunting law was introduced in Norway for the purpose of exterminating all the big predators (SNL, 2009). The following year, 219 bears, 238 wolves and 1,055 golden eagles were killed (hunting records are one of the oldest forms of data available in Norway, exemplifying the cultural role that hunting has had in Norway [Statistisk Sentralbyrå, 2004]). Today, political leadership determines what the 'viable' population is for different species. The hierarchy of governmental wildlife management includes, from top to bottom, the Ministry of Environment, the Norwegian Environment Agency and the County Conservation Commissions (*Rovviltnemnder*). The top three governmental levels determine national policy and create and enforce laws. The eight regional *rovviltnemnder* are loosely accountable to the Ministry of Environment. These boards formulate conditions for predators (e.g. whether they are allowed to pass through an area or will be killed) within the overall framework provided by the Parliament and government and with the assistance of professional managers (*Fylkesmenn*, directorate and county governors) who act as secretariats (Foreningen Våre Rovdyr, 2012). These boards are criticised for allowing or instigating the killing of more predators than what is sustainable for their population survival. They are often composed of people with interests in keeping predator populations down because they themselves are hunters and/or farmers (Haltbrekken, 2010). This is an important point concerning legal versus illegal predator theriocide.

Both the legal and illegal killing of predators in Norway reflect a conflict between farmers, who want to let their sheep/reindeer graze freely without herding, and predators, who regard the livestock as easy prey (Hagstedt and Korsell, 2012; Skogen et al., 2013; Sollund, 2015c). For decades, a political goal in Norway has been to populate the entire country with humans (where possible). The only way to achieve this is by expanding agricultural areas, which means that farmers and their sheep necessarily invade predator territory. Farmers receive very generous compensation by the state when they claim livestock that has been eaten by predators (Lovdata, 2014). These claims far exceed the actual numbers of livestock these few remaining predators could possibly take.

As mentioned, Norway is party to both the CITES and Bern Conventions. These conventions, which both operate with lists of non-human animal species that are accorded protection depending on their vulnerability, are followed up in national legislation such as the Wildlife Law and the Law of Biodiversity. List II of the Bern Convention identifies 700 European non-human animal species that are protected, while the CITES Convention lists 5,600 animal species. Norwegian Bern list II species include 145 bird species and 30 mammal species under protection. The Wildlife Law regulates organised theriocide (hunting and 'harvesting') based on the Law of Biodiversity. Regarding CITES, several laws come into play and are used interchangeably, such as the two aforementioned laws; the Animal Welfare Law and the Customs Law regarding importation and exportation, as well as laws concerning Svalbard (the Norwegian CITES regulation), are also included.[13]

13 See the CITES regulation at https://lovdata.no/dokument/SF/forskrift/2002-11-15-1276.

## Penal cases concerning predator theriocide

### *Case 1: LF-2005–30140 – RG-2006–266*

Although so far I have addressed the framework for wildlife crimes in Norway more generally, in this section I will exemplify predator theriocides through concrete penal cases. The first case, from Frostating Lagmansrett (appeals court) dated 14 July 2005, differs from the others I have analysed (Sollund, 2015c) concerning the laws applied in the two courts (lower and appeals). In this case, two men were charged with breach of the Wildlife Law for killing a lynx illegally. A lynx entered a mink farm, and the two offenders claimed that they were afraid the lynx would kill the minks and so shot her. The man who first noticed the lynx called the other by phone. When the second man arrived after half an hour, he shot the lynx. They claimed an emergency right under the Wildlife Law.[14] The lower court acquitted both men based on the forensic examination of the lynx, which established that it was a young animal who probably would not have survived the winter. According to the court, the offenders had freed the non-human animal from suffering, thus following Section 4 of the Animal Welfare Act. The appeals court, however, did not accept this verdict, as the motivation of the men was not to help the lynx but to kill her in order to prevent her from killing their minks. Curiously, this court did not apply the emergency right paragraph claimed by the men, and the verdict from the previous court was suspended according to procedural law.

In a new trial in the first instance, the two men were convicted and fined 3,000 NOK each, the rifle was not confiscated, and hunting rights were not withdrawn, even though the court found that the minks were not under direct attack and that the emergency right did not apply. The court also emphasised that general deterrence was important in order to prevent people from killing protected species illegally.

### *Case 2: Høyesterett – HR-1992–42-B – Rt-1992–346*

This case from the Supreme Court, heard in 1992, concerned the illegal trapping of two wolverines with a trap banned under the Bern Convention. The case was appealed all the way to the Supreme Court. A man was first convicted with a 60-day suspended prison sentence and a fine of 30,000 NOK for a breach of the Wildlife Law – killing two protected non-human animals by using an illegal trap. The trap was confiscated, but his hunting rights were not withdrawn. In the Supreme Court trial, the prosecutor argued for a 120-day unsuspended prison sentence, a fine of 30,000 NOK, confiscation of the trap and withdrawal of hunting rights for two years. The five judges did not agree, however, and a majority of three voted to keep the suspended prison sentence from the first instance. While the minority argued for the need for a sentence sufficiently harsh enough to be a deterrent, the majority emphasised the importance of not enlarging the conflict between sheep owners and the public predator management, as this would reduce the farmers' respect for the law in regards to protected predators. The two judges in the minority stated, however, that the

14 According to Section 17 of the Law of Biodiversity (Naturmangfoldloven), animals can be killed if it is considered necessary to remove a current and considerable danger to a person. The owner, or someone acting on behalf of the owner, can kill animals during a direct attack on livestock, domesticated reindeer, pigs, dogs or poultry (Lovdata, 19 June 2009b). This paragraph replaces the previous paragraph 11 of the Wildlife Law which was the applicable paragraph when this trial took place.

conflict should not be regarded as an excuse for the crime because this conflict would likely continue until wolverines were extinct. They argued that the offender had, after careful consideration, placed the trap during a season when wolverines have pups and thus had no control over which non-human animal would be killed. They also emphasised that the area where he killed the wolverine was a central wolverine breeding spot and that the population was very small and vulnerable. Twice he found a dead wolverine in the trap, then left it open so that more non-human animals could be killed.

## Parrot and reptile trafficking and theriocide

I will now turn to another kind of crime against non-human animals: the abduction and theriocide of free-born, non-human animals as part of the wildlife trade. These non-human animals are taken for the 'pet' trade, to enhance collections and to be used in the cosmetic and medical industries. These crimes share features with the organised theriocides of predators – for example, they are committed both legally and illegally and states consider themselves to be the owners of non-human animals. But while the hunting and predator theriocides discussed thus far were motivated by protecting livestock (and in other predator theriocide cases, revenge, the thrill of being in control, comradeship or adventure seeking; Sollund, 2015a), the trade in free-born, non-human animals is primarily, though not exclusively, motivated by economic gain, depending on where in the chain the offenders are (whether they are killers/abductors, middlemen, organisers of the crimes or consumers).

I will briefly describe two kinds of cases. The first concerns the trafficking of parrots for profit. There are several cases in my material that concern individuals who were stopped at the Sweden-Norway border or who arrived by ferry from Denmark and were caught with trafficked parrots (Sollund, 2013a, 2015a). The second concerns a typical case in which reptiles were discovered when the police searched a house in relation to other offences. Reptiles that are not native to Norway are illegal here, with a few exceptions, and keeping one is a breach of the Animal Welfare Act concerning the prohibition of importing and keeping exotic species (Lovdata, 1976).

### *Parrot trafficking cases*

One offender has been convicted several times for parrot trafficking and wildlife crimes. There are four verdicts pertaining to this man concerning three incidents. The man has, according to a note made on one of the confiscation reports from customs, also been caught in Gothenburg, Sweden, for trafficking parrots in 2000 (27 individuals) and in 2007. In the verdict from Halden Tingrett from 3 December 2013, he was sentenced for two smuggling attempts: one on 21 November 2010 for trafficking four African grey parrots and one on 20 November 2011 for trafficking eight African grey parrots. For these offences, he was fined 25,000 NOK (£1,923), which he apparently did not pay, as this case was added to the second in the sentence. (The police may impose a fine, but if the fine is not paid by the offender, the case will be brought to trial.) Although the court argued that, for preventative reasons, an unsuspended prison sentence should be applied, the delay in the judicial system resulted in the 30-day prison sentence being commuted to a two-year suspended sentence. In addition, he was fined 5,000 NOK (£384) and the birds were confiscated. The birds seized in 2010 were all killed by the authorities. The outcome for the victims of the 2011 trafficking is not clarified in the verdict, but according to an interview with veterinarians from the Food Safety Authority data, some were saved and others were killed.

In a second verdict pertaining to the same man, dated 20 January 2014, he was convicted for breach of the Wildlife Law and also for breach of the Law of Biodiversity for taking a sea eagle egg from a nest. Because he had been convicted before for similar crimes, aggravating circumstances were taken into account, and thus he received an unsuspended prison sentence of 45 days. In addition, he had to pay 2,000 NOK (approximately £188) for procedural expenses. The third and fourth verdicts pertaining to the man concern sentences from appeals courts, as both the parrot trafficking and sea eagle egg cases were appealed by the offender. In the verdict regarding the parrots from *Borgarting lagmannsrett*, the judges engaged in a lengthy discussion of whether the parrots were or were not 'wildlife' as defined by the Wildlife Law. They concluded that the parrots were not 'wildlife' but 'cage birds' due to the parrots' inability to survive should they be released in Norway. It is therefore stated in the sentence that

> when importation of the parrots is not punishable under the Wildlife law, breach of the CITES regulation's §5 shall be punished according to this regulation's §18, 3rd part, cfrLaw about Import and export of 6 June 1997 nr 32, §4.

This dictates a maximum six-month prison sentence; if he had been found guilty of breaching the Wildlife Law's section, this would have dictated a maximum two-year prison sentence under aggravating circumstances – even three years if the offence is also a breach of the Law of Biodiversity. The trafficker was sentenced to 60 days in prison, 45 of which were suspended (he had already spent 15 days in custody, so he was released). In the verdict from *Gulating lagmannsrett* regarding the sea eagle egg, the prison sentence was reduced to a suspended 30-day prison sentence because of the delay in judicial processing.

In most cases, however, this kind of offence is punished by means of a fine. For example, on 12 August 2014, a man caught arriving in Kristiansand with six African greys was fined 20,000 NOK (£1,677). On 30 March 2014, another man arrived in Kristiansand with 44 parrots; he only had the necessary CITES permits for 36 of them. The offender was fined 20,000 NOK (just under £2000).

### *A typical reptile/combination case*

There are hundreds of cases from my research material where an offender is convicted of violence- or drug-related offences in which the police also seized one or more reptiles. The offender is also charged for breach of the Animal Welfare Act under the regulation against the importation and keeping of 'exotic' species. In all these cases, the non-human animals are killed by the authorities – whether these are CITES species is often omitted from the verdicts. I will give one example. On 16 July 2014, a man was fined 10,000 NOK for breach of the Animal Welfare Act's Section 37 (cf. Regulation of 20 November 1976 regarding exotic species) 'for in a period prior to October 16th 2013 to have kept six snakes as domestic animals'. In addition, he was fined for breach of Weapon Law Section 33 for not having permission to purchase or acquire ammunition and for buying pepper spray. He was also found in breach of the Drug Law for being in possession of amphetamines.

Very often, the species of the seized reptiles are not named and, as in this case, the outcome for the non-human animal is not recorded, but it is very unlikely that they were rescued. As a general rule, all seized reptiles are killed, except when they are found to be very rare (e.g. the CITES listed), in which case they are offered to Kristiansand Zoo or Oslo Reptile Park prior to being killed. The seizure reports and tracking of the outcome of these cases in the judicial system suggest that parrots are more likely than reptiles to be rescued, although in the two aforementioned parrot trafficking cases, the six African greys in the first case were killed, and the eight surplus birds (one *Barnardius zonarius* parrot and seven *Agapornis* parrots) in the second case, after being rejected by Kristiansand Zoo, were also killed.

## Othering and non-human animal objectification

The treatment of the non-human animal victims in the cases I have presented have several common features; I will start by discussing the predator cases. These common features are also present in the other verdicts analysed (Sollund, 2015c), despite involving non-human animals from different species and taking place in different parts of Norway under varying circumstances. Even though their non-human animal livestock were not under direct attack, the offenders claimed to kill for purposes of protection (Sollund, 2015c). The non-human animal keepers are in conflict with the predators who want to eat their livestock and thus are regarded as an enemy – the ultimate other. Another common feature – in fact, a prerequisite to the crime – is that these theriociders are hunters, are therefore experienced killers, and have access to weapons.

Several factors indicate that the offenders may have little compassion for the non-human animals they kill. First, they keep non-human animals to exploit them and therefore are unlikely to attribute intrinsic value to their non-human animals, let alone predators. For example, in the first case discussed earlier, the offenders bred mink for fur. (Fur farming is a highly subsidized and very much critiqued form of non-human animal abuse and is outlawed in several countries, including the UK, the Netherlands, Austria, Italy, Switzerland and Croatia. Sweden has implemented rules so strict in regards to non-human animals' 'need for movement that it is no longer profitable there' [Noah, n.d.].) These offenders keep a thousand minks in small cages until they are old enough to be anally electrocuted or 'furred' (the term used when they anally electrocute them before they are skinned) (Sollund, 2008). It should also be noted that Norwegian fur farms have been repeatedly exposed for not treating injured minks and foxes (e.g. feet eaten off, ears eaten off, open wounds). This includes video footage of injured animals taken by non-human animal rights activists at the offenders' mink farm. One may assume that the offenders may have been as interested in protecting their capital – the minks' fur – from the lynx as much as protecting the minks themselves.

The verdict in this case also identified both offenders as licensed hunters who had previously participated in state-licensed lynx theriocides. Therefore, when they killed the lynx, they were doing something they have practiced regularly, something they do with impunity. Killing non-human animals is not only condoned by the state but is also encouraged through subsidies paid to fur farmers. Furthermore, being trained to kill and to engage in the violence necessary for such an act, they are able to focus on the act of killing itself – which, in regards to predators and other free-born non-human animals, is the ultimate goal of the hunt – rather than on the harm they cause when they kill. Yet this goal may still have broader significance. In many cases, the theriocide may have additional instrumental value in what surrounds the hunt. The comradeship of the accomplices is increased and the enhanced sense of masculinity (Brandth and Haugen, 2006; Bye, 2003) and the sensation of power and reward through beating and killing the non-human animal may give a special satisfaction (Bye, 2003; Presser and Williams, 2011). As the hunter William Taylor says in conversation with researcher Lois Presser, what he enjoys most is the 'challenge, being present in the moment, excitement, learning, the beauty of the surroundings and the social bonding' (Presser and Taylor, 2011: 488; see also Bye, 2003). It should be added that what further facilitates this act of violence is that in the moment of killing, ordinary feelings of compassion may be switched off – what is referred to as 'hunter insensibility' (Børresen, 1996).

Hunting by tracking and use of firearms is, however, not comparable to the deliberate killing of non-human animals by use of traps, as in the wolverine case. What comes into play here is the othering of the wolverine as the enemy, whereby the offenders showed an extreme lack of compassion. The mechanisms through which the offenders abuse and kill their sheep and minks in the other case and those leading them to kill predators are not the same. The minks and sheep are othered as property, commodities and capital which require protection until they are killed for processing. The wolverines and lynxes are othered in a different way, as competitors and enemies of the offenders, justifying the violent theriocides. Paradoxically, this may imply that the lynxes and wolverines are accorded more subjective value by the offenders, as they have become the *evil other*, thus meriting attention as individuals rather than being killed merely to 'harvest the capital'.

Killing is violence and cannot be discussed without taking into consideration the psychological mechanisms involved (Agnew, 1998), such as the pleasure of power (Presser and Taylor, 2011; Sollund, 2001), the reduction of the victim and denial of the victim (Cohen, 2001; Derridá, 2002; Sollund, 2012; Sykes and Matza, 1957). It must also be understood sociologically: the social support of hunting peers and friends for these acts on the micro-level (Smith, 2015); the frequent licensed hunting of predators to protect livestock at the state level; and the anthropocentric, speciesist norms guiding human and non-human animal relationships (or lack thereof) – thus speciesism on the societal level (Nibert, 2002).

An important reason why these theriocides are occasionally licensed and encouraged while usually being illegal is that the predators are accorded no individual, intrinsic value. This is despite Norwegian Animal Welfare Law Section 3, which states that non-human animals do indeed have intrinsic value and therefore should be treated well and protected from unnecessary harms (Lovdata, 19 June 2009a). However, this law has little value in protecting non-human animals because being killed is not regarded as harm – what matters is *how* they are killed. Their intrinsic value seems to be afforded no weight when licenses are distributed or when sheep and minks are slaughtered in the process of meeting humans' 'needs'.

Stan Cohen's (2001: 50–75) work *States of Denial* is useful when discussing this kind of abuse. According to Cohen, initially there is normalisation; the abuse and theriocide first of the minks, then of the lynxes, is part of normal, routine activities for the offenders. If they have ever felt concern for the minks, it is likely that such concerns will have been minimised by their commodification of the minks and the ways in which they routinely kill both them and the non-human animals they hunt. This normalization of harm is part of macro-denial, which one must assume is an underlying factor when the state encourages this kind of systemic abuse. Part of this is the justification of their behaviour. Cohen describes ideological justifications as 'active, unapologetic and offensive; they deny pejorative meanings, ignore accusations or appeal to different values and loyalties' (2001: 59). The offenders did not deny that they kept minks or killed the lynx and other non-human animals; in a newspaper article for which they were interviewed about their mink farm and in court in regards to the killing of the lynx, they justified this harm by claiming that it was not harmful. This can be categorised as ideological justification, which frequently appears in an anthropocentric world.

Consequently, there are several social and psychological mechanisms involved when offenders kill predators: competition for prey, the joy of power through the use of a weapon, the power to kill, the thrill of the hunt and the joy in defeating the non-human animal. Furthermore, precisely because the offenders own and exploit non-human animals, when they kill the predators, they are also likely vindictive, and while killing they are also acting routinely, something which, according to Cohen (2001), makes it easier to commit atrocities.

Just as predators are othered, so, it seems, are reptiles. This may be the result of reptiles having little of the 'fluffy bunny' factor; they receive less sympathy from humans than many other non-human animal species. Speciesism is strongly connected to physical difference, like phenotypical differences among humans being a factor in racism (Sollund, 2008). While humans sympathize with the familiar, such as dogs, cats and parrots, who are known for being intelligent, beautiful and sociable (Pepperberg, 2009), reptiles are not usually associated with such properties. Rather, they are objects of fascination (Sollund, 2013a) and are regarded as alien. Perhaps this alienation is one reason for state-sanctioned theriocide against them.

Parrots, on the other hand, who are generally perceived as charming, are also killed. This may be due to objectification but interestingly may also be the consequence of them *not* being regarded as alien 'wildlife' but as something familiar – the domesticated 'cage bird'. The argument for not including African grey parrots under the Wildlife Law in the trial discussed earlier was that if they were to be included, then guinea pigs, hamsters and budgerigars would also have to be considered wildlife, and that would be problematic because of the tradition of keeping these species in cages. So wildlife was defined as *Norwegian* natural wildlife, excluding non-human animals born elsewhere. The very probable likelihood that these particular African greys were wild when caught and thus protected under the CITES Convention (of which the Norwegian CITES regulation is also based on the Wildlife Law and the Law of Biodiversity) was not discussed by the judges. Instead, Customs Law, which governs what goods may be imported, is usually applied in such rulings, and trafficking victims are regarded as illegal goods. Because these confiscated non-human animals are usually killed and thus revictimised, it is also evident that they are not regarded as individuals whose interests should be respected. Ironically, parrots are killed precisely to enforce CITES, as in the aforementioned recidivist case, where the necessity of enforcing CITES was the argument used in the lower court for confiscating the parrots and thereafter killing them. They were not only othered but had also become mere objects which could be disposed of to make the point that importing CITES species is unacceptable and thus create a deterrent effect.

## Legal versus illegal theriocides – 'non-human animals as nature' versus 'non-human animals as individuals'

A common feature of predator killing cases (Sollund, 2015c) is that the methods by which the victims are killed are the same as those used when the state licenses hunters to kill predators legally. The line dividing 'killings without a license' that are regarded as a crime and 'killing with a license' which is not considered a crime is very blurred because the means, the act and the victim are identical. The state sends a mixed message; on some occasions, hunters like these offenders are hired to do the killing, and on other occasions, they are punished as offenders for doing so. An act of theriocide is not regarded as abuse when done in accordance with legislation, but when it is in conflict with legislation, the Animal Welfare Act comes into play. For example, chasing wolves with cars is illegal and abusive, but chasing and killing them in a helicopter is state practice and legal. One must assume that this is not regarded as a breach of Section 19 of the Wildlife Law, which states that animals shall not be exposed to unnecessary suffering.

In all these cases, non-human animals are regarded as state property. Even if the Norwegian Animal Welfare Act can be referred to in verdicts at times, the Wildlife Law that governs the killing of animals and the Biodiversity Law, which protects biodiversity more than it protects individuals from harm, takes precedence (cf. Nurse, 2015). When the species involved is vulnerable rather than critically endangered, the crimes are regarded as far less severe. If the methods used in illegal killings are the same as those utilized by the state in legal killings, the act itself is not regarded as a breach of the Animal Welfare Act, and one must assume that non-human animal suffering is regarded as insignificant. In the judicial system, free-born animals are regarded as nature, not individuals – they are 'mass wildlife' rather than 'wild' lives.

The protection that endangered species should enjoy in Norway under the Bern and CITES Conventions is not reflected in the ways in which individual non-human animals are treated when they are trafficking victims or 'trespassers' on human-owned territory (Sollund, 2015c). A wolf, wolverine, lynx or bear will be protected in accordance with the Bern Convention in Norway only to the extent that the non-human animal does not threaten the broad interests of humans – e.g. in relation to meat production.

Free-born 'wild animals' are only accorded value and thus deserving of protection as being one 'specimen' of a protected species. As in other wildlife legislation (Nurse, 2015), they are protected for conservation reasons, for anthropocentric reasons, not because they have rights as individuals. But in Norway, even if protected as a species, their value as 'specimens' is downplayed in favour of the 'capital' – that is, livestock.

I have criticised the CITES regulation before for legitimising and thus prolonging and encouraging non-human animal abduction, trafficking and theriocide (Sollund, 2011). For example, according to the Norwegian CITES regulations Sections 4 and 6 regarding export or re-export of CITES-listed species, the shipping of live individuals must not be done in a way that causes the non-human animal 'unnecessary suffering' (Lovdata, 15 November 2002). This implies that some suffering caused by trafficking is acceptable, and nothing is said about suffering during import. Non-human animals are consistently regarded as 'natural resources' which can be 'harvested' for human benefit. To over-exploit them, though, is unacceptable, principally because the loss of biodiversity will harm humans. Whether legal or illegal, the crimes of non-human animal abductions and theriocides have tremendous consequences in terms of individual (and species) suffering.

This suffering is a consequence of protecting 'wildlife' under the Wildlife Law, the CITES and Bern Conventions, and the Law of Biodiversity (and also under the Customs Law), without also paying attention to Section 3 of the Animal Welfare Act, which establishes the intrinsic value of non-human animals. Therefore, the regulatory framework that is applied offers no real protection for the individuals. According to my data, with very few exceptions, the non-human animals who are found in trafficking crimes are killed, as they are only valuable to the degree that their species is in danger.

As also mentioned, in many of the trafficking cases in Norway, the CITES Convention is often not referred to, and paradoxically the regulation that is applied is the regulation based on the Animal Welfare Act concerning the keeping and import of 'alien, exotic' species. But even when applying this regulation, welfare is not a concern.

A stance against non-human animal exploitation is neither reflected in the CITES regulation nor other legislation that should protect animals generally and 'wildlife' specifically, such as the Norwegian Wildlife Law. There are several reasons for this: (1) because non-human animals are regarded as exploitable natural resources and trade is regulated through CITES in order to prolong the exploitation (Sollund, 2011) and to protect state property; and (2) because animals are regarded as a 'mass' or as 'nature', as 'specimens' pertaining to a species more than 'individuals with interests'. Although free-born predators in Norway are protected under the Bern Convention, Norwegian authorities consistently disrespect this convention by keeping these species at the brink of extinction. Furthermore, the methods which are used to kill predators are often extremely cruel. The state thus signals a total lack of respect for these non-human animals as individuals and also for their species value and thus their value to the ecosystems they are a part of. It is difficult to see how such attitudes should not also be reflected amongst Norwegian hunters.

All the verdicts on illegal predator theriocides I have examined show that these are committed by hunters. The punishments in these cases are extremely lenient, usually consisting of fines in the trafficking cases or fines combined with a withdrawal of hunting rights and confiscation of weapons in the predator cases. As seen in the parrot recidivist case, such lenient punishment has no individual deterrent effect and consequently no general preventative deterrent effect. The general climate in Norwegian society for protecting wildlife and desisting from participating in the international wildlife trade is absent or inadequate in its support for the protection of non-human animals; this in turn seemingly also affects the potential punishment dictated in the laws and vice versa (Sollund, 2012).

## Conclusion

The legality, instigation and acceptance of theriocides through state policy when it comes to predators may serve to legitimise illegal predator theriocides. When trafficking victims are regarded as 'goods' without any status as protected (wildlife) species and their species' degree of endangerment is the only factor which would save them from being killed by the state, non-human trafficking victims have no legal protection when seized. In such a climate, even legally trafficked victims have little protection. Due to the anthropocentrism reflected in the enforcement of the Bern and CITES Conventions through Norwegian legislation and the manner in which these conventions are interpreted by the Norwegian judicial system, predator theriocides and trafficking crimes are legitimised rather than prevented.

Again, this is caused by the failure to recognise that non-human animals are our fellow beings rather than the ultimate other, merely objects or nature, and as our fellow beings they should be entitled to compassion and concern rather than alienation and disregard. They are here in their own right, not as our property to abuse and kill.

## References

Adams, C. (1990). *The Sexual Politics of Meat: A Feminist-Vegetarian Critical Theory*, New York: Bloomsbury.

Agnew, R. (1998) 'The causes of animal abuse: A social psychological analysis', *Theoretical Criminology*, **2**(2): 177–210.

Artsdatabanken (2010) *Carnivora: Rødlistevurderinger*. [Redlist assessments]. Retrieved from http://www.artsportalen.artsdatabanken.no/#/Rodliste2010/Vurderinger/Carnivora/296.

Aubert, V. (1954) *Om straffens sosiale funksjon* [The social function of punishment], Oslo: Akademisk forlag.

Beirne, P. (1999) 'For a nonspeciesiest criminology: Animal abuse as an object of study', *Criminology: An Interdisciplinary Journal*, **37**(1): 117–149.

Beirne, P. (2007) 'Animal rights, animal abuse and green criminology'. In P. Beirne and N. South (eds.) *Issues in Green Criminology: Confronting Harms against Environments, Humanity and Other Animals*, Cullompton, England: Willan, pp. 55–87.

Beirne, P. (2009) *Confronting Animal Abuse*, Plymouth, England: Rowman & Littlefield.

Beirne, P. (2011) 'Animal abuse and criminology: Introduction to a special issue', *Crime, Law and Social Change*, **55**(5): 349–357.

Beirne, P. (2014) 'Theriocide: Naming animal killing', *International Journal for Crime, Justice and Social Democracy*, **3**(2): 50–67.

Beirne, P. and South, N. (eds.) (2007) *Issues in Green Criminology: Confronting Harms against Environments, Humanity and Other Animals*, Cullompton, England: Willan.

Børresen, B. (1996) *Den ensomme apen: Instinkt på avveie* [Instinct at astray], Oslo: Gyldendal Norsk Forlag.

Brandth, B. and Haugen, M. (2006) 'Changing masculinity in a changing rural industry: Representations in the forestry press'. In H. Campbell, M. Bell and M. Finney (eds.) *Country Boys: Masculinity and Rural Life*, Philadelphia: Pennsylvania State University Press, pp. 217–234.

BrØseth, H., Heggberget, T. and Landa, A. (2010) *Fakaark: Jerv gulo gulo.* Retrieved from http://www2.artsdatabanken.no/faktaark/Faktaark100.pdf.

Bye, L. (2003) 'Masculinity and rurality at play in stories about hunting', *Norwegian Journal of Geography*, **57**(3): 145–153.

Cazaux, G. (1999) 'Beauty and the beast: Animal abuse from a non-speciesist criminological perspective', *Crime, Law and Social Change*, **31**: 105–126.

Christie, N. (1975) *Hvor tett et samfunn? Bind 2: Tabeller mm; Bind 1: Hvor tett et samfunn?* [How densely knit a society?], Oslo: Universitetsforlaget.

CITES (2013) *How CITES works.* Retrieved from https://cites.org/eng/disc/how.php.

Cohen, S. (2001) *States of Denial: Knowing about Atrocities and Suffering*, Oxford: Wiley.

Council of Europe (2014) *Convention on the conservation of European wildlife and natural habitats (Bern Convention).* Retrieved from http://www.coe.int/t/dg4/cultureheritage/nature/Bern/default_en.asp.

Derridá, J. (2002) 'The animal that therefore I am (more to follow)', *Critical Inquiry*, **28**(2): 369–418.

Farmer, A., Mitsilegas, V., Faure, M., Philipsen, N., Gerstetter, C., Klaas, K., . . . Blanc, N. (2015) *Evaluation of the strengths, weaknesses, threats and opportunities associated with EU efforts to combat environmental crime.* Draft report for the European Communities (EC) from the European Union Action to Fight Environmental Crime (EFFACE) project. Retrieved from http://efface.eu/search/node/Evaluation%20of%20the%20strengths%2C%20weaknesses%2C%20threats%20and%20opportunities%20associated%20with%20EU%20efforts%20to%20combat%20environmental%20crime.

Fitzgerald, A. (2010) 'The underdog as "ideal victim": The attribution of victimhood in the 2007 pet food recall', *International Review of Victimology*, **17**: 131.

Foreningen Våre Rovdyr (2012) *Om forvaltning.* Retrieved from http://fvr.no/fvr_page/om-forvaltning.html.

Francione, G. (2008) *Animals as Persons: Essays on the Abolition of Animal Exploitation*, New York: Columbia University Press.

Francione, G. L. (2010) 'Animal welfare and the moral value of nonhuman animals', *Law, Culture and the Humanities*, **6**(1): 24–36.

Gålmark, L. (2008) 'Aristotle revisited: Anthro-androcentrism and meat normativity'. In R. Sollund (ed.) *Global Harms: Ecological Crimes and Speciesism*, New York: Nova Science, pp. 87–109.

Hagstedt, J. and Korsell, L. (2012) 'Unlawful hunting of large carnivores in Sweden'. In R. Ellefsen, R. Sollund and G. Larsen (eds.) *Eco-Global Crimes: Contemporary Problems and Future Challenges*, Farnham, England: Ashgate, pp. 209–233.

Hall, M. (2013) 'Victims of environmental harms and their role in national and international justice'. In R. Walters, D. Westerhuis and T. Wyatt (eds.) *Emerging Issues in Green Criminology: Exploring Power, Justice and Harm*, Hampshire, England: Palgrave Macmillan, pp. 218–241.

Haltbrekken, L. (2010) *Skyteglade rovviltnemder.* Retrieved from http://naturvernforbundet.no/moreogromsdal/moere-og-romsdal/skyteglade-rovviltnemder-article19120–1825.html.

Hillyard, P., Toomb, D. and Pantazis, C. (eds.) (1996) *Beyond Criminology: Taking Harm Seriously*, London: Pluto Press.

Ingstad, H. (1965) *Pelsjegerliv blant Nord-Canadas indianere* [Fur-hunterlife among North Canada's indigenous population], Oslo: Gyldendal.

Johansen, P. (1984) *Oss selv nærmest: Norge og jødene, 1914–1943*, Copenhagen: Gyldendal.

Lovdata (1976) *Forskrifter om forbud mot at fremmedartede (eksotiske) dyr innføres, omsettes eller holdes som husdyr, selskapsdyr eller i fangenskap på annen mate* [Regulations against the trade, importation and keeping in captivity of exotic animal species in Norway]. Retrieved from https://lovdata.no/dokument/SF/forskrift/1976–11–203.

Lovdata (1981) *Lov om jakt og fangst av vilt (viltloven)* [Law about hunting and capture of wildlife]. Retrieved from https://lovdata.no/dokument/NL/lov/1981–05–29–38.

Lovdata (2002) *Forskrift til gjennomføring av konvensjon 3. mars 1973 om internasjonal handel med truede arter av vill flora og fauna (CITES)* [Regulation for the enforcement of the Convention of 3 March 1973 about international trade in endangered flora and fauna]. Retrieved from https://lovdata.no/dokument/SF/forskrift/2002–11–15–1276.

Lovdata (2005) *Forskrift om forvaltning av rovvilt* [Regulation about predator management]. Retrieved from rovvilthttps://lovdata.no/dokument/SF/forskrift/2005–03–18–242.

Lovdata (2009a) *Lov om dyrevelferd* [Law about animal welfare]. Retrieved from https://lovdata.no/dokument/NL/lov/2009–06–19–97.

Lovdata (2009b) *Lov om forvaltning av naturens mangfold (naturmangfoldloven)* [Law about management of nature biodiversity]. Retrieved from https://lovdata.no/dokument/NL/lov/2009–06–19–100.

Lovdata (2014) *Forskrift om erstatning når husdyr blir drept eller skadet av rovvilt* [Law about compensation when livestock is killed or injured by predators]. Retrieved from https://lovdata.no/dokument/SF/forskrift/2014–05–30–677.

Natali, L. (2015) 'A critical gaze on environmental victimization'. In R. Sollund (ed.) *Green Crimes and Harms: Critical Criminology in a Changing World*, London: Palgrave, pp. 63–79.

Nationen (2013) *Revejakt i gang om to uker* [The fox hunt starts in two weeks]. Retrieved from http://www.nationen.no/tunmedia/revejakt-i-gang-om-to-uker/.

Newitz, A. (2013) *The mysterious tool-making culture shared by crows and humans.* Retrieved from http://io9.com/the-mysterious-tool-making-culture-shared-by-crows-and-1460350033.

Nibert, D. (2002) *Animal Rights/Human Rights: Entanglements of Oppression and Liberation*, Plymouth, England: Rowman & Littlefield.

Noah, P. (n.d.) *Pelsdyr-forbud* [Furfarm prohibition]. Retrieved from http://www.pelsut.no/pelsmotstand/forbud-mot-pelsdyroppdrett/.

Nurse, A. (2015) *Policing Wildlife: Perspectives on the Enforcement of Wildlife Legislation*, London: Palgrave.

Pepperberg, I. (2009) *The Alex Studies: Cognitive and Communicative Abilities of Grey Parrots*, Boston: Harvard University Press.

Presser, L. and Taylor, W. V. (2011) 'An autoethnography of hunting', *Crime, Law and Social Change*, **55**(5): 483–494.

Regan, T. (1999) *Djurens rättigheter: En filosofisk argumentation.* Translated from English by Britt-Maria Thieme, Falun: Bokförlaget Nye Doxa.

Rovviltportalen (2015a) *Ekstraordinære uttak av jerv i 2015* [Extraordinary taking out of wolverine in 2015]. Retrieved from http://www.rovviltportalen.no/content/500048636/Ekstraordinare-uttak-av-jerv-i-2015.

Rovviltportalen (2015b) *50 Jerver felt i vinter* [50 lynx killed this winter]. Retrieved from http://www.miljodirektoratet.no/no/Nyheter/Nyheter/2015/Mars-2015/50-jerver-felt-i-vinter/.

Rovviltportalen (2015c) *Kan felle 87 gauper under årets kvotejakt* [87 lynx can be hunted during this years' licensed hunt]. Retrieved from http://www.rovviltportalen.no/content/500048625/Kan-felle-87-gauper-under-arets-kvotejakt.

Ryder, R. (2010) 'Speciesism again: The original leaflet', *Critical Society*, **2**: 1–2.

Schneider, J. (2012) *Sold into Extinction: The Global Trade in Endangered Species*, Santa Barbara: ABC-CLIO.

Skinnider, E. (2011) *Victims of Environmental Crime: Mapping the Issues*. Vancouver: International Centre for Criminal Law Reform and Criminal Justice Policy.

Skogen, K., Krange, O. and Figari, H. (2013) *Ulvekonflikter: En sosiologisk studie* [Wolf conflicts: A sociological study], Oslo: Akademika.

Smith, P. (2015) 'Dehumanisation, social contact and techniques of othering: Combining the lessons from Holocaust studies and prison research'. In A. Eriksson (ed.) *Punishing the Other: The Social Production of Immorality Revisited*, London: Routledge, pp. 11–29.

Sollund, R. (2001) 'Political refugees' violence in Norway', *Journal of Scandinavian Studies in Criminology and Crime Prevention*, **2**(1): 84–103.

Sollund, R. (2008) 'Causes for speciesism: Difference, distance and denial'. In R. Sollund (ed.) *Global Harms: Ecological Crime and Speciesism*, New York: Nova Science, pp. 109–131.

Sollund, R. (2011) 'Expressions of speciesism: The effects of keeping companion animals on animal abuse, animal trafficking and species decline', *Crime, Law and Social Change*, **55**(5): 437–451.

Sollund, R. (2012) 'Speciesism as doxic practice, or valuing plurality and difference'. In R. Ellefsen, R. Sollund and G. Larsen (eds.) *Eco-Global Crimes: Contemporary Problems and Future Challenges*, Farnham, England: Ashgate, pp. 91–115.

Sollund, R. (2013a) 'Animal trafficking and trade: Abuse and species injustice'. In R. Walters, D. Westerhuis and T. Wyatt (eds.) *Emerging Issues in Green Criminology: Exploring Power, Justice and Harm*, Hampshire, England: Palgrave Macmillan, pp. 72–92.

Sollund, R. (2013b) 'Selskapsdyr: Vennskap versus utnytting' [Companion animals: Friendship versus exploitation]. In R. Sollund, M. Tønnessen and G. Larsen (eds.) *Hvem er villest i landet her? Råskap mot dyr og natur I antropocen, menneskets tidsalder*, Oslo: Spartacus SAP, pp. 112–129.

Sollund, R. (2013c) 'The victimisation of women, children and non-human species through trafficking and trade—Crimes understood through an ecofeminist perspective'. In N. South and A. Brisman (eds.) *The Routledge International Handbook of Green Criminology*, London: Routledge, pp. 317–330.

Sollund, R. (2015a) 'The illegal wildlife trade from a Norwegian outlook: Tendencies in practices and law enforcement'. In R. Sollund (ed.) *Green Harms and Crimes: Critical Criminology in a Changing World*, London: Palgrave, pp. 147–170.

Sollund, R. (2015b) 'Introduction: Critical green criminology – An agenda for change'. In R. Sollund (ed.) *Green Harms and Crimes: Critical Criminology in a Changing World*, London: Palgrave, pp. 1–27.

Sollund, R. (2015c) 'With or without a license to kill: Human-predator conflicts and theriocide in Norway'. In A. Brisman, N. South and R. White (eds.) *Environmental Crime and Social Conflict: Contemporary and Emerging Issues*, Farnham, England: Ashgate, pp. 95–125.

Sollund, R. and Maher, J. (2015) *Illegal wildlife trade: A case study report on the illegal wildlife trade in the United Kingdom, Norway, Colombia and Brazil*. Retrieved from http://efface.eu/sites/default/files/EFFACE_Illegal%20Wildlife%20Trade_revised.pdf.

South, N., Brisman, A. and Beirne, P. (2013) 'A guide to a green criminology'. In N. South and A. Brisman (eds.) *Routledge International Handbook in Green Criminology*, London: Routledge, pp. 1–25.

Statistisk Sentralbyrå (2004) *Fra skuddpremier til fredning og irregulær avgang*. Retrieved from http://www.ssb.no/a/histstat/artikler/rovdyr/art-2004-05-05-01.html.

Statistisk Sentralbyrå (2015) *Registrerte jegere, 2014/2015* [Registered hunters]. Retrieved from https://www.ssb.no/jegerreg/.

Store Norske Leksikon [SNL] (2009) *Jakt* [Hunt]. Retrieved from http://snl.no/jakt.

Stretesky, P., Long, M. and Lynch, M. (2013) *The Treadmill of Crime: Political Economy and Green Criminology*, London: Routledge.

Sykes, G. and Matza, D. (1957) 'Techniques of neutralization: A theory of delinquency', *American Sociological Review*, **22**(6): 664–670.

Ulvund, F. (2015) 'Jødeparagrafen': [The Jew paragraph] *I store norske leksikon.* Retrieved from https://snl.no/J%C3%B8deparagrafen.

Walters, R. (2010) 'Toxic atmospheres air pollution, trade and the politics of regulation', *Critical Criminology*, **18**: 307–323.

White, R. (2013) *Environmental Harm: An Eco-Justice Perspective*, Bristol, England: Polity Press.

Wyatt, T. (2013) *Wildlife Trafficking: A Deconstruction of the Crime, the Victims, and the Offenders*, London: Palgrave Macmillan.

# 6 Environmental victimization

## A case study of citizens' experiences with oil and gas development in Colorado, USA

*Tara O'Connor Shelley and Tara Opsal*

Crimes against the environment have been historically under-studied by social scientists. However, a burgeoning body of work from – especially – green criminologists has begun to shift this trend, highlighting, for example, the costs associated with environmental problems such as e-waste, air pollution, and climate change (Bisschop, 2014; Jarrell and Ozymy, 2010; White, 2012); the rights of animals and the crimes committed by humans against them (Beirne, 2009; Crow et al., 2013; Wyatt, 2010); and the enforcement of environmental regulations by government agencies (Atlas, 2001; Long et al., 2012; Stretesky et al., 2013). Additionally, green criminologists prioritize examining environmental harms; that is, actions and results that are not formally understood as violations of the law (South et al., 2013; White, 2013a). Thus, a number of researchers have positioned their work on pollution, environmental degradation, and the expansion of industry within this 'harm perspective' and illuminate the vast array of actions that negatively impact humans, animals, and the broader ecosystem (Carrington et al., 2011; Lynch and Stretesky, 2001; Ruggiero and South, 2013; White, 2013b). This socio-legal conceptualization is advantageous because it acknowledges that power is connected to who or what our government defines as criminal or crime (Quinney, 1972; Reiman and Leighton, 2010) and that even legal activities can create quite harmful impacts.

A critical understanding of crime, especially in the context of environmental harm and degradation, can disguise the systemic roots of the harm (White, 2003), create inadequate response and enforcement by governmental agencies (Mennis, 2005; Opsal and Shelley, 2014), and lessen the chance that victims are understood as such (Williams, 1996). Regarding this, in his work on environmental victimology, Williams (1996) explains that there are a variety of shortcomings to legalistic understandings of victimhood, especially when considering the environment. For example, he notes that because direct causes and effects are central to legally establishing 'victim status', existing law is particularly 'weak at conceptualizing the indirect nature of environmental victimization' (Williams, 1996: 202). As a result, he posits that environmental victims are 'those of past, present, or future generations who are injured as a consequence of change to the chemical, physical, microbiological, or psychosocial environment, brought about by deliberate or reckless, individual or collective, human acts or acts of omission' (Williams, 1996: 21). Although Williams's work provided criminologists with a framework to think about and examine the experiences of environmental victims, Hall (2014) recently explained that 'victims of environmental harms have largely been overlooked' (139) by green criminologists and especially by victimologists. Regarding this, Hall states that 'the most notable absentees from the vast majority of work carried out in relation to environmental victimization so far are the voices of the environmental victims themselves' (25). The data we present in this chapter begin to address this gap.

More specifically, this chapter explores and analyzes victims' experiences of harm that resulted from energy development and extraction in the state of Colorado. As we discuss in more detail in the next section, Colorado – as well as a number of other U.S. states – has experienced a significant boom in oil and natural gas activity over the last few years because of advancing drilling technology. Thus, the present study not only highlights victims' experiences with industrial expansion but also contributes to the small body of research that explores harms resulting from energy development. In the next section, we describe the political and economic context of oil and gas development in the state to set the stage for the findings of the research. Then, because social scientists have begun to turn their attention toward examining oil and natural gas activity in the United States, we briefly review their work.

## The political and economic context of oil and gas activity in Colorado

Global production of petroleum and natural gas has increased steadily over time. Historically, the United States has been one of the production and consumption leaders of these natural resources, recently becoming the largest producer in the world (U.S. Energy Information Administration [USEIA], 2015). Although a number of social and environmental factors have shaped these production trends (for example, weak economic markets and a warming climate), increased U.S. production is also connected tightly to technological advancements that have provided industry access to undeveloped oil formations and shale gas once thought to be untouchable. In particular, horizontal hydraulic fracturing – a recently refined drilling technique that involves sending millions of gallons of water, sand, and chemicals thousands of feet below the earth's surface through cement-lined pipes – has been central to this rapid development (Weiner, 2014).

A handful of states are home to the specific geological features that produce the vast majority of these fossil fuels; Colorado, a western U.S. state located along the Rocky Mountains, is one of these places. Historically, the San Juan and Raton basins located in the southern part of the state produced much of the region's natural gas through coalbed extraction (Weiner, 2014). More recently, however, development and extraction from the Piceance and Denver-Julesberg basins – two of the largest resource plays (i.e. group of oil fields) in the United States located on the west and east sides of the state – have driven and expanded the production of oil and gas. Specifically, between 2000 and 2012,[1] natural gas production in the state increased by 137%, while crude oil production increased 167% during the same time period (USEIA, n.d.).

This development has not gone uncontested in Colorado. A variety of stakeholders, including property owners, citizen groups, local municipalities, and scientists, have expressed worry and caution about a variety of issues, including unexplored environmental harms and public health concerns. For example, hydraulic fracturing is an intensive drilling process, as it takes months to explore, develop, drill, and eventually 'frack' a well pad.[2] Because extraction increasingly takes place in close proximity to where people live and work, citizens have had to contend with heavy truck traffic as well as the constant noise and

1 We use this time frame as it represents a similar period of time as the data we utilize for this research.
2 The Colorado Oil and Gas Association (COGA) reports that preparing a well pad, drilling and hauling, and the fracturing process can range from 41 to 66 days (COGA, 2015).

light that accompany development. Additionally, especially because in Colorado development has moved into urban and suburban areas, industry increasingly exposes humans to air and water pollutants created by this process of energy extraction (Adgate et al., 2014). Because this development has occurred so rapidly, scientists have had little time to fully evaluate the potential impact of these pollutants on people or the broader ecosystem (Finkel and Law, 2011).

Other stakeholders point to and problematize the broader political-social context in Colorado that, many would argue, facilitates oil and gas development and extraction. For example, Colorado property is subject to split estate whereby residents own land but another person likely owns the rights to develop the minerals beneath the surface. The split estate requires that surface owners provide mineral rights owners access to the resources that lie below the surface. Thus, while energy companies typically financially compensate surface owners to some degree when they access the land or build a well pad on it, landowners are 'clearly at a disadvantage' to both mineral rights owners as well as oil and gas companies who will be more likely to be vested in development because of the economic benefits they receive (Davis, 2012: 186).

In addition to a split estate system that facilitates access to natural resources below the surface, a number of stakeholders in Colorado view the Colorado Oil and Gas Conservation Commission (COGCC) – the state agency charged with regulating oil and gas development and activity – as an agency invested in enhancing opportunities for development. For example, it was only in 2007 – with the passage of the Colorado Habitat Stewardship Act – that the mission of the COGCC widened beyond development to marginally include protections for wildlife, the environment, and public health. Moreover, prior to 2009, the then seven-member commission contained only industry-associated representatives; at this time, Democratic Governor Bill Ritter added two members to the COGCC to begin to diversify the backgrounds of the Commission. Because the Commission is charged with a number of important duties, including rule-making sessions that determine regulatory policy, settling disputes between stakeholders (including holding adjudicatory hearings), and inspecting and enforcing industry violations, the fact that the mission of the COGCC remains focused on the development of oil and gas resources raises suspicion among many Coloradoans (Opsal and Shelley, 2014).

## Emerging research on oil and natural gas development

Because fracking has expanded so quickly across the United States as well as internationally, and because stakeholders have contested this expansion so publicly, researchers across a variety of disciplines have begun to study the phenomenon in order to empirically assess potential impacts of drilling activity. For example, some public health and environmental research examines the health impacts of development on the environment and people and suggests that drilling may impact local air quality (Colburn et al., 2014; Gilman et al., 2013), drinking water (Environmental Protection Agency [EPA], 2015; Llewellyn et al., 2015; Osborn et al., 2011), and the healthy development of newborns (McKenzie et al., 2014).

Along with this research, a number of social scientists have examined the perceived and actual social impacts of development and activity. Much of this work examines citizens' and stakeholders' attitudes toward natural gas development in different areas of the country (for example, Brasier et al., 2011; Ladd, 2013). Additionally, some of this research builds on existing social science work on 'boomtowns' (Freudenburg, 1981; Lawrie et al., 2011) and explores the benefits and risks of shale energy development to communities facing intense growth pressure due to development. For example, in her research on one Pennsylvania county that experienced rapid social and economic changes due to local natural gas drilling, Perry (2012) identified a number of community-level impacts, including evidence of collective trauma (Erikson, 1976) resulting from industrialization of the natural landscape, distrust of local officials, and being bullied by industry representatives. Building on this last finding, Malin (2014) points out how small-scale farmers in her ethnographic research in the same state experience pressure to lease out their land for oil and gas development due to, in part, their own economic marginalization.

A green criminological perspective adds an additional lens to understanding the consequences of recent oil and gas development and activity. While most green criminologists have not examined hydraulic fracturing (for an exception, see Opsal and Shelley, 2014), a handful of researchers have examined harms associated with energy development. For example, in a series of pieces, Jarrell and Ozymy (2010, 2011, 2012) analyze the quantity and type of emissions that petroleum refineries produce during 'upset events' which, as the authors explain, are (legal) releases of unscheduled and unauthorized emissions of air contaminants that can produce significant pollution with serious health consequences. White (2013a) and Carrington and colleagues (2011) examine the current mining boom in Australia, identifying a variety of negative social impacts that affect communities and individuals, including an increase in crime and violence (see also Archbold et al., 2014; Ruddell, 2011). Some of these authors point out that these harms often remain hidden or are excused by individuals and state actors because of the economic benefits the industry provides. Our own research (Opsal and Shelley, 2014) on citizens' perceptions of state response to harms they experienced from oil and gas activity confirms these latter findings.

Thus, the central goal of this chapter is to contribute to the growing body of social science research that explores the dynamics and impacts of development related to hydraulic fracturing. An additional focus is to contribute to the green criminological literature on harm and victimization resulting from energy development. In particular, by drawing on data we collected from semi-structured interviews with 65 Coloradoans as well as findings from a content analysis of formal complaints citizens filed with the COGCC due to problems they experienced with oil and gas activity, we respond to Hall's (2014) recent call for a greater understanding of the experiences of environmental victims.

## Methodology

What are the nature and extent of environmental harm and victimization that occur as a result of oil and gas activity? To address this research question, we examined a range of citizen-reported harms associated with oil and gas activity using a green criminological framework, as it allows for a more inclusive operationalization of environmental victimization (Hall, 2014; Williams, 1996; White, 2003, 2013a). Thus, as we described earlier, we examine a wide range of harms that lead to environmental victimization, even though such harms may or may not be violations of criminal law (though some are considered administrative rule violations).

To examine our research question, we utilized a mixed-methods approach that included (1) a content analysis of formal complaints filed by citizens to the state of Colorado regarding oil and gas activity and (2) interviews with 65 environmental victims. These two data sources give us a general understanding of the nature and extent of harms related to energy extraction while also providing us with an in-depth understanding of the victimization experience. We describe each of these data sources in more detail in the following sections.

### *Content analysis of COGCC complaint database*

When citizens experience problems with oil and gas activity, they can contact the Colorado Oil and Gas Conservation Commission (COGCC) and file a complaint as a way to seek relief. Citizens are able to document their own complaints by completing COGCC paperwork themselves, or they can phone in their complaint whereby a COGCC staff member documents the complaint(s). They are also able to file complaints via local government oil and gas liaisons, though this method is less common. Once a complaint is filed, the COGCC investigates and, if rule violations are found, takes enforcement action (COGCC, n.d.). The COGCC makes these complaints available online, and in June 2013, we ran a statewide query and requested the maximum number of records allowable for a search. This resulted in 2,500 complaints dating November 2, 2001, to June 10, 2013. Because the COGCC database does not allow for a download of aggregate records, it is extremely difficult to access and analyze records for longitudinal analyses. Thus, each of the 2,500 complaints was opened individually, and our research team copied and pasted relevant information to create our own complaint database. During this process, we identified and removed duplicate records, which resulted in a total of 2,444 complaints.

Once the complaint database was developed, we read each complaint narrative and conducted a content analysis of it using an open coding philosophy to identify emergent themes (Emerson et al., 1995). Our coding strategy involved two stages. In the first stage, one researcher read the complaint narrative and then applied a broad code to signify an emergent theme. In the second stage, two researchers jointly reviewed each complaint and then compared it to the initially assigned code. During this stage, the two researchers refined and replaced broad thematic codes with more detailed categories. At the end of the process, we identified 19 forms of environmental harms that occur as a result of oil and gas activity in Colorado.

### *Interviews with environmental victims*

To gain a deeper understanding of the victimization experience, we sent letters to individuals in the COGCC database who had a working address ($n$ = 732) and invited them to participate in face-to-face interviews during the summer and fall of 2013. We were able to conduct interviews with 65 participants of whom 32 were male and 33 were female. The majority of our participants were middle class, though a small handful were upper class or living in poverty. They lived in rural areas where most (but not all) oil and gas activity occurs in Colorado and, like most Coloradoans, only a small handful owned the mineral rights under the surface of their properties.

Most of the interviews began with a tour of the property and, when the problem occurred on the participant's property, the well pad to fully document the nature of the victimization experience. During this tour, we took detailed field notes and photographs. After the tour, interviews were typically conducted in the home of the respondent and were informed by an open-ended, semi-structured interview guide that covered the events that led up to the complaint, the nature and extent of the problem, and harms experienced by the respondent and other non-human victims (i.e. wildlife, domestic animals, ecosystems). All but one participant[3] allowed us to record and make a formal transcription of the interview.

A central goal of the Findings section of this chapter is to illuminate *how many times* a particular kind of complaint was filed to the COGCC from 2001 to 2013. Additionally, though, we use the qualitative data described herein to illuminate what the problems

3 This participant would not consent to a recorded interview because he was in business with the oil and gas industry and feared backlash.

associated with these complaints looked and felt like from the 'on-the-ground' perspective of our participants. Thus, in the findings we present next, we identify specific representative cases from our interviews that elucidate this connection.

## Findings

For simplicity, we present our findings by first detailing the results of the content analysis of the COGCC complaints and then draw illustrative quotes from our qualitative interview data to demonstrate the nature of environmental problems associated with oil and gas activity.

Of the 2,444 citizen complaint reports, we found that approximately 275 (11%) of them constitute what victimization scholars would consider repeat victims (i.e. those who had filed reports at different dates and times) (Weisel, 2005). Moreover, we also observed that some individual complaint records actually contained several nested concerns whereby one complaint report often produced several conceptually unique victimization events. For example, a respondent might report in his or her complaint that he or she was concerned with noise from drilling operations, a produced water spill on his or her property, and harm to a domestic animal. Thus, of the 2,444 total complaint reports we found, 556 nested concerns, resulting in 3,000 total recorded harms.[4]

Citizens identified an extensive range of harms that we coded into 19 distinct categories.[5] Table 6.1 provides a listing of each complaint with a brief explanation, total count, and percentage of total complaints. The most common harms involved well water issues (24%), dumping/spills/leaks (11%), air quality (10.7%), noise (10.4%), and land use (7.5%), while complaints about royalties (0.8%) and orphaned wells (0.7%) occurred less frequently.

Due to space limitations, for the remainder of the chapter, we will only discuss the 10 most common harms associated with oil and gas activity (see Figure 6.1). These 10 categories constitute 87% of all complaints.

### *Well water*

As shown in Figure 6.1, well water issues were the most common concern noted by citizens and constituted 24% of complaints ($n$ = 721). A number of these complaints involved preemptive requests for baseline water tests. Specifically, prior to oil and gas development occurring, some citizens requested that the COGCC perform a baseline water test so that if water quality issues arose after development commenced, they had a point of comparison. However, a sizeable number of these complaints were related to changes in well water quality that often accompanied drilling activity. The data from our qualitative interviews illustrate that 'water quality' complaints often centered on a change in (1) odor (smells that participants described as hydrocarbons, rotten eggs, or sulfur like); (2) appearance (for example, foamy, milky, oily sheen, effervescent); and (3) combustibility (being able to light water on fire).

For example, Libby details her experience with well water problems that she felt were directly related to neighboring oil and gas development:

*Libby:* Somethin's goin' on here . . . it has changed from delicious, clean, wonderful water to nasty, black, it has sulfur-forming bacteria, slime-forming bacteria. It smells horrible of sulfur. . .
*Do you think it's related to oil and gas activity?*

4 For simplicity, these nested concerns will also be referred to as complaints and/or harm events.
5 We had to code some complaints into a missing category due to lack of detailed information.

*Table 6.1* Type of Concern by Count and Percentage of Total

| *Concern* | *Brief Explanation of Concern* | *Count* | *Percentage of Total* |
|---|---|---|---|
| Well water issues | Problem/request concerning a well: baseline tests, contamination, odor, appearance, lighting on fire, water quantity | 721 | 24.0% |
| Dumping/ spills/leaks | Produced water, oil, contaminated mud, and other substances dumped/spilled/leaked onto ground | 330 | 11.0% |
| Air quality | Odor, air pollution, venting, flaring | 320 | 10.7% |
| Noise | Noises from oil and gas activity | 312 | 10.4% |
| Land use | Surface owners' concerns about oil and gas activity on their land | 226 | 7.5% |
| Reclamation issues | Problems returning disturbed land to its original state as a result of oil and gas activity, etc. | 183 | 6.1% |
| Surface damage | Property or crop damage, erosion, damaged roads | 169 | 5.6% |
| Other rule compliance | Well pad maintenance/appearance and other rule violations not specified in other categories | 140 | 4.7% |
| Other | Gas tap rights, explosions, fires, information requests, etc. | 130 | 4.3% |
| Surface water issues | Contamination, odor, appearance, dumping/ spills/leaks into surface water | 103 | 3.4% |
| Domestic animals | Death, illness, birth defects, endangerment of livestock and other animals | 83 | 2.8% |
| Notification | Failure to notify surface owner of oil and gas activity | 49 | 1.6% |
| Truck/road dust | Excessive road dust related to oil and gas vehicles | 48 | 1.6% |
| General environmental concern | Potential environmental problems due to oil and gas activity | 43 | 1.4% |
| Idle well issues | Lack of production, lack of activity, etc. | 32 | 1.1% |
| Traffic concern | Oil- and gas-related traffic: road congestion, speeding, careless driving, aggressive driving | 32 | 1.1% |
| Wildlife concern | Wildlife quantity, migration, and health | 26 | 0.9% |
| Royalties | Dishonest, stalled, or inconsistent payments | 25 | 0.8% |
| Orphaned well issues | Wells improperly plugged, unidentifiable responsible party | 21 | 0.7% |
| Missing | Not enough information | 7 | 0.2% |
| Total | | 3,000 | 100% |

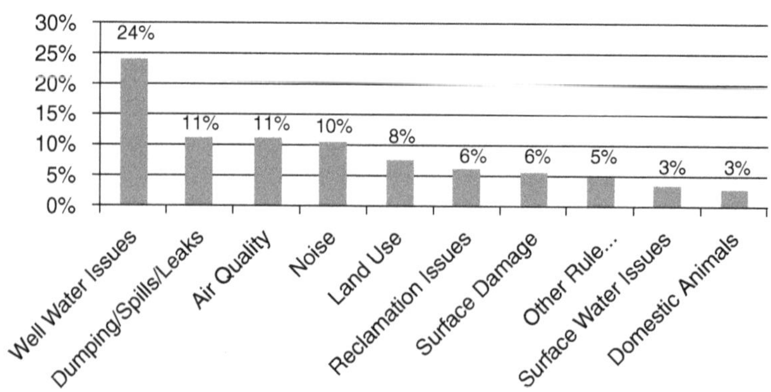


*Figure 6.1* The Most Frequent Citizen Complaints about Oil and Gas Activity

*Libby:* Yeah, I do. There were crummy wells here, sulfury-smellin' wells all around, so I understand that that can be a natural condition. But it was clean, and it was clean for years. And the reason that I think it's associated with the development is because I've seen it happen to all my friends' wells. And it happens as they move out. And I know it's anecdotal and it doesn't meet their scientific criteria of cause and effect, but I don't know a single person out here who doesn't have a reverse osmosis system on your water because you can't drink it otherwise, and that wasn't how it used to be.

As shown in this exchange, Libby suspects that her well water is polluted, but she has not obtained relief from industry or the COGCC; as such, she eventually invested approximately $10,000 into a water treatment system.

Most complaints were related to water quality problems, but some respondents also revealed concerns about water quantity. Most often, these respondents were concerned with the possibility of water shortages associated with oil and industrial activity, though some reported explicitly experiencing such shortages. Eva – as well as another respondent, Seth – reported concerns with the possibility of water shortages:

*Eva:* When you get into the sheer statistics of the amount of water that's being pumped out of the ground and we live in a semi-arid area, average rainfall 14 inches or whatever, you start to realize, this is stupid. What we're doing here doesn't make sense. We can live without gas. We can't live without water.

*Seth:* There is an energy company that has bought some property up here at the end of the creek. They're tryin' to get our adjudicated agricultural water, and they're wantin' to use that for drilling activities . . . we have fought it for at least three years, it just recently went to court, and the judge has not ruled on it yet, and they want our water rights. In other words, they're wantin' to take water out of the creek that is ours, it's adjudicated. It's not just mine, it's all of the water users who have adjudicated rights off of the creek for irrigation. That's our biggest concern right now, and it is a major concern.[6]

As demonstrated by the following excerpts, Rosanne and Oscar experienced water quantity problems shortly after drilling began near their property.

*Rosanne:* We literally ran out of water. We had to turn the pump off, because we ran out of water.

*Did you have to drill another water well?*

*Rosanne:* No. It came back eventually, but I was in the shower and it just quit.

*Oscar:* And back when we ran out of the water, we weren't necessarily in a drought at that time. We had a lot of rain and a lot of snow those few years. I don't know. It just doesn't make sense. . . . I asked them to help me with my cistern and to either put in a cistern or help me with the cost of it. They said no way, they wouldn't help me. I said, at least that way I could get the water into here, as far as because of [sic] we're talkin' quality and quantity. As far as the quantity, I wouldn't have to worry about it running dry because of whatever they did.

6 Like a number of states in the arid western United States, Colorado's water is adjudicated through a prior appropriation system. In basic terms, this means that those individuals who own senior rights can begin to draw water from rivers, streams, and ditches before those who own more junior rights. For information about this, see Wolfe et al. (2012).

Oscar and Rosanne continue to haul water to their home as a result of water quantity (and quality) problems that they associate with oil and gas operations. As noted by Oscar, this created a financial hardship for them: 'Let's put it this way. We're still buyin' water every week. It's costing us several hundred dollars every week, hauling water back and forth.'

These respondents' complaints about water quantity are not without merit, as research indicates that the volume of water required for new oil and natural gas development in Colorado in a single year could serve the water needs of 44,000 to 72,000 households (the population equivalent of the fourth-largest city in Colorado) (Western Resource Advocates, 2012). Of additional concern, water used in oil and gas activity is 100% consumptive – that is, it cannot be treated and returned to streams for future use (Western Resource Advocates, 2012). In light of this information, Eva's concerns are particularly salient, as she realized that there could be more than just water shortages but a boom-bust economy as well: 'But this is not goin' on forever. They're gonna go. But this time when they go, they're not only takin' the jobs, they're takin' the water.'

## *Dumping, spills, and leaks*

The next most frequent complaint involved concerns related to dumping, spills, and leaks (11% or $n$ = 330). This category contained an array of harms associated with produced water[7] spills and improper/illegal dumping of contaminated soil/mud/water or any substance that can be spilled or leaked onto the ground. Harms associated with dumping/spills/leaks entering directly into a water source were coded as either surface water issues or well water issues. Consider the following quotes from Mike and Paul:

*Mike:* Tankers from all over Colorado are now dumping on the site. . . . Truck drivers destroyed all vegetation on my property. Their mud and contaminants are mixed in with the snow and ice. They continue to dump for another month before stopping – all in an area of 40 acres. Hundreds of tons of drilling rig mud mixed into the top soil.

Words cannot convey the full extent of the dumping that occurred on Mike's property, and this was particularly apparent to us while we viewed several of Mike's photos, which showed rickety trucks hauling in hazardous soil that was subsequently dumped into large mounds in excess of 10 feet.

In contrast to Mike's encounters with hazardous waste dumping, Paul experienced a spill of produced water on his property located within 10 feet of a ditch that flows into a nearby spring.

*Paul:* A semi truck transporting produced water, fracking fluids, drove off the road. There were no circumstances. It was dry. He drove right off the road and rolled a semi truck over. That's what led to us filing a complaint or a spill notification.

7 Produced water is a waste generated by the oil and gas industry and consists of a mixture of organic and inorganic compounds. Because produced water is brought to the surface during oil and gas production, it can contain hydrocarbons. It is typically stored in holding tanks until it can be treated and disposed of using different physical, chemical, and biological methods (see Fakhru'l-Razia et al., 2009).

Paul also reported concern with the initial response to the spill; as he put it:

*Paul:* I got there just minutes after it had happened, and the volunteer fire department was just arriving as I was arriving. There were – there's no spill response in this area. The gas companies have provided little trailers with absorbent and that type of thing to the fire department. They did not bring that equipment with them. So by the time that trailer – actually, the gas industry employee was the one who had to go get that trailer, and then there was very little equipment in it, not anything to handle the magnitude [of the] spill that was taking place.

The COGCC estimates that in 2014, there were 769 reportable spills associated with oil and gas activity. According to the COGCC (2014), operators are only required to report spills that achieve a certain magnitude (i.e. in excess of 210 gallons). When spills of this magnitude occur, it is the responsibility of industry to report, respond, and remediate damage with support from government agencies in emergencies. A slow or inadequate response has the potential to exacerbate harms associated with spills, and Paul reported feeling frustrated with industry response and a lack of government oversight of spills generally: 'The problem there was that there is no one to verify how much fluids were spilt, so the reporting process is just totally dependent to whether the gas company is willing to report or not.'

### *Air quality*

Air pollution and air quality complaints were only slightly less common than dumping/spills/leaks (10.7% or $n$ = 320 vs. 11% or $n$ = 330, respectively). Citizens reported excessive flaring, strange and/or strong odors (i.e. hydrocarbons, rotten eggs, sulfur-like smells), and air pollution concerns more generally. Seth offers an example of the typical complaint associated with air pollution.

*Seth:* Couldn't believe it. I thought, here we'd been breathin' this all this time. We'd have to shut the house up at night so we wouldn't get quite as much smell, 'cause we don't have air conditioning. And all of this stuff is very bad for your health, and it's goin' right up into the air, and you can't tell me this is the only well pad in the world [laughs]. There are millions of 'em.

It was not uncommon for participants to associate air pollution problems with health concerns – some of which included stinging eyes, headaches, coughing, bloody noses, and an array of other illnesses. With that said, not all air pollution complaints were linked to health concerns; some were linked to general concerns about pollution and visibility as well as flaring practices and climate change.

*Athena:* It's still polluting the air, it's still creating methane, it's still causing climate change. They can't capture enough emissions to stop the methane that's being dumped right now on a daily basis.

*Georgia:* The oil and gas industry has not made the Western Slope of Colorado a better place in which to live. Our pristine air now has a visible brown cloud and big air pollution problems. . . .

Complaints about air pollution may partially explain recent changes in Colorado's regulation of air pollution whereby industry must reduce fugitive volatile organic compounds (VOCs) and hydrocarbon emissions from condensate tanks and other sources (Colorado Department of Public Health and Environment [CDPHE], 2014).

### *Noise*

While only 10% of complaints ($n$ = 321) filed to the state were related to noise associated with oil and gas activity, this was the most common form of co-occurring harm participants reported to us in our interviews. Noise complaints were associated with a variety of sources, including excessive sound from drilling, compressors, workers, trucks, and other activities to support drilling or maintenance of the well pad. Some noise complaints were associated with short-term operations (particularly during drilling), while others reported long periods of noise pollution that can accompany the full life of a well. Cierra explains this well: 'At first, of course it's really very, very disruptive and noisy and all that stuff, but it's an ongoing thing; that noise from those wells never stops.'

Most participants experienced the noise in significant ways that led to a decline in their quality of life. For example, Billie Jean reported noise from a well pad:

> It was a buzzing, and I'm deaf in one ear, but it sounded like *ngngngn*, and at night when I'm going to sleep, *ngngngn*. It just drove me nuts. I'd be in there in the family room watchin' TV, and the thing, *ngngngng*. . . .

Roman and Carol also complained about noise and took extreme measures to escape the negative impacts associated with it.

*Roman:* It took several years for them to get it done, and all the time, of course, I was sufferin' from the noise. The noise bothers me so much because I worked in the mines quite a bit, underground, surveyin'. It affected my hearing, and I hear the low frequencies that fit the noise from the compressors a lot better than most people. They wouldn't even hear them. So it really bothered me.
*You had trouble sleeping. Were there other effects from that noise on you?*

*Carol:* It gets to you. It really gets to you. We go around – we closed all the windows, we wouldn't open the door. We even do now because of the dust and the odors.

*Roman:* Well, I had to – on our bedroom back there, I put a piece of – at night I have insulation in there, two 2-inch pieces of Styrofoam. That's helped.

The noise got so intolerable that at one point Roman began to sleep in the closet.

*Carol:* When I come back, he had the mattress in the closet, was sleepin' in the closet. They put the compressors in, and especially in this canyon, he couldn't even sleep. And you'd go to bed at night, *rrmm! Rrmm!* It was constant. So that's been a big thing.

### *Land use conflicts*

As we explained earlier in this chapter, Colorado is a split estate whereby surface and mineral rights are split from each other. This system creates conflicts between surface owners who find themselves at odds with those who own mineral rights below the surface and the oil and gas operators who wish to extract these resources or lay pipeline to transport natural gas. Land use conflicts constituted about 7.5% of the complaints ($n = 226$) and took on a variety of forms, such as putting a well pad on a property even when the surface owner objects, the physical location of the well pad, accessing surface owners' land without permission, and storing heavy industrial equipment on the land or in improper locations. Both Phil's and Will's experiences exemplify land use conflicts.

*Phil:* The surface person is subservient to the mineral estate, so it's like, we're coming in. We're gonna drill on this spot.

*Will:* I got a letter in March 2012 sayin' that they wanted to have some landmen come in and cut a right-of-way for a new pipeline, and I told 'em I wasn't interested. They wrote me one more letter sayin' that they were going to run a pipeline through there, and I said, 'I'm not gonna allow that.' Next thing I got was a notice of intent to condemn the property. This is all in about three weeks. I still told 'em, 'I'm gonna fight you. I'm not interested.'

Other landowners report issues with oil and gas workers trespassing or storing equipment on their land without permission. Consider Wonda's account:

*Wonda:* I happened to go over one day, and they had a bunch of equipment here. They were trying to bore and go down and get the pipe buried four feet below. They had all this equipment here. I caught 'em and went and padlocked the gates. They left it there that night. And they showed up the next morning to work, and I said, 'You're not trespassing on my land. Get the hell out of here.' 'We want our equipment!' I said, 'You put your equipment on my land without permission. Get the hell out of here.' The guy here in __ who's the subcontractor hates me to this day.

### *Reclamation*

In Colorado, oil and gas companies are required to reclaim or restore land around inactive wells. Reclamation may mean taking action to reduce erosion, loosening compacted soil, controlling invasive weeds, and planting seeds (Finley and Murphy, 2015). About 6.1% of complaints ($n = 183$) were related to reclamation issues. Most typically, this involved oil and gas operators not properly returning disturbed land to its original state as a result of their industrial activities. In addition to being aesthetically unpleasing, for some respondents, this can be economically devastating when land can no longer be farmed or used to support grazing activity for livestock. Jason, a Colorado rancher whose family has ranched in Colorado for several generations, sums up the typical sentiment about failed reclamation work.

*Jason:* But then they closed it down, they closed it off, and in my – the way I see things, the way things are supposed to be, when they close the dang thing down, they're supposed to clean everything back up, take everything off of it, and then reseed it. And that hasn't happened.

Though reclamation did not account for the majority of complaints, it is worth noting that a recent investigation revealed that it is a pressing problem, as oil and gas companies have not restored land around half of the inactive well sites in Colorado (Finley and Murphy, 2015).

### *Surface damage*

It was not uncommon to learn about an assorted array of damages involving surface owners' property or crops, erosion problems, and road damage that respondents believed were caused by oil and gas activity. Surface damages represented 5.6% of all complaints filed ($n$ = 169). Many participants reported that surface damage was rarely an isolated incident but rather a series of incidents causing ongoing damage. Debbie and her husband, Buck, reported investing significant time into getting operators to fix damages to their private road, fences, and fields.

*Debbie:* Every time they came in with a gas well, they'd pay us, what, $10,000, I think that was their going rate. Ten thousand dollars plus surface damages. And by the time you deal with them for months on end and contracts and talks and negotiations and fighting with 'em about stupid little stuff, that $10,000 wouldn't pay for a second of what you have dealt with.

When Debbie and Buck were successful in getting operators to fix damages, they often found that the repair work was sub-standard, and they ended up fixing the damages themselves.

*Buck:* They were just gonna do some rough road in there, and they dug their heels in and said, 'That's the way it's gonna be.' I finally just said, 'To hell with you guys. I'm tired of fightin' with you. We're gonna build the road like we know it should be,' and we did that.

Given that surface damage was rarely an isolated incident and was not always corrected (or corrected properly), it created significant frustration and sometimes led to verbal and physical altercations between surface owners and operators. For example, Wayne recounted a tense encounter with an oil and gas employee that eventually led to a series of events that culminated in a restraining order being filed against him.

*Wayne:* He asked me how I was doin'. I said, 'I'm not doin' worth a dang. Some sorry outfit come down here and drove across my newly planted field.' He said, 'Well, that was me. I had to get in here. I got a right-of-way to go anywhere I want on your place, and we can even put in barracks and put in people and move 'em in and let 'em stay here in this place.' And I said, 'No, you can't. You're lucky that I wasn't here when you come drivin' across that field, because I'd been ready to shoot you. Anybody would have.'

### *Other rule violations*

There were a series of complaints about various COGCC rule violations by operators, and these constituted about 5% of all complaints. These most often dealt with problems with well pad maintenance. For example, people complained about problems with the appearance of the site due to noxious weed growth on the well pad site, the height of berms (raised banks), rusty storage tanks, and damage to berms, as well as how often – or in what manner – weed control was done. For example, Herman and Cindy reported several problems with weed control on their property that were associated with well pad maintenance.

*Herman:* There have been a few times in the past where they've come and sprayed for weeds. They don't just spray the ground. They spray the gates, everything. So you have to open the gate and you get this green anti-weed crap.
*Cindy:* Yeah, they coated the gate with green herbicide.
*Herman:* We complained about that . . . a couple of times.

Other rule violations included harms that many might consider less serious or benign. Notably, though, we would argue that the category illustrates the very wide variety of harms citizens must navigate when confronted with oil and gas activity on or near their property.

### Surface water issues

As previously noted, surface water complaints involve dumping, spills, or leaks into a water body, which most often included lakes, rivers, and irrigation ditches. Seth's and Dexter's experiences exemplify typical complaints about surface water.

*Seth:* We haul our drinkin' water.
*Have you always done that?*
*Seth:* No. When we first moved to this country, there was very few neighbors above me and the creek water was real good pristine water. Not no more. You can't trust it, because of all the oil and gas activity.
*You feel like the water quality has changed?*
*Seth:* Absolutely.
*Have you had your water tested?*
*Seth:* We had that water tested.
*The creek water?*
*Seth:* The creek water. There was some hydrocarbons, but mostly bacteria. And those guys could care less about where this water goes to or how it's used.

Seth's sentiments about the nearby creek water were not unusual, as several respondents noted concerns about the water quality in rivers and creeks. In contrast, Dexter reported concerns about the pollution of ditch water.

*Dexter:* They were dumpin' whatever water content was left, but still, if there's any backwash, any chemicals in there, they'd be there. So they should have pumped all that dry and did something else with it, took it to a contamination site or put it in a semi and hauled it away. So I don't know, even though they were hauling semi stuff, how much contaminants are in that water, and here you are dumping it in a ditch.

It should be noted that Colorado is an agricultural state often ranking in the top 10 states for production of field crops (National Agricultural Statistics Service [NASS], 2014) and in the top five states when ranked by the market value of agricultural products sold (U.S. Department of Agriculture [USDA], 2012); thus, farmers are particularly watchful of the ditch water they use to irrigate their crops.

### *Non-human animals*

A green criminological approach requires one to move beyond anthropocentric perspectives (Sollund, 2013, 2014) and consider harms to non-human animals. As such, we reviewed the complaint database and queried our respondents about harms to non-human animals, including pets, livestock, and wildlife. Wildlife complaints (0.9% or $n$ = 26) occurred less frequently than concerns about domestic animals (2.8% or $n$ = 83). With respect to domestic animals, citizens reported deaths, illnesses, birth defects, and endangerment. Endangerments most often constituted negligence of some kind on the part of the oil and gas operator – for example, leaving gates open so cattle roamed outside of fenced grazing areas onto highways (causing loss of cattle, injury to cattle, and loss of work time for ranchers retrieving cattle); animals being run over by oil and gas trucks; and deaths or ill health (hair falling out) of animals living near well pads. Consider Buck and Debbie's report:

*Buck:* So he [their family pet] wanders up there to that well up there, and whatever they were doin', here's this pit with all that black water and everything in there.
*Debbie:* And they're supposed to keep it fenced to keep our livestock out of it.
*Buck:* And them guys watched that dog –
*Debbie:* – fall into the pit.
*Buck:* Made no effort to –
*Debbie:* So here he comes back, into the house, and he's just gross. I mean, like, toxically gross, kind of oily, black, just as if he'd been a white dog, he'd have been black.

## Discussion

Environmental victimization related to energy extraction is an emerging area of interest among green criminologists. This chapter contributes to that developing work by examining the nature and extent of environmental harm and victimization associated with energy development. We documented a range of environmental harms by (1) drawing from content analysis of formal complaints filed by citizens to the Colorado Oil and Gas Conservation Commission (COGCC) and (2) supplementing the content analysis with intensive interviews with citizens seeking relief from problematic or abusive industry practices.

Our study revealed that there are clear patterns in the nature and extent of energy-related harms, with concerns about well water, dumping/spills/leaks, and air quality being the most common harms reported by citizens. Furthermore, we documented a wide range of concerns that were coded into 19 distinct categories, revealing that these types of environmental victimization are complex as well as contextual. For example, our study discovered that these energy-related harms are not isolated, one-time occurrences but rather tend to be persistent and patterned. In addition, many of the problems we uncovered represent 'quality of life' concerns (e.g. noise, increased traffic, poor road conditions, speeding industry trucks, discourteous industry employees, etc.), but such a label does not illustrate the full experience or consequences of the problem. Indeed, citizens experience quality of life concerns as quite harmful. Respondents often reported significant stress, anxiety, depression, and economic loss from repeated instances of surface damage to their property, followed by tense (and sometimes hostile, as seen in Wayne's experience) interactions with industry as they sought relief for such damages. While not all quality of life concerns might rise to the level of an actual crime per se, we are reminded of Hall's (2014) point that the earliest victims movements' highlighted victimization beyond that which was officially recognized as *criminally* perpetrated.

This is an important contribution of our study, as quality of life concerns should be conceptualized as a legitimate form of environmental victimization. We recognize that to some observers, quality of life concerns are scientifically unverifiable, and therefore time would be better spent investigating 'real' impacts on water, land, and air. We reject such a notion, as criminologists have been scientifically measuring quality of life concerns in high-crime communities for decades, and these concerns often precede and/or accompany criminal activity (Katz et al., 2001; Skogan, 1990, 2015; Wilson and Kelling, 1982). Our work provides compelling evidence that quality of life issues do accompany other traditional conceptions of green crimes (e.g. pollution). As argued by Lynch and colleagues (2013), green crimes are motivated by the treadmill of production and produce environmental or ecological disorganization as well as indirect victimization of species living in these areas. Our work lends support to this argument, though we also concede that it is feasible that quality of life–related harms can contribute to and/or aggravate such ecological disorganization as well. Future research should examine how green crimes and green quality of life issues co-occur and document the ways in which they may produce environmental disorganization.

This task will not be an easy undertaking, as collecting data on green crime is difficult, and energy-related harms are no different. There are a number of logistical limitations that contribute to the paucity of research in this area (and in Colorado particularly), including a lack of easily retrievable electronic data; a regulatory agency that legally complies with information requests but in a manner that is not in the spirit of full transparency; and inconsistent, incomplete, and contradictory data. As we illustrate elsewhere, officially recorded complaints have a variety of shortcomings (Opsal and Shelley, 2014), particularly in areas that represent quality of life concerns. For example, it was not uncommon to hear about excessive truck traffic and road dust in our interviews but, curiously, this was not a frequent occurrence in the COGCC complaint data (i.e. 1.6% of complaints or $n = 48$). This may be because higher-order concerns get reported (or recorded) above and beyond truck traffic and road dust. Nonetheless, the frequency and/or severity of these quality of life complaints should not be underestimated, despite a low occurrence in the official COGCC complaint data. For example, some estimates indicate that it can take as many as 1,160 to 1,600 trucks[8] to develop and complete a fracking job (Murawski, 2015; U.S. Bureau of Land Management [USBLM], 2006). The volume of trucks to support energy development is likely to produce increased $CO_2$ emissions in areas with oil and gas activity while also generating a significant amount of dust, noise, and traffic. Consider the following accounts:

*Cierra:* But I have called X company and said, you know, I don't want to die comin' home from the grocery store. Tell your people to stay on their own side of the road and slow down, and that sort of thing. Sometimes they do and sometimes they don't. That company is owned by one of the people who profited heavily from the oil and gas presence here. And he kind of runs his company like a – he's kind of an outlaw kind of a guy.

8 This figure is often operator- and site-specific, making it difficult to report an exact number. Murawski (2015) reports that the North Carolina Department of Transportation (DOT) estimated that between 1,290 and 1,650 trucks would be needed for each site, along with approximately $11 million in road maintenance and repairs to accommodate such a volume statewide.

*Georgia:* I don't know how many kinds of trucks are needed from the beginning to the end of just starting one gas well, but the impact of the pollution from all the trucks and the dust they produce and the emissions from the diesel drilling engines and natural gas compressor engines is significant.

Moreover, these formal COGCC complaint records help construct a picture of what is – and what is not – happening in Colorado and thus what citizens are and are not experiencing. When the official data fail to illuminate the full extent of the consequences of oil and gas activity in Colorado, they also function to dilute the real and cumulative costs of energy development.

While our findings are compelling and represent an important first step to understanding the nature and extent of energy-related harm and victimization, our research also revealed that there is still much left to uncover in what is likely a dark figure of energy crime and harm. This dark figure is due to several co-existing factors. First, we learned that many citizens are unaware that they can contact the COGCC to help them with their problems. Second, for those citizens who are aware of the COGCC, some report receiving a lackluster – or what is perceived as a biased – bureaucratic response, so they simply stop reporting harm entirely (see Opsal and Shelley, 2014, for extended documentation of this). Third, Colorado is a western state composed of residents with a distrust of government, coupled with a rugged western identity of 'fix it yourself', so citizens often contact industry directly to resolve concerns about energy-related harms. Fourth, on occasion, some citizens receive relief from the harms they have experienced and are unable to report or discuss these events due to non-disclosure agreements with corporations. Fifth, the array of harms experienced by non-human animals can never be fully examined via human complaint data, as humans are not in a position to continuously monitor or be aware of such harm. Finally, many citizens report feeling powerless in the wake of multi-national corporate interests and are reticent or outright fearful about filing a complaint. When these factors are taken together, it is likely that our results only skim the surface of the actual nature and extent of energy-related harm and victimization.

## References

Adgate, J., Goldstein, B. and McKenzie, L. (2014) 'Potential public health hazards, exposures and health effects from unconventional natural gas development', *Environmental Science & Technology*, **48**(15): 8307–8320.

Archbold, C., Dahle, T. and Jordan, R. (2014) 'Policing the patch: Police response to rapid population growth in oil boomtowns in western North Dakota', *Police Quarterly*, **17**(4): 386–413.

Atlas, M. (2001) 'Rush to judgment: An empirical analysis of environmental equity in U.S. Environmental Protection Agency enforcement actions', *Law & Society Review*, **35**(3): 633–682.

Beirne, P. (2009) *Confronting Animal Abuse: Law, Criminology, and Human-Animal Relationships*, Lanham, MD: Rowman & Littlefield.

Bisschop, L. (2014) 'How e-waste challenges environmental governance', I*nternational Journal for Crime, Justice, and Social Democracy*, **3**(2): 82–96.

Brasier, K., Filteau, M., McLaughlin, D., Jacquet, J., Stedman, R., Kelsey, T. and Goetz, S. (2011) 'Residents' perceptions of community and environmental impacts from development of natural gas in the Marcellus Shale: A comparison of Pennsylvania and New York cases', *Journal of Rural Social Sciences*, **26**(1): 32–61.

Carrington, K., Hogg, R. and McIntosh, A. (2011) 'The resource boom's underbelly: Criminological impacts of mining development', *Australian & New Zealand Journal of Criminology*, **44**(3): 335–354.

Colborn, T., Schultz, K., Herrick, L. and Kwiatkowski, C. (2014) 'An exploratory study of air quality near natural gas operations', *Human and Ecological Risk Assessment: An International Journal*, **20**(1): 86–105.

Colorado Department of Public Health and Environment (CDPHE) (2014) *Air quality control commission regulations.* Retrieved from https://www.colorado.gov/pacific/cdphe/aqcc-regs.

Colorado Oil and Gas Association (COGA) (2015) *The basics.* Retrieved from http://www.coga.org/pdf_Basics/Basics_DrillTime.pdf.

Colorado Oil and Gas Conservation Commission (COGCC) (n.d.) *Rules of practice and procedure.* Retrieved from https://cogcc.state.co.us/RR_Asps/500Series.pdf.

Colorado Oil and Gas Conservation Commission (COGCC) (2014) *Spill analysis by year 1999 – 4th quarter 2014.* Retrieved from http://cogcc.state.co.us/documents/data/downloads/environmental/SpillAnalysisByYear.pdf.

Crow, M., Shelley, T. and Stretesky, P. (2013) 'Camouflage-collar crime: An examination of wildlife crime and characteristics of offenders in Florida', *Deviant Behavior*, **34**(8): 635–652.

Davis, C. (2012) 'The politics of "fracking": Regulating natural gas drilling practices in Colorado and Texas', *Review of Policy Research*, **29**(2): 177–191.

Emerson, R., Fritz, R. and Shaw, L. (1995) *Writing Ethnographic Fieldnotes*, Chicago: University of Chicago Press.

Environmental Protection Agency (EPA) (2015) *Assessment of the potential impacts of hydraulic fracturing for oil and gas on drinking water resources: Executive summary.* Washington, DC: Office of Research and Development, Environmental Protection Agency. Retrieved from: http://www2.epa.gov/sites/production/files/2015-06/documents/hf_es_erd_jun2015.pdf.

Erikson, K. (1976) *Everything in Its Path: Destruction of Community in the Buffalo Creek Flood*, New York: Simon & Schuster.

Fakhru'l-Razi, A., Pendashteh, A., Abdullah, L., Biak, D., Madaeni, S. and Abidin, Z. (2009) 'Review of technologies for oil and gas produced water treatment', *Journal of Hazardous Materials*, **170**(2): 530–551.

Finkel, M. and Law, A. (2011) 'The rush to drill for natural gas: A public health cautionary tale', *Public Health*, **101**(5): 784–785.

Finley, B. and Murphy, J. (2015) 'Colorado land impact of oil and gas boom: Scars spread and stay', *The Denver Post.* Retrieved from http://www.denverpost.com/News/Local/ci_27618385/Colorado-land-impact-of-oil-and-gas-boom:-scars-spread-and-stay?source=infinite.

Freudenburg, W. (1981) 'Women and men in an energy boomtown: Adjustment, alienation, and adaptation', *Rural Sociology*, **46**: 220–244.

Gilman, J., Lerner, B., Kuster, W. and De Gouw, J. (2013) 'Source signature of volatile organic compounds from oil and natural gas operations in northeastern Colorado', *Environmental Science & Technology*, **47**(3): 1297–1305.

Hall, M. (2014) 'Environmental harm and environmental victims: Scoping out a "green victimology"', *International Review of Victimology*, **20**(1): 129–143.

Jarell, M. and Ozymy, J. (2010) 'Excessive air pollution and the oil industry: Fighting for our right to breathe clean air', *Environmental Justice*, **3**: 111–115.

Jarell, M. and Ozymy, J. (2012) 'Real crime, real victims: Environmental crime victims and the Crime Victims' Rights Act (CVRA)', *Crime, Law and Social Change*, **58**: 373–389.

Katz, C., Webb, V. and Schaefer, D. (2001) 'An assessment of the impact of quality-of-life policing on crime and disorder', *Justice Quarterly*, **18**(4): 825–876.

Ladd, A. (2013) 'Stakeholder perceptions of socioenvironmental impacts from unconventional natural gas development and hydraulic fracturing in the Haynesville Shale', *Journal of Rural Social Sciences*, **28**(2): 56–89.

Lawrie, M., Tonts, M. and Plummer, P. (2011) 'Boomtowns, resource dependence and socio-economic well-being', *Australian Geographer*, **42**(2): 139–164.

Llewellyn, G., Dorman, F., Westland, J., Yoxtheimer, D., Grieve, P., Sowers, T. and Brantley, S. (2015) 'Evaluating a groundwater supply contamination incident attributed to Marcellus Shale gas development', *Proceedings of the National Academy of Sciences*, **112**(20): 6325–6330.

Long, M., Stretesky, P., Lynch, M. and Fenwick, E. (2012) 'Crime in the coal industry: Implications for green criminology and treadmill of production', *Organization & Environment*, **25**(3): 328–346.
Lynch, M., Long, M., Barrett, K. and Stretesky, P. (2013) 'Is it a crime to produce ecological disorganization?' *British Journal of Criminology*, **53**: 997–1016.
Lynch, M. and Stretesky, P. (2001) 'Toxic crimes: Examining corporate victimization of the general public employing medical and epidemiological evidence', *Critical Criminology*, **10**(3): 153–172.
Malin, S. (2014) 'There's no real choice but to sign: Neoliberalization and normalization of hydraulic fracturing on Pennsylvania farmland', *Journal of Environmental Studies and Sciences*, **4**(1): 17–27.
McKenzie, L., Guo, R., Witter, R., Savitz, D., Newman, L. and Adgate, J. (2014) 'Birth outcomes and maternal residential proximity to natural gas development in rural Colorado', *Environmental Health Perspectives*, **122**(4): 412–417.
Mennis, J. (2005) 'The distribution and enforcement of air polluting facilities in New Jersey', *The Professional Geographer*, **57**: 411–421.
Murawski, J. (2015) 'DOT: More than 1,600 trucks could be required for one NC fracking site'. *The News and Observer*. Retrieved from http://www.newsobserver.com/news/business/article10216172.html.
National Agricultural Statistics Service (NASS) (2014) *Colorado Agricultural Statistics 2014*. Lakewood, CO: United States Department of Agriculture, NASS Mountain Regional Office. Retrieved from http://www.nass.usda.gov/Statistics_by_State/Colorado/Publications/Annual_Statistical_Bulletin/Bulletin2014.pdf.
Opsal, T. and Shelley, T. (2014) 'Energy crime, harm, and problematic state response in Colorado: A case of the fox guarding the henhouse?' *Critical Criminology*, **22**: 561–577.
Osborn, S., Vengosh, A., Warner, N. and Jackson, R. (2011) 'Methane contamination of drinking water accompanying gas-well drilling and hydraulic fracturing', *Proceedings of the National Academy of Sciences*, **108**(20): 8172–8176.
Ozymy, J. and Jarrell, M. (2011) 'Upset over air pollution: Analyzing upset event emissions at petroleum refineries', *Review of Policy Research*, **28**(4): 365–382.
Ozymy, J. and Jarrell, M. (2012) 'Upset events, regulatory drift, and the regulation of air emissions at industrial facilities in the United States', *Environmental Politics*, **21**(3): 451–466.
Perry, S. (2012) 'Development, land use, and collective trauma: The Marcellus Shale gas boom in rural Pennsylvania', *Culture, Agriculture, Food and Environment*, **34**: 81–92.
Quinney, R. (1972) 'Who is the victim?' *Criminology*, **10**(3): 314–323.
Reiman, J. and Leighton, P. (2010) *Rich Get Richer and Poor Get Prison: Ideology, Class and Criminal Justice*, 9th edition, Boston: Allyn & Bacon.
Ruddell, R. (2011) 'Boomtown policing: Responding to the dark side of resource development', *Policing: A Journal of Policy and Practice*, **5**(4): 328–342.
Ruggiero, V. and South, N. (2013) 'Toxic state–corporate crimes, neo-liberalism and green criminology: The hazards and legacies of the oil, chemical and mineral industries', *International Journal for Crime, Justice and Social Democracy*, **2**(2): 12–26.
Skogan, W. (1990) *Disorder and Decline: Crime and the Spiral of Decay in American Neighborhoods*, Los Angeles: University of California Press.
Skogan, W. (2015) 'Disorder and decline: The state of research', *Journal of Research in Crime and Delinquency*, **52**(4): 464–485.
Sollund, R. (2013) 'Animal trafficking and trade: Animal abuse and species justice'. In D. Westerhuis, R. Walters and T. Wyatt (eds.) *Emerging Issues in Green Criminology: Exploring Power, Justice and Harm*, Hampshire: Palgrave Macmillan, pp. 72–92.
Sollund, R. (2014) 'Wildlife trafficking, speciesism and crimes against animal life'. In G. Bruinsma and D. Weisburd (eds.) *Encyclopedia of Criminology and Criminal Justice*, New York: Springer-Verlag, p. 295.

South, N., Brisman, A. and Beirne, P. (2013) 'A guide to a green criminology'. In N. South and A. Brisman (eds.) *The Routledge International Handbook of Green Criminology*, London: Routledge, pp. 27–42.

Stretesky, P., Long, M. and Lynch, M. (2013) 'Does environmental enforcement slow the treadmill of production? The relationship between large monetary penalties, ecological disorganization and toxic releases within offending corporations', *Journal of Crime and Justice*, **36**(2): 233–247.

U.S. Bureau of Land Management (BLM), Glenwood Springs Field Office (2006) Final Roan Plateau Planning Area (Including Naval Oil Shale Reserves Numbers 1 & 3) Resource Management Plan Amendment and Environmental Impact Statement, August 2006.

U.S. Department of Agriculture (USDA) (2012) *USDA Census of Agriculture*. Retrieved from http://www.agcensus.usda.gov/Publications/2012/Online_Resources/Rankings_of_Market_Value/Colorado/.

U.S. Energy Information Administration (USEIA) (2015) *U.S. remained world's largest producer of petroleum and natural gas hydrocarbons in 2014*. Retrieved from http://www.eia.gov/todayinenergy/detail.cfm?id=20692.

U.S. Energy Information Administration (USEIA) (n.d.) *Energy production estimates in trillion Btu, Colorado, 1960–2013*. Retrieved from http://www.eia.gov/state/seds/sep_prod/pdf/PT2_CO.pdf.

Weiner, C. (2014) *Oil and gas development in Colorado: Fact Sheet 10.639*. Fort Collins, CO: Colorado State University, CSU Extension.

Weisel, D. (2005) *Analyzing repeat victimization: Tool Guide No .4*, Center for Problem Oriented Policing. Retrieved from http://www.popcenter.org/tools/repeat_victimization/.

Western Resource Advocates (2012) *Fracking our Future: Measuring Water and Community Impacts from Hydraulic Fracturing*, Boulder, CO: Western Resource Advocates. Retrieved from http://www.westernresourceadvocates.org/frackwater/WRA_FrackingOurFuture_2012.pdf.

White, R. (2003) 'Environmental issues and the criminological imagination', *Theoretical Criminology*, 7(4): 483–506.

White, R. (ed.) (2012) *Climate Change from a Criminological Perspective*, New York: Springer-Verlag.

White, R. (2013a) *Crimes against Nature: Environmental Criminology and Ecological Justice*, New York: Routledge.

White, R. (2013b) Resource extraction leaves something behind: Environmental justice and mining, *International Journal for Crime and Justice*, **2**(1): 50–64.

Williams, C. (1996) 'An environmental victimology', *Social Science*, **23**(1): 16–40. Reprinted in R. White (ed., 2009) *Environmental Crime: A Reader*, Cullompton, England: Willan, 200–222.

Wilson, J. and Kelling, G. (1982) 'Broken windows'. *The Atlantic*. Retrieved from http://www.lantm.lth.se/fileadmin/fastighetsvetenskap/utbildning/Fastighetsvaerderingssystem/BrokenWindowTheory.pdf.

Wyatt, T. (2010) 'The illegal trade of raptors in the Russian Federation', *Contemporary Justice Review*, **14**(2): 103–123.

# 7 Pirates or protectors?

## A critical perspective on extreme environmental activism

*Angus Nurse*

Green criminological discourse identifies the importance of non-governmental organisations (NGOs) to achieving effective environmental protection via law enforcement (Nurse, 2013b, 2015; White, 2012). Environmental enforcement often falls outside the remit of mainstream policing policy and practice. Instead, it is often the responsibility of state environmental departments and specialist environmental regulators rather than mainstream policing agencies (Situ and Emmons, 2000; Stallworthy, 2008). This reflects an ideological and policy view of mainstream crime control as being primarily about addressing interpersonal violence, street crimes and property crimes as the dominant societal threats (Lea and Young, 1993). Accordingly, environmental harm and its associated criminality is arguably the subject of a less stringent enforcement and policy regime that sees environmental wrongdoing as an environmental protection and sustainable use problem rather than as a criminal justice one (Heyes, 2000; Nurse, 2012b, 2015; Ruhl, 1997).

This chapter examines the legitimacy of 'extreme' environmental activism and the use of allegedly illegal means to pursue a legitimate environmental protection goal. NGOs play a vital role in regards to campaigning for better environmental legislation; developing policy; monitoring the implementation of existing legislation; and, in some cases, carrying out practical law enforcement activities to plug the gaps in enforcement inadequacy (Nurse, 2013b; White, 2012; Williams, 2013). At the most basic level, NGOs will frequently challenge government ideology through campaign publications or seek to influence policy through parliamentary lobbying and campaigning aimed at influencing decision makers (Jacobson and Saxonberg, 2013; Nurse, 2013b). However, some NGOs and civil society groups employ direct action as a means of enforcing wildlife and environmental laws. Activism is primarily aimed at activities perceived as being illegal (or morally wrong) through means such as interfering with the progress of fisheries operations; disrupting the planting of crops or the use of animals for scientific experimentation; or, in extreme cases, the use of violent means of protest (Eagan, 1996; Foreman, 1991). Such actions may be ideologically driven, reflecting an eco-centric stance that considers the primacy of animals or the environment over human interests and that views animals' and environmental needs as requiring extreme action (Cianchi, 2015). Such actions may also be influenced by a belief that mainstream enforcement action is inadequate and that NGO or citizen action is required to address a perceived enforcement deficit. NGOs may also take action where legislative structures arguably imply that they may do so and provide legitimacy for NGO direct action (Nurse, 2015; Roeschke, 2009).

This chapter argues that the use of illegal methods as an integral strategy – not just in pursuit of environmental or wildlife protection but also as a business, campaigning or organisational strategy – risks being problematic for activist organisations which employ them for a number of reasons. Through a green criminological examination of a recent US case involving the Sea Shepherd Conservation Society and the ongoing debate about the legitimacy of Japanese whaling, this chapter examines how branding activists as eco-terrorists arguably undermines their legitimacy and marginalises social acceptance of their cause. It also examines the justifications for extreme actions such as the alleged use of violence and the extent to which such actions may not achieve NGO or activist objectives. When activists appear to consider themselves above the law or believe that they should not be subject to certain aspects of the law, one man's freedom fighter becomes society's eco-terrorist.

## Environmental activism and green movements

Critical discussion of environmental activism and a homogenous 'green movement' is slightly misleading and risks suggesting that activism serves a common unified purpose. Far from there being one integrated green movement pursuing a common goal of environmental protection, environmental NGOs come from different ideological and socio-economic perspectives and operate in different ways. Some NGOs employ mainstream fundraising and public awareness campaigning as their main tool; others are heavily involved in political lobbying. Others may employ an activist or even practical law enforcement approach in order to achieve their goals (Nurse, 2013b). Activism can thus be distinguished as being 'hard' or 'soft' activism, characterised in part by the perceived legitimacy of the activist organisation and its approach – in particular, the extent to which 'soft' lawful and socially acceptable methods of campaigning are used (e.g. letter writing, media appeals, policy briefings) or whether the activist group is perceived as using 'hard' illegitimate and arguably unlawful means (e.g. vandalism, property destruction, violence). In the latter case, a question might be asked as to whether the activists' tactics risk having a negative impact on public sympathies and also risk attracting a punitive law enforcement approach.

From a green criminological perspective, extreme direct action might be justified on species justice and ecological justice grounds where traditional domestic enforcement activity has failed or where transnational animal harm is taking place and international enforcement efforts are non-existent but international NGOs or NGO consortia are able to intervene (Nurse, 2015; Smith and Klass, 2015). Ellefsen (2012) identifies how laws aimed at 'traditional' organised crime are being used to criminalise the actions of certain animal activists. A wider green criminological discourse now exists concerning the extent to which animal and environmental activists are perceived as being a threat to private and commercial interests and should be the target of law enforcement activity (Joosse, 2012; Moore and Ireland, 2005; Smith, 2008). In the United States and elsewhere, the label 'eco-terrorist' has been used to demonise those who take extreme action on behalf of the environment and, in doing so, challenge the primacy of neo-liberal markets (Hirsch-Hoefler and Mudde, 2014). However, the case study at the heart of this chapter identifies how NGO activity can itself have negative impacts and risks undermining legitimate environmental concerns, particularly in regards to activities that are ostensibly legal (such as allegedly 'scientific whaling' or the development of GMO crops) but whose legality is, in reality, questionable or contested by activists. Arguably, legal challenges to environmental activism and the attention of law enforcement bodies that treat activists as being deviant are now a feature of the battle between environmentalism and state and commercial interests. Subjecting activists to law-and-order attention that delegitimises environmental activism and brands activists as criminals provides a means through which environmental concerns can be marginalised in policy discourse.

Statutory enforcement failures and the perceived inadequacy of policy leave a vacuum that has increasingly been filled by NGOs adopting policy development and practical enforcement roles (Nurse, 2013b). NGOs may also take direct action to prevent a green crime or to punish an 'offender' seen as causing environmental harm, which can include taking enforcement action when the statutory regulator is perceived as having failed in his or her duty or where the existing regulatory scheme is perceived as being inadequate (Nurse, 2013b; Roeshke, 2009). This is particularly the case when regulatory schemes are predicated on allowing harmful corporate activities to continue, such as pollution (albeit within regulated limits) or growing GMO crops. Law enforcement and regulatory regimes may be perceived as being ineffectual where, rather than preventing such activities, regulatory justice simply regulates the activities in accordance with neo-liberal market principles (Stallworthy, 2008). Sanctions are also seen to be ineffectual if the underlying purpose of a regime is to allow activities to continue because the sanctioning regime ultimately allows offenders to continue with the offending behaviour despite multiple infractions. NGOs may thus work within regulatory and enforcement regimes, acting as policy advisors; researchers; field investigators; expert witnesses at court; scientific advisors; casework managers; and, in the case of a small number of organisations, independent investigators and prosecutors. But NGOs may also work outside of regulatory and enforcement regimes, acting as independent policy monitors to scrutinise policy and enforcement activity (Gemmill and Bamidele-Izu, 2002; Slapper and Kelly, 2011: 15). In their campaigning capacity, NGOs also contribute greatly to public debates on environmental harm (including pollution and climate 'crimes', food crimes and wildlife crimes). Particularly in the area of environmental crime and environmental law enforcement, NGOs have a role to play in identifying contemporary environmental threats and the potential flaws in policy and enforcement practice that allow these to continue. NGOs generate considerable publicity for environmental problems and their associated criminality and are active in identifying enforcement deficits and coordinating (and undertaking or funding) much of the research into contemporary environmental problems and some possible solutions to these. Some NGOs take a hands-on approach to prosecution and challenging government enforcement inadequacies, while others view themselves as primarily having an advisory or scientific role (Nurse, 2013b). Thus, NGOs such as Earthjustice and the Sierra Club, which operate in a broad environmental field, may differ from those such as Defenders of Wildlife or National Audubon, which occupy a species-specific wildlife-based remit, or others such as World Wildlife Fund (WWF) and Friends of the Earth, which operate globally and as part of international networks rather than solely within a national framework.

However, the role of NGOs in environmental enforcement attracts scrutiny, and the effectiveness of NGOs can sometimes be called into question. For example, in the UK, the Royal Society for the Prevention of Cruelty to Animals (RSPCA) has been criticised for allegedly wasting money on unnecessary prosecutions and faced claims that it misuses the law to achieve its own ends, operating from an ideological rather than purely criminal justice perspective (Hope, 2013). Scrutiny of the organisation's investigative and prosecutions function also raised concerns about some aspects of the NGO's operating practices and the robustness of these when compared to those of the public prosecutor, the Crown Prosecution Service (CPS) (Wooler, 2014). The UK government's 'Big Society' agenda, which envisaged greater use of NGOs in environmental law enforcement (Cabinet Office, 2011), risked over-reliance on NGOs; this is potentially problematic without considering why NGOs take on certain work, especially where their aims and objectives may not be compatible with those of government or public policy and may be ideology based (discussed later in this chapter).

Elsewhere, some NGOs and activist groups have also begun to use more extreme direct action mechanisms in order to achieve their goals, reflecting the conception that 'one man's freedom fighter is another man's terrorist' (Ganor, 2002: 295) and that the understanding of activism and extremism is very much in the eye of the beholder. NGOs may enjoy public support from an environmentalist or animal-sympathetic supporter base. But actions that interfere with commercial or dominant social interests may put them into conflict with law enforcement agencies and underlying public policy priorities (Lovitz, 2010; Potter, 2011). This chapter explores the concept of extreme activism and what happens when NGO activity and environmental activism move beyond enforcing the law and advocating certain policies into areas which are alleged to constitute illegal activity. Some activists may consider it appropriate to use unlawful or 'violent' means in order to pursue the greater good of environmental or animal protection, but this raises the question of whether species justice or ecological justice concerns (Beirne, 2007, 2009; Benton, 1998) outweigh the limitations of the existing civil and criminal law, providing a legitimate basis for pursuing extreme direct action.

## Environmental citizenship and environmental activism

The role of environmental NGOs is linked to notions of environmental citizenship and Beck's (1992) risk society theory. Beck argues that events such as the Chernobyl nuclear meltdown require us to reconsider our conceptual framework, the role of scientific knowledge and our policy responses. Thus, our social and political institutions and mechanisms need to transform, particularly concerning how they deal with contemporary environmental risks. In this respect, there is arguably a need for a new form of environmental citizenship that focuses not just on developing environmental policy to deal with obvious risks such as climate change, food shortages and the harmful impact of over-reliance on fossil fuels. In contemporary society, there is a need for ecological citizenship which looks at the potential unity between legal, political and moral systems, and it is here that a range of NGOs operate, from the small community grassroots group to the major 'conservation corporation' that combines professional activism and policy development with local action (Nurse, 2016).

Contemporary NGOs sometimes combine policy development and advocacy with practical enforcement roles in addition to sometimes taking direct action to prevent a green crime or to address regulatory shortfalls. Previous research (Nurse, 2013b) examined the policies and practices of different NGOs involved in wildlife crime, finding that wildlife NGOs could be broadly categorised into the following different types:

- Campaigning NGOs
- Law enforcement NGOs
- Political lobbying NGOs

Although in principle NGOs can operate in more than one of these areas, NGOs generally prioritise one of these areas (e.g. direct law enforcement) in regards to their response to animal harm and environmental offending (Nurse, 2013a, 2013b). The approach taken (campaigning, enforcement or lobbying) dictates how their environmental protection goals are pursued, even though a secondary objective (e.g. political lobbying to improve wildlife protection legislation) may be followed alongside this. Analysis of the available literature on NGO policies and their ideological perspectives reveals that environmental NGOs develop their policies from the primary ideological positions of the following:

- Moral culpability: censuring activities that they believe are morally wrong.
- Political priorities: censuring activities that they believe should be given a higher profile in public policy (which may include issues that they consider worthy of a higher law enforcement priority or those which should be the subject of law enforcement activity and/or legislative change).
- Environmentalism/animal rights: a belief in ensuring and protecting environmental rights or rights for animals, which includes policies that demonstrate either the case for animal/environmental rights or that demonstrate breaches of these existing rights (Nurse, 2013b).

There is inevitably some overlap in these policy objectives, and the extent to which they apply to particular campaigns or policy initiatives varies. But analysis of the background illustrates how NGOs develop their policing policies and priorities and whether active law enforcement or assistance to statutory agencies is pursued in order to put policy objectives into effect.

Previous research (Nurse, 2013b) has identified that at one end of the spectrum, there are large NGOs existing as 'conservation corporations' with legitimacy within social structures such that they are seen as part of the establishment and are significant players in policy development and debates. Such organisations gain legitimacy through Royal Charters in the UK (e.g. the Royal Society for the Protection of Birds [RSPB], the Royal Society for the Prevention of Cruelty to Animals [RSPCA]) or by achieving recognized charity or non-profit status. This risks their being viewed by other, more activist NGOs as 'illegitimate' by virtue of their standing within the establishment and their adherence to societal norms and acceptance of 'soft' activism as the appropriate tools to combat environmental threats. More activist NGOs are frustrated by the perceived lack of effectiveness of mainstream NGOs and a failure to use direct action or protest tactics, as their drive for mainstream legitimacy distances them from 'hard' grassroots activism (Carmin and Bast, 2009; Carter, 2007; Plows, 2008; Rawcliffe, 1998). Jasper (1997), in discussing 'post-material' social movements, explained that mainstream environmental organisations are composed mainly of people who have already integrated into their society's political, economic and educational systems and who, by virtue of their affluence, did not need to campaign for basic rights for themselves but could pursue protections and benefits for others. Thus, one danger of mainstream environmental organisations is that they become representative of (mainly white) middle-class concerns and interests and risk only partially representing those who are marginalised by uneven access to environmental justice (Gibson-Wood and Wakefield, 2012; Sandler and Pezaullo, 2007; Schlosberg, 2007: 3). The major environmental NGOs illustrate this perspective, having grown from their activist roots to embrace animal protection and conservation corporations with considerable economic and political power, representing a mainstream socio-economic supporter base that may be at odds with the ideals of their activist brethren.

At the other end of the spectrum, some NGOs and civil society groups employ direct action as a means of enforcing environmental laws (Nurse, 2013b), directly challenging actions that are either illegal or which they perceive as such through means such as interfering with the progress of fisheries operations, the planting of crops or the use of animals for scientific experimentation. Civil disobedience can be a useful tool in forcing governments to reconsider a policy or re-evaluate public support for a policy. Persen and Johansen (1998) argue that an action can be called 'civil disobedience' when it meets the following five requirements:

- Openness;
- Non-violence;
- Breaking a law or norm;
- Serious personal conviction; and
- Societal and/or ethical objectives.

However, in extreme cases, violence (or the threat of violence) is used to promote the animal rights or environmental cause. The question then becomes: are these NGOs legitimate activists, or do they become eco-terrorists?

A further consideration is the extent to which those engaged in extreme direct action represent those from the middle strata of activist groupings who disproportionately have the means to engage in extreme action and defend themselves against legal action by the state when they do so. Commensurate with Jasper's (1997) theory, Lowe and Ginsberg (2002) concluded that the (US) animal rights movement's membership is disproportionately well educated, reflecting what Parkin called 'middle class radicalism' (1968). In effect, the ability to undertake environmental activism and the means through which to do so are inextricably linked to socio-economic concerns and reflect the existence of societal privilege. Ethnic minority groups are frequently disadvantaged when it comes to enjoying their environmental rights and knowing what these are or should be (Schlosberg, 2007). Indeed, environmental justice and environmental racism discourse demonstrate that ethnic minority groups disproportionately feel the effects of environmentally damaging development such as the siting of waste recycling plants and polluting factories in poor urban areas with a high concentration of residents who are black, are in an ethnic minority or have lower socio-economic status. Stephens et al. (2001) identify that ethnic minority groups, while suffering disproportionately from poor environmental conditions, often lack access to processes which could affect these conditions – in part by being excluded by the language and perceptions of environmental groups (2001: 20) but also by being denied access to legal recourse mechanisms. Nocella (2012: 142) also argues that the animal rights movement remains dominated by people who identify as 'white', with the consequence that people of colour remain marginalised within this form of activism. Arguably, extreme direct action is often the purview of middle-class radicals with the means and education to conduct such activities. This is particularly the case when considerable resources are required to conduct extreme activism, as is the case with the case study discussed later in this chapter.

White (2012) applies contemporary regulation theory to environmental crime, recognising the poor level of resources, meagre budgets and low staffing levels that exist in environmental law enforcement given the size and scale of environmental problems. Such statutory enforcement failures add to the marginalisation of environmental crime and leave a vacuum that has increasingly been filled by NGOs adopting policy development and practical enforcement roles (Nurse, 2013b; White, 2012), with a number of NGOs actively investigating and prosecuting environmental and wildlife crimes. While environmental NGO approaches often emphasise the importance of criminal law and frequently include calls for tougher sentences and more punitive measures for wildlife crime (Nurse, 2012a, 2012b), they also employ a regulatory approach to compliance that is heavily dependent on monitoring, sanctioning and reactive enforcement through existing mechanisms. However, more activist NGOs adopt a more preventative and arguably aggressive enforcement approach. This is sometimes constructed as being deviant or illegitimate or even representing a societal threat and can itself attract sanction by mainstream justice agencies and policymakers. The following section and subsequent case study explore this in more detail.

## Criminalising NGOs and animal rights activists

Cianchi (2015) argues that radical environmental groups are generally grassroots organizations that are committed to participatory forms of decision making and are strongly anti-institutional (Carter, 2007: 155–156; Doyle, 2000: 45). Yet the radical nature of such groups sometimes makes them a target of an extreme state response and subject to labelling as terrorists.

Terrorism is generally defined according to notions that view its goals and ideals as rooted in the use of violence or the threat of violence and the pursuit of specific ideological goals. However, Terry (2009) states that there is no single agreed-upon definition of terrorism or of what constitutes a terrorist, noting also that terrorism can be domestic or international, based upon single issues or broad ideologies, with or without a religious foundation. Thus, US law defines terrorism as an act 'calculated to influence or affect the government by intimidation or coercion, or to retaliate against government conduct' (US Code Title 18, §2331), whereas Section 1 of the UK's 2000 Terrorism Act defines terrorism as 'the use or threat [of action] designed to influence the government or an international governmental organisation or to intimidate the public or a section of the public'. UK law also requires that 'the use or threat [be] made for the purpose of advancing a political, religious, racial or ideological cause'. Thus, an extreme animal rights position that uses or threatens the use of violence to pursue policy change can arguably be classified as terrorism according to both US and UK terrorism laws.

Ellefsen (2012) offers an analysis of the perceived threat that green movements pose to the state, observing how several green movements have recently been criminalised and subject to state sanctions. He identifies a rise in threat assessments over the last 15 years, evident in reports from American and European state institutions and private security firms. Ellefsen identifies how an anti-Mafia law intended to be used in regards to human trafficking was applied in the case of a prominent Austrian animal rights movement which had been successful in banning fur farming and pushing through progressive animal welfare legislation. Use of the law in this way arguably represents an attempt by the state to criminalise a civil society organisation seen as challenging dominant social ideas or the established political order. White (2007) states that 'political economy' is at the heart of the exploitation of animals and environments and that property values assigned to animals and the environment are important in a capitalist system. Thus, animal rights and environmental organisations that threaten such property 'rights' risk being affected by crime control policies, especially when they use direct action techniques that go against social norms and break or subvert existing law. Ellefsen concludes that criminalisation of animal rights movements reflects the fact that 'important societal interests are being challenged by such movements' (2012: 202) but also that animal advocates 'threaten the role and place of humans on our planet' (2012: 203). Thus, state power is being used to criminalise animal activists as a means of political oppression and to prevent animal activists from challenging the dominant ideas about animal exploitation. However, where animal or environmental activists are themselves using allegedly illegal means to address wider wrongdoing and non-compliance with environmental or animal protection laws, the merits of using the criminal law to address their activities might be justified. Species justice and mainstream criminal justice may well be in conflict where eco-centric and bio-centric views held by activists challenge normative law enforcement perspectives. The following case study illustrates this.

## Case study: Sea Shepherd Conservation Society versus the Institute for Cetacean Research (ICR)

In principle, the 1982 World Charter for Nature adopted by the United Nations (UN) provides a mechanism for protecting animals from harm by providing a conservation framework that would prevent animal harm through species protection measures (Nurse, 2013a). In practice, implementation of the Charter relies on national animal protection legislation, although Sections 21–24 provide authority for individuals to enforce international conservation laws that could provide animal protection. This provision has been used by NGOs as a basis on which to conduct direct action to prevent animal harm (Roeschke, 2009).

The Sea Shepherd Conservation Society (SSCS) is an international non-profit marine wildlife conservation organisation. Its mission states that the organisation seeks an end to the destruction of habitat and slaughter of wildlife in the world's oceans. Sea Shepherd uses innovative direction action tactics to investigate, document and take action to expose and confront illegal activities on the high seas. This includes aggressive and allegedly violent action (Hoek, 2010) to combat perceived illegal action by the Japanese whaling fleet. In 1986, the International Whaling Commission (IWC) passed a temporary moratorium banning commercial whaling. However, Japan continues to whale on a commercial level thanks to a loophole in the IWC Convention that allows whales to be hunted in the name of scientific research. Sea Shepherd contends that Japanese whaling is illegal and that the World Charter for Nature gives it authority to act on behalf of and enforce international nature conservation laws. In the absence of effective international legal enforcement action, Sea Shepherd uses direct action to enforce the law and prevent Japanese whaling. However, it is arguable whether the direct action employed by Sea Shepherd is lawful; Roeschke (2009) states that Sea Shepherd techniques include 'chasing, harassing, scuttling and in some cases ramming illegal whaling and fishing vessels on the high seas' (99).

Hoek (2010) argues that it is likely that both the Japanese whaling fleet and Sea Shepherd have broken the law during the long running conflict over Japanese whaling. As of 2008, Sea Shepherd's Captain Watson has claimed responsibility for sinking ten illegal whaling ships. Hoek (2010) states that the battles between Sea Shepherd and the Japanese whalers are certainly 'life threatening' but that little has been done to regulate the actions of either party (161). The issue of legality is a complex one; Japan's whaling activities are theoretically legal where they are 'covered' by the legislative and policy loophole that allows whaling for research. However, Sea Shepherd and other conservation organisations contend that Japan is misusing the loophole to engage in commercial whaling and a whale meat trade that subverts the whaling ban and represents an 'abuse of right'. Sea Shepherd, on the other hand, 'is arguably violating the law by engaging in eco-terrorism on the high seas' (Hoek, 2010: 162) in those cases where its direct action techniques create risk or cause damage to other marine vessels or their crews.

Both sides have used legal action. Sea Shepherd's Captain Paul Watson was reportedly arrested in Germany in 2012 on a warrant issued by Costa Rica for an alleged violation of shipping traffic (i.e. endangerment of a ship and its crew) in Costa Rica (Interpol, 2012). The incident related to a confrontation with an illegal shark-finning operation in 2002.

Watson was released on bail but allegedly failed to report to Frankfurt police on a daily basis as he was required to do. Interpol (2012) issued a red notice requiring countries to identify or locate Watson with a view to his provisional arrest and extradition in accordance with the country's national laws. Japanese whalers have also been successful in obtaining injunctions against Sea Shepherd, making it illegal for SSCS ships to approach Japanese whaling ships in some areas.

Sea Shepherd has also used legal action to pursue its case alongside its allegedly illegal action. For example, in 2010, Sea Shepherd lodged writs to sue the crew of Japanese whaling ship Shonan Maru 2 for piracy in the Dutch court system for threatening the lives of the six crew members of the Ady Gil and destroying their vessel. Sea Shepherd has also taken various legal actions in an attempt to have whaling activities declared illegal. However, in a recent US Court of Appeals ruling (Institute of Cetacean Research, Kyoda Senpaku Kaisha Ltd, Tomoyuki Ogawa and Toshiyuki Miura v Sea Shepherd Conservation Society and Paul Watson No. 12–35266 D.C. No. 2:11-cv-02043-RAJ), Chief Judge Alex Kozinski of the Ninth US Circuit Court of Appeals stated:

> You don't need a peg leg or an eye patch. When you ram ships; hurl glass containers of acid; drag metal-reinforced ropes in the water to damage propellers and rudders; launch smoke bombs and flares with hooks; and point high-powered lasers at other ships, you are, without a doubt, a pirate, no matter how high-minded you believe your purpose to be.
>
> (2014: 2)

While the appeal ruling turns on some specific legal points and concerns an attempt by Japanese whalers to obtain an injunction, it is nevertheless of interest in clarifying and contributing to the debate on the legitimacy of environmental activism. The court contested the public interest nature of Sea Shepherd's actions, citing case law and legal opinion that suggested that environmental activism was a private endeavour. Accordingly, the court commented that 'the activities that Cetacean alleges Sea Shepherd has engaged in are clear instances of violent acts for private ends, the very embodiment of piracy' (2014: 6).

The conclusion that activism constitutes a private endeavour arguably undercuts the species justice perspective employed by activists which is situated within public good and wildlife trust discourse (Nurse, 2015). These hold that protection of wildlife is a public good, as wildlife belongs to all, and that there is benefit to the wildlife itself, to society as a whole and to future generations by keeping wildlife safe for the future. Public good arguments identify that sometimes interventionist activity and precautionary principles should be employed. They also have the potential to allow those alleged to have transgressed the law to argue that their actions were justified and should not be subject to sanction because they serve a wider purpose and benefit more than just themselves. However, irrespective of the merits of direct action, a court ruling of environmental activism as a private endeavour becomes problematic where it suggests that the activists' behaviour pursues private ends rather than the public good and thus arguably amounts to self-serving action. Thus, the court may consider that it is justified in weighing the competing merits of two different private interests where one is ostensibly legal (the Japanese whaling) and the other (the activists' direct action) seemingly is not. Thus, the US District Court found grounds to grant an injunction to prevent Sea Shepherd from engaging in further activity while at the same time effectively sanctioning the perceived wrong of the direct action tactics. Subsequently (December 2014), Sea Shepherd was found to be in contempt of an injunction prohibiting Sea Shepherd, Watson and 'any party acting in concert with them' from physically attacking or coming within 500 yards of the whaling and fuelling vessels of the Institute of Cetacean Research and other plaintiffs on the open sea (Filisko, 2015). The injunction's contempt issue was eventually settled in 2015 (Marine Executive, 2015), reportedly by Sea Shepherd agreeing to pay the ICR $2.55 million and the ICR agreeing to dismiss its $4.1 million claim for damages in respect of the contempt and to drop all claims against Sea Shepherd's former board of directors.

## Eco-activism or eco-terrorism?

The Sea Shepherd case illustrates both a theoretical and practical dilemma. Where an NGO engages in civil disobedience which escalates into illegality, can its activities be justified as legitimate under environmental, ecological or species justice concerns? Does the 'alleged' or actual illegality of the NGO's actions negate the legitimacy of the concern, or should 'eco-terrorism' by an NGO which nevertheless exposes wider illegality and serious environmental crimes be exempt from criminal prosecution?

Eco-terrorism is, to a certain extent, in the eye of the beholder and is both socially constructed and subject to interpretation. Behind the labelling of NGOs and activists as 'criminal' lie complex questions about the role of the state and NGO challenges to societal norms. But illegal actions by NGOs also raise questions about the appropriateness and effectiveness of direct action, especially extreme direct action. Does the end justify the means?

## Pirates or protectors? Some provisional conclusions

The Sea Shepherd case discussed herein is undoubtedly a specific, if not unique, example that relates to both a particular form of activism and a specific area of international law. It should also be noted that the recent decision of the US Ninth Circuit Court of Appeals does not constitute a binding ruling that Sea Shepherd's activities are unlawful and amount to piracy and unlawful environmental activism. However, the decision is useful in clarifying judicial attitudes towards 'extreme' environmental activism and ultimately in determining whether such activities represent a legitimate form of activism within socially constructed notions of 'hard' and 'soft' activism. The decision also provides context on whether, through the use of illegal means, such activities actually damage the cause they aim to promote. Hoek (2010) acknowledges that environmental activists such as Sea Shepherd serve a purpose by drawing attention to the issue of illegal whaling but argues that 'engaging in eco-terrorism is not helping to end Japanese whaling in the long-term, but rather adding fuel to the fire' (193). While Japanese 'scientific' whaling is – at least on paper – legal (despite the fact that it is widely argued by campaigners that, in reality, it is a commercial whaling operation and thus 'unlawful'), the actions of Sea Shepherd or other activists are not when they cross into activities clearly proscribed by international law. It should be noted that the International Court of Justice (ICJ) has ruled that Japanese Southern Antarctic whaling was not scientific and thus was not covered by the provisions of the whaling convention (ICJ, 2014). Thus, in some respects, activists may feel vindicated in that they were combating 'unlawful' activity, or at least activity whose legitimacy has now been negated by an international court's judgement.

But, in a broader context, what the US Ninth Circuit's appeal ruling has done is clarify what has long been suspected: that public interest animal protection concerns may not be accepted as such by jurists. Thus, while the World Charter for Nature arguably provides legitimacy for NGOs/activists to commit minor transgressions or civil wrongs in order to gain evidence of more serious conservation crimes, it would not provide cover for blatantly illegal acts, acts which endanger life or acts that are themselves prohibited within criminal law. In addition, a failure to observe the legal systems of democratic nation-states such as Germany (as was alleged in Paul Watson's case) arguably allows the state to contextualise animal activists as eco-terrorists (Ellefsen, 2012).

For environmental activists, this raises the spectre that some of their actions, while deemed illegal, will not harm their cause, while more serious transgressions will. So, environmental activists might, for example, trespass on shooting estates or enter onto private land in order to gain evidence of illegal activity by shooting enthusiasts or illegal hunting activities and the trespass would not by itself render any evidence inadmissible and could be defended as 'necessary' trespass. But the alleged ramming and potential sinking of whaling ships goes beyond being a 'minor' civil dispute and arguably undermines the legitimacy of any activity carried out under the protection of the UN Charter. Indeed, the ICJ, in its ruling on Australia's case against Japan, commented on an IWC resolution which condemned the alleged dangerous acts of campaigners as follows:

> In this context, the Court recalls IWC Resolution 2011–12, which was adopted by consensus. That resolution notes reports of the dangerous actions by the Sea Shepherd Conservation Society and condemns 'any actions that are a risk to human life and property in relation to the activities of vessels at sea'.
>
> (Para 206 of Whaling in the Antarctic, IWC Judgment of 31 March 2014)

Enders (2015) also notes that certain direct actions have an alienating effect on the public and policymakers and thus can backfire. Thus, what might be intended as necessary extreme direct action or even well-meaning environmental vigilantism risks being called 'eco-terrorism'. This is particularly so when the use of illegal methods is perceived as an integral strategy not just in pursuit of the protection of the environment or wildlife but also as a business or organisational strategy such that the activists appear to consider themselves above the law or believes that they should not be subject to aspects of the law. Where such 'illegal' strategies are also perceived to show disregard for the safety or well-being of others, the state risks turning protectors into pirates and ultimately may feel justified in labelling activists as eco-terrorists.

## References

Beck, U. (1992) *Risk Society: Towards a New Modernity*, London: Sage.

Beirne, P. (2007) 'Animal rights, animal abuse and green criminology'. In P. Beirne and N. South (eds.) *Issues in Green Criminology: Confronting Harms against Environments, Humanity and Other Animals*, Devon: Willan.

Beirne, P. (2009) *Confronting Animal Abuse: Law, Criminology and Human-Animal Relationships*, Lanham, MD: Rowman & Littlefield.

Benton, T. (1998) 'Rights and justice on a shared planet: More rights or new relations?' *Theoretical Criminology*, **2**(2): 149–175.

Cabinet Office (2011) *Red tape challenge*, London: Cabinet Office. Retrieved from http://www.redtapechallenge.cabinetoffice.gov.uk/home/index.

Carmin, J. and Bast, E. (2009) 'Cross-movement activism: A cognitive perspective on the global justice activities of US environmental NGOs', *Environmental Politics*, **18**(3): 351–370.

Carter, N. (2007) *The Politics of the Environment: Ideas, Activism, Policy*, Cambridge: Cambridge University Press.

Cianchi, J. (2015) *Radical Environmentalism: Nature Identity and More-Than-Human Agency*, Basingstoke, England: Palgrave Macmillan.

Doyle, T. (2000) *Green Power: The Environmental Movement in Australia*, Sydney: University of New South Wales Press.

Eagan, S.P. (1996) 'From spike to bombs: The rise of eco-terrorism', *Studies in Conflict and Terrorism*, **19**(1): 1–18.

Ellefsen, R. (2012) 'Green movements as threats to order and economy: Animal activists repressed in Austria and beyond'. In R. Ellefsen, R. Sollund and G. Larsen (eds.) *Eco-Global Crimes: Contemporary Problems and Future Challenges*, Farnham, England: Ashgate, pp. 181–208.

Enders, C. (2015) 'Can Sea Shepherd survive its own success?' *The Guardian*. Retrieved from http://www.theguardian.com/environment/2015/jun/05/sea-shepherd-whale-wars-animal-planet.

Foreman, D. (1991) *Confessions of an Eco-Warrior*, New York: Harmony Books.

Filisko, G. (2015) 'Sea Shepherd law firm won't make waves like the protest group', *ABA Journal*. Retrieved from http://www.abajournal.com/magazine/article/sea_shepherd_law_firm_wont_make_waves_like_the_protest_group.

Ganor, B. (2002) 'Defining terrorism: Is one man's terrorist another man's freedom fighter?' *Police Practice and Research: An International Journal*, **3**(4): 287–304.

Gemmill, B. and Bamidele-Izu, A. (2002) 'The role of NGOs and civil society in global environmental governance'. In D. Esty and M. Ivanova (eds.) *Global Environmental Governance: Options and Opportunities*, New Haven, CT: Yale School of Forestry and Environmental Studies, pp. 1–24.

Gibson-Wood, H. and Wakefield, S. (2012) '"Participation", white privilege and environmental justice: Understanding environmentalism among Hispanics in Toronto', *Antipode*, **45**(3): 641–662.

Heyes, A. (2000) 'Implementing environmental regulation: Enforcement and compliance', *Journal of Regulatory Economics*, **17**(2): 107–129.

Hirsch-Hoefler, S. and Mudde, C. (2014) '"Ecoterrorism": Terrorist threat or political ploy?' *Studies in Conflict & Terrorism*, **37**(7): 586–603.

Hoek, J. (2010) 'Sea Shepherd Conservation Society v. Japanese whalers, the showdown: Who is the real villain?' *Stanford Journal of Animal Law and Policy*, **3**: 159–193. Retrieved from https://journals.law.stanford.edu/sites/default/files/print/issues/hoek.pdf.

Hope, C. (2013) 'RSPCA warned on hunt prosecutions by charities watchdog', *The Telegraph*. Retrieved from http://www.telegraph.co.uk/news/politics/9809362/RSPCA-warned-on-hunt-prosecutions-by-charities-watchdog.html.

ICC (2014) *Whaling in the Antartic: Judgment of 31st March 2014*. Retrieved from http://www.icj-cij.org/docket/index.php?p1=3&p2=1&case=148&p3=4.

ICJ (2014) *Whaling in the Antarctic, Australia v Japan: New Zealand intervening, judgment of 31 March 2014*. Retrieved from http://www.icj-cij.org/docket/files/148/18136.pdf.

Interpol (2012) *Red notice issued for Paul Watson at Japan's request*, Lyon, France: Interpol. Retrieved from http://www.interpol.int/News-and-media/News-media-releases/2012/N20120914.

Jacobson, K. and Saxonberg, S. (eds.) (2013) *Beyond NGO-ization: The Development of Social Movements in Central and Eastern Europe*, Farnham, England: Ashgate.

Jasper, J.M. (1997) *The Art of Moral Protest: Culture, Biography, and Creativity in Social Movements*, Chicago: University of Chicago Press.

Joosse, P. (2012) 'Elves, environmentalism, and "eco-terror": Leaderless resistance and media coverage of the Earth Liberation Front', *Crime, Media, Culture*, **8**(1): 75–93.

Lea, J. and Young, J. (1993) *What Is to Be Done about Law and Order?* London: Pluto Press.

Lovitz, D. (2010) *Muzzling a Movement: The Effects of Anti-Terrorism Law, Money & Politics on Animal Activism*, Brooklyn, NY: Lantern Books.

Lowe, B.M. and Ginsberg, C.F. (2002) 'Animal rights as a post-citizenship movement', *Society & Animals*, **10**(2), Washington, DC: Society & Animals Forum, pp. 203–215.

Marine Executive (2015). Retrieved from http://www.maritime-executive.com/.

Moore, A. and Ireland, N. (2005) 'Caging animal advocates' political freedoms: The unconstitutionality of the Animal and Ecological Terrorism Act', *Animal Law Review*, **11**: 255–282.

Nocella, Anthony J. II (2012) 'Challenging whiteness in the animal advocacy movement', *Journal for Critical Animal Studies*, **10**(1): 142–154.

Nurse, A. (2012a) 'Red tape and regulation: Rolling back environmental enforcement in contemporary Britain', *Criminal Justice Matters*, **90**(1): 14–15.
Nurse, A. (2012b) 'Repainting the thin green line: The enforcement of UK wildlife law', *Internet Journal of Criminology*, **October**.
Nurse, A. (2013a) *Animal Harm: Perspectives on Why People Harm and Kill Animals*, Farnham, England: Ashgate.
Nurse, A. (2013b) 'Privatising the green police: The role of NGOs in wildlife law enforcement', *Crime Law and Social Change*, **59**(3): 305–318.
Nurse, A. (2015) *Policing Wildlife: Perspectives on the Enforcement of Wildlife Legislation*, Basingstoke, England: Palgrave Macmillan.
Nurse, A. (2016) *An Introduction to Green Criminology and Environmental Justice*, London: Sage.
Parkin, F. (1968) *Middle Class Radicalism: The Social Bases of the British Campaign for Nuclear Disarmament*, Manchester, England: Manchester University Press.
Persen, A. B. and Johansen, J. (1998) *The Necessary Disobedience*, Oslo: Folkereisning Mot Krig.
Plows, A. (2008) 'Towards an analysis of the "success" of UK green protests', *British Politics*, **3**: 92–109.
Potter, W. (2011) *Green Is the New Red: An Insider's Account of a Social Movement under Siege*, San Francisco: City Lights Books.
Rawcliffe, P. (1998) *Environmental Pressure Groups in Transition (Issues in Environmental Politics)*, Manchester: Manchester University Press.
Roeschke, J. E. (2009) 'Eco-terrorism and piracy on the high seas: Japanese whaling and the rights of private groups to enforce international conservation law in neutral waters', *The Villanova Environmental Law Journal*, **XX**(1): 99–136.
Ruhl, J. D. (1997) 'The case of the speluncean polluters: Six themes of environmental law, policy, and ethics', *Environmental Law*, **27**: 343–373.
Sandler, R. and Pezzullo, P. (2007) *Environmental Justice and Environmentalism: The Social Justice Challenge to the Environmental Movement*, Cambridge, MA: MIT Press.
Schlosberg, D. (2007) *Defining Environmental Justice: Theories, Movements, and Nature*, Oxford: Palgrave Macmillan.
Situ, Y. and Emmons, D. (2000) *Environmental Crime: The Criminal Justice System's Role in Protecting the Environment*, Thousand Oaks, CA: Sage.
Slapper, G. and Kelly, D. (2011) *The English Legal System: 2011–2012*, London: Taylor & Francis.
Smith, L. and Klaas, K. (2015) *Networks and NGOs relevant to fighting environmental crime: Study in the framework of the EFFACE Research Project*, Berlin: Ecologic Institute. Retrieved from www.efface.eu.
Smith, R. K. (2008) '"Ecoterrorism"?: A critical analysis of the vilification of radical environmental activists as terrorists', *Environmental Law*, **38**(2): 537–576.
Stallworthy, M. (2008) *Understanding Environmental Law*, London: Sweet & Maxwell.
Stephens, C., Bullock, S. and Scott, A. (2001) ESRC Global Environmental Change Programme, *Environmental Justice: Rights and Means to a Healthy Environment for All*, Special Briefing No. 7, University of Sussex.
Terry, K. (2009) 'Terrorism', *Oxford Bibliographies*. Retrieved from http://www.oxfordbibliographies.com/view/document/obo-9780195396607/obo-9780195396607-0023.xml.
White, R. (2007) 'Green criminology and the pursuit of ecological justice'. In P. Beirne and N. South (eds.) *Issues in Green Criminology*, Cullompton, England: Willan.
White, R. (2012) 'NGO engagement in environmental law enforcement: Critical reflections', *Australasian Policing*, **4**(2): 7–12.
Williams, C. (2013) 'Strategy and tactics in the environmental movement', *Climate & Capitalism*. Retrieved from http://climateandcapitalism.com/2013/09/21/strategy-tactics-environmental-movement/.
Wooler, S. (2014) *The independent review of the prosecution activity of the Royal Society for the Prevention of Cruelty to Animals*. Retrieved from http://www.rspca.org.uk/webContent/staticImages/Downloads/WoolerReviewFinalSept2014.pdf.

# 8 Eco-crime and fresh water

*Hope Johnson, Nigel South and Reece Walters*

## Introduction

> 'Companies proclaim water the next oil in a rush to turn resources into profit.'
> (Suzanne McGee, *The Guardian*, 28 July 2014)

> 'Access to water should not be a public right.'
> (Mr Peter Brabeck-Letmathe, CEO of Nestlé, cited in Samson, 2015)

The unsustainable and exploitative use of one of the most important but scarce resources on the planet – fresh water – continues to create conflict and human dislocation on a grand scale. Instead of witnessing nation-states adopting more equitable and efficient conservation strategies, powerful corporations are permitted to privatise and monopolise diminishing water reservoirs based on flawed neo-liberal assumptions and market models of the 'global good'. The commodification of water has enabled corporate monopolies and corrupt states to exploit a fundamental human right – as discussed in the following – and, in the process, create new forms of criminality.

In recent years, both developing and affluent industrialised nations have experienced violent rioting as protestors express opposition to government 'fresh water taxes' and to corporate investors seeking to privatise drinking water. These water conflicts have included unprecedented clashes with police and deaths of innocent civilians in South Africa (BBC News, 2014a); the United Nations (UN) intervention in Detroit, Michigan, after weeks of public protest (Burns, 2014); and the hundreds of thousands of people protesting in Ireland (BBC News, 2014b; *Irish Times*, 2015). Subsequently, the commodification of fresh water has become a criminological issue for water-abundant rich states and highly indebted, water-scarce nations.

Criminological research examining fresh water has tended to focus on the pollution of local waterways and tablelands from industry, transportation and mining (Grabosky, 1989; Smandych and Kueneman, 2010); the contamination of water from exploitative and illegal industrial enterprises (Pearce and Tombs, 1998); or the privatisation of water for corporate interests (Benton, 1998; White, 2003). In order to advance criminological scholarship, this chapter adopts a green criminological perspective underpinned by political economy theories – primarily ecological Marxism and the treadmill of production theory – to explore the ways in which corporate power, supported and sponsored by government initiatives and legal frameworks, monopolises an essential global resource with devastating environmental and human consequences (Lynch et al., 2013; Stretesky et al., 2014).

## Market models, human rights and fresh water scarcity

An estimated one billion people worldwide continue to have irregular access to safe drinking water (The Water Project, 2014). In line with this, the UN Department of Economic and Social Affairs (DESA) identified 45 countries that currently experience severe water stress or scarcity, the majority of which are in Africa. Moreover, by 2030, humanity's annual water requirements will exceed current sustainable supplies by forty per cent (UNDESA, 2013).

The UN Water Report outlined the top drivers of water scarcity as agriculture; climate change and variability; demography, economy and security; ethics, society and culture (for example, equity); governance and institutions; infrastructure; politics; technology; and water resources (including groundwater and ecosystems) (UNESCO, 2012: 4). Accordingly, the major causes of water scarcity (for example, agriculture and climate change) stem back to the overriding emphasis on economic growth, as part of capitalist ideologies, over environmental and human health.

Water scarcity has been cast by the UN in economic terms of excess demand and limited supply. More specifically, the Food and Agriculture Organization of the United Nations (FAO) has identified several dimensions of water scarcity. These dimensions are (i) scarcity in water availability where there is a physical lack of fresh water (for example, during droughts); (ii) deficiencies in the infrastructure required for controlling, storing, distributing and accessing water; and (iii) institutional inability to deliver the required water services ('economic water scarcity') (FAO, 2008).

One result of scarcity is that fresh water becomes an increasingly lucrative investment. As one hedge fund advisor remarked, emerging worldwide fresh water scarcity is providing

> serious profit opportunities for those in the know. . . . The Aqueduct Alliance database / maps will show where those opportunities are located. . . . If you play it right . . . the results of this impending water crisis can be very good.
>
> (Nelson, 2012)

The burgeoning fresh water industry is estimated to be worth US$1 trillion a year and has produced major new corporate conglomerates such as the Aqueduct Alliance (a database operated by Goldman Sachs, General Electric, Coca-Cola, Dow Chemicals, United Technologies, Talisman Energy and Bloomberg). These large transnational corporations (TNCs), some with dubious and reprehensible records of water abuse and contamination, are now creating databases that chart water supplies and identify risks and opportunities for business.

The Institute for Water Management suggests that the main reason for insecurity or scarcity regarding fresh water supply is poor governance and a lack of commitment, as well as the ineffectiveness of those institutions that could address and mitigate the aforementioned drivers of water scarcity (Molden, 2003: 17). This leads to the suggestion that current modes of water governance can result in water scarcity – although improved governance could also be a critical tool for challenging prevalent unsustainable and unjust uses (Good, 2011). Efficient and effective governance requires, amongst other factors, rights-based approaches to law as well as transparency in decision making; meaningful public participation; and a responsive, accountable public sector (Office of the United Nations High Commissioner for Human Rights, 2015).

However, individualist market-based solutions are generally seen as the preferred governance arrangements for dealing with fresh water issues. This is evidenced in international water policies, such as Principle 4 of the *Dublin Statement on Water and Sustainable Development 1996*,[1] which states that 'past failure to recognise the economic value of water has led to wasteful and environmentally damaging uses of the resource'. It is also clear in the inclusion of water in the world trade regime through the General Agreement on Trade in services and the promotion of water privatisation by international financial institutions. For instance, the World Bank (1993) has had a major role in promoting water privatisation to developing countries as part of its structural adjustment programs (see, for example, McDonald and Ruiters, 2005: 32). Specifically, those promoting water privatisation as a response to fresh water issues include international water companies,[2] consultancy firms,[3] state organs and international financial institutions.

Because corporations cannot be held directly accountable for human rights breaches or acts that might be conceived as 'ecocide' (Higgins et al., 2012), it is questionable whether deregulation through neo-liberal state governance is the 'good governance' response required for providing and sustaining water access on an equitable basis. Regulatory preferences for market-based responses tend to reflect the interests of powerful TNCs over those of water users (encompassing human and non-human animals). Lynch and Stretesky (2003) argue that such an approach stems from a corporate 'emphasis on reduced self-regulation, greater corporate control, a reduction in law and a greater reliance on forms of power for influencing law and its enforcement' (233). To expand on this, the focus on market-based approaches to fresh water issues is aligned with how good governance and 'common sense' are currently constructed in mainstream discourses. This construction takes place through the mobilisation of images and messages of pro-environmental concern and corporate social responsibility. Such an approach directs attention away from the fact that it is corporate interests that both drive the degradation and devastation of water sources and create selective and exclusionary forms of control over access to fresh water.

## Fresh water governance and the 'treadmill of production'

Fresh water governance is underpinned by the following legal doctrines: sovereignty, property (including private property and common property), and rights and entitlements to water (Fisher, 2009: 61). Granting private property rights over water is one way in which states enable corporate entities to expand the fresh water economic sector, which in turn both increases withdrawals of fresh water and decreases access to fresh water for others. Accordingly, capital accumulation and profit maximisation are environmentally damaging means of production, which can be encapsulated in the treadmill of production (ToP)

1 The International Conference on Water and the Environment (ICWE) in Dublin, Ireland, on 26–31 January 1992.

2 The three largest international water companies are Veolia Environment (France), Suez Environment (France) and the ITT Corporation (United States). These companies are primarily involved in water supply and waste management. See ETC Group (2012), 'World's 10 Largest Water Companies' (18 January), available at: http://www.etcgroup.org/content/worlds-10-largest-water-companies. In terms of bottled water, Nestlé is currently the largest bottled water company in the world. See Nestlé: The Healthy Hydration Company, *Nestlé Waters in a Few Facts*, available at: http://www.nestle-waters.com/aboutus.

3 For instance, international consulting firm KPMG supports the privatization of water. See KPMG (December 2012), *Financing Water Infrastructure Beyond 2015*, available at: http://media.aws.stwater.co.uk/upload/pdf/KPMG-Financing-Water-Infrastructure.pdf.

theory. The ToP theory is, according to Lynch and Stretesky (2014), useful for 'explaining the political economy of environmental crime and lends important insights into explaining green behaviorism' (139). The ToP theory is grounded in the fact that capitalism needs to be constantly expanding in order to maximise profits, and in order to expand, increasing amounts of environmental resources will need to be used and commodified for consumer societies based on free trade ideologies. Consumption must increase as a result of greater amounts of production. For instance, the uptake of bottled water in developed nations as a response to increased marketing and availability is an example of a way in which consumption has increased along with production (see, for example, Brisman and South, 2014: 72–78; Lynch, 2014).

In relation to private property, corporate entities that control fresh water sources are owners of a means of production, which gives them the ability to profit from such production (for example, from water use or supply). These actors are then able to reinvest these profits into production systems (for example, increased irrigation, expanded bottled-water markets or value-added water products) that in turn expand both consumption and production (Blonquist, 1998). In the context of water, this means ever-increasing withdrawals. Schnaiberg et al. (2000) explain that underpinning this regulatory approach is the 'untenable, almost magical, sense that any type of economic expansion will reduce social and ecological problems'. Within a broader view of crime adopted by green criminology, states and corporate entities are perpetrators of water degradation and scarcity.

The commons is an approach to fresh water governance that provides an alternative to private property– and market-based solutions and one that, depending on the situation, is more likely to align with good governance principles. This is because when global commons such as water become commodities for commercial exchange, not only are the essentials of human life unevenly accessed and distributed, but such global commons are also threatened by governance models that prioritise trade over preservation (Ostrom et al., 1994; Ostrom and Hess, 2007). Recognising water as part of the commons and so subject to common property rights requires collaborative management of water sources between the people who drink and otherwise use that water source. Accordingly, the commons approach to governance differs from, for instance, private governance, where corporations own water and decide how it is distributed, while states externally enforce rules on water use. Furthermore, the commons approach holds that water is ultimately 'a public trust, a common heritage of people and nature and a fundamental human right' (Barlow, 2007: 102). If such an approach were to result in the sustainable and equitable use of a water source, then it seems unlikely that it would become an area for criminological inquiry.

## Conflicting rights

The appropriation of fresh water under property rights regimes can be incompatible with guaranteeing human rights, particularly the right to water and food (Bakker, 2007). The human right to safe drinking water and sanitation is defined as 'the right of everyone to sufficient, safe, acceptable and physically accessible and affordable water for personal and domestic uses' (United Nations Committee on Economic Social and Cultural Rights, 2002: 2). The privatisation of water supplies undermines this right and access, increasing the price of water and reducing affordability; those who cannot afford the higher prices have their connections cut (see, for example, Bayliss, 2003). McClanahan (2014: 408) argues that the privatisation of water raises 'issues of equitable access' and also fails to deliver the kind of effective service that private sector investment and control are supposed to deliver. In fact, according to McClanahan, 'privatization can result in reduced water quality', a point supported by White, who argues that

> corporatization of state agencies – the processes by which agencies are managed as corporate, profit-seeking entities – has led to serious issues of water quality in the developing world. Either by mismanagement of treatment operations in the pursuit of profits, or in the denial of safe water to impoverished populations unable to afford the high costs of privatized water, as many as 5 million people – primarily children – die each year from illnesses caused by poor-quality drinking water or reduced access to affordable clean water.
>
> (2009: 68–69)

The issues of private control and human rights breaches indicate a conflict between private property and human rights and suggest that a rights-based, comprehensive, criminological inquiry into the impacts of water privatisation is needed. Significantly, the privatisation of water under private property regimes has fuelled state and corporate unwillingness to support the recognition of a human right to water. For example, countries such as Canada and companies such as Nestlé were opposed to such a human right, allegedly because of concerns that it may create a legal barrier to privatising water sources (Clark, 2010). Despite progress, the human right to water is at present only recognised in non-binding legal instruments, so the enforceability of the right is still debatable. While the construction of water as a commodity has flourished due to the privatisation of water, the acceptance of a human right to water has struggled for recognition.

If, in the future, a human right to water is to be recognised and strengthened at the international level, then states will be under more pressure to fulfil this right (Shue, 1996: 62). Under the right to water, states would be obligated to facilitate access to water and ensure that corporate entities do not interfere with that right whether they are involved in water pollution or in providing access to water. This presupposes that the state will try to meet human rights obligations as a response to international pressure and that the state has the resources to do so. Meanwhile, corporate entities are still able to operate in a regulatory void where they are generally not held liable for human or environmental harms.

While international actors have been somewhat successful in creating a human right to water in recent times, implementing such a right in the context of the globalised capital accumulation model is incredibly problematic. The trend towards states creating private property rights over water and the ensuing corporate control in order to accumulate capital and wealth is at odds with redistributing and sustainably using fresh water sources. More broadly, the inability of human rights to protect fresh water users again illustrates an underlying conflict between capital accumulation and environmental and human health. In this way, green criminologists, the authors included, need to heed the argument of Lynch et al. (2013) and not 'shy away from connecting capitalism to ecological crime' (1009).

The trend described herein represents the successful neo-liberal commodification of nature, new in its breadth and implications but reflecting ToP theory and ecological Marxism more generally. Regulatory discourses related to the privatisation of water are based on the idea that capital accumulation and profit maximisation in relation to water will increase access and improve equality and efficiency. This 'common sense' is reinforced by the discourses that construct water privatisation as a legitimate policy objective for the attainment of water security and through the existing legal frameworks that have created this ability to privately own water. The inability of human rights to protect access to water, illustrated by the difficulties of enforcing human rights more generally and of holding corporate actors accountable for human rights breaches, shows how such resistances are weakened by the globalised capitalist model.

## Green criminology and the manipulation of fresh water

In order to build upon this emerging analysis, the following sections provide two cases that illuminate the injustices and inequities related to something as simple yet precious as water. The first case study concerns the corporate exploitation of fresh water via the development of privatised markets for public water supply using the example of the London water company Thames Water. The second case study gives examples of water theft and smuggling as phenomena that show how water scarcity, poverty and privatisation produce troubling responses and challenges.

### *Pollution, corporate negligence and tax evasion*

In the UK, examining the record of privatised water companies, the investigative journalist Nick Cohen (2013) argues that successive governments have been negligent by allowing 'dubious companies . . . to take over a vital national interest'. In line with the conflict between fundamental human rights and capital accumulation, as well as the legally attributed goal of profit maximisation, these companies have not behaved with probity or in the best interests of their customers. Cohen (2013) finds that these water corporations are involved in

> widespread tax avoidance . . . hidden . . . behind the high walls of commercial confidentiality [and] [m]ost egregiously, they have loaded their books with debt, not to improve Britain's decaying network of sewers and pipes, but to provide fantastic returns to investors from a captive market of consumers.

Although Cohen's criticisms extend to all the privatised water companies in the UK, he focuses on the example of Thames Water, which is the provider of water and wastewater services for most of Greater London and several counties of South East England. Similar to the situation in developing countries, the privatisation of Thames Water generated high profits and returns to shareholders, but the logic of privatisation as a way to draw in private investment, thereby freeing public funds for other projects, was proven to be false. Thames Water has required government funding to enable it to build a new and much needed super-sewer through London. Nor was the average citizen a beneficiary of this privatisation through dividends. This is because what followed was not a share-owning democracy (as promised by advertising campaigns and capitalist ideologies more generally) but rather share ownership concentration among investment institutions and consortia. In this particular case, Cohen observes that Thames is still 'controlled by a consortium led by Macquarie, an Australian bank':

> Despite making healthy profits for years, the company is too enfeebled by debt to fund a major building project without taxpayer support. . . . If it were a respectable company operating in any kind of functioning marketplace, Thames Water would have had to have changed its ways years ago or go bust.

This example highlights the dysfunctional state of the water market as a result of corporate concentration. Furthermore, it indicates that the privatisation of water is very functional for a few, but much rests on financial behaviour that in other contexts and to other audiences might be construed as close to fraud and criminal tax avoidance. In relation to Thames Water, Cohen found that

> the level of debt is the thread that ties incompetence, negligence, tax avoidance and over charging together. It allows private equity firms to leverage their original investment and increase their returns exponentially. It also allows them to escape tax. If they raise equity, they must pay tax on profits before they can give dividends to shareholders. If they raise loans, however, they can charge the interest payments against tax.

Carrington and Barnes (2013) reported on an investigation by *The Observer* newspaper in November 2012. This investigation 'revealed that three of Britain's biggest water companies paid little or no tax on their profits in 2012 while generously rewarding their executives and investors.' Likewise, Boffey (2012: 6–7) draws on research commissioned by the MP Simon Hughes and carried out by Martin Blaiklock, a former director of utilities at the European Bank for Reconstruction and Development. This research investigated the 'workings of the maze that was Thames Water's company accounts and others', and the findings of this exercise are particularly stark. Blaiklock (cited in Boffey, 2012: 6–7) discovered

> a system that . . . is letting down the customers and the taxman and one that appears to be repeated across the UK, where 75% of water companies are owned by private equity firms. The first part of the jigsaw is an annual bumper dividend paid to investors or to companies which are often their own subsidiaries, sometimes offshore, and which rip out funds that publicly owned waterworks might once have kept aside for infrastructure investment.

In addition to setting up convoluted ownership structures, including subsidiary holdings based in tax havens such as the Cayman Islands, the water companies deliberately pursue a twin strategy of paying out large dividends (to external investors but also to their owners) and also paying off the large debts incurred by these same owners when they borrowed the money needed to buy the water companies. As Blaiklock concluded, the result 'was undoubtedly a severely weakened balance sheet' (Boffey, 2012: 6). This in turn means that the profits of the water companies have been diverted away from their liabilities, so they become 'unable to invest in large-scale projects and . . . ever more reliant on rises in water bills to pay their way' as well as on the support of government to subsidise major infrastructure projects (Boffey, 2012: 6).

In addition to all this, corporate tax arrangements building on these high levels of debt repayment and capital allowances allow companies to be exempt from, defer or off-set various taxes. As Boffey (2012: 6) reports, the examination of the UK water industry pursued by Blaiklock and Hughes 'discovered that little corporation tax is being paid by . . . major water companies – in some years none at all'. For example:

> Thames water enjoyed a tax rebate of £79.6m in 2011–12 and paid just £26m in tax the previous year, despite a net cash inflow for that year of £943.1m. Yorkshire paid just £2.9m [in 2011] and £11.1m in the year before, despite an operational profit of £303m. In 2012, for the regulated part of Anglian water's business, the company paid

> no corporation tax at all. In 2011 it paid £500,000 corporation tax on the profits and in 2010 it was £1.4m.
>
> (Boffey, 2012: 6)

For Hughes, the MP who raised this issue with the House of Commons Public Accounts Committee, the question was whether there is 'a particular problem in the water industry, which is a regulated monopoly with high capital requirements and which allows companies to reduce the capital stock of the utility while lowering their tax liabilities' (quoted in Boffey, 2012: 6).

This question aligns with the role – and weakness – of regulatory oversight or intervention. The Thames Water example illustrates a lack of effective governance arrangements in line with ideals of transparency and equality before the law. The environmental record of the various privatised water companies emphasises the ineffectiveness of regulatory decision making. Cohen (2013) noted that in nine years up to 2013, these companies 'polluted waterways and beaches about 1,000 times' but that 'two-thirds of the spillages resulted in a caution without further punishment. The remaining third attracted fines of £10,800 on average.' Cohen's acerbic judgement is that 'no private equity manager will wake up screaming at such sanctions'.

This record has drawn political attention from some but little or no action. Carrington and Barnes (2013) have reported that cases of pollution caused by water companies 'have included sewage illegally pouring into a harbour for more than a year' and cover-ups occurring when managers destroyed data and 'coerced colleagues to falsify records'. The authors argue that according to data gathered from the Environment Agency (EA) under freedom of information rules, such offending shows no sign of decline. This shows not only poor decision making by regulators when choosing which companies to lease public water systems to but also a lack of effective law enforcement. Responding to this record, Joan Walley, MP, Chair of the Parliamentary Environmental Audit Committee, has said:

> In law, the 'polluter pays' principle is supposed to deter companies from damaging the environment, but in this case the penalties appear to be so pitiful that water companies seem to be accepting them as the price of doing business. The [UK] Sentencing Council must ensure that courts take into account the profits made from environmental crimes and that fines have a sufficient deterrent effect.
>
> (Carrington and Barnes, 2013: unpaginated)

These criticisms of privatisation do not imply a naïve belief that water can simply flow, from capturing falling rain to meeting domestic and industrial consumption demands, without cost. Younger (2012) addresses this matter while also pointing out that questions of supply and cost also raise the issue of equity in relation to *how much* access and quantity different consumers can or should have available to them. As Younger (2012) queries, 'While few would argue with the principle of ensuring safe drinking water and basic sanitation for all, where do we draw the line?' (107). The suggested response – which would avoid byzantine and exploitative private arrangements – would be 'a compromise between the principle of universal free access and the need to cover costs' (Younger, 2012: 107), which is

> achieved by mandating that all water supply and sewage disposal operations must remain in public ownership, to be run on a not-for-profit basis. The costs are covered from general taxation, and as long as the taxation system is progressive, the poor should end up paying less, yet still receive all the water they need free at the point of use.
>
> (Younger, 2012: 107)

Such a response could better balance competing issues around fundamental rights to water and the economic rationale behind privatisation.

In line with the ToP approach outlined earlier, the harms and crimes of privatised water can be seen in terms of 'ecological withdrawal' and 'ecological additions', with the former describing the profit-oriented and short-termist gathering, owning and distribution of water and the latter describing the contamination of areas of land, coast or sea by poorly managed discharge and effluent. The market encourages the search for profit, rise in share value and expansion of production and consumption dependent on water supply and use, accelerating and intensifying the conditions of ecological disorganisation (Lynch and Stretesky, 2014; Stretesky et al., 2014). The privatisation of the control of water supply, purification and delivery infrastructures provides one example of contemporary problems arising from turning a public good into a profit-yielding commodity.

### *Stealing water in a world of unequal distribution*

Several decades of initiatives to provide and enhance the availability of clean and disease-free water for drinking and sanitation have had successes and failures. As Gleick reports:

> Despite these efforts, many water-related problems have worsened [on the global scale]. The incidence of cholera soared in the 1990s and expanded in geographic extent. The populations in urban areas without access to clean water and sanitation actually increased between 1980 and 1990.
>
> (1998a: 500)

In this context, when water is privately owned and available only to those who can afford to pay, it attracts the same kind of innovative and desperate solution to the problem of scarcity and inaccessibility that other precious goods do: theft.

A report from Global Initiative (2014) presents an overview of the growth of organised water theft:

> The uneven distribution of water around the world has led to the situation in which the (sic) water theft is on the rise. Water theft includes the illegal acquisition of natural water courses as well as piped or harnessed water, both of which are designated as 'non-revenue water', i.e. water that is 'lost' before reaching its intended consumer. Loss of water through theft can occur in a variety of ways including damaging or removing water meters and physically installing a connection to water distribution pipes as well as stealing aid tanks.

In different contexts, violence, desperation and profiteering are associated with illegal transactions in this precious resource, ranging from the very minor to the significant and major. For example:

> Contracted drivers bringing water supplies in Jordan's Za'atari refugee camp, which currently holds 100,000 Syrian refugees, must fend off theft, vandalism, and aggression, and supplies are often hijacked and redirected to tanks that refugees have stolen. . . . South Africa has been a major locale for water smuggling. In the past decade, several conflicts arose with local farmers accused of illegally extracting up to 1.58 billion

> kiloliters of water per year, the equivalent of the entire yield of the Mohale Dam in neighbouring Lesotho.

And in Kenya,

> where droughts have become more frequent, reports indicate a rise in water theft crimes in urban slums. Disconnections of water pipes by criminals who collect and sell water have become common occurrences in these areas, where there is a lack of sufficient access to piped water. Data from the country's largest slum (approximately 1.5 million inhabitants) estimate that on average there are seventy-five incidents of water theft reported each day.

To consider cases in Kenya in more detail, Njeru (2012) has reported on 'water shortages driving growing thefts' and quotes Professor Makumi Mwagiru of the Institute of Diplomacy Studies at the University of Nairobi, who stated:

> 'What we are witnessing in the slums is very serious. Some think that water theft is petty but we are living with a time bomb.' 'Most cases involving water crimes rarely make it to court,' he said, largely because Kenyan police view water theft as a petty offense. But 'there have been incidents where people have been killed that relate to water,' he said.

According to a Kenyan police officer interviewed by Njeru, in 2011, 16,000 water crimes had been reported to the police, and these 'were taken seriously', with 'many thieves . . . prosecuted' – although a junior officer who was also interviewed observed that 'corruption in the force is a problem in combating water thefts'. This observation would seem to be important because while such theft and its consequences can be local and small scale and hence create a perception of it being a 'petty offence', in fact it can also be systemic, organised, large scale and devastating, as other reports indicate. Odiwuor (2013) writes that

> collusion among government officials, unscrupulous water vendors and large farm owners results in diverted water supply lines, misappropriated funds, and failure to implement laws on protecting water sources from encroachment and pollution. These are just some of the ways corruption is denying millions of poor people in Africa access to safe and clean drinking water, experts say.

Odiwuor quotes those working in local non-governmental organisations (NGOs) such as Bethlehem Mengistu, regional advocacy manager at the NGO Water Aid, to support this analysis: 'The impact of corruption on the water sector is manifested by lack of sustain able delivery, inequitable investment and targeting of resources, and limited participation of affected communities in developmental processes.' In Colombia, the aqueducts and pipelines that the Ranchería River El Cercado Dam was supposed to feed were never built, providing a tragic case study of the consequences of such corruption (Brodzinsky, 2015).

The Global Initiative (2014) report confirms the significance of corruption in relation to water smuggling, as this limits transparency in financial dealing:

> Although corrupt practices vary across countries, the World Bank estimates that between 20–40% of water sector finances are lost to criminal or corrupt activities. Petty bribes to government officials and water suppliers are used to falsify meter readings,

avoiding disconnections, and conceal illegal connections. The rising demand for water only serves to reinforce these corrupt practices and enforce a sense of discretionary power among officials, consequently weakening a country's rule of law.

## Conclusion

Responses to water scarcity are shaped by the capitalist need to maximise profits and accumulate assets. The human right to water, the ecological limits of fresh water sources and the need for genuine sustainable development remain secondary considerations, and the logics of privatisation and economic efficiency prevail (Gleick, 1998b: 571–572). The way in which water is constructed in law and policy – as part of the commons or privately owned – determines what and who drives the agenda.

By using legal doctrines, state and corporate entities have constructed fresh water sources as something that can be owned or leased. For some regions, the privatisation of water has enabled corporate monopolies and corrupt states to exploit a fundamental human right and has created new forms of criminality. Arguing that such matters are of relevance to a criminology that should be concerned with fundamental environmental and human rights, this chapter begins to develop a green criminological perspective on water (see also White, 2003). This involves exploring the ways in which corporate power, supported and sponsored by government initiatives and legal frameworks, monopolises an essential global resource with often devastating environmental and human consequences.

Today, despite the efforts of some international and national bodies and NGOs, many still live in day-to-day conditions where they are unable to meet their water needs. Elsewhere, water is in abundance, and processing, bottling or piping it makes enormous profits for the private 'owners' of a naturally produced 'public good'. Ironically, despite the fact that the market has put a value on the price of water, in places where it is abundant, water is often 'de-valued', wasted and polluted. In terms of crimes or harms against humanity and the planet, what we do to and with water – diverting it, polluting it, withholding it, privatising it, bottling it, stealing it and so forth – provides a substantial and urgent regulatory and research agenda.

The way forward is to work towards legal and governance frameworks that acknowledge water as a public good – that is, as part of the commons. This would involve user self-governance approaches that are informed by the human right to water (Barlow, 2007; Ostrom, 1990). In user self-governance, users of the water create institutional and regulatory arrangements to sustainably use the water. Whether this approach is successful depends on the context, yet it has proven to be effective in relation to water. Regardless, such an approach provides an avenue outside of private property rights that is worth exploring in future research.

## References

Bakker, K. (2007) 'The "commons" versus the "commodity": Alter-globalization, anti-privatization and the human right to water in the global south', *Antipode*, **39**: 430–455.

Barlow, M. (2007) *Blue Covenant: The Global Water Crisis and the Coming Battle for the Right to Water*, New York: New Press.

Bayliss, K. (2003) 'Privatization and poverty: The distributional impact of utility privatization', *Annals of Public and Cooperative Economics*, **73**(4): 603–625.

BBC News (2014a) *South Africa: Four killed at protest over water shortages.* Retrieved from www.bbc.com/news/world-africa-25840703.

BBC News (2014b) *Tens of thousands attend rallies across Ireland to protest against water charges.* Retrieved from http://www.abc.net.au/news/2014–11–02/tens-of-thousands-protest-water-charges-in-ireland/5861108.

Benton, T. (1998) 'Rights and justice on a shared planet: More rights or new relations?' *Theoretical Criminology*, **2**(2): 149–175.

Blonquist, W. (1998) Common property's role in water resource management. In *2nd International Conference on Property Rights*, France, Aix Marseille University, 6–8 July 1998, Bloomington: Indiana University Digital Library of the Commons, pp. 1–14.

Boffey, D. (2012) 'Water companies pay billions to shareholders but little tax: Why?' *The Observer*, 11 November, pp. 6–7.

Brisman, A. and South, N. (2014) *Green Cultural Criminology: Constructions of Environmental Harm, Consumerism, and Resistance to Ecocide*, London: Routledge.

Brodzinsky, S. (2015) 'Colombia's pipes to nowhere: Villagers die of thirst as corruption stalls dam project', *The Guardian*, 18 June. Retrieved from http://www.theguardian.com/global-development/2015/jun/18/colombia-water-drought-rancheria-corruption.

Burns, R. (2014) 'Now the UN is intervening in Detroit's water conflict: Could thirsty cities riot?', *The Guardian*. Retrieved from www.theguardian.com/cities.2014/oct/17/united-nations-detroit-water-cities-riot.htm.

Carrington, D. and Barnes, S. (2013) 'Revealed: How UK water companies are polluting Britain's rivers and beaches', *The Observer*. Retrieved from http://www.theguardian.com/environment/2013/aug/03/water-companies-polluting-rivers-beaches.

Clark, C. (2010) 'Why didn't Australia support the human right to water?' *ABC News*, 2 August. Retrieved from http://www.abc.net.au/news/2010–08–02/35644.

Cohen, N. (2013) 'The water companies and the foul stench of exploitation', *The Observer*, 3 August. Retrieved from http://www.theguardian.com/commentisfree/2013/aug/03/water-industry-exploitation-pollution.

Fisher, D. (2009) *Governance of Water Resources: The Challenge of Sustainability*, London: IWA Publishing.

Food and Agriculture Organization (2008) *Coping with water scarcity: An action framework for agriculture and food security*, Water Report No. 38, Rome: United Nations Food and Agriculture Organization.

Gleick, P. (1998a) 'The human right to water', *Water Policy*, **1**: 487–503.

Gleick, P. (1998b) 'Water in crisis: Paths to sustainable water use', *Freshwater Systems*, **8**(3): 571–579.

Global Initiative (2014) 'Water, water everywhere: Charting the growth of organized water theft', *Analyzing Organised Crime*. Retrieved from http://www.globalinitiative.net/water-smuggling/.

Good, M. (2011) 'Implementing the human right to water in Australia', *University of Tasmania Law Review*, **30**(2). Retrieved from http://www.austlii.edu.au/au/journals/UTasLawRw/2011/14.html.

Grabosky, P. (1989) 'Water pollution and the Yass Shire Council'. In *Wayward Governance: Illegality and Its Control in the Public Sector*, Canberra: Australian Institute of Criminology. Retrieved from http://www.aic.gov.au/publications/previous%20series/lcj/1–20/wayward/ch15.html.

Higgins, P., Short, D. and South, N. (2012) 'Protecting the planet after Rio – The need for a crime of ecocide', *Criminal Justice Matters*, **90**(1): 4–5.

*Irish Times* (2015) *Thousands march in anti-water charges protest in Dublin*, 20 June. Retrieved from http://www.irishtimes.com/news/environment/thousands-march-in-anti-water-charges-protest-in-dublin-1.2257402.

Lynch, M. (2014) 'Treadmill of production theory', *Green Criminology Blog*, 6 September. Retrieved from http://greencriminology.org/glossary/treadmill-of-production-theory/.

Lynch, M., Long, M., Barrett, K. and Stretesky, P. (2013) 'Is it a crime to produce ecological disorganization? Why green criminology and political economy matter in the analysis of global ecological harms', *British Journal of Criminology*, **53**(6): 997–1016.
Lynch, M. and Stretesky, P. (2003) 'The meaning of green: Contrasting criminological perspectives', *Theoretical Criminology*, 7: 217–238.
Lynch, M. and Stretesky, P. (2014) *Exploring Green Criminology: Toward a Green Criminological Approach*, Farnham, England: Ashgate.
McClanahan, B. (2014) Green and grey: Water justice, criminalization and resistance, *Critical Criminology*, **22**(3): 403–418.
McDonald, D. and Ruiters, G. (2005) *The Age of Commodity: Water Privatisation in Southern Africa*, London: Earthscan.
McGee, S. (2014) 'Companies proclaim water the next oil in a rush to turn resources into profit', *The Guardian*, 28 July. Retrieved from http://www.theguardian.com/money/2014/jul/27/water-nestle-drink-charge-privatize-companies-stocks.
Molden, D. (2003) 'A water productivity framework for understanding and action'. In J. Kijne, R. Barker and D. Molden (eds.) *Water Productivity in Agriculture: Limits and Opportunities for Improvement*, Washington, DC: International Water Management Institute.
Nelson (2012). 'Who's profiting from the water crisis?', *New Internationalist Magazine*, Issue 452. Retrieved from https://newint.org/features/2012/05/01/water-crisis-profit-opportunity/.
Njeru, G. (2012) 'Water shortages driving growing thefts, conflicts in Kenya', *Thomson Reuters Foundation*, 6 August. Retrieved from http://www.trust.org/item/?map=water-shortages-driving-growing-thefts-conflicts-in-kenya.
Odiwuor, K. (2013) 'In Africa, corruption dirties the water', IRIN, 14 March. Retrieved from http://www.irinnews.org/report/97642/in-africa-corruption-dirties-the-water.
Office of the United Nations High Commissioner for Human Rights (2015) *Good Governance and Human Rights*, Geneva: Office of the High Commissioner for Human Rights. Retrieved from http://www.ohchr.org/EN/Issues/Development/GoodGovernance/Pages/GoodGovernanceIndex.aspx.
Ostrom, S. (1990) *Governing the Commons: The Evolution of Institutions for Collective Action*, Cambridge: Cambridge University Press.
Ostrom, E., Gardner, R. and Walker, J. (1994) *Rules, Games, and Common-Pool Resources*, Ann Arbor: University of Michigan Press.
Ostrom, E. and Hess, C. (2007) *Understanding Knowledge as a Commons: From Theory to Practice*, Cambridge, MA: MIT Press.
Pearce, F. and Tombs, S. (1998) *Toxic Capitalism: Corporate Crime and the Chemical Industry*, Aldershot, England: Dartmouth.
Samson, K. (2015) 'The privatization of water: Nestlé denies that water is a fundamental human right', *Global Research: Centre for Research on Globalisation.* Retrieved from http://www.globalresearch.ca/the-privatisation-of-water-nestle-denies-that-water-is-a-fundamental-human-right/5332238.
Schnaiberg, A., Pellow, D. and Weinberg, A. (2000) 'The treadmill of production and the environmental state'. In A.P.J. Mol and F. H. Buttel, *The Environmental State under Pressure*, Bingley, England: Emerald Insight, pp. 32–52. Retrieved from http://www.emeraldinsight.com/doi/pdfplus/10.1016/S0196–1152%2802%2980004–7>.
Shue, H. (1996) *Basic Rights: Subsistence, Affluence, and U.S. Foreign Policy*, Princeton, NJ: Princeton University Press.
Smandych, R. and Kueneman, R. (2010) 'The Canadian-Alberta tar sands: A case study of state-corporate environmental crime'. In R. White (ed.) *Global Environmental Harm: Criminological Perspectives*, Cullompton, England: Willan, pp. 87–109.
Stretesky, P., Long, M. and Lynch, M. (2014) *The Treadmill of Crime: Political Economy and Green Criminology*, London: Routledge.

United Nations Committee on Economic Social and Cultural Rights (2002) *General Comment No. 15: The Right to Water (Articles 11 and 12 of the International Covenant on Economic, Social and Cultural Rights)*, E/C.12/2002/11, 20 January 2003, Brussels: EC.

United Nations Department of Economic and Social Affairs (UNDESA) (2013) 'The human right to water and sanitation', *Department of Economic and Social Affairs*. Retrieved from http://www.un.org/waterforlifedecade/human_right_to_water.shtml.

United Nations Educational, Scientific and Cultural Organization (UNESCO) (2012) *Report on the findings of Phase One of the UNESCRO-WWAP: Water scenarios to 2050*. Retrieved from http://www.unesco.org/new/en/natural-sciences/environment/water/wwap/world-water-scenarios/phase-1/.

The Water Project (2014) *Water scarcity and the importance of water*. Retrieved from http://thewaterproject.org/water_scarcity.php?gclid=CNHQhcKszLcCFcZcpgod5iYAKw.

White, R. (2003) 'Environmental issues and the criminological imagination', *Theoretical Criminology*, 7(4): 483–506.

White, R. (2009) 'Toxic cities: Globalizing the problem of waste', *Social Justice*, **30**(3): 107–119.

World Bank (1993) *Water resources management*, Report No. 12334. Retrieved from http://wwwds.worldbank.org/external/default/WDSContentServer/WDSP/IB/2000/02/23/000178830_98101911251888/Rendered/PDF/multi_page.pdf.

Younger, P. (2012) *Water: All that Matters*, London: Hodder & Stoughton.

# 9 The other side of agricultural crime

## When farmers offend

*Joseph F. Donnermeyer*

## Introduction

There is an emerging literature about crimes and harms committed by those who grow food and raise livestock. Previously, the agriculturalist as offender was virtually ignored by mainstream criminology and has only recently been considered by rural and critical scholars.

I define a farmer as anyone who produces food, ranging from those who grow crops, fruits, and vegetables to those who raise livestock, and covering the gamut of farm types, from small, labor-intensive landholders to capital-intensive, large-scale industrialists who own and manage what today are often called "food factories." After briefly describing the diversity of farming systems around the world, crimes that occur to farms, and a typology of farm operations connected to illegal behavior, this chapter reviews five classes of criminal actions common to when farmers offend: property crime, domestic violence, farmworker abuse and trafficking, farm animal abuse, and violations of environmental regulations and laws. Following this, the chapter describes two generalizations about the social structural and social-psychological dynamics of farmers as offenders, considers when the concept of "green-collar crime" should be applied to the illegal actions of farmers, and suggests possible directions for future research and theorizing about the criminal behaviors of farmers.

## Agriculture in a post-modernist world

It is hard to imagine that a greater share of the "real" world's population is still engaged in the production of food than any other profession, especially in the lesser world of criminology, where the focus long ago veered toward an urban bias (Hogg and Carrington, 2006). Perhaps as much as one third of the world's population are agriculturalists, and the majority are small landowners and food producers, mostly involved in subsistence forms of agriculture (World Bank, 2007). Nearly 38 percent of the world's landmass is devoted to growing food and raising livestock (World Bank, 2015), whereas only about 3 percent is given over to urban occupation (The Earth Institute, 2005).

There is a strong correlation between various measures of economic and social development and the proportion of a country's population that lives on agricultural operations. For example, the agricultural population of the United States today is about 2 percent (American Farm Bureau Federation, 2015), which is a nearly total transformation of its people since it conducted its first census in 1790, when 90 percent of approximately 4 million people in the newly established country were classified as agricultural (National Institute of Food and

Agriculture, 2014). Similarly, rural and agricultural populations of other advanced capitalist societies – such as the United Kingdom, France, and Japan – make up only a small share of their total populations and, in contrast, less developed countries – such as Cambodia, Guyana, and the Sudan – have substantially greater non-urban populations and populations that rely on agriculture as their primary source of income (World Bank, 2015).

Nonetheless, the farm population is declining as a percentage of the total population in the vast share of countries around the world, and this trend will persist throughout the 21st century. The background or context for this is obvious but is nonetheless worth restating: urbanization and industrialization. As a result, there is very uneven development of food production systems, and hence a new diversity among agriculturalists exists today (aside from historic, ethnic, regional, cultural, religious, and social differences) that would not have been present only a century ago. This new form of disparity or difference exists in the economic structure of agriculture itself and reflects the various economies within the societies where food is produced. There remain many predominantly agricultural regions of the world, with limited mechanization and types of labor-intensive production modes that are not far removed from centuries-old and traditional forms of agriculture, regardless of climatic variations in rain and temperature. In many societies undergoing rapid urbanization, agriculture is shifting from labor-intensive varieties to more industrialized models, often at the expense of displaced peasant farmers who migrate to cities where income disparities are huge and poverty is high. Sometimes their displacement is a form of land theft (White, 2012). Last, there are highly efficient forms of agriculture embedded within the most economically advanced and most urbanized countries of the world today. Relying on big machines, chemicals, computer technology, genetic modification of plants and animals, and scales of efficiency unimagined even a few decades ago, this mode of agricultural production is as fully globalized as any multi-national corporation in the world today, even though this vast agri-industrial complex continues to promote an ideology of farmers as wholesome stewards of the land and the natural environment (Cheshire et al., 2013).

The diversity of food production and the socio-economic forces behind systems of growing crops and raising livestock, therefore, are necessary for a proper criminological understanding of when farmers offend and the seriousness of the possible harms they inflict on others, their communities, the environment, and society as a whole. Hence, it is not the case that criminal behavior among food producers is unusual or exceptional; rather, it is contextualized and embedded within the fabric of the very changes that affect all peoples, whether they reside in the city or live outside the shadows of skyscrapers and suburbs. To speak of one third of the world's population as "farmers" is a convenient sobriquet, but this is a moniker that masks diversities as extensive as any found when considering urban populations anywhere in the world.

## Victims . . .

Despite the scarcity of criminology research, the documentation of food producers as the victims of crime is relatively extensive when compared to the body of scholarship on farmers as offenders (Armstrong, 2005; Barclay, 2016; Barclay and Bartel, 2015; Bunei and Auya, 2016; Bunei et al., 2013, 2014; Clack, 2013; Mears et al., 2007; Sudgen, 1999). Nearly all of the research – with the exception of that of Bunei et al. (2013) and Clack (2013), among others, which focuses on farm victimization in African countries – is centered on crime in the highly urbanized countries of Australia, England, Northern Ireland, and the

United States.[1] Armstrong's (2005) work is particularly notable because he focused on the dynamics behind the increase in farm crime in a county bordering Ireland after security forces were withdrawn subsequent to the Belfast Agreement of the late 1990s. All of the other aforementioned studies, plus earlier studies within the US context (Donnermeyer et al., 2011), were victimization studies that were not firmly set against the background of broader historical, social, economic, or cultural forces. However, all implied an inherent relationship between farm crime experiences and social change. In particular, much of the farm crime literature searched for statistical correlates of victimization either with various ecological characteristics (e.g. proximity to highways, physical size of the operation, arrangement/distance of farm buildings from the homestead or where the farm family lives, etc.) or the extent of a farm's capitalization (equipment, machinery, supplies, and other production inputs) because most criminal incidents were occurrences of property crimes, such as theft, illegal dumping, and vandalism (Mears et al., 2007). In essence, these studies can be interpreted as indicators of the extent to which the industrialization of farming is associated with increased levels of agricultural crime that are compatible with routine activities (Felson, 1998) and/or a situational crime prevention (Barclay and Donnermeyer, 2009) approach to the subject matter.

## . . . and offenders

One of the first serious attempts to consider farmers as offenders is the collected work of Gerard McElwee and Rob Smith (McElwee et al., 2011; Smith, 2013; Smith et al., 2013). Approaching the topic from a business management viewpoint, they apply the concept of "pluriactivities" – that is, the idea that a farm operation (and other rural enterprises) of any size and type is an ongoing business that seeks to make a profit and may do so by diversifying beyond traditional or exclusively food-producing activities, some of which may simultaneously involve legal and illegal activities. This straightforward and eminently common-sense assumption dispels the ideal that farmers are always "yeoman" – like caretakers of the land (Cheshire et al., 2013; Jones, 2012), hardworking producers, and businesspeople conforming to the norms and standards of their industry and supporting their families in a supposedly more wholesome environment, closer to the land and to nature (Stenholm and Hytti, 2014). To quote: "The entrepreneurial farmer need not only operate in a legal domain and may engage in a criminal act as a form of illegal diversification" (Smith and McElwee, 2016). Further, all farmers as entrepreneurs who commit crime are presumed to "meet or coalesce and network in a central market place . . . they do this either formally or informally and either virtually or physically" (McElwee et al., 2011: 53).

McElwee et al. (2011: 54) developed four types of rural and farm enterprises, all of which involve offending to some degree. The first type is the "legal enterprise," which occasionally engages in "semi-legal" activities. These may include "off-book" economic production activities to avoid taxation, engaging in cash transactions for the same reason, or not conforming to laws and regulations with which the food producer disagrees or perceives as too onerous to do. For example, Enticott (2011) applied techniques of neutralization to

1 One of the best places to find non-Western academic work on farmers as victims is in *Acta Criminologica*. For example, there are articles on violent crime, including homicide and robbery of small landholders (Moolman, 2000; Olivier and Cunningham, 2006) in addition to the work of Clack (2013) and others on property crime.

examine how farmers justify their violations of wildlife laws, specifically the culling of badgers in rural England and Wales, referring to farmer justifications as a type of "drift into deviance" (206), underpinning their "suspicion of authority" (206) and perceived necessity to do what has to be done for the economic survival of the operation. Although not explicitly mentioned, the implication of McElwee et al.'s (2011) framework is that this is the most frequent expression of pluriactivity for rural and farm enterprises. But there are others as well.

The second type is the use of an agricultural operation as a "front" (McElwee et al., 2011: 55) for hiding illegal activities, such as drug production and trafficking. The farmer as owner is not the direct instigator of the illegal behaviors but is aware of the activities, acquiescing or allowing those who rent or use the property to successfully conduct their nefarious affairs.

The third type is similar, but in this case, the property is acquired (rented or sold) specifically for the establishment of drug production, smuggling, operating an organized theft ring, or other kinds of illegal behaviors. McElwee et al. (2011) calls this third type the "illegal enterprise" or "rural retreat" to distinguish it from the second type, which is a "front" operation. Hence, the owner (when rented) or previous owner (when sold) may or may not be aware of the way the farm property is used, but its utility is now dedicated mostly or solely to the illegal activity. The authors also mention that some of the individuals involved may be local, noting that "in a rural context the relationship between the rural entrepreneur and in particular the farming community will be tenuous and symbiotic" (McElwee et al., 2011: 55).

The fourth and final type is labeled the "opportunistic illegal enterprise." It is similar to the first type because these unlawful actions are committed mostly by farmers or by those with farm backgrounds and experience – that is, individuals who know and understand the everyday management and work-related tasks associated with running an agricultural operation. However, it is different from the first type because the farm operator is engaged directly in illegal behaviors of various kinds, ranging from stealing from neighbors to drug production and the abuse of farmworkers.

McElwee et al. (2011) refer to this fourth type as either the "rogue farmer" or, if connected to organized networks, as members of a "rural organized crime group" (Smith and McElwee, 2016). For example, criminological work by Weisheit (1992), Katz and Whitaker (2001), and Potter (2010), among others, points to the frequency of drug production by farm operators in various regions of the world. Indeed, in the case of illicit drugs, farmers are involved in local, national, and multi-national networks, even though they may be poor subsistence producers at the beginning of a long and complex supply chain of illicit drugs to lucrative markets in distant cities (Potter, 2010).

The remainder of this chapter describes types of offenses that the literature has identified specifically as illegal actions and criminal behaviors engaged in by farmers around the world. It does not include every kind of harm or criminal behavior but does attempt to frame the issue so that future scholarly attention can be turned to farmers as offenders.

## Farmers as thieves

One of the first scholarly studies to recognize the illegal behavior of food producers themselves was an examination of farm victimization in New South Wales (Barclay et al., 2004). Unexpectedly,[2] the authors discovered that the reluctance of farmers as victims to report

2 Interpretation of this article stems from my direct participation in some of the data collection and my interpretation of the dynamics underlying crime when one farmer is victimized by another farmer.

livestock theft was associated with a characteristic of the thief and the social and cultural dynamics of small, tight-knit, rural communities in Australia. Namely, the suspect was often a neighbor who was also a livestock farmer. On these large-acreage operations, a great deal of livestock loss can be attributed to predation and harsh environmental conditions, therefore hiding or masking the real culprit – a neighbor who would muster sheep from adjoining operations on to his property for later sale. Fear of "dobbing in" or reporting both the crime and the suspect as a local or neighbor to the police was one finding from the study and was attributed to community pressure to not cause problems, therefore facilitating rather than constraining criminal behavior.

*Gemeinschaft*, a term associated with the 19th-century social theorist Ferdinand Tönnies (1955), is generally translated in mainstream, functionalist criminological theory to mean a highly cohesive rural community where deviance and crime are socially controlled through the high density of acquaintanceship among its members (Donnermeyer and DeKeseredy, 2013). That was the purpose of the article by Barclay et al. (2004): to critique the age-old concept of *gemeinschaft* and its misuse in criminology to stereotype rural areas as crime free, thereby maintaining an urban bias to criminology's theoretical and substantive foci. In retrospect, the article also touched on the farmer as offender.

In essence, this article was describing the fourth type of offender identified by McElwee et al. (2011) – that is, the "rogue farmer" who victimizes others in the local community. There is little systematic scholarship on farmers as thieves, although Bunei et al. (2013, 2014) mention some farmers in Kenya who were concerned about theft by members of their family who worked on the operation. Further, it is difficult to determine if the work of Barclay et al. (2004) is typical of the ways that farmers are thieves or how extensive the problem actually is. A search of web and media reports of organized theft rings for cattle, tractors, farm supplies, and even crops and fruits suggests that some of these crimes are certainly one farmer victimizing a neighboring farm as a form of property predation; others may be thieves who have extensive farm backgrounds, either as former/current farmworkers or from having grown up on a farming operation. One unusual case comes from the Midwestern state of Illinois, where a farmer had an entire field of soybeans valued at $18,000 harvested by thieves (Amelinckx, 2014). It was estimated that about two hours was needed for the perpetrators to complete the harvest, which requires a working knowledge about how to operate a combine. The news item, however, did not indicate if the thieves used their own equipment or the combine of the victim, which may have been parked out in the open near the field of the purloined soybeans in the days immediately prior to when the harvesting was planned.

Regardless, property theft where farmers are the perpetrators is likely to show that other farmers who live nearby are frequently the victims, and although some of the theft may be very opportunistic, other crimes may be much more deliberative and organized, with networks extending out into a clandestine or black marketplace (McElwee et al., 2011).

In regard to the latter, the work of Smith and McElwee (2016) has begun to document the extent to which some agriculturalists in the UK are involved in forms of food fraud. In particular, they describe the Halal Meat Scandal (or "smokies" trade), which is the slaughter of sheep and other animals in unsafe and unsanitary conditions and then marketing the meat as conforming to Islamic standards for butchering and processing of the animal. With the growing Islamic populations of the UK and other European countries, demand for Halal meat makes this form of illegal enterprise quite profitable. This is but one of many recent examples of extensive food fraud, such as the horse meat scandal – which made headlines, especially in Europe, several years ago – that can involve extensive participation on the part of farmers. Smith and McElwee (2016) also cite the Eurovet Scandal (Smith and Whiting, 2013) and the Black Fish Scandal (Smith, 2015) as examples of how black markets include the participation of food producers.

Spencer (2014) recently examined food adulteration from the point of view of routine activities theory (Felson, 1998). His analysis of the complex networks involved in a globalized marketplace emphasized the potential for lack of guardianship to enhance the ability of farmers, food processors, and retailers – either individually or cooperatively – to bypass rules and regulations related to safety inspections, labeling, and other standards set in place to ensure food security. Hence, as market networks grow in complexity, guardianship declines if there are not sufficient investments in inspections and enforcement of standards, increasing opportunities for illicit profits that can include the active participation of farmers themselves.

## Farmers and domestic violence

Farming is not an easy occupation. It is subject to the vagaries of both the weather and the marketplace. It is stressful. And, added to this mix, it remains mostly a family-based business enterprise in most countries of the world, regardless of their urbanization and the structure of their economies (Elder et al., 1994; Food and Agriculture Organization of the United Nations, 2014). Conger and Elder (1994) documented the ways in which the farm financial crisis in the United States affected farm families, including an increase in child abuse. However, their focus was not specifically on forms of family violence by either farm families or the families in rural communities dependent on an agricultural economy.

The most extensive work on family violence among farm families is the Australian work of Carrington et al. (2013). Their thesis centers on the "internalization of violence" among agriculturalists in Australia, which they juxtapose with more external or public forms of violence found in another type of rural community – namely, rural places dominated by resource extractive and other industries that encourage expressions of hyper-masculinity. Their work also illustrates how "one size fits all" neither applies to the great diversity of rural peoples and rural communities throughout the world, nor can generalizations and stereotypes be easily made about violence associated with rural communities alone (Carrington et al., 2010, 2011; Hogg and Carrington, 2006).

In their work, they emphasize the image that farmers – especially men but farm women as well – have of agriculture, an agricultural lifestyle, and themselves. It is one of autonomy, self-reliance, and hard work and in this respect is not dissimilar to what American scholars refer to as the "agrarian ideology" (Lobao and Meyer, 2001; Rohrer and Douglas, 1969). But the image is changing in response to the changing structural conditions of agriculture around the world, which in turn is the backdrop against which to understand the dynamics of domestic violence within farm families.

The focus of Carrington and colleagues' (2011) work is on violence committed by farm men against their spouses but can be interpreted to be more inclusive – that is, to represent how the economic, cultural, and social forces can be much the same for any kind of violence committed by members of a farm family against each other, including child and elder abuse (Wendt, 2016). Carrington et al. (2013) characterize this violence within the farm family as distinctive because it is a form of "internalization" brought about by "the decline of pub(lic) masculinity, the increasing privatisation of drinking and, with this, the increasing isolation of rural men (and women)" (8). Domestic violence is interpreted as a private affair in many farm families, and both men and women (and the community at large, including rural service providers) remain inclined to think that it was the woman's fault. If assistance is provided to abused farm wives in these rural communities, it is often accomplished quietly. In a sense, the very *gemeinschaft* qualities identified by Barclay et al. (2004) to explain the reluctance of farmers to report stock theft when it is committed by their farm neighbors is the same dynamic operating for a completely different type of offending.

## Farmworker exploitation and human trafficking

The abuse of farmworkers covers a large range of criminal behaviors and harms, from physical and verbal abuse to outright slavery. A great deal of this abuse occurs among undocumented workers, who are afforded little legal protection in the countries where they labor (Barrick et al., 2014; Byrne and Smith, 2016).

Zhang et al. (2014) examined undocumented workers in Southern California and found that about one in five were there as agricultural workers. They reported abusive labor practices, threats, restrictions to their physical movements (such as not being allowed to travel beyond the confines of the farm operation or workplace), and assaults. Barrick et al. (2014) conducted a study in North Carolina of both documented and undocumented farmworkers, finding that nearly half were victimized by physical abuse (beatings, kicking, etc.), threats (ranging from physical and sexual harm to deportation and jail), various deceptions (such as being paid less and working longer hours than promised), and working in hazardous conditions without proper protection (from heavy machinery to farm chemicals). Females were more likely to be trafficked than males, but otherwise both Barrick et al. (2014) and Zhang et al. (2014) found little variation in levels of farmworker abuse by age, marital status, educational level, number of children, or other demographic characteristics.

One reason put forth by scholars for farmworker exploitation is the "acculturation hypothesis," which is the cultural isolation of workers, especially workers (both documented and undocumented) who know only a little of the language in the country where they labor and therefore are more vulnerable to abuse and exploitation. Yet both Zhang et al. (2014) and Barrick et al. (2014) found that some knowledge of English was positively associated with victimization. This may be because workers who know the rudiments of the language of owners, managers, and supervisors (in this case, English) are more likely to understand when they have been abused, which means that the method of research is affecting the results. However, another explanation is that more fluent farmworkers are more likely to have contact with farmers who practice various forms of labor abuse to squeeze more profits from their operations.

One form of slavery found in many parts of the world, and of particular relevance to farm operations, is debt bondage. Debt bondage is the condition by which an agricultural worker is laboring to pay off a debt incurred to the person for whom he or she is working. However, the farmworker is over-charged for expenses associated with transportation (legal or illegal) to the worksite or charged excessive amounts for clothes, food, and shelter; visa or work permit expenses; and other mocked-up legal expenses. The result is that the farmworker makes little or no progress in repayment (Barrick, 2016).

Of course, the United States is not alone in the exploitation of farmworkers. Examples can be found in every country of the world. *The Guardian* (McDonald, 2014) filed a news story about arrests in Northern Ireland (in the county of Armagh) for the illegal transportation of Romanian nationals for farm work. Only a few days before, the same news source (Press Association, 2014) reported on a case in the Southampton area of England of workers from Romania, Latvia, and Poland who had been trafficked and detained on a farm there. The police also found stolen industrial equipment hidden on the grounds of the agricultural operation. Farmworkers in the Mexican state of Baja California recently went on strike, not only to improve wages but also to stop abusive work conditions, forced child labor, and sexual harassment (Tuckman, 2015), according to another story in *The Guardian*. Meanwhile, Amnesty International (2014) issued a report of extensive abuse of farmworkers in South Korea. Many of these workers were from Vietnam, Cambodia, and other countries of Southeast Asia. Human Rights Watch (2011) has documented the systematic abuse and sub-standard living conditions of farmworkers in South Africa who work for fruit and wine producers. The stories are often the same – it is merely the setting for farmworker abuse that varies.

All of these examples have two characteristics in common. First, whether the farm operation is small or large, many of these exploited farmworkers plant, cultivate, and harvest food products for sale in globalized markets geared to urban consumers in more affluent countries. This is no different from examples of sweatshops in the textile industry, to which the general public and public institutions in advanced capitalist societies have reacted and for which numerous attempts to curtail purchases of these products have been made. Second, governments and organizations representing farm owners/agricultural corporations frequently ignore the problem or deny that the problem is extensive or serious.

## Abuse of farm animals

In the United States, farm animal abuse is often exempted from laws and regulations used to prevent abuse of pets and companion animals, even though there are stricter regulations in other advanced capitalist societies, such as the animal welfare regulations adopted by the European Union (Lovell, 2016). In large part, this is due to the lobbying efforts of organizations representing farmers and farm-related industries. In fact, state legislatures in the United States have passed more recent laws banning farm animal advocacy groups from secretly videotaping and in other ways investigating and bringing to the public's attention cases of abuse (Lovell, 2014).

Piers Beirne (1999) has been a leading advocate for a "nonspeciesist criminology," but most of the attention so far has focused on animals outside the food production chain. However, Lovell (2016) makes a strong case for a closer examination of the causes and consequences of animal abuse within the food production system, from the farm through to the slaughterhouse. He also links animal abuse to issues of farm employee safety and the conditions of workers both on the farm and at the slaughterhouse. Pointing to the profit motive of farming, especially on a large scale, he attributes current issues with farm animal abuse to both the structural conditions of the marketplace and complex systems of food production (from the field to the table).

Like many other environmental issues (White, 2009), the abusive behaviors of farmers and farmworkers against animals may not be illegal, but the application of the broader concept of harm brings this issue within the purview of concern among criminologists, especially the growing community of rural criminologists. Inevitably, however, there will be difficult debates about what constitutes a proper criminological focus on the abuse of farm animals. Some farming practices, such as branding, have long been part of agriculture, while others, such as confinement operations that restrict the movement of animals, are more recent. When do the actions of a farmer become abusive, whether or not the behavior is illegal? Different cultures have diverse views on how animals of any kind, but especially those that become food, are to be treated; often these cultural differences are based on strongly held religious values. Regardless of differences in definitions, criminological research on animal abuse in general has shown a link to interpersonal violence (Agnew, 1998; Taylor and Signal, 2014) and domestic violence (Volant et al., 2008).

## Environmental regulations and laws

Broadly speaking, there are two types of illegal behaviors related to farmers: farming practices and violation of environmental regulations and laws. One is not very well documented, while the other has been well researched even though the scholarship is not specific to farmers. The former is criminological research and theorizing on the violation of environmental regulations and laws, while the latter is the criminological examination of wildlife and hunting regulations. However, I suggest that the latter can help inform the former about causes and motives.

Barclay and Bartel (2015) note that the drought in Australia has exacerbated water theft in rural and remote regions, illustrating one type of environmental regulation that victimizes farmers and can be committed by agriculturalists as well. It also serves to illustrate the potential motives and rationalizations of farmers for breaking environmental laws associated with soil conservation, pesticide and chemical applications, farm machinery safety procedures, water quality, contamination of food products, and a host of other issues. As farms around the world become increasingly enmeshed in global commodity chains and the demands for greater efficiency, restrictions of any kind can be perceived as increasing production costs and hence limiting profits. Furthermore, the imposition of environmental regulations and laws from national and international governmental and non-governmental organizations can be perceived as a form of injustice on the part of farmers, leading to violations as a form of defiance and protest (Holmes, 2016). All of these constraints combine with uncontrollable features of the natural environment, such as drought (or too much rain, high winds, frost and freezing, extreme heat, etc.) to create risky conditions for individual farmers.

Winter and May (2001), in their analysis of Danish farmers, examined how awareness of compliance and an ability to comply combined with a perceived sense of moral obligation to follow regulations. They concluded that both normative (moral obligation) and social (judgments about the formalism and coercion of enforcers) motivations were "as influential as calculated motivations" (the likelihood of detection and associated penalties) (Winter and May, 2001: 692).

These very dynamics form a great deal of the theorizing and empirical research behind violations of wildlife laws (Enticott, 2011; von Essen et al., 2015) as forms of resistance and defiance. Specifically, when wildlife is perceived as a threat to "livelihood and lifestyle" through degradation of crops or predation of farm animals, both of which are apropos to the way farmers perceive what they do (Cheshire et al., 2013), combined with sympathy and even support for their actions by others in the local community who also resent the imposition of regulations by centralized governments, it becomes easy to rationalize and romanticize these criminal behaviors as noble and righteous. For farmers around the world, especially in Africa and Asia, laws that originate from distant (physically, socially, and culturally) national and international governmental bodies and from non-profit environmental organizations whose members and support are mostly in countries north of the Equator can appear to be a latter-day expression of colonialism. The killing is not for meat or sustenance alone but is a form of political protest (Holmes, 2016).

## Themes

There are two overriding themes associated with the scattered literature on the subject of when farmers offend. First, the normative and social structures of rural and remote communities where most agricultural operations are located often display *gemeinschaft*-like qualities, yet this high degree of solidarity seems to facilitate crime. Specifically, it constrains victims – farmers victimized by other farmers nearby and family members of abusive farmers – from asking for help, either in the form of reporting the crime to the police or seeking medical, counseling, and other services.

Second, the normative and social structures of rural and remote communities may well create a social-psychological climate of support for farmers who engage in illegal behaviors, especially those related to violation of wildlife and environmental rules. Also, to some extent, the abuse of both farmworkers and farm animals is supported by farmer organizations in which these abusers are members because it is their goal to support the profitability of agricultural industries and to reduce the transaction costs associated with government oversight. Taken together, we have another example of the way in which rural criminology critiques mainstream criminological theories – such as social disorganization theory and the theory of collective efficacy – both of which posit crime to be facilitated at places that display high levels of disorder, not social order (Donnermeyer, 2015).

## Discussion: when is it "green-collar crime"?

Several scholars have proposed the concept of "green-collar crime" to refer to both individual and corporate harms and violations of the law that are related to the health and welfare of the environment (Frank and Lynch, 1992; O'Hear, 2004; Wolf, 2011). An analysis of farmers as offenders suggests that the concept also has application to incidents when farmers or farm-based corporations commit crime or harm the environment, other individuals, and the communities where they operate.

In a "critical commentary" published in *The Critical Criminologist* (Donnermeyer, 2014), I proposed expanding the concept of green-collar crime to the illegal behavior of farmers. However, not all offending by farmers should be automatically viewed as "green collar." Certainly, when farmers violate laws and regulations intended to protect the environment and wildlife, they are committing a form of green-collar crime. When they engage in black market activities related to the mislabeling of food, they are green-collar offenders. Even when they steal from other farmers who are their neighbors – hence harming the ability of the victim to make a living – the thefts are a form of green-collar crime. But to assign a green collar to every violent action is problematic. Although the abuse of farm animals can more easily be classified as green-collar crime, violence against farmworkers or a spouse and other family members is not so green. In fact, a label of green may seem to mollify the seriousness with which these latter forms of violence should be taken. Hence, where is the line drawn between distinctively green crime and other offenses committed by farmers – not only violence against other people but also clandestine drug production and other illegal behaviors not directly associated with growing foodstuffs and raising livestock?

A second issue challenging the boundaries of this topic – when farmers offend – is a consideration of agriculture and history. To be sure, almost all societies in the world today have an agricultural heritage that stretches back to times before they began to industrialize and urbanize (Lobao and Meyer, 2001), as well as the period of transition marked by this transformation. Recognizing this helps provide a greater and more critical understanding of the role of agriculture in crimes and harms that may not have explicit and/or primary connections to the farm. Take, for example, the work of Baris Cayli (2013, 2014) on the role of land in the development of the Mafia in Italy and on current anti-Mafia movements that include land confiscation and its re-use by non-governmental groups to produce organic and fresh food for the marketplace. Only by understanding the evolution of the Mafia as overseers of land and how land is used in organized crime – the third type of illegal enterprise described by McElwee et al. (2011) – can a scholarly discourse on attempts to reduce crime associated with the Mafioso be fully understood.

Collins (2016) does much the same as Cayli (2014) in her analysis of piracy in Somalia. Most of the world, especially the most advanced capitalist countries that have a vital interest in protecting shipping lanes on the open seas, frames these pirates as "terrorists." Yet their development is one of the ways in which colonialism and post-colonial interventionist developments displaced thousands of peoples from Somalia who were pastoralists (semi-nomadic herders) to urban centers or who made a living from fishing. In the short span of a generation, piracy evolved from small payments by foreign fishermen and fisherwomen to local fishing communities along Somalia's vast coastline for using local waters to both a form of resistance and protest and as a way to make money to support the extended families (along tribal lines) of the pirates. Piracy also evolved into armed conflict with the United States and other world powers with ships boarded and crew members kidnapped.

A third area where boundaries are fuzzy in any discussion about farmers as offenders is the idea that they are businesspeople who are at the end of a supply chain for genetically modified organisms, pesticides, and other inputs that potentially harm the natural environment and the health and welfare of people in the surrounding community (Walters, 2006). One prominent feature of globalized markets and supply chains is the property of vertical integration – that is, the extent to which someone at the local level is linked to larger networks and structures. To what degree are farmers, as the local purchasers (i.e. local agents/representatives) of products developed by these corporate offenders (Lynch and Stretesky, 2009), culpable for the harms they create? A parallel that some might argue is rather draconian but nonetheless worth posing is the war crime tribunals of World War II, whereby many defendants claimed that they were only following the orders of their superiors or did not understand the extent and seriousness of the crimes they committed. At the very least, research on the motives of farmers about the use of these products rather than employing safer but perhaps less profitable alternatives evokes new forms of research that apply the rationalizations first identified by Sykes and Matza (1957) in their classic article published in the *American Sociological Review*. Hence, two questions should be asked: when is it corporate crime, and when is it a crime committed by an individual? Is there a clear line to be drawn?

## Moving forward

Developing proper scholarship about farmers as offenders will require a great deal of effort. First, the literature is indeed very scattered, but this chapter and other attempts to bring synthesis to the topic will (hopefully) draw attention to the criminal behaviors of food producers. Second, there is a great need for additional research on varieties of criminal behaviors engaged in by farmers. Obviously, survey research and ethnographic interviews are appropriate, depending on the topic. However, one innovative way already brought to the issue of farmers as offenders is the work of Smith and McElwee (2016), in which the authors conduct case analyses through utilization of multiple methods of data collection. Their approach is popular for scholarship in business management, and their innovativeness for applying the same to the pluriactivities of food producers is one fruitful avenue for the advancement of scholarship on farmers as offenders.

In closing, it is time for the serious development of a *criminology of food and agriculture*. Not only will a great share of the world remain agricultural throughout this century, even as the world continues to urbanize, but food security and safety are at the very heart of people's welfare. Regardless of whether the criminological perspective is critical or non-critical, neglecting the offending behavior of food producers should now be at an end.

## References

Agnew, R. (1998) 'The cause of animal abuse: A social-psychological analysis', *Theoretical Criminology*, **2**: 177–209.

Amelinckx, A. (2014) 'The year in farm crime', *Modern Farmer*, 26 December, p. 8.

American Farm Bureau Federation (2015) *Fast Facts about Agriculture*, Washington, DC: Author.

Amnesty International (2014) *Bitter Harvest: Exploitation and Forced Labor of Migrant Agricultural Workers in South Korea*, London: Author.

Armstrong, N. (2005) *The Impact of Crime in Rural Fermanagh*, Belfast: Queen's University, M.S. Thesis, April.

Barclay, E. (2016) 'Farm victimization: The quintessential rural crime'. In J. Donnermeyer (ed.) *The Routledge International Handbook of Rural Criminology*, London: Routledge, pp. 107–116.

Barclay, E. and Bartel, R. (2015) 'Defining environmental crime: The perspective of farmers', *Journal of Rural Studies*, **39**: 188–198.

Barclay, E. and Donnermeyer, J. (2009) 'Crime and security on agricultural operations', *Security Journal*, **24**: 1–8.

Barclay, E., Donnermeyer, J. and Jobes, P. (2004) 'The dark side of gemeinschaft: Criminality with rural communities', *Crime Prevention and Community Safety: An International Journal*, **6**: 7–22.

Barrick, K. (2016) 'Human trafficking, labor exploitation, and exposure to environmental hazards: The abuse of farmworkers in the U.S.'. In J. Donnermeyer (ed.) *The Routledge International Handbook of Rural Criminology*, London: Routledge, pp. 147–156.

Barrick, K., Lattimore, P., Pitts, W. and Zhang, S. (2014) 'Labor trafficking victimization among farmworkers in North Carolina: Role of demographic characteristics and acculturation', *International Journal of Rural Criminology*, **2**: 223–242.

Beirne, P. (1999) 'For a nonspeciesist criminology: Animal abuse as an object of study', *Criminology*, **37**: 117–148.

Bunei, E. and Auya, S. (2016) 'Agricultural crimes in Africa: Trends and perspectives'. In J. Donnermeyer (ed.) *The Routledge International Handbook of Rural Criminology*, London: Routledge, pp. 117–126.

Bunei, E., Rono, J. and Chessa, S. (2013) 'Factors influencing farm crime in Kenya: Opinions and experiences of farmers', *International Journal of Rural Criminology*, **2**: 75–100.

Bunei, E., Rono, J. and Chessa, S. (2014) 'Crime prevention on farms: The opinion of farmers', *International Journal of Rural Criminology*, **2**: 209–224.

Byrne, R. and Smith, K. (2016) 'Modern slavery and agriculture'. In J. Donnermeyer (ed.) *The Routledge International Handbook of Rural Criminology*, London: Routledge, pp. 157–166.

Carrington, K., Hogg, R. and McIntosh, A. (2011) 'The resource boom's underbelly: The criminological impact of mining development', *Australian and New Zealand Journal of Criminology*, **44**: 335–354.

Carrington, K., McIntosh, A., Hogg, R. and Scott, J. (2013) 'Rural masculinities and the internalization of violence in agricultural communities', *International Journal of Rural Criminology*, **2**: 3–24.

Carrington, K., McIntosh, A. and Scott, J. (2010) 'Globalization, frontier masculinities and violence: Booze, blokes and brawls', *British Journal of Criminology*, **50**: 393–413.
Cayli, B. (2013) 'Italian civil society against the Mafia: From perceptions to expectations', *International Journal of Law, Crime and Justice*, **41**: 81–99.
Cayli, B. (2014) 'Renewing criminalized and hegemonic cultural landscapes', *Critical Criminology*, **22**: 579–593.
Cheshire, L., Meurk, C. and Woods, M. (2013) 'Decoupling farm, farming and place: Recombinant attributes of globally engaged family farmers', *Journal of Rural Studies*, **30**: 64–74.
Clack, W. (2013) 'The extent of stock theft in South Africa', *Acta Criminologica*, **26**: 77–91.
Collins, V. (2016) 'The nomadic pastoralist, the fisherman and the pirate: A historical overview of the rural dimensions of piracy in Somalia'. In J. Donnermeyer (ed.) *The Routledge International Handbook of Rural Criminology*, London: Routledge, pp. 93–102.
Conger, R. and Elder, G. (1994) *Families in Troubled Times: Adapting to Change in Rural America*, New York: Aldine de Gruyter.
Donnermeyer, J. (2014) 'On expanding the concept of green collar crime: Some considerations about crimes and harms of food producers', *The Critical Criminologist*, **22**: 2–5.
Donnermeyer, J. (2015) 'The social organisation of the rural and crime in the United States: Conceptual considerations', *Journal of Rural Studies*, **39**: 160–170.
Donnermeyer, J., Barclay, E. and Mears, D. (2011) 'Policing agricultural crime'. In R. Mawby and R. Yarwood (eds.) *Rural Policing and Policing the Rural*, Farnham, England: Ashgate, pp. 193–204.
Donnermeyer, J. F. and DeKeseredy, W. (2013) *Rural Criminology* (Vol. 3), London and New York: Routledge.
The Earth Institute (2005) *The Growing Urbanization of the World*, New York: Columbia University.
Elder, Jr., G. H., Robertson, E. B. and Foster, E. M. (1994) 'Survival, loss, and adaptation: A perspective on farm families', In R. Confer and G. Elder (eds.) *Families in Troubled Times: Adapting to Change in Rural America*, New York: Aldine De Gruyter, pp. 105–126.
Enticott, G. (2011) 'Technique of neutralizing wildlife crime in rural England and Wales', *Journal of Rural Studies*, **27**: 200–208.
Felson, M. (1998) *Crime and Everyday Life*, 2nd edition, Thousand Oaks, CA: Pine Forge Press.
Food and Agriculture Organization of the United Nations (FAOUN) (2014) *What Is Family Farming?* Rome: Author.
Frank, N. K. and Lynch, M. J. (1992) *Corporate Crime, Corporate Violence: A Primer*, New York: Harrow and Heston.
Hogg, R. and Carrington, K. (2006) *Policing the Rural Crisis*, Sydney: Federation Press.
Holmes, G. (2016) 'Conservation crime as political protest'. In J. Donnermeyer (ed.) *The Routledge International Handbook of Rural Criminology*, London: Routledge, pp. 309–317.
Human Rights Watch (2011) *Ripe with Abuse: Human Rights Conditions in South Africa's Fruit and Wine Industries*, New York: Author.
Jones, J. (2012) 'Looking beyond the "rural idyll": Some recent trends in rural crime', *Criminal Justice Matters*, **89**: 8–9.
Katz, R. and Whitaker, S. (2001) 'Explaining accommodation and resistance in Kentucky', *Crime, Law and Social Change*, **35**: 295–318.
Lobao, L. and Meyer, K. (2001) 'The great agricultural transition: Crisis, change, and social consequences of twentieth century US farming', *Annual Review of Sociology*, **27**: 103–124.
Lovell, J. (2014) 'Behind a veil of secrecy: Animal abuse, factory farms and Ag-Gag legislation', Paper presented at the annual meeting of the American Criminological Society, San Francisco, November 2014.
Lovell, J. (2016) 'Understanding farm animal abuse: Legal and extra-legal factors'. In J. Donnermeyer (ed.) *The Routledge International Handbook of Rural Criminology*, London: Routledge, pp. 137–146.

Lynch, M. and Stretesky, P. (2009) 'The meaning of green: Constraining criminological perspectives'. In R. White (ed.) *Environmental Crime: A Reader*, Cullompton, England: Willan, pp. 84–102.

McDonald, H. (2014) 'Police rescue 20 potential victims of people trafficking in Northern Ireland', *The Guardian*, 18 August.

McElwee, G., Smith, R. and Somerville, P. (2011) 'Theorising illegal rural enterprise: Is everyone at it?' *International Journal of Rural Criminology*, **1**: 40–62.

Mears, D., Scott, M. and Bhati, A. (2007) 'Opportunity theory and agricultural crime victimization', *Rural Sociology*, **72**: 151–184.

Moolman, N. (2000) 'Farm attacks: Are there any ulterior motives?' *Acta Criminologica*, **13**: 64–74.

National Institute of Food and Agriculture, United States Department of Agriculture (2014) *Growing a Nation: The Story of American Agriculture*, Washington, DC: Author.

O'Hear, M. (2004) 'Sentencing the green collar offender: Punishment, culpability and environmental crime', *Journal of Criminal Law and Criminology*, **95**: 133–277.

Olivier, J. and Cunningham, P. (2006) 'Victims' perception of attacks on farms and smallholdings in the Eastern Cape, South Africa', *Acta Criminologica*, **19**: 115–126.

Potter, G. (2010) *Weed, Need and Greed: A Study of Domestic Cannabis Cultivation*, London: Free Association Books.

Press Association (2014) 'Eight men rescued from Hampshire farm amid slavery claims', *The Guardian*, 12 August.

Rohrer, W. and Douglas, L. (1969) *The Agrarian Transition in America: Dualism and Change*, Indianapolis, IN: Bobbs-Merrill.

Smith, R. (2013) 'Developing a working typology of rural criminals: From a UK police intelligence perspective', *International Journal of Rural Criminology*, **2**: 126–145.

Smith, R. (2015) 'The UK "Black Fish Scandal" as a case study of criminal entrepreneurship', *International Journal of Sociology and Social Policy*, **35**: 199–221.

Smith, R., Laing, A. and McElwee, G. (2013) 'The rise of illicit enterprise within the farming industry: A viewpoint', *International Journal of Agricultural Management*, **2**: 185–188.

Smith, R. and McElwee, G. (2016) 'Criminal farmers and organized rural crime groups: A UK case study'. In J. Donnermeyer (ed.) *The Routledge International Handbook of Rural Criminology*, London: Routledge, pp. 127–136.

Smith, R. and Whiting, M. (2013) 'Documenting and investigating the entrepreneurial trade in illegal veterinary medicines in the United Kingdom and Ireland'. In H. Kidlington (ed.) *Veterinary Business and Enterprise: Theoretical Foundations and Practical Cases*, Toronto: Elsevier, pp. 59–72.

Spencer, J. (2014) 'Food adulteration: Understanding the dynamic of supply and criminal action', Paper presented at the annual meeting of the American Society of Criminology, San Francisco, November 2014.

Stenholm, P. and Hytti, U. (2014) 'In search of legitimacy under institutional pressures: A case study of producer and entrepreneur farmer identities', *Journal of Rural Studies*, **35**: 133–142.

Sudgen, G. (1999) 'Farm crime: Out of sight, out of mind: A study of crime on farms in the county of Rutland, England', *Crime Prevention and Community Safety: An International Journal*, **1**: 29–36.

Sykes, G. and Matza, D. (1957) 'Techniques of neutralization: A theory of delinquency', *American Sociological Review*, **22**: 664–670.

Taylor, N. and Signal, T. (2014) 'Animal cruelty and delinquency, criminality, and youth violence'. In M. Brewster and C. Reyes (eds.) *Animal Cruelty: A Multidisciplinary Approach to Understanding*, Durham, NC: Carolina Academic Press, pp. 217–231.

Tönnies, F. (1955) *Community and Society* [trans. by C. Loomis], London: Routledge and Kegan Paul.

Tuckman, J. (2015) 'Baja California farm workers demand better pay and working conditions', *The Guardian*, 25 March.

Volant, A., Johnson, J., Gullone, E. and Coleman, G. (2008) 'The relationship between domestic violence and animal abuse: An Australian study', *Journal of Interpersonal Violence*, **23**: 1277–1295.

von Essen, E., Hansen, H., Norström Källström, H., Peterson, M. and Peterson, T. (2015) 'The radicalization of rural resistance: How hunting counterpublics in the Nordic countries contribute to illegal hunting', *Journal of Rural Studies*, **39**: 199–209.

Walters, R. (2006) 'Crime, agriculture and the exploitation of hunger', *British Journal of Criminology*, **46**: 26–45.

Weisheit, R. (1992) *Domestic Marijuana: A Neglected Industry*, New York: Greenwood Press.

Wendt, W. (2016) 'Intimate violence and abuse in Australian rural context'. In J. Donnermeyer (ed.) *The Routledge International Handbook of Rural Criminology*, London: Routledge, pp. 191–200.

White, R. (2009) 'Introduction: Environmental crime and eco-global criminology'. In R. White (ed.) *Environmental Crime: A Reader*, Cullompton, England: Willan.

White, R. (2012) 'Land theft as rural eco-crime', *International Journal of Rural Criminology*, **1**: 203–217.

Winter, S. and May, P. (2001) 'Motivation for compliance with environmental regulations', *Journal of Policy Analysis and Management*, **20**: 675–698.

Wolf, B. (2011) '"Green collar crime": Environmental crime and justice in the sociological perspective', *Sociology Compass*, **5**: 499–511.

World Bank (2007) *World Development Report 2008: Agriculture for Development*, Washington, DC: The International Bank for Reconstruction and Development/The World Bank.

World Bank (2015) *Data: Agriculture and Rural Development*. Washington, DC: The International Bank for Reconstruction and Development/The World Bank.

Zhang, S.X., Spiller, M.W., Finch, B.K. and Qin, Y. (2014) 'Estimating labor trafficking among unauthorized migrant workers in San Diego', *The Annals of the American Academy of Political and Social Science*, **653**: 65–86.

# Part III

# Questions and agendas in green criminology

# 10 A new benchmark for green criminology

## The case for community-based Human Rights Impact Assessments of REDD+ programmes

*Malayna Raftopoulos and Damien Short*

### Introduction: green criminology, alternative benchmarks to crime and REDD+

Climate change is one of the defining challenges of the twenty-first century and is a considerable threat to both natural and human systems (IPCC, 2014). It has become increasingly clear that climate change will severely impact the enjoyment of human rights, such as the right to life, adequate food, the highest attainable standard of health, adequate housing, self-determination, and access to safe drinking water and sanitation. Furthermore, the impact of climate change on human rights will not be felt equally, with the poorest and most politically marginalised communities affected the most (Roht-Arriaza, 2010). The increasingly apparent human rights implications of climate change have led many observers to explore how to incorporate human rights institutions, practices and discourses into debates on environmental harm, environmental laws and environmental regulation. One such opportunity has emerged in the area of criminology and the development of the green perspective in recent years.

Criminology's traditional concern with crime per se meant that discussions on environmental crimes, laws and harms were largely absent from the vast majority of criminological approaches until the relatively recent development of 'green criminology' (O'Brien and Yar, 2003: 231). The discourse of green criminology, developed by Lynch in 1990, forged a link between environmental issues and criminology, recognising the plundering of the Earth's resources and the degradation of the environment as 'activities that might be considered criminal or at least seriously harmful with intergenerational consequences and transnational impacts' (Higgins et al., 2013: 255). As White (2008) notes:

> In this relatively new area of research and scholarship the concern is to stretch the boundaries of mainstream criminology to accommodate issues of global significance, while also utilising the insights of conventional criminology to illuminate ways in which to understand and to respond to environmental harm.
>
> (3)

In defining the meaning of the term 'green' in the framing of green criminology, Lynch and Stretesky (2003) take the view that 'green crimes, like other crimes, are social constructions influenced by social locations and power relations in society' (218). Green criminology serves as a means of alerting criminologists to

> the types of major environmental harm and damage that can result from environmental harms; the conflicts that arise from attempts at defining environmental crime and

> deviance; and the controversies still raging over possible solutions, given extensive environmental regulations already in place.
>
> (Lynch and Stretesky, 2003: 231)

The green criminology paradigm provides a useful lens through which scholars can critique and theorise discourses related to environmental harm, laws and regulation within a model of environmental justice that places human beings and their well-being at the centre of analysis. Furthermore, the incorporation of green criminology into the discipline serves as an interface with other disciplines concerned with environmental issues and allows scholars to use a variety of analytical tools that are theoretical, empirically grounded and politically active (Walters, 2006: 39). Acknowledgement of the degradation and destruction of the environment by criminologists concerned with social injury and regulation has led to the emergence of new interests, conceptualisations and techniques of analysis, as well as a greater awareness of the interconnectedness of social and environmental issues such as indigenous rights, corporate business misdealings and state corruption. In conjunction with this increased awareness of the interconnectedness between such issues, green criminologists have openly recognised the need for multi-disciplinary approaches, involving cooperation between different areas of expertise both academic and non-academic, in the study of environmental harm (White, 2008: 31).

In the green criminology literature, examples of environmental harm and crime have been organised into two categories and classified as either resulting directly from the destruction and degradation of the Earth's resources (primary) or as being symbiotic with or dependent upon such destruction and efforts made to regulate or prevent it (secondary). According to Higgins et al. (2013), the distinction drawn between 'crime' and 'harm' portrays the long-standing challenge that criminologists have faced over whether they should primarily concern themselves with legally defined crimes or also incorporate 'those activities that lie within lawful practice but evidently, at least to some and by some measures of evidence, have harmful consequences that might merit legal proscription and response' (256). An extension of this approach has led to suggestions of alternative 'benchmarks' to legal definitions of crime. As Potter points out,

> some have argued that we should think of crime differently – in terms of human rights abuses, or in terms of social harm. These other instances of societal harm are considered as crimes by many criminologists. Green criminologists make the point that most, if not all, environmental harms incorporate harms to individuals and social groups and that many entail human rights abuses. People lose their livelihoods, property and way of life as traditional lands are cleared for agriculture or development. We can count millions of avoidable deaths around the globe that are linked to preventable environmental problems, such as the absence of clean drinking water or exposure to pollutants.
>
> (2010: 11)

Taking Potter's observation a stage further, we suggest that green criminologists should utilise an emerging methodological approach from the field of human rights: the Human Rights Impact Assessment (HRIA). There are numerous strengths to this approach which we will elucidate later in this chapter, but for green criminology, in essence, an HRIA can be viewed as a useful benchmark sitting somewhere between legally codified, nationally and internationally defined 'crime' and the much more nebulous notion of 'harm'. While human rights are socially constructed, they are codified legal norms that have a long history, are relatively universal in acceptance and are widely endorsed. Moreover, an HRIA can accommodate – and in fact wholeheartedly embrace – the interconnectedness between social and environmental issues and actively seek cooperation between experts to produce suitable impact 'indicator data', which can then feed into a green criminological framework. Taking an HRIA approach can also help inform the methodological practice of green criminology by providing a research methodology and an internationally agreed-upon normative framework for assessing the often interconnected nature of environmental and social harms. As will be explored further in this chapter, impact assessments act as a means of improving the knowledge of both policymakers and those affected about the potential impacts of policy programmes such as the United Nations' (UN's) REDD+ programme, encourage debate on current and future policies, promote evidence-based policy making, build capacity for policy analysis, and help facilitate adjustment to policies to help mitigate against the negative impacts and consider other alternatives (Hunt and MacNaughton, 2006). This model of analysis provides a socio-legal framework in which the nature of regulatory mechanisms and the social control of environmental harm can be measured and observed through interdisciplinary insight and collaboration. As we shall see, given the concerns surrounding the impact of REDD+ activities, it is necessary to develop strong links with human rights discourses.

Recognising the financial value of stored carbon, REDD+ is a broad framework that sets out to create a system that provides forest users with economic incentives to reduce net emissions of greenhouse gases through enhanced forest management and improved forest carbon stocks. Possible policies include governments strengthening law enforcement or changing the law to stop large-scale logging and forest conversion activities such as establishing protected areas or increasing tree plantations. If designed and governed well, REDD+ has the potential to increase the value of forests and support the constitution of these territories as political, social and economic entities whilst generating co-benefits such as poverty alleviation, biodiversity conservation, financial incentives, technical assistance and facilitated technology transfer (Birrell et al., 2012; Pagiola et al., 2005; Venter et al., 2009).

Split into three phases, REDD+ activities focus on:

1. The development of national strategies or action plans, policies, and measures and capacity building (Phase One).
2. The implementation of national policies and measures that could involve further capacity building, technology, development and transfer, and results-based demonstration activities (Phase Two).
3. Results-based actions that should be fully measured, reported and verified (Phase Three).

(Parker et al., 2009: 97)

Working outside of the United Nations Framework Convention on Climate Change (UNFCCC), international programmes have been created among multi-lateral bodies, such as the World Bank's Forest Carbon Partnership Facility (FCPF), the UN–REDD Programme and the Forest Investment Program (FIP) of the World Bank to provide technical assistance and funding to partner countries to develop Phases One and Two (Thompson et al., 2011: 101). However, questions still remain regarding funding for Phase Three due to the lack of clarity on what a results-based approach would actually include. Currently, funding for REDD+ payments can originate from national funds set up by multi-lateral institutions, major bi-lateral donor countries or non-governmental organisations (NGOs) or from emerging global carbon credit markets (Hall, 2013).

In addition to the use of carbon markets as a way of generating financing for REDD+, there have been two other major areas of contention surrounding REDD+. These have been centered on the inclusion of environmental and social co-benefits, including improving community livelihoods; conserving biodiversity, governance, and rights; and reducing poverty. Another concern is actor participation within REDD+ governance structures at the national level, as well as recognition of indigenous peoples' and other forest dwellers' rights (Espinoza Llanos and Feather, 2011; Kelly, 2010; Savaresi, 2013). The issue of safeguards and their implementation continues to overshadow REDD+, and although small steps have been taken by the UNFCCC to address these problems through the insertion of seven non-mandatory safeguards into Annex 1 during COP 16, concerns still remain regarding the protection of indigenous peoples' and forest dwellers' rights. Although the Cancun Agreement cites the United Nations Declaration on the Rights of Indigenous Peoples (UNDRIP) and acknowledges the need to respect the knowledge, rights and participation of indigenous peoples and local communities, it does not provide a specific legal mechanism through which to achieve these rights (Birrell et al., 2012: 203). Furthermore, there is still no agreement on the inclusion of free, prior and informed consent (FPIC). Establishing FPIC standards for REDD+ would ensure greater procedural rights for affected communities and ensure that 'the interests of national elites and international commercial interests do not override the rights of forest communities' (Brown et al., 2008: 112).

As Raftopoulos (2016) notes, carrying out HRIAs on REDD+ would have a number of potential benefits. First, in addition to increasing the attention focused on those communities connected to REDD+ activities, it can help build political will to compel governments and the international community to implement appropriate procedural standards, including assessment, monitoring and verification mechanisms, into the rhetoric of REDD+. Second, it would provide a thorough understanding of the human rights impact of REDD+ activities, the legal duties and safeguards placed on national and regional governments in regards to the scheme and its potential human rights impacts on future generations. Third, it has the potential to act as an early warning system and provide policymakers and governments with valuable information, enabling them to take prompt action. Fourth, as Hunter (2009) posits, '[a] rights-based perspective can inform a re-prioritisation of policy responses to climate change away from one focused solely on carbon accounting and toward one that considers more fully principles of equity, fairness, and the impact on the most vulnerable' (334–335).

In outlining the case for green criminologists and human rights professionals to collaborate on conducting rigorous, independent HRIAs, this chapter discusses the key areas of concern surrounding REDD+ and the repercussions for the rights and interests of local forest communities. Furthermore, in its discussion on why REDD+ necessitates HRIAs, the chapter explores the implications that a specific link between human rights and REDD+ would have on the promotion and protection of forest peoples' human rights and its potential to change the ways in which REDD+ strategies are devised and implemented. In the context of the climate change crisis, formulating a specific link between human rights and climate change mitigation strategies such as REDD+ is highly pertinent if they are to have a positive impact on a local level, securing the protection of the traditional knowledge, law, customs and lands of those communities in which they operate. In addition, this link would ensure that the most vulnerable and poorest members of society do not bear the negative costs of such policies.

## A critique of REDD+

Since 2007, Payments for Ecosystem Services (PES) and carbon sequestration have gained increasing worldwide attention due to their potential role in climate change mitigation (Corbera, 2012; Stern, 2007). The idea of reducing carbon emissions through avoided deforestation (RED) was first proposed in 2005 at the 11th Conference of the Parties (COP 11) in Montreal. It soon evolved to include avoided forest degradation (REDD), and later, in 2007 at COP 13, the enhancement of carbon stocks was added, finally becoming Reducing Emissions from Deforestation and Forest Degradation plus Conservation and Sustainable Development (or REDD+) (Hall, 2013). Wunder (2007) defines PES as a voluntary transaction where a service buyer (e.g. generated by voluntary or compliance markets) buys a well-defined environmental service from a service provider (governments or sub-national entities in developing countries) when and only when the service provider secures service provision (3). In the case of REDD+, payments by service buyers to service providers are conditional on the adoption of sustainable land use practices and the delivery of reduced emissions from limiting deforestation and degradation in accordance with national or project-based guidelines. However, direct payments from international to sub-national levels are only permitted when these transactions are approved by a national agency (Angelsen and Wertz-Kanounnikoff, 2008: 1; Corbera, 2012: 613).

The emergence of PES schemes such as REDD+ – developed to promote economic growth alongside the protection of ecosystems by ensuring that forest conservation is economically more attractive than forest destruction – have faced increasing ideological opposition. One key area of contention has been finance generation, particularly the use of carbon markets as a way of creating incentives for private sector involvement in order to raise the substantial investments needed to consolidate carbon accounting and capacity building in developing countries (Corbera, 2012: 612). Discussions surrounding the financing of REDD+ have recently moved towards a hybrid model that includes both market-based mechanisms and voluntary donations as potential sources of funding (Hiraldo and Tanner, 2011: 4). Three main avenues are currently under discussion. These include (1) direct carbon market funding through the integration of REDD+ into a global compliance carbon market; (2) market-linked funding through the allocation of auction proceeds and revenues from other fees (e.g. a levy on 'clean development' projects), fines (e.g. non-compliance with the international climate regime), and taxes (e.g. air traffic); and (3) voluntary funding through development assistance (Hiraldo and Tanner, 2011; Parker et al., 2009). While the incorporation of REDD+ into a carbon market–based mechanism would allow companies and national governments to use REDD Certified Emission Reduction credits to meet emission reduction targets in their national cap and trade systems, it could also further exacerbate the impact of REDD+ on indigenous and forest peoples' human rights.

The development of REDD+ as a climate change mitigation strategy has raised grave concerns regarding the impact that its activities will have at a local level. Although academic papers on REDD+ have covered a wide range of topics, from local perspectives of REDD+ (Evans et al., 2014) to the cost effectiveness of REDD+ (Fosci, 2013); implementing, governing, and monitoring REDD+ initiatives (Kanowski et al., 2011; Pettenella and Brotto, 2012; Thompson et al., 2011); operationalising social safeguards in REDD+ (McDerrot et al., 2012); land tenure rights (Larson, 2011); carbon rights (Karsenty et al., 2014); and indigenous rights and engagement (Birrell et al., 2012; Reed, 2011; Wallbott, 2014), an impartial interdisciplinary human rights–based investigation of REDD+ has yet to be carried out. Carrying out an in-depth study of the human rights–impacting activities connected to the scheme is of particular importance considering that the UNFCC has so far failed to establish intergovernmental commitments to rights and equity issues as part of the ongoing climate change policy negotiations.

Given that it is the world's poorest peoples and nations who disproportionately bear the social costs of these socio-economic disparities, 'including the toxic social and environmental fallouts now manifesting as climate crisis, human rights must play a critical role in any response to the climate change crisis' (Grear, 2014: 120). A rights-based analysis is particularly useful as leverage to build more effective political coalitions and pressure for action, especially for marginalised groups such as indigenous peoples and forest communities who are increasingly looking to both international human rights and international environmental law for protection. Furthermore, clarifying the human dimensions of climate change and its impact on individual human rights and interests can help change perceptions that climate change is solely a scientific problem (Knox, 2014: 33).

The negative effects of REDD+ can be separated into four key categories, each of which has a legal basis in human rights and would provide key indicator data if an HRIA were carried out. These are (1) land grabs, land conflicts and violation of customary land rights; (2) exploitative carbon contracts and corruption; (3) marginalisation of indigenous peoples and forest dwellers; and (4) increased poverty and disruption of traditional forest-based lifestyles. It is necessary to examine each of these topics in turn in order to make a case for carrying out an impartial HRIA of REDD+ based on substantial empirical data.

## Land grabs, land conflicts and violation of customary land rights

The infringement of substantive rights through the appropriation of lands and territories through dispossession, forced displacement or the permanent leasing of land by indigenous communities is a key area of concern for opponents of REDD+. Central to achieving an effective and equitable REDD+ mechanism is the clarification and strengthening of land tenure rights. Unless land rights are secured, REDD+ could potentially lead to the exclusion of forest-based communities from the planning and implementation of the scheme, prohibit their access to the forests, and act as an incentive for corruption and land grabbing by either national elites or unscrupulous foreign investors (Lemaitre, 2011). Furthermore, REDD + could slow or reverse improvements to forest governance at the national level by creating incentives for governments or commercial interests to deny forest dwellers access and control over forest resources and block their legal right to benefit financially from the scheme (Griffiths, 2009). In the absence of a legal title, indigenous communities face an uphill struggle to assert FPIC and run the risk that land could be taken away from them by governments to capture REDD+ revenues. In 2012, Via Campesina declared its opposition to REDD+ activities taking place in the Lacandón jungle in Chiapas, Mexico, on the grounds that they are leading to the appropriation, commodification and control of the natural resources on indigenous lands. Ana Valadez, a legal specialist in environmental issues at Via Campesina, maintains that the Chiapas government violated inhabitants' rights by signing an agreement with the California state government, led by Arnold Schwarzenegger, without providing prior information to the populace (Lang, 2012).

Strict rules on forest conservation are leading to large-scale evictions of indigenous and other communities from so-called protected areas and the permanent loss of their rights over their land and resources, together with the right to practice their traditional livelihoods. A report from Oxfam alleges that over 22,000 peasants with land titles were violently evicted from the Mubende and Kiboga districts in Uganda to make way for the UK-based New Forests Company (NFC) to plant trees, earn carbon credits and, ultimately, sell the timber (Grainger and Geary, 2011). Furthermore, the new land use zoning exercises undertaken by the state to capitalise on forest carbon revenues are further marginalising forest-based communities and stalling or reversing the recent trends of decentralising forest ownership and management responsibilities to communities. In the region of San Martín in northern Peru, there are already reports that community land is being restricted. Indigenous people are now forced to hunt in allocated areas, are prohibited from implementing their traditional system of rotational agriculture, and are prohibited from entering the forests without the permission of the regional government. Moreover, land titles are only being given to the area around the community's homes (Forest Peoples Programme, 2012).

## Exploitative carbon contracts and corruption

Concerns over how to reconcile forest carbon sequestration with the protection of indigenous peoples' and forest dwellers' rights are now dominating the discussion of REDD+ activities. The failure of REDD+ to clarify the nature of 'carbon rights' in legal terms has not only raised the question about who holds the rights to emissions reductions and the associated benefits but has also made REDD+ more susceptible to unfair practices (De Jong et al., 2014). Under scrutiny is the issue of whether carbon rights should be considered a land interest separate from the land upon which the carbon is situated, questioning the established common law presumption that the carbon contained within those trees is a natural part of the land and therefore belongs to the landowner. Currently, there are very few countries that have developed laws relating to carbon sequestration as an environmental service or as a resource produced by forests, one of the few exceptions being Australia (Karsenty et al., 2014). Consequently, parties are entering into carbon rights agreements without a legal framework or independent support in place to safeguard against the exploitation of those involved. Indigenous communities are being convinced to sign away their rights to land and carbon under terms that are highly favourable to commercial interests. These terms offer little or no guarantee for the protection of indigenous peoples' and forest dwellers' rights, including their right to use and access natural resources and the principle of FPIC.

The lack of national guidelines has resulted in the explosion of carbon piracy and the emergence of unregulated sub-national projects in indigenous territories as project developers rush to snap up the legal rights to trade carbon. Communities are unknowingly handing over considerable control to project developers for financial and project administration and for intellectual property. Moreover, they are accepting payments that undervalue the true opportunity costs of land use forgone and assuming liability of forest loss (Espinoza Llanos and Feather, 2011). With incidents of carbon piracy already occurring in countries such as Peru and Papua New Guinea, organisations such as the Forest Peoples Programme have been quick to denounce current practices, stating that no carbon contracts should be signed with communities until their fundamental rights are guaranteed and measures are in place at a national level to ensure that these rights are safeguarded (Espinoza Llanos and Feather, 2011: 56).

## Marginalisation of indigenous peoples and forest dwellers

One of the main criticisms of the REDD+ programme has been its failure to include and involve indigenous peoples and forest communities in the planning and implementation of the scheme, undermining their right to self-determination (Espinoza Lanos and Feather, 2011; Freudenthal et al., 2011). Organisations such as Friends of the Earth have also complained about the lack of transparency surrounding REDD+ programmes, reporting instances of closed meetings and the issuing of invitations so late that the relevant stakeholders were unable to make travel arrangements in time (Hall, 2012). Increasing evidence such as the study carried out by the Forest Peoples Programme in 2013 on the conditions of the implementation of the Takamanda National Park project in Cameroon, especially regarding FPIC, echoed these concerns. Findings from two enclave villages, Obonyi I and Obonyi III, showed that FPIC-based procedures required in REDD+ projects were being ignored, and local representatives stated very clearly that they had neither been informed nor consulted on the issue (Ndobe and Mantzel, 2014). With forest dwellers being sidelined from the process of negotiations by governments as they seek to push through national REDD+ strategies, there is a real danger that these communities will be excluded from their land. Furthermore, their inadequate involvement in REDD+ policies and practices threatens to infringe on their procedural rights, including the right to public participation and access to justice and information as expressed in International Labour Organization (ILO) Convention 169 and the UN Declaration on the Rights of Indigenous Peoples (UNDRIP) declaration. The issue of participation and exclusion of local communities has led some indigenous and human rights organisations to withdraw their support from REDD+ projects. One such example is the indigenous peoples' organisations in Panama that withdrew from the UN–REDD National Joint Programme (NJP) in 2013 due to the inadequate attention to rights issues by the government and UN agencies, as well as the lack of full and effective consultations with indigenous peoples during the various stages and implementation of the programme (Forest Peoples Programme, 2013).

## Increased poverty and disruption of traditional forest-based lifestyles

The incorporation of forest dwellers and indigenous communities into the design of REDD+ has been widely acknowledged by observers as being critical to the success of the scheme. In addition to contributing crucial expertise and traditional knowledge about the forests they inhabit, forest-based communities are also best placed to monitor and protect forests. While it is vital that they play an active role in developing and implementing REDD+ programmes, as stewards of their lands, they must also receive the majority of benefits from these initiatives. However, there are fears that the violation of indigenous customary land rights could result in a loss of access to forests for subsistence and income generation needs, disrupting traditional lifestyles and livelihoods and displacing local people (Lawlor and Huberman, 2009).

REDD+ is threatening the enjoyment of these peoples' economic, social and cultural rights as well as their civil and political rights. Under REDD+ programmes, traditional forms of land use practiced by indigenous peoples, such as the collection of fuel wood, the controlled burning of forests to improve habitat diversity and shifting cultivation (despite sustainable rotational agriculture and agroforestry systems being protected under international environmental and human rights laws), are now considered forms of 'forest degradation'. REDD+ also fails to distinguish between permanent and temporary forest loss and fails to acknowledge that many of the traditional practices used by forest-based communities are often carbon neutral. Given that forest dwellers rely heavily on the forests for shelter, food and all other aspects of their livelihoods, REDD+ activities could lead to an increase in rural poverty and undermine some of the ecosystem services that local people depend on to survive. Moreover, without efficient and open forest governance and effective systems in place, benefits of REDD+, such as the payments of compensation, will not reach the communities that manage the forests and will instead be captured by national elites or unscrupulous foreign investors, leaving local communities without a sustainable income (Lawlor and Huberman, 2009; Roht-Arriaza, 2010; Savaresi, 2013).

With many environmentally destructive development practices taking place on traditional lands and severely impacting native and indigenous communities' cultures, the struggle to protect the environment is very often intertwined with their struggle for their own protection. Factors such as their geographical location; natural resource dependency; historical marginalisation from decision making and public policies; insecurity of rights to lands, territories and resources; low income; and institutions and customary laws that are not respected by dominant governance systems make indigenous peoples and forest communities highly vulnerable to climate change mitigation strategies such as REDD+. As the most universally accepted ethics system in the world, a human rights approach helps focus attention on these situations as well as increasingly detailed legal obligations (Knox, 2014: 25). Furthermore, the inclusion of explicit human rights language in current and future climate change policy would serve as a 'bridge' between the climate change regime and international human rights law, prompting states to consider their human rights commitments when implementing relevant mitigation and adaptation policies (Roht-Arriaza, 2010: 226).

## Green criminology and the potential for REDD+ Human Rights Impact Assessments

The last ten years have seen a growth in HRIAs as a policy tool; HRIAs have been developed by a variety of actors as an extension of – or improvement on – Social Impact Assessments (SIAs) and Health Impact Assessments (HIAs), which in turn developed from Environmental Impact Assessments (EIAs). Increasingly, HRIAs are being applied to areas of environmental concern such as the production of shale gas, coalbed methane and 'tight oil', known colloquially as 'fracking'. A recent article called 'Extreme Energy, "Fracking" and Human Rights' written by Short et al. (2015) called for an HRIA to be carried out on fracking activities as a matter of urgency, arguing that there is significant evidence to show that fracking development poses a significant risk to a range of key human rights. In discussing the value of carrying out HRIAs, Short et al. (2015) note that current social scientific research on extreme energy production tends to explore community 'perceptions' of developmental opportunity/threat conundrums which provide very limited insight into the field, as

> they do not utilize an interdisciplinary approach that would engage with scientific findings that speak to an empirical reality beyond individual's 'perceptions', nor do they systematically interrogate how individual perceptions and behaviours are affected by wider social structures and institutionalised power.
>
> (Short et al., 2015: 701)

A green criminological approach with a human rights benchmark, however, offers not just an important means of analysing REDD+ and its impact on forest-based communities but also provides the tools for acting on that analysis. As Harrison (2011) notes, 'HRIAs are inherently valuable processes because of the human rights values and ethos that underpin them' (180). The international legal framework of human rights, given that it has become increasingly embedded within states' practices and adopted into national and international constitutions and agreements, is an excellent alternative benchmark for green criminology and provides a useful avenue to analyse REDD+. More than ever now, practitioners and policymakers need to understand the impact of what they advocate and do. An HRIA would permit the gap between state commitments and the ability of individuals, groups and communities to enjoy these rights – otherwise known as the compliance gap. Moreover, given that REDD+ involves some of the world's most marginalised and disadvantaged communities, including many indigenous peoples, it is essential that such groups can understand and exercise their rights if such schemes are to generate and deliver their purported co-benefits, such as poverty alleviation and biodiversity conservation.

With a lack of legislation and clarity surrounding REDD+ and carbon sequestration, forest groups have increasingly begun to look to rights that go beyond civil and social rights, including the rights to self-determination, economic and social development, cultural heritage, natural resources and a satisfactory environment as a means to bring about environmental and social justice. An increasing focus on the human rights implications of REDD+ has provided indigenous peoples and forest communities with an important opportunity to campaign for wider rights and entitlements, secure land tenure and engage in more participatory policy-making processes. Additionally, since the Convention on Biological Diversity came into force in 1993 – along with the United Nations Declaration on the Rights of Indigenous Peoples in 2007 – indigenous and minority groups have begun to make the crucial connection between the right to self-determination and environmental conservation while demanding legal recognition of their role as 'guardians of the Earth's ecosystems' and the rights to ecological stewardship. Moreover, biodiversity conservation is now being linked to securing indigenous and forest peoples' bio-cultural rights and the protection of their way of life, culture and customary law decision making.

The HRIA approach provides an alternative benchmark for green criminology that is normatively based on international human rights standards and operationally engaged in promoting and protecting human rights. This normative framework is built on the Universal Declaration of Human Rights; the International Covenant on Civil and Political Rights; and the International Covenant on Economic, Social and Cultural Rights. The methodological approach to HRIAs involves an evidence-based evaluation of key rights indicator data (e.g. where the right to water is concerned, key indicators would be access levels, privatisation, quality, purity and the like) against international human rights norms; this would be carried out in eight steps: screening, scoping, evidence gathering, consultation, analysis, conclusions and recommendations, publications and, lastly, monitoring and review. Importantly, HRIAs can occur before an activity has taken place or (*ex ante*) or after (*ex post*) (Harrison, 2011). HRIAs involve the assessment of 'activities which directly and intentionally aim at changing a human rights situation (such as the activities of a human rights NGO) or activities which may have unintended human rights consequences (such as the activities of a multinational company)' (Harrison, 2011: 166). An HRIA of REDD+ would call for the participation of all stakeholders, and the assessment would seek to identify all community harms and evaluate the status of corresponding rights. It would highlight the rights that are not respected and any suggestions that they may be in jeopardy in the future in order to suggest satisfactory solutions. An HRIA would also seek to assist forest-based communities to document the human rights impacts of REDD+ activities as they are experienced by members of the community. Thus, HRIAs are far from value-free social science and seek to take a stance on the issues; they are wholeheartedly normative and seek to promote human rights compliance. Moreover, they aim to provide people with an opportunity to contribute to their own development and strengthen direct democracy by giving those affected a platform to express their concerns regarding policies that affect them – moving beyond research *on* human rights to research *for* human rights.

A human rights framework is based on a number of principles. First, individuals have the right to participate in the planning and implementation of decisions that affect their human rights and have the right to have access to the information they need to participate in the process. Second, governments are accountable for the implementation of their human rights commitments, and citizens must have access to effective remedies in the event that their human rights are violated. Third, there must be a commitment to the belief that all human beings are equal and that no person should be subjected to discrimination. Lastly, there must be an understanding that all human rights – social, economic, cultural, civil and political – are indivisible, inter-related and interdependent (Brodeur, 2011).

Conducting a harm-based HRIA, informed by green criminological insight, would make a number of potentially important contributions to promoting and protecting the human rights of indigenous peoples and forest-based communities. First, taking a human rights–based approach is particularly useful, as it uses a set of norms and standards that are based on shared values and therefore represent a solid normative foundation on which to base an impact assessment (Walker, 2009: 43). Since the adoption of the Universal Declaration of Human Rights in 1948, the UN has constantly reaffirmed the importance of human rights and has become the most universally accepted ethical system in the world due to its ability to continually adapt to new circumstances without compromising its principles (Knox, 2014). Recent UN-based developments regarding the human rights of indigenous and tribal peoples such as UNDRIP and International Labour Convention No. 169 (ILO 169), as well as other international human rights instruments such as the International Covenant on Economic, Social and Cultural Rights and the International Covenant on Civil and Political Rights, are particularly relevant to REDD+. Indeed, both ILO 169 and UNDRIP provide a strong framework for indigenous peoples to assert their rights regarding activity on their customary lands, particularly the right to exercise control over their own economic, social and cultural development by giving their FPIC for any activities on, or their resettlement from, their lands. As Lawlor and Huberman (2009) suggest, 'the requirement that states grant legal title is especially important since the vast majority of forest area is still owned by the state in most tropical countries' (278). Where 'legal' title is absent, indigenous peoples face a significant struggle to assert FPIC and run the risk that land could be taken away from them by governments to capture REDD+ revenues.

Second, given that many human rights norms are incorporated into states' legal obligations, HRIAs may compel duty bearers to act to protect the rights of rights holders (Harrison, 2011: 167). The legal codification of human rights has led to an increasingly large and detailed body of jurisprudence that outlines human right obligations and also allows courts and other institutions to apply these norms to a wide range of issues. As Knox (2014) notes, through the two International Covenants and many other agreements at the global and regional level, as well as through national laws, the international community has created a body of human rights law that sets out obligations in much more detail.

Importantly, almost every state belongs to at least one human rights treaty, whilst more than 160 states belong to both the International Covenant on Civil and Political Rights and the International Covenant on Economic, Social and Cultural Rights. Third, HRIAs will seek to disaggregate impacts to ensure that the effects on vulnerable groups, such as indigenous peoples, are identified. Finally, the human rights approach encourages respect for stakeholder rights to information, participation, transparency and accountability alongside a firm commitment to the improvement of lives and a desire to influence policy and practice (MacNaughton and Hunt, 2011: 361).

Carrying out an evidence-led HRIA on REDD+ would therefore allow for:

- A clear scientific examination of human rights–impacting activities connected to REDD+;
- An in-depth analysis of the legal duties and safeguards placed on national and regional governments in regards to REDD+;
- A thorough and thoughtful human rights–based assessment of the balance of public interest in regards to the uncertain economic benefits of REDD+ and the potential risk of serious and irreversible human and environmental damage; and
- A thorough analysis of the potential human rights impacts of REDD+ on future generations.

A review of academic and practitioner writing on existing HRIA practice reveals an 'overlapping consensus of good practice . . . involving eight core methodological elements' (Harrison, 2011: 169) – screening, scoping, evidence gathering, consultation, analysis, conclusions and recommendations, publication of findings, and monitoring and review. Stages One and Two – screening and scoping – will frame the assessment by identifying the legal, political and cultural context of REDD+, as well as affected populations, enabling the identification of possible human rights impacts. The task at the scoping stage will be to narrow down the rights to be analysed to those most impacted by REDD+ activities. It is important at this stage to gain a firm understanding of REDD+ and identify the possible human rights impacts so that 'the assessment process can be directed towards identifying whether negative or positive impacts have occurred with regard to the rights in question' (Harrison, 2011: 173–174). A preliminary indication of those rights includes (1) procedural rights (e.g. the right to participate in decision making, acquire information and access justice); (2) substantive rights (e.g. the right to life, personal security, health, an adequate standard of living, education, freedom to practice culture and freedom from all forms of discrimination); (3) the right to self-determination (e.g. the ability to exercise their inalienable right to full sovereignty over all their natural wealth and resources) and (4) tenure and resource rights (e.g. the right to secure tenure rights and equitable access to land and resources). Other international commitments and legal obligations will also be relevant, such as carbon emission reduction targets and multi-lateral environmental agreements which relate to both the notion of sustainable development and the notion of human rights more broadly due to the projected global impacts on people from climate change.

Stages Three and Four would focus on evidence gathering and consultation. For the study to yield sufficient quality data, significant community-based research should take place in countries where REDD+ activities are taking place in indigenous or forest peoples' territories in order to inform emerging contexts both within those countries and internationally. The collection of information is at the centre of an impact assessment methodology: 'Without gathering evidence about the (potential) impacts of a policy, the conclusions of the decision-maker are likely to reflect simply their own knowledge, experience and prejudices' (Harrison, 2011: 174). The use of a combination of quantitative and qualitative research methods will enhance data richness in analysing the impacts on those countries and communities involved in Phases One and Two of REDD+. This approach will facilitate the analysis and comparison of current evidence of both 'positive' and 'negative' impacts across a range of physical environments; social, political and legal contexts; and stages in order to identify short-, medium- and longer-term impact patterns and trends, especially potential developing impacts. For example, government, NGO, think tank and others' reports and community-based consultations can help develop a comprehensive picture of the current documented impacts of REDD+ activities to gain a better understanding of multiple perspectives within communities. The centrality of the community in this kind of research is one of the key differences that distinguishes an HRIA from other impact studies that tend to focus on aggregated impacts without paying due consideration to the 'impacts on vulnerable groups' (Harrison and Goller, 2008: 599). Furthermore, an HRIA will enable communities to interact with both political and corporate management structures, flag up potential community resistance to their practices, and shed light on the methods used to garner local support and counter community opposition.

Stage Five will involve the analysis and assessment of human rights impacts. A key strength of utilising a human rights lens as an analytical tool for impact assessment is that impacts are evaluated against codified legal standards, international norms and governmental obligations (Harrison, 2011: 176). A legal analysis should begin with a framework of rights established for the country in question based on its human rights commitments (treaty ratifications and customary legal obligations) but should also be mindful of broader international human rights norms and a wider rights context. Rights of both immediate and progressive realisation (including the minimum core obligations of economic, social and cultural rights) should be analysed. Stage Six involves the development of clear conclusions and recommendations and, where necessary, a series of policy alternatives. The aim of carrying out an HRIA on REDD+ is to have an effect on actual policy and practice by formulating conclusions and recommendations that decision makers can act upon (Harrison, 2011). As Harrison (2011) notes, 'a lack of any concrete recommendations at all hugely reduces the chance of the HRIA being acted upon' (188). An HRIA acts as a means of informing a large group of people about the reality of a situation and communicating the concerns of those communities involved to the relevant people and organisations.

The outcomes of HRIAs can potentially make important contributions to the debates surrounding REDD+, especially the debate on safeguards, which has increasingly become an opportunity for indigenous peoples and civil society to further enhance their calls for respect of internationally recognised rights and standards. The final report and recommendations will provide the stakeholders involved with the opportunity to engage in a dialogue with the various people, agencies and organisations involved in REDD+, both during and after the assessment has been completed. HRIAs have the potential to shape how REDD+ safeguards should be measured, reported and verified throughout the implementation of activities and to help militate against the harmful negative impacts of REDD+ on forest-based communities. REDD+ could be potentially used as a tool for strengthening human rights in the countries in which it operates by imposing obligations upon the state and incorporating them into its design criteria. An explicit link between human rights and the REDD+ mechanism would allow forest-based communities to rely on the law and guidance developed by human rights bodies as well as provide a legal avenue for action against any violations. It would also enable state parties to identify the relevant measures in the domestic legal order and to build appropriate links between the two. Lastly, an explicit reference to human rights would enable parties to rely on relevant capacity for monitoring and evaluating REDD+ (Saversi, 2013).

Stage Seven of an HRIA involves publishing the results. This is a critical part of the impact assessment process, as it ensures that those undertaking the assessment can be held accountable by rights holders and other interested parties. Furthermore, it can help increase the attention focused on indigenous and forest-based communities that are connected to REDD+

activities and build political will to compel governments and the international community to implement appropriate procedural standards, including assessment, monitoring and verification mechanisms, into the rhetoric of REDD+. Importantly, the published results can act as an early warning system and provide policymakers and governments with valuable information and enable them to take prompt action. Lastly, the inclusion of Stage Eight allows for some form of monitoring process to be incorporated into the assessment process. HRIAs should not be a one-off event but rather an ongoing process that documents human rights progress over time. Monitoring is crucial when recommendations are implemented to understand what the actual ongoing human rights impacts are and if further change is needed.

As the fields of criminology and human rights move into new areas of such vital importance to humanity as the environment and ecological crisis, there is an increasing burden on the scholarly community to move beyond simply identifying the problem and make a greater contribution to the solution (Gready, 2009). HRIAs, in addition to measuring human rights standards and the gap between those standards and the reality on the ground, have the potential to develop 'new and potentially transformative interventions [that] can be made into key policy debates where other interests prevail and human rights concerns are traditionally marginalized' (Harrison, 2011: 183).

Rising concerns regarding the impact of REDD+ on indigenous and forest-based communities' interests, rights and traditional knowledge present an urgent need to carry out an impartial, interdisciplinary community-based human rights assessment of the effects, impacts and changes brought about by REDD+ activities on those communities involved with the scheme. As REDD+ proposals and projects continue to gather momentum, there is a general consensus among observers that the program's success will depend on whether these groups' interests are integrated into policy deliberations and decision-making processes and whether their rights, including the principle of FPIC and respect for customary land rights, are recognised. Given the evidence that is emerging from those countries already undertaking REDD+ activities such as Peru and Mexico, it is clear that further academic research is needed into the impact of REDD+ policies and measures on local communities.

Taking a green criminological approach, which embraces human rights impacts as alternative benchmarks to 'crime', 'either explicitly, by referencing rights; or implicitly, by referencing principles or adopting policies that have a normative basis in human rights law' (Lawlor and Huberman, 2009: 282), can reduce the risks associated with REDD+ and help ensure that forest dwellers benefit from the scheme by guaranteeing that their procedural and substantive rights in particular are respected. As noted, currently absent from both academia and public policy making is an impartial, interdisciplinary, community-based HRIA. As noted by Short et al. (2015) in their discussion on fracking, in order to fully comprehend the range and extent of the impact of REDD+, as well as the potential human rights impact for future generations, it is vital that research include data collected from sites at different stages of the REDD+ process. For example, data should be collected from those countries more advanced in REDD+ activities, such as Peru and the Republic of Congo, which are currently Forest Carbon Partnership Facility (FCPF) and readiness grant holders and have a carbon fund, and from those countries such as Papua New Guinea and Ecuador that are currently undertaking the UN–REDD+ readiness process.[1] It is imperative that research begin immediately, given that many countries will complete Phases One and Two of the REDD+ process in the coming years and move into the final phase. REDD+ is

1 See the UN–REDD Programme Collaborative Online Workspace at http://www.unredd.net/index.php?option=com_content&view=featured&Itemid=103.

continuing to develop at pace despite the lack of research into its social and human rights impacts. With its architecture still yet to be finalised, the next few years represent a critical period for the development of REDD+ policies and measures. Whether the results of REDD+ are positive or negative will largely depend on the incorporation of a rights-based approach into the scheme. Carrying out a community-based HRIA can greatly aid this cause by facilitating the participation of all stakeholders, such as local communities and civil society organisations, and encouraging them to meaningfully engage with those proposing REDD+ activities.

## Conclusion

In recent years, REDD+ has taken centre stage in international climate change discussions. How REDD+ works in practice is proving to be highly controversial, raising complex and emotive issues of national sovereignty, human rights and corruption. With the world's tropical forests home to some of the poorest and most politically marginalised communities in the world, their management not only has economic and environmental consequences but also has considerable social implications. Therefore, policies such as REDD+ will have profound consequences for the rights and welfare of indigenous peoples and forest dwellers whose livelihoods, culture and way of life rely on forests. In particular, as this chapter has demonstrated, concerns have been raised regarding the possible harmful impacts of the REDD+ initiative's activities at a local level on the protection and promotion of indigenous and forest peoples' human rights and the initiative's potential to act as a form of neo-colonialism, further transferring forest resources out of the hands of forest communities. If REDD+ is incorporated into carbon markets in the future, these concerns will be amplified and there would be a considerable risk that forest dwellers would be further excluded from directly participating in the design and implementation of REDD+ activities as well as receiving their share of the benefits.

Although it is still unclear how deforestation will ultimately be addressed in the international climate change regime, REDD+ will undoubtedly play an important role. Concerns about the social impact of REDD+ highlight the need for an independent, comprehensive, evidence-based and community-based interdisciplinary HRIA to be carried out. The insights of green criminology can be invaluable in framing such assessments, which can be a vital tool for both forest-based communities and policymakers as REDD+ activities move ahead in the future. The success of REDD+ will depend on the incorporation and protection of indigenous peoples and forest dwellers at all stages of REDD+'s implementation. Therefore, understanding the potential environmental and social harms connected to REDD+ and the current legal duties and safeguards placed on national and regional governments in regards to the scheme and its potential human rights impacts on future generations is crucial to developing appropriate safeguards and incorporating procedural standards into the rhetoric of REDD+ in the future. Furthermore, the process of identifying and documenting human rights violations, as an alternative benchmark within green criminology, brings with it the improved possibility of holding those who violate indigenous and forest peoples' rights responsible and accountable.

## References

Angelsen, A. and Wertz-Kanounnikoff, S. (2008) 'What are the key design issues for REDD and the criteria for assessing options?' In A. Angelsen (ed.) *Moving Ahead with REDD: Issues, Options and Implications*, Bogor Barat, Indonesia: Force for Change (CFOR), pp. 1–11.

Birrell, K., Godden, L. and Tehan, M. (2012) 'Climate change and REDD+: Property as a prism for conceiving indigenous peoples' engagement', *Journal of Human Rights and the Environment*, **3**(2): 196–216.

Brodeur, C. (2011) *Introducing . . . Human Rights Impact Assessments*, Montreal: Rights and Democracy. Retrieved from http://hria.equalit.ie/pdf/en/index/Getting%20Started.pdf.

Brown, D., Seymour, F. and Peskett, L. (2008) 'How do we achieve REDD co-benefits and avoid doing harm?' In A. Angelsen (ed.) *Moving Ahead with REDD: Issues, Options and Implications*, Bogor Barat, Indonesia: Force for Change (CFOR), pp. 107–119.

Corbera, E. (2012) 'Problematizing REDD+ as an experiment in payments for ecosystem services', *Current Opinion in Environmental Sustainability*, **4**: 612–619.

De Jong, W., Castillo Torres, D. and Salazar, A. (2014) 'Carbon cowboys in Peru and the prospects of local REDD governance', *Portes*, **18**(16): 61–83.

Espinoza Llanos, R. and Feather, C. (2011) 'The reality of REDD+ in Peru: Between theory and practice', *Forest Peoples Programme*. Retrieved from http://www.forestpeoples.org/sites/fpp/files/publication/2011/11/reality-redd-peru-between-theory-and-practice-website-english-low.res.pdf.

Evans, K., Murphy, L. and de Jong, W. (2014) 'Global versus local narratives of REDD: A case study from Peru's Amazon', *Environmental Science & Policy*, **35**: 98–108.

Forest Peoples Programme (2012) 'The return of fortress conservation: REDD and the green land grab in the Peruvian Amazon', *Forest Peoples Programme*. Retrieved from http://www.forestpeoples.org/topics/redd-and-related-initiatives/news/2012/10/return-fortress-conservation-redd-and-green-land-gr.

Forest Peoples Programme (2013) 'Indigenous peoples' organisations in Panama pull out of UN-REDD National Joint Programme (NJP)', *Forest Peoples Progamme*. Retrieved from http://www.forestpeoples.org/topics/un-redd/news/2013/03/indigenous-peoples-organisations-panama-pull-out-un-redd-national-joint-.

Fosci, M. (2013) 'Balance sheet in the REDD+: Are global estimates measuring the wrong costs?' *Ecological Economics*, **89**: 196–200.

Freudenthal, E., Nnah, S. and Kenrick, J. (2011) 'REDD and rights in Cameroon: A review of the treatment of indigenous peoples and local communities in policies and projects', *Forest Peoples Programme*. Retrieved from http://www.redd-monitor.org/wp-content/uploads/2011/02/redd-cameroon-report-final-online.pdf.

Grainger, M. and Geary, K. (2011) 'The New Forests Company and its Uganda plantations', *Oxfam International*. Retrieved from https://www.oxfam.org/sites/www.oxfam.org/files/cs-new-forest-company-uganda-plantations-220911-en.pdf.

Gready, P. (2009) 'Reasons to be cautious about evidence and evaluation: Rights-based approaches to development and the emerging culture of evaluation', *Journal of Human Rights Practice*, **1**(1): 380–401.

Grear, A. (2014) 'Towards "climate justice"? A critical reflection on legal subjectivity and climate injustice: Warning signals, patterned hierarchies, directions for future law and policy', *Journal of Human Rights and the Environment*, **5**: 103–133.

Griffiths, T. (with contributions from Francesco Martone) (2009) *Seeing "REDD"? Forests, climate change mitigation and the rights of indigenous peoples and local communities*. Retrieved from http://www.rightsandre-sources.org/documents/files/doc_923.pdf.

Hall, A. (2013) *Forests and Climate Change: The Social Dimensions of REDD in Latin America*, Cheltenham, England: Edward Elgar Publishing.

Hall, R. (2012) 'REDD: The realities in black and white'. *Friends of the Earth*. Retrieved from http://www.foei.org/wp-content/uploads/2014/01/REDD-ingles-final-17–11.pdf.

Harrison, J. (2011) 'Human rights measurement: Reflections on the current practice and future potential of human rights impact assessment', *Journal of Human Rights Practice*, **3**(2): 162–187.

Harrison, J. and Goller, A. (2008) 'Trade and human rights: What does "impact assessment" have to offer?' *Human Rights Law Review*, **8**(4): 587–615.

Higgins, P., Short, D. and South, N. (2013) 'Protecting the planet: A proposal for a law of ecocide', *Crime, Law and Social Change*, **59**(3): 255–266.

Hiraldo, R. and Tanner, T. (2011) 'The global political economy of REDD+ engaging social dimensions in the emerging green economy occasional paper four social dimensions of green economy and sustainable development'. *United Nations Research Institute for Social Development*. Retrieved from https://www.ids.ac.uk/files/dmfile/Hiraldo-Tanner3.pdf.

Hunt, P. and MacNaughton, G. (2006) *Impact assessments, poverty and human rights: A case study using the right to the highest attainable standard of health*, Health and Human Rights Working Paper Series No. 6, New York: World Health Organization and United Nations Educational, Scientific and Cultural Organization (UNESCO).

Hunter, D. (2009) 'Human rights implications for climate change negotiations', *Oregon Review of International Law*, **11**: 331–363.

IPCC (2014) *Climate Change 2014: Synthesis Report: Contribution of Working Groups I, II and III to the Fifth Assessment Report of the Intergovernmental Panel on Climate Change*, Geneva: Intergovernmental Panel on Climate Change (IPCC).

Kanowski, P., McDermott, C. and Cashore, B. (2011) 'Implementing REDD+: Lessons from analysis of forest governance', *Environmental Science & Policy*, **14**(2): 111–117.

Karsenty, A., Vogel, A. and Castell, F. (2014) 'Carbon rights, REDD+ and payments for environmental services', *Environmental Science & Policy*, **35**: 20–29.

Kelly, D. (2010) 'The case for social safeguards in a post-2012 agreement on REDD', *Law Environment and Development Journal*, **6**(1): 63–80.

Knox, J. (2014) 'Climate ethics and human rights', *Journal of Human Rights and the Environment*, **5**: 22–34.

Lang, C. (2012) 'Via Campesina declares its opposition to REDD in the Lacandón Jungle', *REDD Monitor*. Retrieved from http://www.redd-monitor.org/2012/09/21/via-campesina-declares-its-opposition-to-redd-in-the-lacandon-jungle/.

Larson, A.M. (2011) 'Forest tenure reform in the age of climate change: Lessons for REDD+', *Global Environmental Change*, **21**: 540–549.

Lawlor, K. and Huberman, D. (2009) 'Reduced emissions from deforestation and forest degradation (REDD) and human rights'. In J. Campese, T. Sunderland, T. Greiber, T. Oviedo and G. Oviedo (eds.) *Rights-Based Approaches: Exploring Issues and Opportunities for Conservation*, Bogor Barat, Indonesia: Force for Change (CFOR), pp. 269–287.

Lemaitre, S. (2011) 'Indigenous peoples' land rights and REDD: A case study', *Review of European Community of International Environmental Law*, **20**(2): 150–162.

Lynch, M. (1990) 'The greening of criminology: A perspective on the 1990s', *The Critical Criminologist*, **2**(3): 1–4.

Lynch, M. and Stretesky, P. (2003) 'The meaning of green: Contrasting criminological perspectives', *Theoretical Criminology*, 7(2): 217–238.

MacNaughton, G. and Hunt, P. (2011) 'Human rights-based approach to social impact assessment'. In F. Vanclay and A. Esteves (eds.) *New Directions in Social Impact Assessment: Conceptual and Methodological Advances*, Cheltenham, England: Edward Elgar, pp. 355–369.

McDermott, C., Coad, L., Helfgott, A. and Schroeder, H. (2012) 'Operationalizing social safeguards in REDD+: Actors, interests and ideas', *Environmental Science & Policy*, **21**: 63–72.

Ndobe, S. and Mantzel, K. (2014) 'Deforestation, REDD and Takamanda National Park in Cameroon – a case study'. *Forest Peoples Programme*. Retrieved from http://www.forestpeoples.org/topics/un-redd/publication/2014/deforestation-redd-and-takamanda-national-park-cameroon-case-study.

O'Brien, M. and Yar, M. (2003) *Criminology: The Key Concepts*, London: Routledge.

Pagiola, S., Arcenas, A. and Platais, G. (2005) 'Can payments for environmental services help reduce poverty? An exploration of the issues and the evidence to date from Latin America', *World Development*, **33**(2): 237–253.

Parker, C., Brown, J., Pickering, J., Roynestad, E., Mardas, N. and Mitchell, A. (2009) 'The little climate finance book', *Global Canopy Programme*. Retrieved from http://www.globalcanopy.org/sites/default/files/lcfb_en%20(1).pdf.

Pettenella, D. and Brotto, L. (2012) 'Governance features for successful REDD+ projects organization', *Forest Policy and Economics*, **18**: 46–52.

Potter, G. (2010) 'What is green criminology?' *Sociology Review*, **8**: 12.

Raftopoulos, M. (2016) 'REDD+ and human rights: Addressing the urgent need for a full community-based human rights impact assessment', *International Journal of Human Rights*, **20**(4): 509–530.

Reed, P. (2011) 'REDD+ and the indigenous question: A case study from Ecuador', *Forests*, **2**: 525–549.

Roht-Arriaza, N. (2010) 'Human rights in the climate change regime', *Journal of Human Rights and the Environment*, **1**(2): 211–235.

Savaresi, A. (2013) 'REDD+ and human rights: Addressing synergies between international regimes', *Ecology and Society*, **18**(3): 5–13.

Short, D., Elliot, J., Norder, K., Lloyd-Davies, E. and Morley, J. (2015) 'Extreme energy, fracking and human rights: A new field for impact assessments', *International Journal of Human Rights*, **19**(6): 697–736.

Stern, N. (2007) *The Economics of Climate Change: The Stern Review*, Cambridge: Cambridge University Press.

Thompson, M., Baruah, M. and Carr. E. (2011) 'Seeing REDD+ as a project of environmental governance', *Environmental Science & Policy*, **14**(2): 100–110.

Venter, O., Laurance, W., Iwamura, T., Wilson, K., Fuller, R. and Possingham, H. (2009) 'Harnessing carbon payments to protect biodiversity', *Science*, **326**(5958): 1368.

Walker, S. (2009) *The Future of Human Rights Impact Assessments of Trade Agreements*, Brussels: Intersentia.

Wallbott, L. (2014) 'Indigenous peoples in UN REDD+ negotiations: "Importing power" and lobbying for rights through discursive interplay management', *Ecology and Society*, **19**(1): 21.

Walters, R. (2006) 'Crime, bio-agriculture and the exploitation of hunger', *British Journal of Criminology*, **46**(1): 26–45.

White, R. (2008) *Crimes against Nature: Environmental Criminology and Ecological Justice*, Cullompton, England: Willan.

Wunder, Sven. (2007) 'The efficiency of payments for environmental services in tropical conservation', *Conservation Biology*, **21**(1): 48–58.

# 11 Implementation and enforcement of environmental law

## The role of professional practitioners

*Grant Pink*

## Introduction

This chapter considers the important role that regulatory professionals play in the effective implementation and enforcement of environmental law. For the purposes of this chapter and in respect to environmental and transnational environmental crime, regulatory professionals operate within three types of agencies: police agencies, customs and border agencies, and environmental regulatory agencies. This chapter critically compares the three organisational contexts of the regulatory professions to identify inconsistencies and to explore possible improvements. The aim of this chapter is to provide information, options, and strategies to enable more effective recruitment, training, and continuing professional development of regulatory staff. This research has particular relevance for environmental regulatory agencies, as they, like all public service agencies, are continually seeking efficiencies and effectiveness in the performance of their various roles and functions. Finally, this chapter considers the possibility of there being greater recognition of environmental regulatory professions, a process that may already have begun.

The chapter is in four parts and draws upon initiatives and case studies from around the world. The first part provides background and context regarding environmental regulation and some of the drivers behind recruiting, training, and continuing professional development. The second part provides an insight into the current state of how environmental regulatory professionals are recruited, trained, and undertake continuing professional development. The third part looks at current indicators and trends impacting environmental regulatory professionals (including the regulatory profession more broadly). The fourth part – the conclusion – makes a number of observations regarding the benefits for environmental regulatory agencies more fully considering the various elements of the professional development of staff.

## Background

Environmental regulation is complex and multi-faceted. Therefore, environmental regulatory agencies (ERAs) must be flexible and adaptive while remaining cognizant of institutional resourcing and cultural limitations.

It is extremely difficult to find a single agency that is equipped and has the staff, resources, and mandate to respond to the various forms of non-compliance and illegality emanating from breaches of environmental regulation (BoER), environmental crime (EC), and transnational environmental crime (TEC). As a result, the majority of activities associated with responding to BoER – but especially so in terms of EC and TEC – are shared across three core agencies: police agencies, customs and border protection agencies, and environmental regulatory agencies (Pink, 2015b).[1]

Previous research which considered how these three core agencies, individually and collectively, applied law enforcement responses in the context of EC and TEC highlighted that organizational culture and preferences played a prominent role (Pink, 2015b). The research indicated that there were subsequent cultural challenges when mainstream law enforcement agencies (such as police agencies and customs and border agencies) and non-mainstream law enforcement agencies (such as environmental regulatory agencies) worked together. Reference to a lack of training or the inadequacy of training of environmental regulatory agency staff to undertake high-level enforcement work involving the use of coercive powers[2] was both directly and indirectly raised as both an issue and a barrier to interoperability (Pink, 2015b).

One way in which environmental regulatory agencies have attempted to address these challenges, while maximizing the effectiveness of their regulatory responses, is by ensuring that they have a highly skilled workforce in key operational positions. While challenges and difficulties around recruiting, training, and continuing professional development are not unique to environmental regulatory agencies, this chapter suggests that they encounter additional challenges (particularly in terms of the inspectorate function) when compared to other parts of the public service.[3] More specifically, the chapter suggests that these additional challenges are cultural and are compounded by the fact that some public service agencies/departments, which have principally been established to implement 'client-focused' programs, find themselves performing regulatory roles for a variety of reasons.

Even though the focus of this chapter is on considering improvements from the perspective of environmental regulatory agencies, from time to time references to models and approaches used by police agencies and customs and border agencies will be made for comparison purposes.

Before considering the current state, the following quote from the Organisation for Economic Co-operation and Development (OECD) emphasizes the importance placed upon the recruiting, training, and continuing professional development of regulatory and enforcement staff:

> Inspectors should be trained and managed to ensure professionalism, integrity, consistency and transparency: this requires substantial training, focusing not only on technical but also on generic inspection skills, and official guidelines for inspectors to help ensure consistency and fairness.
>
> (OECD, 2014b: 63)

1 For examples of the three core agencies coming together to combat specific forms of environmental crime and transnational environmental crime such as electronic waste and tropical timber, see Bisschop (2015: 81–90); for wildlife trafficking, see Wyatt (2013: 115–119).

2 Coercive powers tend to be 'police-like' powers, which include arresting suspects, executing search warrants (on people and premises), and the ability to compel persons to provide information and/or answers to questions.

3 In some countries, the public service is referred to as the civil service.

Equally, regulators themselves acknowledge the importance of staff capability, noting that

> a modern and effective regulator requires authorised officers with a high standard of competency and professionalism. The effectiveness of . . . a regulator will to a large extent be judged on the experience of business and community members who interact with . . . authorised officers, investigators and other field staff.
>
> (Krpan, 2011: 228–229)

## Current state

This section considers the issues of recruiting, training, and continuing professional development from the general to the specific. Its focus is on how environmental regulatory agencies are approaching these issues.

### *Recruiting*

Using Australia as an example, Table 11.1 highlights the differences in recruiting pathways into the three core agencies engaged in environmental regulation and enforcement.

The three core agencies have very different approaches to recruiting staff for regulatory or enforcement roles. It is clear that the core discipline of police agencies is involved with or directed toward enforcement work. In comparison, while not a core discipline, a more common and central theme for customs and border agencies is responding to serious non-compliance and involves enforcement. The variation within environmental regulatory agencies is by far the most extensive. As such, the remainder of this section will consider recruiting within environmental regulatory agencies in greater detail.

#### *Recruiting within the public service*

There are many similarities when recruiting within both the public sector and the private sector. This is because, at its most basic level, recruiting refers to the selection processes used to identify staff with the requisite knowledge, skills, and attributes to undertake roles that advance the objectives of the employer.

Similarly, recruiting within and across the public sector involves a number of similarities, including the use of common selection criteria.[4] Differences tend to relate to additional requirements around qualifications, skills, and experience for specialist or technical roles.

#### *Recruiting for regulatory, compliance, and enforcement roles*

There can be additional differences depending on the nature and focus of the particular public service agency undertaking the recruiting. For the purposes of this chapter, the three common pillars of public service activity are policy, programmatic, and regulatory.

4 For example, common selection criteria cover issues such as shapes strategic thinking, achieves results, exemplifies personal drive and integrity, cultivates productive working relationships, and communicates with influence. For more information, see http://www.apsc.gov.au/publications-and-media/current-publications/ses-jobs.

*Table 11.1* Approaches to Recruiting across the Three Core Agencies

| *Police* | *Customs* | *Environment* |
|---|---|---|
| For policing and investigation roles:<br>• *Recruitment* is a fixed process with high levels of consistency across the nine police forces in Australia | For enforcement and investigation roles:<br>• *Recruitment* is a fixed and single national process across Australia for the front-line border officers | For compliance and enforcement roles:<br>• *Recruitment* occurs via numerous streams, with differing focus and priority given to policy, programmatic, and regulatory/enforcement experience |
| Testing includes:<br>• Written assessments<br>• Psychometric assessments<br>• Physical assessments | Testing includes:<br>• Psychological aptitude<br>• Literacy and numeracy skill measurement<br>• Problem solving/teamwork aptitude assessment<br>• Broad life skills assessments<br>• Physical fitness increasing ahead of 'Border Force' concept | Testing includes:<br>• Written assessments<br>• Work-/scenario-based assessments |
| Educational requirements:<br>• Year 12/ matriculation | Educational requirements:<br>• No specific educational qualifications required | Educational requirements:<br>• Highly variable from nil to post-graduate qualifications |
| Additional information:<br>• Each police force has its own academy and most have a partnership with universities | Additional information:<br>• Customs has a single point of entry (Customs College from July 2015) | Additional information:<br>• The diversity is compounded due to the fact that the nine jurisdictions on average have four agencies with environmental regulatory and enforcement responsibilities – which quickly takes the number of agencies up to several dozen.<br>• This number climbs to many hundreds when the local level of government is added. |

Of particular relevance to this chapter is the fact that a number of recent publications (ANAO, 2014; IPAA, 2015; NZPC, 2014;[5] OECD, 2014a, 2014b; PC, 2014; PM&C, 2014a) have provided guidance by more clearly defining (in some areas, unequivocally so – e.g. permitting and environmental impact assessment [ANAO, 2014: 33–38]) what 'regulatory activities' are and which roles and functions within agencies are captured by the definitions and guidance. Whether agencies embrace this guidance and modify their operations, business models, and delivery methods is a different question and beyond the scope of this chapter.

5 Including the version it replaced, see ANAO (2007).

It is also important – for this chapter – to recognize that regulatory activities can be further split into those which are administrative and operational. As such, there are three broad options when recruiting staff for regulatory, compliance, and enforcement roles:

- Agencies recruit externally
- Agencies recruit internally
- Agencies choose to 'grow their own'

### *External recruiting*

When recruiting externally, the focus is usually more directed toward recruiting staff who already possess regulatory, compliance, and enforcement expertise. As a result, those undertaking the recruiting and the managers and executives that they represent prefer that this expertise be 'proven' in the sense that staff have or would be comfortable with undertaking regulatory and enforcement work in an *environmental* context. If this is not possible, the next best preference is to recruit staff from other regulatory or mainstream law enforcement agencies who can then transfer/translate their existing regulatory and enforcement experience and apply it in an *environmental* setting. The least preferred option is to recruit staff who have no regulatory or enforcement experience.

### *Internal recruiting*

When recruiting internally, in addition to the aforementioned factors, recruiters and managers will be looking for staff with skills, knowledge, and experience who possess a nexus with or can complement regulatory, compliance, and enforcement activities. For example, staff with scientific training may be well placed to undertake assessment and inspection work; staff with accounting and audit training may be well placed to perform monitoring and quality assurance activities.

### *Recruiting by 'growing their own'*

This method of recruiting is a variation on *internal recruiting*. The main difference is that it is more akin to skills transferral and transitioning non-regulatory or enforcement staff into regulatory or enforcement roles. This 'recruiting' often occurs as a result of organizational changes and/or the changing nature of the way in which environmental regulation is undertaken or delivered within and by the agency. Examples of the former occur when organizational restructures result in several organizational groups or divisions, with mixed disciplines, merging into a single regulatory and enforcement group or division. In this instance, non-regulatory or enforcement staff[6] are subsequently required to perform support or actual regulatory and enforcement roles. An example of the latter occurring would be when 'hands-on' activities undertaken by regulatory and enforcement officers within an agency are then delegated to another entity. These other entities could be a regulatory body in another level of government, a peak industry body, or a third party, and these

6 For examples of communicating and building capacity among non-inspectors within an environmental regulatory agency, see Marshall and Pink (2011).

officers often move from having operational practitioner roles to having roles which are more administrative in nature and reflect monitoring, auditing, and quality assurance of the regulatory delivery of the aforementioned entities.

## *Training*

This section considers training of staff who perform regulatory, compliance, and enforcement roles within environmental regulatory agencies. It specifically considers issues associated with generalist and specialist training, delivery methods and assessment, and the type and level of qualifications.

Again using Australia as an example, Table 11.2 highlights the differences in the initial training and qualifications for the three core agencies engaged in environmental regulation and enforcement.

*Table 11.2* Approaches to Initial Training and Qualifications across the Three Core Agencies

| *Police* | *Customs* | *Environment* |
|---|---|---|
| • *Initial training* occurs over a 12-month period at a police academy | • *Initial training* takes the form of a 6-month course at the Customs College combined with various work placements | • *Initial training* is highly variable, from nil to a 2- to 3-day awareness course up to approximately 6 months[7] to achieve a nationally accredited qualification (see immediately below) |
| • *Initial qualification* satisfies or substantially contributes toward a post-graduate qualification in Policing or Justice Studies | • *Initial qualification* comprises internal qualification only[8]<br>• At least one university in Australia offers post-graduate qualification in Border Control[9] | • *Initial qualification*, generally speaking, satisfies the accepted standard for compliance and enforcement practitioners is the Certificate IV in Government (Statutory Compliance) or Diploma in Government (Investigations) |
| Assessment method:<br>• Combination of examinations and competency based (portfolio of work) | Assessment method:<br>• Combination of classroom assessment and work-based practical assessments | Assessment method:<br>• Combination of classroom assessment and competency based (portfolio of work) |

7 This variability in duration depends on the intensity of the method of delivery and whether or not the participant can demonstrate and therefore access any credits/standing under the Recognition of Prior Learning (RPL) provisions.

8 Noting that many of the activities could be 'mapped to' and satisfy a number of the learning outcomes for various qualifications within the Government stream within the Australian Qualification and Training Framework (AQTF). For more information on the AQTF, see http://www.training.com.au/government-courses/.

9 For more information on these courses, see https://www.csu.edu.au/faculty/arts/centres/cces/courses.

The three core agencies have vastly different approaches to training staff for regulatory or enforcement roles. Moreover, the depth and breadth of regulatory, compliance, and enforcement roles undertaken by staff in environmental regulatory agencies means that determining, implementing, and maintaining generalist and specialist training is challenging. The remainder of this section will consider recruiting within environmental regulatory agencies in greater detail.

### *Generalist and specialist training*

Staff undertaking regulatory, compliance, and enforcement activities require various forms of training (Farmer, 2007; Van der Schraaf, 2005, 2008).

In relation to training and determining generalist standards and specialist requirements, it is important to map agency/departmental needs and roles against staff capability. Farmer states:

> It is first necessary to identify the key competencies necessary for staff to undertake the various tasks. It is, therefore, helpful to undertake a competency audit. This identifies the specific tasks of individual staff (permitting, inspection, personnel management, etc.) and what skills are necessary to deliver these tasks.
>
> (2007: 231)

By way of practical application, Van der Schraaf (2008) describes how the Dutch Environmental Inspectorate developed a strategic methodology for the capacity building of its inspectors. The initiative involved a 3-year plan which set capacity objectives for various competencies for its 550 inspectors. More specifically, each competency was further broken down in terms of content, scope, and corresponding qualification across three levels: 'operational, specialist, and super specialist' (Van der Schraaf, 2008: 247).

The training that staff require can span and be informed by a 'regulatory spectrum' (Pink, 2013).[10] The regulatory spectrum (or variations of it) is generally recognizable within environmental regulatory agencies, and it often assists in broadly describing groups and staff roles as involving activities such as:

- Education and outreach
- Licensing and permitting
- Monitoring and auditing
- Assessing compliance
- Responding to non-compliance
- Enforcement and litigation

It should also be noted that the regulatory work described in the aforementioned roles intersects, to a greater or lesser extent, with a number of other disciplines which include or relate to areas such as:

- Legal
- Investigative

10 See Diagram 4 (Pink, 2013), noting that this is referred to as 'the compliance and enforcement spectrum' (10).

- Scientific
- Supervisory and managerial
- Technical[11]

### *Generalist training*

Generalist training courses correlate with the activities/roles outlined across the regulatory spectrum (Pink, 2013: 10). The subject matter (theory, content, and practice) can be confined to a single function or two contiguous functions or might even involve full-spectrum training. Examples would include a course in Auditing, a course in Auditing of Licensing and Permit conditions, and the Certificate IV in Government (Statutory Compliance)[12] course, respectively.

## Overview of Case Study 1 – Australia

The Authorised Officer Training and Re-authorisation Program 2012/13 saw in excess of 80 staff within a provincial environment protection agency undertake training. Moreover, these staff occupied seven distinct roles (for authorized and unauthorized officers) – namely, environment protection officers, investigators, team leaders, managers, compliance strategists, planning officers, and staff responsible for regulatory programs.[13]

Conversely, while specialist training courses also correlate with the activities/roles outlined across the regulatory spectrum, they do so to a greater level of specificity in terms of both commodities and discrete disciplines. Continuing the auditing training example, a specialist course would relate to auditing which focused on the mining sector or even possibly a subset of the mining sector such as offshore petroleum or coal-seam gas.

Equally, and again continuing the Certificate IV in Government (Statutory Compliance) example from earlier, participants of that course can then advance and specialize within the specific discipline of investigations[14] and complete the Diploma in Government (Investigations).[15]

11 See also Farmer, 2007: 230.

12 The Certificate IV in Government (Statutory Compliance) is a qualification that covers the regulatory spectrum sufficiently to enable those who achieve the qualification to make a contribution in a number of functions and roles. For more information regarding learning outcomes of this course, see https://training.gov.au/Training/Details/PSP41412. The 'learning outcomes are the expression of the set of knowledge, skills and the application of the knowledge and skills a person has acquired and is able to demonstrate as a result of learning' (see AQF at http://www.aqf.edu.au/wp-content/uploads/2013/05/AQF_glossary_Jan2013.pdf).

13 See Hudson (2013).

14 With investigations being a function which, depending on the agency, can appear within the 'regulatory spectrum' either in Responding to Non-compliance or Enforcement and Litigation.

15 The Diploma in Government (Investigations) is a specialist qualification that covers the specific competencies required of persons responsible for the coordination and conduct of complex and protracted investigations and/or supervising other inspectorate or investigations staff. For more information concerning the outline, contents, and learning elements/outcomes of this course, see https://training.gov.au/Training/Details/PSP51704.

## Overview of Case Study 2: the Netherlands

Environmental prosecution training involves two to three staff within a provincial environment agency undertaking training, provided by the relevant prosecuting authority, which enables them to attend court in the capacity of a prosecutions officer who is able to progress and resolve matters on behalf of both the environmental agency and the prosecuting authority. This is extremely rare in environmental regulation.

In terms of the delivery method, training tends to be delivered face to face but is increasingly online[16] and in a combination of these two methods. The last decade has seen the traditional face-to-face classroom or lecture style of content delivery being supplemented by more interactive work-based scenarios and activities. Participants work through, and sometimes extend, the activities back into their workplace through completion of a qualification portfolio. This style of delivery feeds into an assessment which is more interested in meaningful learning and comprehension based upon whether or not the participant can actually use and apply the learning, as opposed to learning (information and processes) by rote in order to simply pass an exam and move on to the next, which can be pejoratively referred to as 'learn and forget'.

The change in the method of content delivery has seen a corresponding shift in assessment methods. Previous assessment, irrespective of the level of qualification, almost exclusively took the form of written exams. Written exams, or comprehensive written assignments, are still prominent in the higher (and especially post-graduate) qualifications, but assessments relating to vocational qualifications have become competency based. Under this form of assessment, a participant is deemed to be 'competent' or 'not yet competent'; this often involves demonstration of theory and applied knowledge.

The relative newness of environmental legislation, with most being introduced during the last 10 to 20 years (Bates, 2006; Du Rées, 2009); the complex scientific and technical elements of the legislation; and the particular nature of agency requirements have meant that training tends to require harnessing internal and external expertise. In relation to the use of internal experts, Jones and Honarto (2016) warn against 'prophet syndrome', which is a reference to the fact that despite a long career of successful experience and expertise, many people will not recognize and respect the expertise and skills of their immediate colleagues or countrymen and countrywomen.[17] When considering external expertise, this can come from academic institutions or consultants. On academic institutions, and based on the experiences of the South African environmental department, Jardine (2011) states that

> collaborating with tertiary education institutions can provide a successful model for delivering basic training to environmental inspectors on [the] condition that key aspects, such as standardisation, quality assurance, career development,

16 For example, the Environment Agency in England has over 300 courses for its staff ranging from 1 day to 1 week in duration, many of which use 'teach yourself' materials in CD-ROM format or via the department's intranet site (OECD, 2009: 159).

17 This, they say, can be a real obstacle for local trainers. It is often associated with various versions of sayings associated with someone being a prophet in his own land.

> academic credibility, accessibility and cost effectiveness are clearly defined, monitored and evaluated.
>
> (681)

Gemmell et al. (2016) note that both traditional consultancies and academic consultancies have often struggled to meet the needs of the regulator, especially at the more technical level. In an attempt to address this, they note that some consultancies have purposively:

> developed particular skills in education and communication . . . but at the core is a team of ex-regulators. This expert understanding of the regulatory regime allowed the consultants proactively to come up with ideas and proposals and to deliver a timely, fit for purpose output. This positive experience was very much related to their background in regulation.
>
> (130)[18]

To highlight this point, the Graduate Certificate in Environmental Compliance (GCEC) provides an example of a post-graduate qualification delivered in partnership between a tertiary/vocational institution and a university. The GCEC uses both face-to-face and online delivery and assessments which have written and work-based components.

### Overview of Case Study 3: Australia

This is a post-graduate Certificate in Environmental Compliance qualification in environmental compliance and enforcement (ECE), with three topics delivered online using the university's teaching and learning platform and the fourth topic (Investigating Environmental Crime) taught face to face during a 4-day intensive program with presenters who are experienced environmental (or mainstream law enforcement) investigators.[19]

## *Type and level of qualifications*

In terms of type, qualifications are either in house or external. In-house qualifications tend to be highly role and agency specific. They can often form part of an induction process (Farmer, 2007: 234) into the agency proper or when the staff member moves to another area within the agency. Generally speaking, they take the form of a Statement of Attendance and are not considered to be a formal qualification.[20] Instead, this is something that

18 Gemmell et al. also note that increasingly in contracts, regulatory clients will specify and require a named individual consultant as the lead or specialist input provider.

19 For more information on this course, see http://www.flinders.edu.au/courses/rules/postgrad/gcec.cfm.

20 The exception to this would be if the agency is a registered training organisation (RTO) or uses an RTO to endorse aspects of this training, noting that this is only possible when they matriculate into an approved training course.

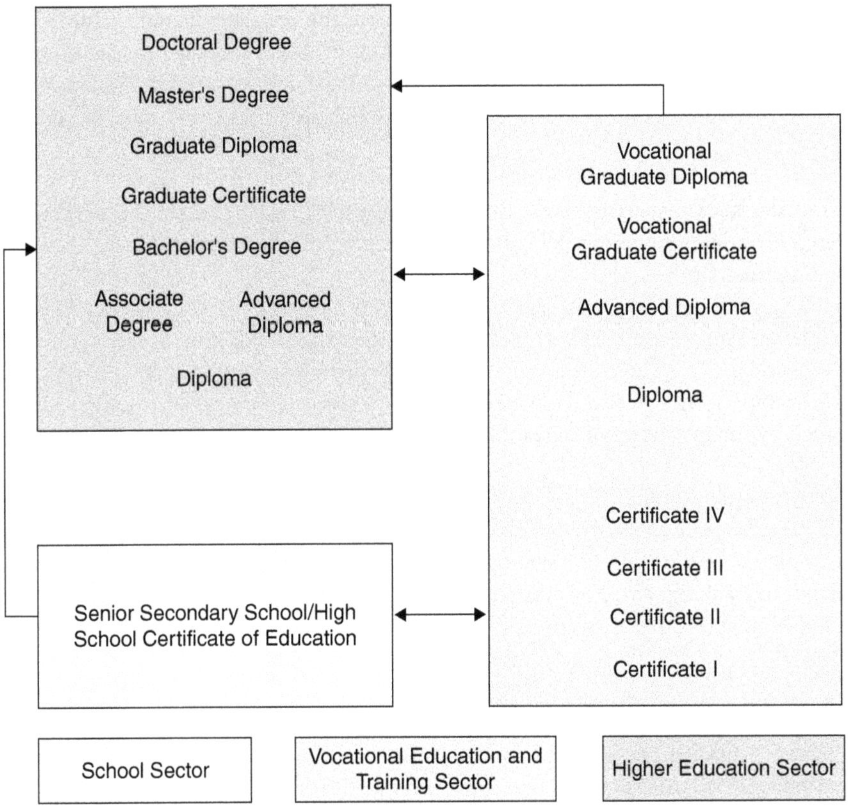


*Figure 11.1* Approaches to Recruiting across the Three Core Agencies

Source: adapted from Atlasindia (n.d.).

is endorsed on the staff member's personnel file. External qualifications, however, have broader application (discipline, function, sector, and industry) and rarely go to agency specificity, with exceptions coming from a few well-resourced and large environmental enforcement agencies with a commitment to training (see Farmer, 2007: 234–235).

In terms of level, qualifications vary greatly. Some training coordinators in ERAs advise that there are no qualification requirements for staff (even in clearly defined roles that deal with serious non-compliance and enforcement), while others indicate that there are prescriptive and mandatory post-graduate qualification requirements for similar roles. Figure 11.1 provides an example of the learning and qualification pathways available under the Australian Qualification Framework.

Anecdotally, qualifications can be a polarizing issue in an emerging area such as environmental regulation and enforcement. Some consider qualifications to be overrated, too theoretical, and not giving due regard to practical and 'life' experiences. However, the point is that qualifications, whether vocational or academic, provide a foundation from which practical experience can be added to develop a rounded and hopefully professional practitioner. The reverse can equally be true too, such that one does not preclude the other.

Sparrow[21] frequently highlights the importance of 'the regulatory craft' (2000)[22] and the benefits of the 'craftshop' approach to tool selection, problem solving, and regulatory interventions (2008). Sparrow's point, and the imagery associated with the craftsperson analogy, is not only that knowledge and skill are required but also that these must be continually honed and refined by practice.

Balancing theory and practice is necessary – especially so when providing training to adult learners in the workplace (Merriam, 2008; Mezirow and Taylor, 2009). This is reflected by the changes to training content delivery and assessment mentioned previously. On this issue, Taylor suggests that:

> Academic knowledge alone is insufficient to meet the development needs of regulatory professionals. . . . Thus although academic theory is used and discussed, at all times its role in improving practice is stressed. This emphasis on practical knowledge will be reinforced by the involvement of leading practitioners as guest lecturers on the programme. (1996: 41)

On a positive note, as Case Studies 1, 2, and 3 highlight, a number of agencies and countries, while taking different approaches, are developing comprehensive and innovative approaches to training staff. For more information, see also IMPEL (2003), Jardine (2011), Jones and Honarto (2016), and USEPA (n.d.).[23]

### *Continuing professional development*

This section considers the issue of continuing professional development in terms of how environmental regulatory agencies are approaching the issue and draws upon examples used within other professions.

Continuing with the Australian example, Table 11.3 highlights the differences in the approaches to continuing professional development across the three core agencies engaged in environmental regulation and enforcement.

There are substantial differences in the approaches to continuing professional development across the three core agencies engaged in environmental regulation and enforcement. The remainder of this section will consider recruiting within environmental regulatory agencies in greater detail.

### *What is continuing professional development?*

Continuing professional development (CPD)[24] is the means by which people maintain their knowledge and skills related to their professional roles. CPD can be self-directed (as part of self-development in terms of professional growth) or structured and involve a mandatory element (which is required to continue as a member of or to practice in a profession). While CPD activities and obligations are common to most professions, they range from

21 Malcolm Sparrow is Professor of the Practice of Public Management at the John F. Kennedy School of Government at Harvard University.

22 See Part II – The Emergence of Regulatory Craftsmanship, pp. 79–203.

23 In respect to the USEPA, see the work of the Office of Criminal Enforcement, Forensics and Training (OCEFT) at http://www2.epa.gov/aboutepa/about-office-enforcement-and-compliance-assurance-oeca#oceft.

24 CPD is sometimes referred to as continuing professional education (CPE).

*Table 11.3* Approaches to Continuing Professional Development across the Three Core Agencies

| *Police* | *Customs* | *Environment* |
|---|---|---|
| • Maintenance of current skills and currency of law<br>• Ongoing professional development as a police officer involves high-risk activities such as the use of firearms, use of force, and high-speed pursuit driving, etc.<br>• Progressing to other specialist streams and other work functions (e.g. detective, forensics, prosecution) | • Maintenance of current skills and currency of law<br>• Ongoing professional development as an officer progresses and streams to other work functions<br>• Specialist qualifications (Investigations, Operational Command, Technology [e.g. X-ray, ion scan], Dog Handler) | • Maintenance of current skills and currency of law<br>• To date (for most), this is non-existent or ad hoc<br>• Increasing interest in competency-based annual assessments<br>• Specialization tends to be across the various:<br>  • Environmental commodities (air, water, waste, land, etc.) and/or by<br>  • Discipline (investigations, inspections, monitoring/ auditing) |

self-directed and informal to structured and formal. Regardless of approach, its purpose is to advance learning and competence to practice.

### *What constitutes a profession?*

General community expectations and the existing literature (Kizlik, n.d.), including the charters and mission statements (CIMA, n.d.) of professional associations, suggest that three key components assist in defining a profession:

- Qualifications, whether academic or technical;
- Working to agreed standards and a commitment to continuing professional development; and
- That the activities of the profession are overseen or supported by a dedicated/discrete/ specific identifiable professional association or 'peak'[25] trade or industry body.

In research relating to hazardous waste enforcement, White and Heckenberg (2012) suggest that:

> The hallmarks of a profession include occupational autonomy, pre-service and continued professional development in terms of training and education, social status, and an ethos of service to the community. For those working in the broad area of environmental law enforcement, including the policing of hazardous waste disposal, work-related issues included, among other things, financial remuneration, status, a career path and adequate professional training.
>
> (12)

25 'Peak' being an term used widely in Australia to describe a leading or major industry or sectoral representative body.

The three key components and the description written by White and Heckenberg (2012) can be directly aligned with the literature on communities of practice (CoP).[26] Lave and Wenger (1998) suggest that a CoP requires three components: domain, community, and practice:

- *Domain:* 'A CoP has an identity defined by a shared domain of interest. . . . Membership implies a commitment to the domain.'
- *Community:* 'A necessary component is that members of a specific domain interact and engage in shared activities, help each other, and share information with each other.' 'They build relationships that enable them to learn from each other. In this way, merely sharing the same job does not necessitate a CoP.'
- *Practice:* 'A CoP is not just people who have an interest in something (e.g. sports or agriculture practices). The third requirement for a CoP is that the members are *practitioners*.'

(Lave and Wenger, n.d.)

### *Approaches to continuing professional development by established professions*

Lawyers, accountants, and engineers are professions that have made CPD a core part of their profession. This sample group, like other professions, tends to be composed of well-established and recognized professions in their own right. Moreover, these professions are recognized and associated as being an identifiable group, and membership of the group requires certain pre-conditions such as existing academic or technical qualifications. Members are actively practicing in their field or discipline, and they are required to undertake activities that maintain the requisite knowledge and skill sets of the profession, with the latter often, but not exclusively, facilitated or supported by a professional or peak industry body or association.

The legal profession provides an example of an approach to CPD. In many parts of the world, lawyers who have undertaken the necessary academic and practical training and who have then been admitted to practice[27] are required to maintain professional learning. This is done through various forms of CPD where as part of their membership to their peak or industry body, they must achieve a certain number of CPD points/credits per year. These CPD points/credits are earned by attending seminars, conferences, and professional short courses.

### *Approaches to continuing professional development by environmental regulators*

As the previous section on training outlined, many ERAs are still determining, developing, or consolidating their training requirements. As this is a more immediate need, most ERAs have not yet commenced meaningful work in the area of CPD. While some agencies have made modest efforts in the area of CPD for regulatory staff, these bespoke and internal endeavors are the exception. Most ERAs are limited to accessing the more general

26 See also Lave and Wenger, 1991; Wenger et al., 2002, 2011).
27 Admitted to practice in this context is a reference to the 'bar table' or 'bench' in a court of law.

opportunities provided or facilitated by the environmental enforcement networks they are associated with.

However, several examples of CPD do exist. Some of the training case studies mentioned previously have aspects or components which go to CPD.[28] We now briefly consider CPD initiatives specifically developed for ERA practitioners, specialists, managers, and executives.

## Overview of Case Study 4: New Zealand

The *Basic Investigative Skills for Local Government Reference Manual* has been developed and updated to provide assistance and direction to staff (outside of formal accredited training) as part of continuing professional development in the areas of investigative skills.[29]

## Overview of Case Study 5: Australia

The Expertise Framework Program provides a mechanism which identifies, recognizes, and rewards experts in environmental areas (air quality, water quality, contaminated land, odor, noise, and the waste industrial area). Experts are given additional responsibilities in terms of advice provision, staff mentoring, and dealing with the media. Part of the recognition comes with some additional funding to attend conferences and seminars for experts to present in their area of expertise and practice.[30]

## Overview of Case Study 6: Belgium

The Environmental Inspectors Help Desk assists local environmental supervisors/inspectors. The Help Desk has two staff providing technical expertise and support to generalist environmental supervisors and inspectors. In addition to providing telephone and online support for queries, the Help Desk also distributes a monthly digital newsletter which provides information on issues such as changes to legislation and upcoming training courses.[31]

The following case studies contribute to the continuing professional development of managers and executives.

## Overview of Case Study 7: the Netherlands

The Dutch Environment and Transport Inspectorate runs a 2-day workshop every 6 months with team leaders/managers and senior executives to advance the regulatory profession within the agency through 'action learning'. A particular focus of these events is how to learn from the field 'what the real problems actually are' and how middle and upper management can assist in terms of implementation.

28 By way of example, the Dutch Environment Inspectorate (VROM) allocated €1100 and 10 working days annually per inspector for continuing professional development/capacity building (OECD, 2009: 146).

29 See Environment Waikato (2009).

30 For more information on the Expertise Frameworks, see http://www.epa.vic.gov.au/about-us/expertise-framework-program.

31 See De Schutter (2014).

### Overview of Case Study 8: international (delivered in the United States and Australasia)

Professor Malcolm Sparrow runs courses for managers and senior executives in the form of the Strategic Management of Regulatory and Enforcement Agencies course[32] in the United States (through Harvard University) and the Managing Regulation, Enforcement and Compliance course[33] in Australasia (through the Australia and New Zealand School of Government [ANZSOG]).

Within established professions (e.g. lawyers, accountants, and engineers), continuing professional development is inseparable from recognition of the profession as a distinct field of labor, endeavor, and practice. It is also evident that being a *practitioner* and *practicing* is a central part of identifying with a profession as much as it is being part of a community of practice.

## Indicators and trends

The previous discussion has highlighted that the three core agencies have widely differing approaches to recruiting, training, and continuing the professional development of regulatory or enforcement staff. This occurs at a time when the three core agencies are increasingly required to work together in order to effectively and efficiently respond to BoER, EC, and TEC (Pink, 2015b; Pink and White, 2015).

### *Drivers for enhancing regulatory professionalism*

The last few years have seen a number of widespread activities that have resulted in a greater focus on an identifiable professional stream for regulators generally and environmental regulators specifically.

### *Drivers for enhancing general regulatory professionalism*

Delivery of regulatory services as a public administration function has gained increased notice both internationally and in Australia, as have issues associated with the performance of regulators.

In the international context, the OECD has played a key role through a number of publications, including:

- The Recommendation of the Council on Regulatory Policy and Governance (OECD, 2012),
- Regulatory Enforcement and Inspections (OECD, 2014b), and
- The Governance of Regulators (OECD, 2014a).

32 For more information on this course, see https://exed.hks.harvard.edu/Programs/smre/overview.aspx.
33 For more information on this course, see https://www.anzsog.edu.au/executive-workshops/executive-workshops/managing-regulation-enforcement-and-compliance.

In Australasia, the Australian and New Zealand national governments have released a number of publications, including:

- The Regulatory Professional Capability Guidance (IPAA, 2015),
- The Australian Government Guide to Regulation (PM&C, 2014a),
- The Regulatory Audit Framework (PC, 2014),
- The Regulator Performance Framework (PM&C, 2014b),
- Regulatory Institutions and Practices (NZPC, 2014),
- Achieving the Right Balance (ANAO, 2014),
- Regulator Engagement with Small Business: Research Report (PC, 2013),
- Performance Benchmarking of Australian Business Regulation: The Role of Local Government as Regulator: Research Report Volume I and Volume II (PC, 2012), and
- Achieving Compliance: a Guide for Compliance Agencies in New Zealand (CCCP, 2011).

### *Drivers for enhancing environmental regulatory professionalism*

Specific drivers can then further inform the operating environment for regulators. In response, regulators then develop documents and supporting material to a finer level of detail for application in specific regulatory domains (e.g. consumer protection, taxation, and transport). In the area of environmental regulation and enforcement, this has occurred through initiatives and publications such as:

- The Modern Regulator Improvement Tool (AELERT, 2015),
- Choosing appropriate interventions alongside inspections to ensure compliance and achieve environmental outcomes: Phase 1 – Developing principles and features of a model for choosing interventions (IMPEL, 2013),
- The National Environmental Security Task Force: Bringing Compliance and Enforcement Agencies Together to Maintain Environmental Security (Interpol, 2012),
- The Principles of Environmental Compliance and Enforcement Handbook (INECE, 2009), and
- Best practices concerning training and qualification for environmental inspectors (IMPEL, 2003).

### *Role and influence of environmental enforcement networks*

During the last 20 years when attempting to build capability and capacity, environmental regulatory agencies have looked to their peers for support and guidance (Farmer, 2007; Faure et al., 2015; Pink, 2011, 2015a). Notably, training of regulatory and enforcement staff has been a common and recurring issue raised by member agencies (Gemmell and Circelli, 2015; INECE, 2011; Jardine, 2011; Klein, 2005; Pink, 2008; Van der Schraaf, 2008) with environmental enforcement networks.

Research into environmental enforcement networks (EENs), including the analysis of their mission statements, charters, and activities, reveals that EENs have made training and capacity building of staff prominent areas of focus and attention (Farmer, 2007; Pink, 2010, 2015a).

For example, at the international level, during its triennial conference in Cape Town, South Africa, in 2008, the International Network for Environmental Compliance and

Enforcement (INECE) established the International Network for Environmental Compliance Training Professionals (2008: 4). This group 'is a practitioner knowledge community that shares information and best practices, supports trainer education and exchanges, and promotes the importance of effective environmental compliance training' (INECE, n.d.). At its next conference in 2011 in Whistler, Canada, INECE dedicated a stream to the 'Development of Core Competency for Environmental Compliance Professionals' (INECE, 2011: 121–124).

Similarly, at the regional level, Gemmell and Circelli (2015) describe how the Australasian Environmental Law Enforcement and Regulators neTwork (AELERT) 'has used its collective membership to review available T&D [training and development] programmes for the specialised skills necessary for modern regulatory practitioners' (182). Moving to practical implementation, AELERT, through leadership provided by two member agencies, has developed the AELERT Professional Development & Training Program (the AELERT PD&TP). The AELERT PD&TP offers a suite of operational, technical, and regulatory training, which is[34]

> delivered on a cost-recovery basis to other network members, and is able to be quickly tailored to reflect any individual strategic development focus and/or to account for particular jurisdictional environmental statues. The network allows for this programme to remain in the close control of the regulators that need it, and provide additional scope and scale to ensure it remains viable over time.
>
> (Gemmell and Circelli, 2015: 182)

### *Establishing an environmental regulatory profession*

Two questions emerge from the considerations presented in this chapter:

- Is environmental regulation a profession in its own right?
- If not, then what further work might be required to make it so?

Definitive answers to these questions are beyond the scope of this chapter. They are, however, questions that would benefit from a discourse between practitioners, academics, training providers, and professional associations. Therefore, in an attempt to commence such a discourse (and by using the aforementioned three key components that assist in defining a profession as a frame), the following observations are offered. Specifically, it is suggested that, in terms of:

- 'qualifications, whether academic or technical', this is probably the area that is most advanced across the board within environmental regulatory agencies. It is also an area which can be leveraged relatively quickly.
- 'working to agreed standards, and a commitment to continuing professional development', this is an area where there is increasing interest within environmental regulatory

34 In 4 years of operation between 2011–2012 and 2014–2015 (the first of which was the pilot), the AELERT PD&TP has delivered over 148 training and awareness courses/sessions to over 2477 staff from member agencies in nearly every member jurisdiction across Australasia. During this time, the AELERT PD&TP has significantly expanded and now offers 17 different courses. For more information on the various courses, see http://pdt.aelert.com.au/.

agencies, but as yet commitment to continuing professional development is patchy and ad hoc. It is likely that this area will progress when greater consistency has been achieved in the area of qualifications.

- 'the activities of the profession are overseen or supported by a dedicated/discrete/specific and identifiable professional association or peak body' – first, most environmental regulatory agencies are connected to and supported by a variety of EENs.[35] Second, the majority of EENs operate at an informal or semi-formal level, and even those that operate at a formal or highly formal level do so at an agency, not individual member, level.

While much of the foundational work is in place for an environmental regulatory profession to be established in its own right, there is still further work and research to be done to make this a reality. It is anticipated that one of the most significant challenges will be moving to a professional association model which has membership fees (usually joining and annual thereafter) which are payable by the individual practitioner. An interesting situation could occur where at the same time that practitioners are being asked to put a personal value on 'their profession', they will be asking others to recognize it as a stand-alone profession.[36]

## Conclusion

This chapter has demonstrated that dealing with breaches of environmental regulation, and responding to instances of environmental crime and transnational environmental crime, is a complex and multi-faceted area of operations for environmental regulatory agencies. It is also an area of operations that increasingly requires public servants in environmental regulatory agencies to work alongside more highly trained mainstream law enforcement agencies such as police agencies and customs and border agencies.

The differences in training type and intensity between these agencies lead to increased challenges when environmental regulatory agencies, which have been established to implement 'client-focused' policy and programs, find their regulatory roles now requiring them to adopt adversarial postures. More specifically, these coercive powers are often used when working alongside mainstream law enforcement agencies as part of a joint investigation.[37] This juxtaposition of roles reinforces the importance of improving the capacity and capability of environmental regulatory agency staff.

A trained, skilled, motivated, and well-maintained workforce has multiple benefits. There are significant benefits across environmental, social, and economic activities when environmental law is implemented effectively. This chapter offers a starting point for the discourse and ongoing research into advancing environmental regulatory professionalism.

35 There are at least 20 major environmental enforcement networks around the world. They operate at sub-national, national, regional, and international levels, and their focus can be shaped by commodity, geographic, or regulatory discipline. See Pink and Bartel (2015).

36 A good example of a profession emerging in the last 20 years is that of the Professional Intelligence Analyst. Staff were originally seen as data entry personnel or collators. With established and industry-accepted training, a commitment to CPD, establishment of peak bodies at the national and international level and, perhaps most critically, their ability to demonstrate where their role has added value, a 'profession' emerged. See, for example, the Australian Institute of Professional Intelligence Officers at http://www.aipio.asn.au/ and the International Association of Law Enforcement Intelligence Analysts at http://www.ialeia.org/.

37 Joint investigations are also referred to as multi-disciplinary teams or task forces.

## References

Australasian Environmental Enforcement and Regulators neTwork (AELERT) (2015) *Modern regulator improvement tool – An introduction* [Video presentation]. Retrieved from https://vimeo.com/120322944.

Australian National Audit Office (ANAO) (2007) *Administering Regulation: Better Practice Guide*, Canberra: Author.

Australian National Audit Office (ANAO) (2014) *Administering Regulation: Achieving the Right Balance – Better Practice Guide*, Canberra: Author.

Atlasindia (n.d.) *Australia education system: Australian qualifications frameworks*. Retrieved from http://www.atlasindia.net/study-abroad-australia-education-system.htm.

Bates, G. (2006) *Environmental Law in Australia*, 6th edition, Sydney: LexisNexis Butterworths.

Bisschop, L. (2015) *Governance of the Illegal Trade in E-Waste and Tropical Timber: Case Studies on Transnational Environmental Crime*, Farnham, England: Ashgate.

Chartered Institute of Management Accountants (CIMA) (n.d.). *What makes you a professional?* Retrieved from http://www.cimaglobal.com/Documents/Professionalism%20%282%29%20pdf.pdf.

Compliance Common Capability Programme (CCCP) (2011) *Achieving Compliance: A Guide for Compliance Agencies in New Zealand*, Wellington: Author.

De Schutter, G. (2014) 'Capacity building within environmental enforcement', Paper presented at PIH – Antwerp, Antwerp, Belgium, 4 July 2014.

Du Rées, H. (2009) 'Can criminal law protect the environment?' In R. White (ed.), *Environmental Crime: A Reader*, Cullompton, England: Willan.

Environment Waikato (2009) *Basic Investigative Skills for Local Government: With Particular Emphasis on Enforcement of the Resource Management Act*, Waikato: Author.

Farmer, A. (2007) *Handbook of Environmental Protection and Enforcement: Principles and Practice*, London: Earthscan.

Faure, M., De Smedt, P. and Stas, A. (eds.) (2015) *Environmental Enforcement Networks: Concepts, Implementation and Effectiveness*, Cheltenham: England, Edward Elgar.

Gemmell, C., Bingham, S. and Isarin, N. (2016) 'Collaboration and consultancy: Tackling environmental crime and delivering environmental protection'. In G. Pink and R. White (eds.) *Environmental Crime and Collaborative State Intervention*, Basingstoke, England: Palgrave Macmillan, pp. 119–137.

Gemmell, C. and Circelli, T. (2015) 'Environmental regulation and enforcement networks operating in tandem: A very effective vehicle for driving efficiencies and facilitating knowledge exchange and transfer'. In M. Faure, P. De Smedt and A. Stas (eds.) *Environmental Enforcement Networks: Concepts, Implementation and Effectiveness*, Cheltenham, England: Edward Elgar, pp. 119–137.

Hudson, J. (2013) 'Authorised Officer Training & Re-authorisation Program 2012/13', Paper presented at the Australasian Environmental Law Enforcement and Regulators neTwork Conference, Melbourne, Australia, 13–14 November 2013.

European Union Network for the Implementation and Enforcement of Environmental Law (IMPEL) (2003) *Best Practices Concerning Training and Qualification for Environmental Inspectors*, Brussels: Author.

European Union Network for the Implementation and Enforcement of Environmental Law (IMPEL) (2013) *Choosing Appropriate Interventions Alongside Inspections to Ensure Compliance and Achieve Environmental Outcomes: Phase 1 – Developing Principles and Features of a Model for Choosing Interventions*, Brussels: Author.

Institute of Public Administration Australia (IPAA) (2015) *Regulatory Professional Capability Guidance*, Canberra: Author.

International Network for Environmental Compliance and Enforcement (INECE) (2008) *Cape Town Statement*, Washington, DC: Author, pp. 3–5.

International Network for Environmental Compliance and Enforcement (INECE) (2009) *Principles of Environmental Compliance and Enforcement Handbook*, Washington, DC: Author.

International Network for Environmental Compliance and Enforcement (INECE) (2011) *Workshop F5: Development of Core Competency for Environmental Compliance Professionals*, Washington, DC: Author, pp. 121–124.

International Network for Environmental Compliance and Enforcement (INECE) (n.d.). *International Network for Environmental Compliance Training Professionals*. Retrieved from http://inece.org/topics/capacity-building/trainers-network/.

International Criminal Police Organisation (Interpol) ((2012) *National Environmental Security Task Force: Bringing Compliance and Enforcement Agencies Together to Maintain Environmental Security*, Lyon, France: Author.

Jardine, M. (2011) 'Collaborating with tertiary education institutions to provide basic training to environmental management inspectors', *9th International Conference on Environmental Compliance and Enforcement*, Whistler, British Columbia, Canada, 24 June 2011: Proceedings, Washington, DC: INECE, pp. 681–690.

Jones, D. and Honarto, I. (2016) 'Capacity building and collaboration: Enforcement training to build capacity that ensures environmental protection'. In G. Pink and R. White (eds.) *Environmental Crime and Collaborative State Intervention*, Basingstoke, England: Palgrave Macmillan, pp. 39–56.

Kizlik, B. (n.d.) *What makes a profession?* Retrieved from http://www.adprima.com/profession.htm.

Klein, W. (2005) 'Minimum criteria for a professional environmental enforcement process'. In INCE (ed.) *7th International Conference on Environmental Compliance and Enforcement: 9–15 April 2005, Marrakech, Morocco, Proceedings Volume 1*, Washington, DC: INECE.

Krpan, S. (2011) *Compliance and Enforcement Review: A review of EPA Victoria's approach*, Melbourne, Australia: EPA, February 2011.

Lave, J. and Wenger, E. (1991) *Situated Learning: Legitimate Peripheral Participation*, Cambridge: Cambridge University Press.

Lave, J. and Wenger, E. (1998) *Communities of Practice: Learning, Meaning, and Identity*, Cambridge: Cambridge University Press.

Lave, J. and Wenger, E. (n.d.) *Learning theories: Communities of practice*. Retrieved from http://www.learning-theories.com/communities-of-practice-lave-and-wenger.html.

Marshall, M. and Pink, G. (2011), 'Internal communication strategies for building capacity among non-inspectors'. In *9th International Conference on Environmental Compliance and Enforcement: 24 June 2011*, Whistler, British Columbia, Canada: Proceedings, Washington DC: INECE, pp. 704–716.

Merriam, S. (2008) 'Adult learning theory for the twenty-first century', *New Directions for Adult and Continuing Education*, **2008**: 93–98.

Mezirow, J. and Taylor, E. (2009) *Transformative Learning in Practice: Insights from Community, Workplace, and Higher Education*, Chichester, England: Wiley.

New Zealand Productivity Commission (NZPC) (2014) *Regulatory Institutions and Practices*, Wellington: NZPC.

Organisation for Economic Co-operation and Development (OECD) (2009) *Ensuring Environmental Compliance: Trends and Good Practices*, Paris: OECD Publishing.

Organisation for Economic Co-operation and Development (OECD) (2012) *Recommendation of the Council on Regulatory Policy and Governance*, Paris: OECD Publishing.

Organisation for Economic Co-operation and Development (OECD) (2014a) *The Governance of Regulators, OECD Best Practice Principles for Regulatory Policy*, Paris: OECD Publishing.

Organisation for Economic Co-operation and Development (OECD) (2014b) *Regulatory Enforcement and Inspections, OECD Best Practice Principles for Regulatory Policy*, Paris: OECD Publishing.

Productivity Commission (PC) (2012) *Performance Benchmarking of Australian Business Regulation: The Role of Local Government as Regulator: Research Report Volume I and Volume II*, Canberra: Author.

Productivity Commission (PC) (2013) *Regulator Engagement with Small Business: Research Report*, Canberra: Author.

Productivity Commission (PC) (2014) *Regulator Audit Framework*, Canberra: Author.

Pink, G. (2008) 'Building regulatory capacity in environmental agencies: Through tailored training'. In J. Gerardu, D. Jones, S. Reeves, T. Whitehouse and D. Zaelke (eds.). *8th International Conference on Environmental Compliance and Enforcement: 5–11 April 2008 Cape Town, South Africa, Proceedings*, London: Cameron May Ltd., pp. 225–233.

Pink, G. (2010) 'Environmental enforcement networks: A qualitative analysis', unpublished master's thesis. Retrieved from http://ssrn.com/abstract=1803179.

Pink, G. (2011) 'Assessing the utility of environmental enforcement networks: Maximising benefits to members'. In J. Gerardu, R. Grabiel, B. Koparova, L. Markowitz and D. Zaelke (eds.). *9th International Conference on Environmental Compliance and Enforcement: 24 June 2011, Whistler, British Columbia*, Washington, DC: International Network for Environmental Compliance and Enforcement, pp. 797–804.

Pink, G. (2013) *Law enforcement responses to transnational environmental crime: Choices, challenges and culture*, Transnational Environmental Crime Project Working Paper 4/2013, Department of International Relations, Australian National University Canberra.

Pink, G. (2015a) 'Environmental enforcement networks: Theory, practice and potential'. In M. Faure, P., De Smedt and A. Stas (eds.) *Environmental Enforcement Networks: Concepts, Implementation and Effectiveness*, Cheltenham, England: Edward Elgar, pp. 234–251.

Pink, G. (2015b) 'Regulatory responses to transnational environmental crime: An overview of choices, challenges and culture'. In T. Spapens, R. White and W. Huisman (eds.) *Environmental Crime and the World: Global Issues in Green Enforcement and Criminology*, Farnham, England: Ashgate, pp. 101–123.

Pink, G. and Bartel, R. (2015) 'Regulator networks: Collaborative agency approaches to the implementation and enforcement of environmental law', In P. Martin and A. Kennedy (eds.) *Implementation of Environmental Law*, Cheltenham, England: Edward Elgar, pp. 1–20.

Pink, G. and White, R. (2015) 'What is collaboration and why does it matter?' In G. Pink and R. White (eds.) *Environmental Crime and Collaborative State Intervention*, Hampshire: Palgrave Macmillan, pp. 26–38.

Prime Minister and Cabinet (PM&C) (2014a) *Australian Government Guide to Regulation*, Canberra: Author.

Prime Minister and Cabinet (PM&C) (2014b) *Regulator Performance Framework*, Canberra: Author.

Sparrow, M. (2000) *The Regulatory Craft: Controlling Risks, Solving Problems, and Managing Compliance*, Washington, DC: Brookings Institution Press.

Sparrow, M. (2008) *The Character of Harms: Operational Challenges in Control*, New York: Cambridge University Press.

Taylor, M. (1996) Are good compliance officers made or are they born? *The Compliance Digest*, April/June, pp. 40–42.

United States Environment Protection Agency (USEPA) (n.d.) *National Enforcement Investigations Center*. Retrieved from http://www2.epa.gov/enforcement/national-enforcement-investigations-center-neic.

Van der Schraaf, A. (2005) 'The compliance strategy in the Netherlands'. In J. Gerardu, D. Jones, K. Markowitz and D. Zaelke, *7th International Conference on Environmental Compliance and Enforcement: 9–15 April 2005, Marrakech, Morocco, Proceedings Volume 1*, Washington DC: INECE, pp. 89–94.

Van der Schraaf, A. (2008) 'Capacity building in the Dutch Inspectorate: Bridging the gap'. In J. Gerardu, D. Jones, K. Markowitz and D. Zaelke, *8th International Conference on*

*Environmental Compliance and Enforcement: 5–11 April 2008 Cape Town, South Africa, Proceedings*, London: Cameron May Ltd., pp. 225–233.

Wenger, E., McDermott, R. and Snyder, W. (2002) *Cultivating Communities of Practice: A Guide to Managing Knowledge*, Boston: Harvard Business School Publishing.

Wenger, E., Trayner, B. and de Laat, M. (2011) *Promoting and Assessing Value Creation in Communities and Networks: A Conceptual Framework*, Ruud de Moor Centrum, Open Universiteit, Rapport 18 2011. Retrieved from http://www.open.ou.nl/rslmlt/Wenger_Trayner_DeLaat_Value_creation.pdf.

White, R. and Heckenberg, D. (2012) *Policing hazardous waste disposal: Key trends and issues*, Briefing Paper No. 7. Retrieved from http://www.utas.edu.au/__data/assets/pdf_file/0018/284202/Briefing_Paper_7_-_Policing_Hazardous_Waste_Disposal_Key_Trends_and_Issues_-_July_2012.pdf.

Wyatt, T. (2013) *Wildlife Trafficking: A Deconstruction of the Crime, the Victims, and the Offenders*, Basingstoke, England: Palgrave Macmillan.

# 12 Examining secondary ecological disorganization from wildlife harms

*Michael J. Lynch, Michael A. Long, Kimberly L. Barrett and Paul B. Stretesky*

## Introduction

Green criminologists have successfully demonstrated that a variety of harms that non-human animals endure are a result of human activities. Many of the more compelling descriptions of harm in the literature focus on poaching and wildlife trafficking. While it is clear that a significant volume of wildlife harm is a direct result of humans, indirect consequences – that is, those that are a result of ecological destruction – also exist but have not yet been sufficiently examined by green criminologists. Importantly, ecological destruction feeds back to ecosystems and causes further ecosystem and wildlife harm. In the present discussion, we draw attention to these indirect wildlife harms that stem from ecological disorganization through systemic feedback and how indirect wildlife and ecosystem harms intersect within the context of ecosystems to produce secondary ecological harms. In exploring the analysis of secondary ecological harms, we also draw attention to the need for a political economic analysis of those harms which illustrates how wildlife harm and secondary ecological harm produce forms of ecological disorganization tied to the expansion of capitalism and the capitalist treadmill of production.

## Examining secondary ecological disorganization from wildlife harms

The study of harms against non-human animals has become a central concern within green criminology (Beirne, 2007; Beirne and South, 2007; Cazaux, 2007; Ngoc and Wyatt, 2013; Nurse, 2013; Regan, 2007; Wyatt, 2009, 2011, 2013; Yates, 2007). The core theoretical issues associated with harming non-human animals were well defined by Beirne (1999), who identified how examinations of non-human animal harms could be accomplished within criminology while addressing important criminological issues such as the definition of crime. A number of studies have built upon that approach by exploring specific harms against non-human animals that often involve forms of violence initiated by humans (Cazaux, 1999; Hughes and Lawson, 2011; Ngoc and Wyatt, 2013; Nurse, 2013; Sollund, 2013; Wyatt, 2009, 2013; Yates et al., 2001). These studies include research on poaching, hunting, wildlife trade and animal abuse.

Green criminologists have noted ways in which wildlife trade impacts ecosystems indirectly through, for example, introduction of invasive species and diseases (White and Heckenberg, 2014: 131) and have explained how wildlife trafficking victimizes humans, the state, non-human animals, plants and the environment (Wyatt, 2013: 59–81). We contribute to this literature by exploring, in detail, the ecological context in which non-human animal harms occur and how that context can amplify non-human animal harms by impeding ecosystem stability and producing additional harm to ecosystems and wildlife. Here, we label that additional form of harm *secondary ecological harm*. Within the context of ecological systems analysis, harms against ecosystems and wildlife can produce ecological feedback mechanisms that amplify ecological harm and generate secondary ecological harm. For example, when a wildlife species is harmed directly (for example, poached), that harm can generate secondary impacts on ecosystems that threaten ecosystem stability and viability, producing further wildlife harm that may also threaten species viability.

This analysis explores the concept of secondary ecological harm against wildlife. To illustrate this point, we draw attention to relevant biological and ecological science research that has examined the effects of species loss and richness on ecosystem stability. Of particular importance in those studies is the relationship between species endangerment and ecosystem sustainability and viability. In drawing attention to that connection, a broader contextual understanding of harms against wildlife emerges in which a greater spectrum of harms posed by harming wildlife can be elucidated. Before beginning that review, we examine Beirne's (1999) position on non-speciesist criminology as one of the anchoring points for such an analysis. After reviewing the relevant biological and ecological literature, we examine how political economic conditions set this harm process in motion, how that political economic context explains the origins of these harms, and the role capitalism plays in producing forms of ecological disorganization that facilitate these harms.

## The relevance of criminological studies of non-human animal harm

Beirne (1999) produced the first significant and perhaps the most important theoretical discussion of the relevance of studies of harms against non-human animals in the green criminological literature. At the time that the article was published, Beirne observed that no major criminological journal had ever published an article on animal harm. Beirne also noted that criminologists had yet to offer a cogent theoretical analysis of animal abuse and that the omission of animal abuse as a form of crime limited the criminological understanding of crime and violence. Beirne linked the tendency to exclude animals as an object of criminological study to criminology and law's propensity to construct harm in anthropocentric or human-centered terms (120). Given their anthropocentric orientations, criminology and law were largely restricted to views of animals as property/commodities (121) – or as indicators of interhuman conflict and violence – and to biosocial criminology's effort to produce generalizations about human behavior from animal behavior studies (122).

Legally, abuse of animals has long been addressed and codified in numerous legal statutes (Beirne, 1999: 126). Those statutes, however, are restrictive with respect to the types of animal harms they recognize: numerous acts of animal cruelty are omitted from legal statutes as acceptable social practices (Beirne, 1999: 128). Given these omissions, Beirne suggested that the problem for criminologists is defining the scope of animal abuse so that it can be defined as crime for the purpose of criminological investigations of animal abuse. In this sense, Beirne argues that animals lack 'standing' as legal or criminological subjects. In that argument, Beirne (1999: 130) draws attention to creating a criminologically relevant understanding of the definition of animal harm and crime as the infliction of intentional suffering on animals by humans. Beirne reviews several arguments (for example, utilitarianism, animal rights and feminist theory) to support this contention and emphasizes:

> A criminology that ignores animal abuse will be a speciesist discourse utterly irrelevant to the understanding of much harm and suffering inflicted by humans on nonhuman, but nevertheless valuable, forms of life. Rather than cede the study of it to other disciplines, criminologists should with confidence apply their theoretical expertise to the understanding of animal abuse.
>
> (1999: 140)

The idea that criminology must resist becoming speciesist has been well received by green criminologists and has promoted the development of the study of non-human animal harms. Unfortunately, one of the neglected observations offered by Beirne is that

> in the United States and in Britain and in its former colonies, the emergence of legal safeguards against animal abuse at the beginning of the nineteenth century was associated *with the growth of capitalist economic relations* and with the social, ideological, and juridical processes that sustained them.
>
> (1999: 129, footnote 11; emphasis added)

Elsewhere, green criminologists have followed up on this observation, noting how, for example, capitalism can produce various forms of widespread animal harm (Stretesky et al., 2013). As we shall argue in the following sections, the capitalist treadmill of production and the forms of ecological disorganization it generates have relevance for exploring the intersection of wildlife harm, ecological disorganization and deleterious feedback (secondary) harms associated with that intersection.

We begin our analysis by building on the important work of Beirne (1999) and other green criminologists who study wildlife crime to then suggest an expansion of the criminological research on wildlife harms by drawing on the concept of secondary ecological harm. As previously noted, the criminological analysis of non-human animal harm largely focuses on *direct harms* against non-human species. Our goal is to illustrate that those harms can initiate an additional array of harms against ecosystems and wildlife that should not be overlooked. In offering this argument, we seek to include a broader array of animal harms and the secondary consequences of animal harms for ecosystems and wildlife as a valid analytic subject.

## Ecological context, wildlife harm and secondary ecological effects

In this section, we explore the concept of secondary ecological harm associated with or produced by wildlife and ecological harm. In order to appreciate this concept, it is first necessary to consider that these secondary ecological harms occur within the ecological web of interdependency in which all species and ecosystems are enmeshed. In that view, wildlife harms have ecological relevance to secondary ecological harm to the extent that harms against wildlife and ecosystems have a 'ripple effect' on ecosystem stability and functionality that impacts the health and viability of wildlife species (see, for example, Flather and Sieg, 2000; Western, 2001). Thus, it is important to draw attention to these secondary ecological affects associated with wildlife harm to expand discussions of the ways in which wildlife harms feedback on ecosystems and to produce additional negative ecological system outcomes within the broader context of ecosystem analysis.

Theoretically, it is also necessary to appreciate that the nature and distribution of both wildlife harm and secondary ecological harms have a relationship with what is more generally referred to in ecological literature as 'human development'. Human development is a general term used to describe the well-being of society and is judged on a variety of quality of life indicators (Alkire, 2002). One of the indicators often referenced in the human development literature is the quality and concern placed on ecosystems and wildlife. While human development is widely employed, we adopt a more specific meaning for that term and frame the theoretical argument concerning the secondary ecological impacts associated with wildlife harm in relation to the growth of capitalism, the capitalist world economic system and the treadmill of production as specific manifestations of human development. Thus, in our view, it is not some generic form of human development that is at issue but more specifically the expansion of capitalism and its connection to secondary ecological harm that should be the focus.

Treadmill of production theory posits that numerous human activities associated with the expansion of capitalism generate ecological disorganization. Ecological disorganization is a broad term used to refer to the negative ecological outcomes that disrupt ecological stability and function as the treadmill of production expands and accelerates (Schnaiberg, 1980; Stretesky et al., 2013). In the context of the current argument, ecological disorganization is an important form of harm that occurs in relation to harms against wildlife and ecosystems and can be employed to explore the secondary ecological harms produced by wildlife harm. From the perspective of ecosystem analysis, wildlife harms not only create direct harms against wildlife (for example, from poaching) but also produce secondary ecological impacts related to the effect the decline of species has on ecosystem stability and functionality. Declining wildlife species status, as illustrated in the following, produces ecological disorganization and can reduce wildlife species sustainability that in turn accelerates ecosystem disorganization.

It is widely recognized in the ecological and biological literatures that any given wildlife species plays specific and important roles in ecosystem management and maintenance. When a species is harmed to the extent that its influence on an ecosystem is transformed, it can lead to ecosystem damage and reduced ecosystem viability that we define as a form of ecological disorganization. Numerous examples of how this process operates in ecosystems can be found in the biological and ecological literatures. We review examples of this process in the following sections.

## Species decline and secondary ecosystem impacts

A number of studies indicate that species health in ecosystems is related to ecosystem health and that declining wildlife species viability feeds back to reduce ecosystem viability. In that view, special attention is given to species richness as an important dimension of ecosystem health (Loreau et al., 2002; for a critique of the species richness argument, see Schwartz et al., 2000). In recent years, interest in this subject has expanded significantly, often under the heading of biodiversity and ecosystem function (for example, Cardinale et al., 2011). Studies like these illustrate the ways in which wildlife species decline can promote negative (disorganized) ecosystems and diminished ecosystem health. This general observation reinforces our argument that wildlife harms can have secondary effects on ecosystems that diminish ecosystem viability and reproduction, which in turn generates feedback on wildlife viability. Our argument is also reinforced by scientific discussions which posit that 'biodiversity-ecosystem function (BEF) is important because socio-economic development is almost always accompanied by the loss of natural habitat and species' (Midgley, 2012: 175).

As an example of this species-ecosystem interaction, Worm et al. (2006) discussed the effect of species loss on marine ecosystem health. As they note, numerous studies examine marine ecosystems as a location where species/wildlife decline plays an important role in ecosystem viability. Worm et al. (2006) indicate that species loss and impaired species diversity in marine ecosystems produce negative ecosystem effects that can be observed across both time and place. Moreover, there is an association between species loss and biodiversity decline with respect to marine ecosystem resource collapse. Evidence from this study also indicates that marine species decline has important ecosystem consequences because it has been associated with a decline in marine ecosystem water quality. With respect to our argument, this study supports the contention that species harm (decline) causes a feedback effect (secondary ecological harm) that impairs ecosystem viability and that impaired ecosystem viability impacts species health.

The relationship between species richness and ecosystem stability and viability can also be addressed by examining the positive effects of ecosystem restoration. Studies of species biodiversity restoration on ecosystem viability and sustainability have found that as species biodiversity is restored, marine ecosystem quality improves (Stachowicz et al., 2007). Indeed, as Stachowicz et al. note, in ecosystems with sufficient species presence, ecosystem productivity of ecological resources increased by a factor of four (for evidence related to 'no-take' fishing zones on ecosystem viability, see Lester et al., 2009). This produces enhanced ecosystem quality, which can contribute to further species recovery.

The effect of biodiversity and species presence on ecosystem functionality is complex and involves understanding how both horizontal and vertical integration in ecosystems is promoted by species diversity, presence or richness (Duffy et al., 2007). In reviewing relevant research, Duffy et al. (2007) identified a number of different ecosystem outcomes affected by species presence and diversity. For example, horizontal species diversity increases the volume of biomass produced in marine ecosystems (see also DeVries et al., 1997). Interestingly, they also note that biodiversity among prey species is promoted by species richness and decreases the likelihood that any individual prey species is adversely impacted by the presence of predator species. Thus, marine ecosystems damaged by human activity can suffer serious adverse consequences that lead to a decline in marine ecosystem viability.

As noted, species loss has a significant impact on ecosystem viability. Of special concern in this research is the effect of rising rates of animal extinction on ecosystems. Summarizing the effects of humans on marine ecosystems (for example, through over fishing, climate change, ocean acidification, nutrient runoff and toxic pollution), Jackson (2008) explored the significant impacts that Anthropocene extinctions in oceans have on marine ecosystems. Loss of species diversity is transforming rich ocean ecosystems such as coral reefs and kelp forests into dead zones and ocean deserts. One consequence of these species loss impacts is the creation of ocean 'boom and bust' ecological cycles. These boom and bust ecological cycles are, in comparison to normal ocean/marine system cycles, extraordinarily quick and non-linear. These boom and bust cycles intersect with species harm and can be magnified (creating detrimental ecosystem feedback) by harming species that, under other conditions, improve marine ecosystem quality, thereby averting boom and bust conditions in favor of marine ecosystem stability.

Deep sea ecosystems are recognized as the largest type of ecosystem on earth. As Danovaro et al. (2008) note, these large ecosystems are of great importance because they also contain the largest concentration of biomass found throughout the world. Danovaro et al. reviewed the content of 116 studies on deep sea ecosystems to address the relationship between deep sea ecosystem functionality and species biodiversity and loss. From those studies, they concluded that increased deep sea biodiversity is linked to expanded deep sea ecosystem efficiency and health.

The association between ecosystem health and biodiversity is seen across various ecosystems and is sometimes seen for ecosystems we do not ordinarily entertain as requiring green criminological research attention, such as grasslands, which serve a number of important ecological functions such as water filtration (Carlier et al., 2009). Reviewing the species-ecosystem health connection for grasslands, Hector and Bagchi (2007) note that, in general, the greater the biodiversity in grasslands, the healthier the grassland becomes. Indeed, they argue that protecting ecosystem multi-functionality in grasslands requires the presence of a very large number of species types. The large number of species necessary for grassland ecosystem viability reflects the fact that different species play specific roles in ecosystems and that the functions of those species in preserving ecosystem health do not broadly overlap (see also Tilman et al., 2006).

One of the issues raised in these types of studies focuses on 'functionally redundant species' – those species that perform the same ecosystem roles as other species present in the same ecosystem. It could be argued that due to the presence of functionally redundant species, species diversity and richness *are not* the most important concerns in maintaining healthy ecosystems because other species can 'fill in' when another species is in limited supply. To address this issue, Wohl et al. (2004) performed a laboratory experiment to examine the relationship among species richness, the presence of functionally redundant species and ecosystem health using cellulose decomposition in an artificial ecosystem. They hypothesized that increased species richness would have no impact on ecosystem health and that over time species richness would decline because the existence of functional redundancy among species in an ecosystem would be shaped by ecological survival mechanisms that would limit the presence of functionally redundant species. Their laboratory results rejected both of these hypotheses, suggesting instead that both species richness and functional redundancy were important to ecosystem health, suggesting that green criminologists need to pay particular attention to secondary ecological harm (for additional empirical laboratory support, see Naeem and Li, 1997; for an empirical review of fifty years of research, see Balvanera et al., 2006).

Much of the species diversity and richness literature focuses on plant species, aquatic environments and grassland ecosystems. As Duffy (2002) noted, this focus has generated a lack of knowledge concerning the effects of declines in species richness among 'consumer' species – that is, how predators and other top-of-the-food-chain species affect ecosystem health. The effect of a decline in top-level consumer animals in ecosystems is also summarized in biological literature on what is called 'trophic downgrading' (Estes et al., 2011) – or the effect on an ecosystem of removing large apex consumers/predators from that ecosystem. This is an important area of research because, as Duffy noted, top-level species tend to be more adversely impacted by human development and the threat of species extinction (see also Estes et al., 2011). This is also an important concern because consumer species have 'disproportionate' ecosystem impacts, and the loss of such species can therefore have magnified ecological impacts (Duffy, 2002). Among the most significant impacts on consumer species is human encroachment on natural spaces that results in habitat loss (for example, urbanization and deforestation). Such encroachment leads to consumer species harm, limits consumer species richness and vitality, and feeds back on ecosystem vitality in negative ways (Laurance et al., 2012).

This brief review of relevant literature illustrates how species richness and ecological decline are linked. These studies support our assertion that forms of human development promoted by the expansion of capitalism have numerous adverse impacts on the presence of wildlife species and that causing harm to wildlife species promotes secondary harm to ecosystem and wildlife. These secondary ecosystem impacts are widespread and are seen across a variety of wildlife species and different types of ecosystems. In the following section, we expand upon these observations to illustrate the importance of considering the capitalism-ecological disorganization connection and why green criminologists ought to direct greater attention to the political economy of ecological disorganization and the secondary adverse ecological impacts that wildlife destruction promotes.

## Discussion: political economy and secondary ecology harm from wildlife harm

The aforementioned studies suggest that species richness impacts ecosystem viability and illustrate that wildlife harm can have detrimental secondary ecological impacts. In terms of our argument, species richness or its absence is a function of harms against wildlife promoted by the continual expansion of global capitalism and the ecological disorganization that capitalism produces through ecological additions (pollution) and ecological withdrawals (for example, mining, deforestation, changing land use patterns, etc.). These effects can also be seen in local ecosystems impacted by extensive, deleterious treadmill of production impacts. This review of the scientific literature suggests that greater attention should be paid to the secondary impacts wildlife harm has on ecosystems.

Our focus on secondary ecological harms related to wildlife destruction draws attention to how the green criminology literature can be expanded to illustrate the significance of wildlife harm within the context of ecosystem viability analysis (for example, Laurance, 2008). In other words, the analysis of secondary ecological harms should become more relevant to green criminological analyses of wildlife harm and should draw attention to the ways in which wildlife harms cause ecological system feedbacks that can accelerate ecological disorganization and additional wildlife harm. Secondary wildlife harm needs to be placed in a more central position with respect to the political economic analysis of ecological disorganization. In the treadmill of production literature, emphasis has been devoted to how the treadmill produces ecological disorganization through ecological withdrawals (resource withdrawals and ecosystem disruption and destruction) and ecological additions (pollution). Omitted from that analysis is a fuller appreciation of the deleterious impacts the withdrawal of wildlife from nature has on accelerating ecological disorganization and further wildlife harm. In framing the analysis of the secondary ecological impacts of wildlife harm from a political economic perspective, it is important to emphasize that the ecological withdrawal of wildlife from ecosystems occurs under the influence of capitalism in a variety of ways. Some forms of wildlife withdrawals are indirect or caused by the expansion of the treadmill of production into ecological areas in ways that destroy ecosystems and transform human-ecosystem interactions in a manner that promotes further wildlife species decline. From that view, it could be argued that the ecological withdrawal of wildlife from ecosystems is an important outcome of the expansion of the global capitalist treadmill of production. It is possible to discuss direct harm to wildlife in areas damaged by the expansion of the treadmill of production with respect to specific economic activities such as mountaintop mining, deforestation and forest fragmentation caused by expanded urbanization.

Secondary ecological effect analysis can also become part of studies related to issues that green criminologists have explored, such as wildlife poaching and trafficking. Such efforts can include a discussion of how the treadmill of production shapes ecological disorganization and secondary ecological destruction (Stretesky et al., 2013). In this view, it is necessary to understand that under capitalism, the distribution of production and access to the means of production are unequally distributed geographically and that the unequal distribution of production is a function of the structure of the global capitalist world system. That system transforms relations of production globally and, in doing so, redefines ownership and access to nature across the nations of the world. This transformation of ownership and production is of special concern in developing and under-developed nations/regions where some portion of the population must adjust to the expansion of the capitalist treadmill of production and adapt to these new productive and ecological access relations (for example, Moore, 1993; South, 2007; Wyatt, 2014). In those locations, capital may be quickly consuming nature in ways that are qualitatively different than nature had been previously consumed by peoples in developing and under-developed areas before the expansion of capitalism. This new, expanded form of ecological consumption associated with capitalism generates a conflict between the effort of the expanding treadmill of production to assert its dominance and control over natural resources and the rights and traditions of native peoples who once determined how local natural resources were consumed (Anguelovski and Alier, 2014; Hooks and Smith, 2004). As an example, in areas of Africa, the expansion of global agriculture and the treadmill of production have caused extensive ecological disorganization and in the process have limited the volume of nature available to the promotion of traditional ways of life (Wilson, 2002). To protect those ecologically sensitive areas, new legal rules have emerged, some of which protect species from being hunted or poached. That legal protection, however, has a political economic or class dimension linked to the commodification of the right to hunt through the sale of high-priced hunting licenses. This process has removed the rights of native peoples to access wildlife, a political economic relation long ago addressed by Karl Marx (1842) in his analysis of laws related to the theft of wood and class relationships. Thus, in a rather invisible way, the expansion of the capitalist treadmill of production generates all types of wildlife harm that contribute to ecological disorganization and secondary ecological harm from direct wildlife harms.

It is also necessary to discuss the rather nondescript, general assertion scientists tend to make about the connection between wildlife harm and the secondary impacts of wildlife harm in the absence of a theory concerning the organization of society. In scientific research, ecological destruction has been linked to human development and the expansion of human societies. There is little reason to object to making such a link. Absent from that description, however, is a theoretical position or explanation about the nature of 'human development' or the causes of the 'expansion of human societies'. Typically, scientific studies simply assume that human development occurs (that is, it is an empirical reality), and no theoretical explanation for development is offered. From the perspective of political economic analysis, human development and the expansion of human societies can be explained in relation to the inherent organizational principles of capitalism and its quest to continually expand and accelerate the production of profit. In short, from a political economic perspective, human development/expansion is explained via the profit growth orientation of capitalism. As ecological Marxists have observed, expanding capitalism and profit making requires continuous expansion of the consumption of nature, and hence each 'advance' in capitalism (that is, 'human development') must be understood as producing a contraction of nature (Burkett, 2008; Foster, 1992, 1999, 2000, 2002; Foster and Clark, 2008; Foster et al., 2011). In other words, we can say that the continuous expansion of the treadmill of production (that is, human development) produces forms of ecological disorganization (that is, the destruction of nature).

Theoretically, we believe that it is also necessary to point out that over the past century and a half, the tremendous expansion of ecological disorganization related to wildlife destruction and escalating rates of extinction (Steffen et al., 2007, 2011; Stork, 2010) has been generated by the conversion of land through deforestation for production and agricultural and urban land use within the global capitalist economy. This long-term form of ecological destruction illustrates the contentions of ecological Marxism concerning the influence of capitalism on ecosystem viability. This long-term process generates wildlife harm (that is, extinction), which feeds back on ecosystem viability, accelerating ecological disorganization. This view is also reinforced by global measures of ecological disorganization such as the global ecological footprint, its expansion and its association with a variety of adverse ecological outcomes associated with ecological disorganization (Baer, 2008; Clark and York, 2005; Hoffman, 2004; Jorgenson, 2003, 2008, 2009).

In exploring these arguments, it is also useful to consider the ways in which this view of secondary ecological effects sits with other green criminological analyses. The global nature of this form of ecological disorganization can be integrated into research that has built on White's (2011) argument concerning the global nature of ecological crime and the development of eco-global green criminology. To be sure, it is possible to discuss wildlife harm in relation to its local ecosystem effects. Ignoring the global prevalence of this kind of harm, however, may present a misleading image that these harms are isolated rather than global in their origins and impacts.

## Conclusion

We have argued that green criminology should expand its scope of analysis by addressing the secondary ecological harms caused by wildlife harm and destruction and that wildlife harm has broad ecosystem impacts that expand ecological disorganization. This is an important global issue, and as research in the biological and ecological literatures notes, the consideration of the broad impacts wildlife destruction has on ecosystem viability tells us much about the ways in which wildlife harm feeds back on ecosystems to cause extensive ecosystem viability concerns.

The study of wildlife harms by green criminologists is an important area of research. In undertaking that research, however, green criminologists should not overlook feedback mechanisms or the ways in which wildlife harms contribute to the acceleration of ecological disorganization. Thus, while wildlife harms are certainly important, they have greater importance when placed within a larger ecological context that illustrates how wildlife harm and ecological disorganization intersect and how wildlife harm is not only itself a form of ecological disorganization but also contributes to additional ecological disorganization through the withdrawal of wildlife from ecosystems.

In taking this view, we explored the need to examine the context of secondary ecological harm from wildlife harm from the perspective of political economic analysis. Political economic analysis provides a useful way of framing ecological disorganization and linking patterns of ecological disorganization together so that the global process of ecological disorganization and its connection to the expansion of capitalism become more apparent (Lynch et al., 2013; Stretesky et al., 2013). The absence of an analysis of the influential role that capitalism plays in ecological disorganization is important to consider because it also impacts the kinds of policy responses to ecological disorganization that green criminologists may propose. A political economic analysis of green crime makes it clear that the diverse array of ecological issues facing the world cannot be solved by piecemeal legislation related to controlling any specific form of ecological destruction. Rather, there is a need to recognize that these ecological harms intersect with the expansion of capitalism and that the solution to ecological destruction lies in controlling or replacing capitalism with a different system of economic and social relationship conducive to the protection of global and local ecosystems.

## References

Alkire, S. (2002) Dimensions of human development, *World Development*, **30**(2): 181–205.

Anguelovski, I. and Alier, J. (2014) 'The "environmentalism of the poor" revisited: Territory and place in disconnected glocal struggles', *Ecological Economics*, **102**: 167–176.

Baer, H. (2008) 'Global warming as a by-product of the capitalist treadmill of production and consumption – The need for an alternative global system', *The Australian Journal of Anthropology*, **19**(1): 58–62.

Balvanera, P., Pfisterer, A., Buchmann, N., He, J.-S., Nakashizuka, T., Raffaelli, D. and Schmid, B. (2006) 'Quantifying the evidence for biodiversity effects on ecosystem functioning and services', *Ecology Letters*, **9**(10): 1146–1156.

Beirne, P. (1999) 'For a nonspeciesist criminology: Animal abuse as an object of study', *Criminology*, **37**(1): 117–148.

Beirne, P. (2007) 'Animal rights, animal abuse and green criminology'. In P. Beirne and N. South (eds.) *Issues in Green Criminology: Confronting Harms against Environments, Humanity and Other Animals*, Cullompton, England: Willan, pp. 55–86.

Beirne, P. and South, N. (eds.) (2007) *Issues in Green Criminology: Confronting Harms against Environments, Humanity and Other Animals*, Cullompton, England: Willan.

Burkett, P. (2008) *Marxism and Ecological Economics: Toward a Red and Green Political Economy*, Chicago: Haymarket Books.

Cardinale, B., Matulich, K., Hooper, D., Byrnes, J., Duffy, E., Gamfeldt, L., . . . Gonzalez, A. (2011) 'The functional role of producer diversity in ecosystems', *American Journal of Botany*, **98**(3): 572–592.

Carlier, L., Rotar, I., Vlahova, M. and Vidican, R. (2009) 'Importance and functions of grassland', *Notulae Botanicae Horti Agrobotanici Cluj-Napoca*, **37**(1): 25–30.

Cazaux, G. (1999) 'Beauty and the beast: Animal abuse from a non-speciesist criminological perspective', *Crime, Law and Social Change*, **31**(2): 105–125.

Cazaux, G. (2007) 'Labelling animals: Non-speciesist criminology and techniques to identify animal harm'. In P. Beirne and N. South (eds.) *Issues in Green Criminology: Confronting Harms against Environments, Humanity and Other Animals*, Cullompton, England: Willan, pp. 87–113.

Clark, B. and York, R. (2005) 'Carbon metabolism: Global capitalism, climate change, and the biospheric rift', *Theory and Society*, **34**(4): 391–428.

Danovaro, R., Gambi, C., Dell'Anno, A., Corinaldesi, C., Fraschetti, S., Vanreusel, A., Vincx, M. and Gooday, A. (2008) 'Exponential decline of deep-sea ecosystem functioning linked to benthic biodiversity loss', *Current Biology*, **18**(1): 1–8.

DeVries, P., Murray, D. and Lande, R. (1997) 'Species diversity in vertical, horizontal and temporal dimensions of a fruit-feeding butterfly community in an Ecuadorian rainforest', *Biological Journal of the Linnean Society*, **62**: 343–363.

Duffy, J. (2002) 'Biodiversity and ecosystem function: The consumer connection', *Oikos*, **99**(2): 201–219.

Duffy, J., Cardinale, B., France, K., McIntyre, P., Thébault, E. and Loreau, M. (2007) 'The functional role of biodiversity in ecosystems: Incorporating trophic complexity', *Ecology Letters*, **10**(6): 522–538.

Estes, J., Terborgh, J., Brashares, J., Power, M., Berger, J., Bond, W., Carpenter, S., Essington, T., Holt, R., Jackson, J., Marquis, R., Oksanen, T., Paine, R., Pikitch, E., Ripple, W., Sandin, S., Scheffer, M., Schoener, T., Shurin, J., Sinclair, A., Soulé, M., Virtanen, R. and Wardle, D. (2011) 'Trophic downgrading of planet earth', *Science*, **333**(6040): 301–306.

Flather, C. and Sieg, C. (2000) 'Applicability of Montreal process Criterion 1 – conservation of biological diversity – to rangeland sustainability', *The International Journal of Sustainable Development and World Ecology*, 7(2): 81–96.

Foster, J. (1992) 'The absolute general law of environmental degradation under capitalism', *Capitalism, Socialism, Nature*, **3**(3): 77–81.

Foster, J. (1999) 'Marx's theory of metabolic rift: Classical foundations for environmental sociology', *American Journal of Sociology*, **105**(2): 366–405.

Foster, J. (2000) *Marx's Ecology: Materialism and Nature*, New York: Monthly Review Press.

Foster, J. (2002) 'Capitalism and ecology: The nature of the contradiction', *Monthly Review*, **54**(4): 6–16.

Foster, J. and Clark, B. (2008) 'The paradox of wealth: Capitalism and ecological destruction', *Monthly Review*, **61**(6): 1–18.

Foster, J., Clark, B. and York, R. (2011) *The Ecological Rift: Capitalism's War on the Earth*, New York: New York University Press.

Hector, A. and Bagchi, R. (2007) 'Biodiversity and ecosystem multifunctionality', *Nature*, **448**(7150): 188–190.

Hoffman, J. (2004) 'Social and environmental influences on endangered species: A cross-national study', *Sociological Perspectives*, **47**(1): 79–107.

Hooks, G. and Smith, C. (2004) 'The treadmill of destruction: National sacrifice areas and Native Americans', *American Sociological Review*, **69**(4): 558–575.

Hughes, G. and Lawson, C. (2011) 'RSPCA and the criminology of social control', *Crime, Law and Social Change*, **55**(5): 375–389.

Jackson, J. (2008) 'Ecological extinction and evolution in the brave new ocean', *Proceedings of the National Academy of Sciences*, **105**(1): 11458–11465.

Jorgenson, A. (2003) 'Consumption and environmental degradation: A cross-national analysis of the ecological footprint', *Social Problems*, **50**(3): 374–394.

Jorgenson, A. (2008) 'Structural integration and the trees: An analysis of deforestation in less-developed countries, 1990–2005', *The Sociological Quarterly*, **49**(3): 503–527.

Jorgenson, A. (2009) 'Unequal ecological exchange and environmental degradation: A theoretical proposition and cross-national study of deforestation, 1990–2000', *Rural Sociology*, **71**(4): 685–712.

Laurance, W. (2008) 'Theory meets reality: How habitat fragmentation research has transcended island biogeographic theory', *Biological Conservation*, **141**(7): 1731–1744.

Laurance, W., Useche, D., Rendeiro, J., Kalka, M., Bradshaw, C., Sloan, S., . . . Zamzani, F. (2012) 'Averting biodiversity collapse in tropical forest protected areas', *Nature*, **489**(7415): 290–294.

Lester, S., Halpern, B., Grorud-Colvert, K., Lubchenco, J., Ruttenberg, B., Gaines, S., Airamé, S. and Warner, R. (2009) 'Biological effects within no-take marine reserves: A global synthesis', *Marine Ecology Progress Series*, **384**: 33–46.

Loreau, M., Naeem, S. and Inchuasti, P. (2002) *Biodiversity and Ecosystem Functioning: Synthesis and Perspectives*, Oxford: Oxford University Press.

Lynch, M., Long, M., Barrett, K. and Stretesky, P. (2013) 'Is it a crime to produce ecological disorganization? Why green criminology and political economy matter in the analysis of global ecological harms', *British Journal of Criminology*, **55**(3): 997–1016.

Marx, K. (1842) 'Debates on the law on theft of wood', *Rheinische Zeitung*, 298, 300, 303, 305 and 307. Retrieved from http://www.marxists.org/archive/marx/works/1842/10/25.htm.

Midgley, G. (2012) 'Biodiversity and ecosystem function', *Science*, **335**(6065): 174–175.

Moore, D. (1993) 'Contesting terrain in Zimbabwe's eastern highlands: Political ecology, ethnography, and peasant resource struggles', *Economic Geography*, **69**(4): 380–401.

Naeem, S. and Li, S. (1997) 'Biodiversity enhances ecosystem reliability', *Nature*, **390**(6659): 507–509.

Ngoc, A.C. and Wyatt, T. (2013) 'A green criminological exploration of illegal wildlife trade in Vietnam', *Asian Journal of Criminology*, **8**(2): 129–142.

Nurse, A. (2013) *Animal Harm: Perspectives on Why People Harm and Kill Animals*, Farnham, England: Ashgate.

Regan, T. (2007) 'Vivisection: The case for abolition'. In P. Beirne and N. South (eds.) *Issues in Green Criminology: Confronting Harms against Environments, Humanity and Other Animals*, Cullompton, England: Willan, pp. 114–139.

Schnaiberg, A. (1980) *The Environment: From Surplus to Scarcity*, New York: Oxford University Press.

Schwartz, M., Brigham, J., Lyons, H., Mills, M. and Van Mantgem, P. (2000) 'Linking biodiversity to ecosystem function: Implications for conservation ecology', *Oecologia*, **122**(3): 297–305.

Sollund, R. (2013) 'Animal trafficking and trade: Abuse and species injustice'. In R. Walters, D. Westerhuis and T. Wyatt (eds.) *Emerging Issues in Green Criminology*, New York: Palgrave Macmillan, pp. 72–91.

South, N. (2007) 'The corporate colonization of nature: Bio-prospecting, bio-piracy and the development of green criminology'. In P. Beirne and N. South (eds.) *Issues in Green Criminology: Confronting Harms against Environments, Humanity, and Other Animals*, Cullompton, England: Willan, pp. 230–247.

Stachowicz, J., Bruno, J. and Duffy, J. (2007) 'Understanding the effects of marine biodiversity on communities and ecosystems', *Annual Review of Ecology, Evolution, and Systematics*, **38**: 739–766.

Steffen, W., Crutzen, P. and McNeill, J. (2007) 'The Anthropocene: Are humans now overwhelming the great forces of nature?' *Ambio: A Journal of the Human Environment*, **36**(8): 614–621.

Steffen, W., Grinevald, J., Crutzen, P. and McNeill, J. (2011) 'The Anthropocene: Conceptual and historical perspectives', *Philosophical Transactions of the Royal Society A: Mathematical, Physical and Engineering Sciences*, **369**(1938): 842–867.

Stork, N. (2010) 'Re-assessing current extinction rates', *Biodiversity and Conservation*, **19**(2): 357–371.

Stretesky, P., Long, M. and Lynch, M. (2013) *The Treadmill of Crime: Political Economy and Green Criminology*, London: Routledge.

Tilman, D., Reich, P. and Knops, J. (2006) 'Biodiversity and ecosystem stability in a decade-long grassland experiment', *Nature*, **441**(7093): 629–632.

Western, D. (2001) 'Human-modified ecosystems and future evolution', *Proceedings of the National Academy of Sciences*, **98**(10): 5458–5465.

White, R. (2011) *Transnational Environmental Crime: Toward an Eco-Global Criminology*, New York: Taylor & Francis.

White, R. and Heckenberg, D. (2014) *Green Criminology: An Introduction to the Study of Environmental Harm*, New York: Routledge.

Wilson, D. (2002) 'The global in the local: The environmental state and the management of the Nile perch fishery on Lake Victoria'. In A. Mol and F. Buttel (eds.) *The Environmental State Under Pressure, (Research in Social Problems and Public Policy, Volume 10)*, Bingley: England, Emerald Group Publishing, pp. 171–192.

Wohl, D., Arora, S. and Gladstone, J. (2004) 'Functional redundancy supports biodiversity and ecosystem function in a closed and constant environment', *Ecology*, **85**(6): 1534–1540.

Worm, B., Barbier, E., Beaumont, N., Duffy, J., Folke, C., Halpern, B., . . . Watson, R. (2006) 'Impacts of biodiversity loss on ocean ecosystem services', *Science*, **314**(5800): 787–790.

Wyatt, T. (2009) 'Exploring the organization of Russia Far East's illegal wildlife trade: Two case studies of the illegal fur and illegal falcon trades', *Global Crime*, **10**(1–2): 144–154.

Wyatt, T. (2011) 'The illegal trade of raptors in the Russian Federation', *Contemporary Justice Review*, **14**(2): 103–123.

Wyatt, T. (2013) *Wildlife Trafficking: A Deconstruction of the Crime, the Victims, and the Offenders*, New York: Palgrave Macmillan.

Wyatt, T. (2014) 'Invisible pillaging: The hidden harm of corporate biopiracy'. In P. Davies (ed.) *Invisible Crimes and Social Harms*, New York: Palgrave Macmillan, pp. 161–171.

Yates, R. (2007) 'Debating "animal rights" online: The movement-countermovement dialectic revisited'. On P. Beirne and N. South (eds.) *Issues in Green Criminology: Confronting Harms against Environments, Humanity and Other Animals*, Cullompton, England: Willan, pp. 140–160.

Yates, R., Powell, C. and Beirne, P. (2001) 'Horse maiming in the English countryside: Moral panic, human deviance, and the social construction of victimhood', *Society and Animals*, **9**(1): 1–24.

# 13 Green cultural criminology, intergenerational (in)equity and 'life stage dissolution'

*Avi Brisman and Nigel South*

## Introduction

A proposal for a *green cultural criminology* seeks to bring together green criminology and cultural criminology and to identify points of overlap. More specifically, a green cultural criminology endeavours to illuminate how cultural criminology's attention to space is central to green criminology while attempting to highlight means by which green criminology might adopt a cultural criminological lens by (1) assigning greater consideration to the way(s) in which environmental crime, harm and disaster are constructed and represented by the news media and in popular cultural forms; (2) dedicating increased attention to patterns of consumption, constructed consumerism, commodification of nature and related market processes; and (3) devoting heightened concern to the contestation of space, transgression and resistance in order to analyse the ways in which environmental harms are opposed in/on the streets and in day-to-day living (Brisman and South, 2013a, 2014, 2015; see also Brisman, 2015; Brisman et al., 2014; McClanahan, 2014; Schally, 2014).

In the present article, we seek to extend the idea of a green cultural criminology by drawing on Hayward's (2012) articles 'Pantomime Justice: A Cultural Criminological Analysis of "Life Stage Dissolution"' and '"Life Stage Dissolution" in Anglo-American Advertising and Popular Culture: Kidults, Lil' Britneys and Middle Youths'. We begin with a brief overview of Hayward's key points in these pieces and then attempt to apply them to a concern relevant to the development of a green cultural criminology: intergenerational equity and the responsibility of present generations to take into consideration how their acts, omissions, behaviours and practices will affect the ecological environments for future generations.

## Overview of 'Pantomime Justice: A Cultural Criminological Analysis of "Life Stage Dissolution"' and '"Life Stage Dissolution" in Anglo-American Advertising and Popular Culture: Kidults, Lil' Britneys and Middle Youths'

In 'Pantomime Justice: A Cultural Criminological Analysis of "Life Stage Dissolution"', Hayward (2012) asserts that the opposition between adolescence and adulthood is increasingly challenged as late modern capitalist culture artificially extends the former. In the first part of this article, Hayward introduces the concept of 'life stage dissolution' – and its attendant and overlapping *bi-directional* processes of 'adultification' and 'infantilisation' – to propose that it is becoming difficult for young people to differentiate and disassociate themselves from the generation immediately ahead of them and vice versa. Here, Hayward draws on a wide range of examples to demonstrate the marketing of adulthood (especially sexuality) to kids (such as the British retailer Primark's marketing of padded bikini tops to seven-year-old girls) and of 'childish pleasures' to adults (2012: 216). On the latter, Hayward (2012) explains,

> major advertising campaigns unashamedly align their products with childhood nostalgia, while cartoon tropes are now a staple theme of adult campaigns, used to sell everything from caffeinated energy drinks (Red Bull) to banking services (Lloyds/TSB, Santander). Recent mobile phone network commercials, for example, have utilised kites, crayons and giant ribbons (Orange – 'Good things should never end' campaign), teddy bears, nursery rhymes and toys ($O_2$), singing cherries (3-Mobile), cartwheels and tumbling (T-Mobile), a dollhouse and the 'spin the bottle' game (Orange, Magic Numbers), and inflatable dolphins and balloon animals (Orange, 'Pay as you Go'). The trend is even more pronounced in contemporary Anglo-American car advertising, where adults now happily purchase cars marketed to consumers half their age [what Hayward refers to as the 'toyification' of automobile advertising].
>
> (217)

The result of these processes, according to Hayward, is a sort of 'generational mulch' where shared and interchangeable cultural experiences are now the norm (2012: 216).

In the second half of this article, Hayward looks at the criminological significance of 'intergenerational blurring' and identifies three ways in which 'life stage dissolution' is affecting criminology and criminal justice policy. In the section titled 'The "At Risk" Individual and the "Therapeutic State": Life Stage Dissolution and the Culture of Victimhood', Hayward juxtaposes adult treatment of and for juvenile/teen offenders with the rise of a 'victim culture' in which 'individuals now actively perceive themselves as being "at risk"' (2012: 222). As Hayward explains, 'taking advantage of socio-cultural circumstances in which the infantilised victim is ascendant, politicians and policy-makers are now remoulding the relationship between individual and government through what one might describe as the rise of the "therapeutic state"' (2012: 222–223) – one in which the infantilised adult/parent is replaced by the 'trained professional' of the state. Next, in 'Life Stage Dissolution and the Crime-Media Nexus', Hayward identifies two processes contributing to the demise of what he refers to as 'hard news' and the rise of 'an infantilised soft news':

> The first process is the uncurbed rapidity of (crime) news gathering, which has resulted in a situation whereby the news cycle now moves faster than the news. Consequently, anything longer than a soundbite/meme is dismissed by tech-savvy audiences raised on digital instantaneity as a ponderous intrusion into their world of self-centred information gathering. For the grown-up kidults of late modernity, then, news stories deteriorate to the level of textspeak or Twitter feed – add a smiley or sad face to the story lest it be dismissed as 'TLTR'/'TLDC' ('too long to read'/'too long don't care'). This, of course, contributes to the second process: the erosion of complexity and the dumbing down of debate . . . the distilling down of broadcast news to black-and-white issues stripped of all nuance and subtlety.
>
> (2012: 224)

Finally, in 'The Infantilised Narcissist: Life Stage Dissolution and Aetiology,' Hayward contends that

> consumerism as a cultural ethos [is] propagating new emotional states, feelings and desires that are contributing to *both* the depreciation of mature adulthood (and the roles and responsibilities typically associated with that stage of people's lives), and importantly the adultification of very young teenagers (in terms of lifestyle choices and activities involving sexual activity/drugs/criminality etc.) that previously were the preserve of young adults.
>
> (2012: 226; italics in the original)

This 'depreciation of mature adulthood' and 'adultification of very young teenagers,' Hayward asserts, raises 'aetiological concerns about young people making adult decisions (or, inversely, young adults acting like children)', which has implications for both youth crime and criminal justice responses thereto (2012: 226).

In '"Life Stage Dissolution" in Anglo-American Advertising and Popular Culture: Kidults, Lil' Britneys and Middle Youths', Hayward continues the argument set forth in his earlier piece, focusing here on 'the move by advertisers and markets to actively undermine and erode the inherent *opposition* that exists between established stages of the life cycle in a bid to enhance sales and boost corporate profits' in order to 'outline the tendency in contemporary advertising to blur traditionally demarcated adulthood and childhood roles, differences and oppositions in its promotion of a new message within contemporary consumerism' (2013: 526; italics in the original).

This second article is organised into three parts. In the first part, '"Different Breed of Cat"? Adultification and Infantilization in the Anglo-American Cultural Script', Hayward introduces the inter-related *bi-directional* concepts of 'adultification' and 'infantilisation' to illustrate the ways and extent to which contemporary cultural representations are serving to undermine established life stages. Of particular importance here is the '"reversal of authority" between child and adult' and that 'while kids hurtle at full speed towards adulthood, what awaits them when they arrive is something remarkably familiar' (2013: 530). Hayward (2013) highlights how contemporary films and advertising encourage and celebrate immaturity in adults and a regression to childhood, accompanied by a '"conscious abdication of adult responsibility" in favour of fantasy and play' (531). At the same time, Hayward (2013) maintains, 'one of the most identifiable motifs in advertising today is the role reversal that sees grown-ups positioned in subservient roles to children' (530) – so much so, Hayward asserts, that 'a dominant theme in contemporary television advertising is the way the empowered child is inversely correlated with the passive and stultified adult' (530).

In the second part, 'Extant Explanation: A Sociological Review', Hayward conducts a short sociological review of the social scientific research that has sought to engage with these generational issues. In particular, Hayward criticises Jeffrey Arnett's (2000, 2004; Arnett and Tanner, 2006; Arnett et al., 2010) concept of 'emerging adulthood' that applies to the years 18–29 (which is 'neither adolescence nor young adulthood but is theoretically and empirically distinct from both' [Arnett, 2000: 469]), arguing that rather than the emergence of a distinct or entirely new stage of the life cycle (along the lines suggested by Arnett), what may actually be transpiring within Western society is the *erosion* or *blurring* of established life stages.

In the third part, '"It's the Market, Stupid": Life Stage Dissolution and Lifestyle Consumerism', Hayward (2013) illustrates how the blurring of life stages is reflected and projected within contemporary marketing and advertising logics associated with lifestyle consumerism – a merging that seeks to '[interpolate] people in terms that appeal to their desire for "difference" and "escape"' (541). Hayward (2013) concludes by restating his overall argument: rather than the emergence of a new and distinct life stage (such as Arnett's 'emerging adulthood'), 'what is actually happening is the erosion of established ones; with the result a sort of generational mulch where shared cultural experiences become the norm' (543).

Admittedly – and as Carey (2010) cautions – 'trying to pin down the character of a generation is a controversial and, some say, presumptuous exercise' (D5). Thus, there is some risk in relying too heavily on generational portraits or on representations of the merging landscapes between generations. But if we keep Carey's caveat in mind and if we treat such images as *snapshots*, then we can extend Hayward's line of thinking and consider the application of 'infantilisation' and 'adultification' to various environmental concerns and the implications of 'life stage dissolution' for green criminology.

## 'Life stage dissolution' and intergenerational (in)equity, (in)justice and (ir)responsibility

The 1972 United Nations (UN) Conference on the Human Environment in Stockholm (the Stockholm Conference) was convened by the UN General Assembly 'to serve as a practical means to encourage and provide guidelines for action by Governments and international organizations designed to protect and improve the human environment' (Brisman, 2011b: 1039). Among other things, the Stockholm Conference generated the 1972 Stockholm Declaration of the United Nations Conference on the Human Environment (the Stockholm Declaration), Principle 1 of which provides:

> Man has a fundamental right to freedom, equality and adequate conditions of life, in an environment of a quality that permits a life of dignity and well-being, and he bears a solemn responsibility to protect and improve the environment for present and future generations.
>
> (for a discussion, see South, 2010: 239–240; Thornton and Tromans, 1999: 36; White, 2013: 45)

Twenty years later, the United Nations Conference on Environment and Development (UNCED) (also known as the Earth Summit or the Rio Conference) was held in Rio de Janeiro in June 1992. The Rio Conference, which produced the Rio Declaration on Environment and Development – in many senses, the 'successor' to the Stockholm Declaration (Thornton and Tromans, 1999: 37) – consists of twenty-seven principles intended to guide future sustainable development around the world (for a discussion, see Brisman, 2011a: 960–961; Hall, 2013: 68, 2015: 120–123). Principle 3, The Right to Development, reflects the spirit of Principle 1 of the Stockholm Declaration: 'The right to development must be fulfilled so as to equitably meet developmental and environmental needs of present and future generations.'

The ideas reflected in Principle 1 of the Stockholm Declaration and Principle 3 of the Rio Declaration pre-date their expression in these non-binding international legal documents (see Hiskes, 2008; Schneeberger, 2011). Since then, many scholars working within green criminology and across various other disciplines have attempted to articulate these principles in their own terms. For example, for Ruggiero and South (2010: 254), *intergenerational equity* means 'justice between generations' – that each generation receives a natural and cultural legacy from previous generations that it holds in trust for succeeding ones. This partnership between the living, the dead and the unborn entails 'a duty on mankind to pass onto succeeding generations a planet at least as healthy as the one it inherited so that each generation will be able to enjoy its fruits' (Kofele-Kale, 2006: 324). Heckenberg (2009) explains that 'the principle of intergenerational equity asserts that future generations have the right to environments that are the equal in terms of quality and amenity to that of the present generation' (14). Similarly, for White (2012: 27, 2013: 31; White and Heckenberg, 2014: 41), *intergenerational equity* 'refers to the principle of ensuring that the generations to follow have at least the same or preferably better environments in which to live than those of the present generation.' *Intergenerational equity*, White emphasises, requires a degree of *intergenerational responsibility* such that 'present generations do not act in ways which jeopardise the existence of future generations' (2011: 147, 2013: 45). Even more comprehensively, Wyatt (2013) stresses that our obligation of *intergenerational justice* – 'of leaving not just a sustainable environment, but a healthy flourishing one, extends beyond the next human generations, but also to the generations of non-human animals, plants, fungi, etc. that come after us' (81) (see also Takemura, 2010: 216; Wyatt, 2013: 170). According to Weiss:

> The basic concept is that all generations are partners caring for and using the Earth. Every generation needs to pass the Earth and our natural and cultural resources on in at least as good condition as we received them. This leads to three principles of intergenerational equity: options, quality, and access. The first, comparable options, means conserving the diversity of the natural resource base so that future generations can use it to satisfy their own values. The second principle, comparable quality, means ensuring the quality of the environment on balance is comparable between generations. The third one, comparable access, means non-discriminatory access among generations to the Earth and its resources.
>
> (2008: 616–618)

As future generations become living generations, they inherit the intergenerational obligations to conserve options, quality, and access in relationship to other members of the present generation.

Unfortunately, as Barnett (1999) points out, 'our ethical evolution has a long way to go. The majority does not appear convinced that we need to limit environmental destruction to preserve the world for our children or grandchildren, let alone the seventh generation' (164). In a similar vein, Hiskes observes that

> societal norms and patterns of consumption, corporate decisions about resource usage or production, and family decisions about property use or purchasing all carry effects for the surrounding environment.
>
> The future has little legal standing or real political power to force the living to conserve – future generations are always in the minority in the eyes of those who currently wield

> power. As a result, even in democracies, environmental concerns, especially those that invoke intergenerational justice, languish near the bottom of the political agenda.
>
> (2014: 404–406)

Likewise, Bruni argues that the United States'

> slowness to deal with swelling seas and melting glaciers is just one manifestation of our myopia, just one metaphor for our failure to reckon with the future we're visiting upon today's children, who get more lip service than legislation from us.
>
> (2014: SR3)

To make matters worse, this appears to be a cumulative phenomenon. As Milfont and colleagues (2012) note, 'spatial and temporal biases have practical implications because the more people believe that consequences of environmental problems are far away geographically and temporally, the less willing they may be to take action here and now' (331). We seem, then, to be engaging in 'intergenerational inequity', to use Preston's (2011: 143) term, passing the burden of remediating contaminated land and restoring ecological communities to future generations.

For Shiva (2008) and Leech (2012), the culprit is clear. As Shiva maintains:

> Humanity is playing . . . tricks with itself and the planet because we are locked into the industrial paradigm. Our ideas of the good life are based on production and consumption patterns that the use of fossil fuels gave rise to. We cling to these patterns without reflecting on the fact that they have become a human addiction only over the past 50 years and that maintaining this short-term, non-sustainable pattern of living for another 50 years comes at the risk of wiping out millions of species and destroying the very conditions for human survival on the planet. We think of well-being only in terms of humans, and more accurately, only in terms of human beings over the next 50 years. We are sacrificing the rights of other species and the welfare of future generations.
>
> (2008: 130–131)

Correspondingly, Leech convincingly argues:

> Inevitably, the drive to maximize profits that lies at the root of the logic of capital requires that essential natural resources be exploited in an unsustainable manner – to benefit disproportionately a wealthy minority at the expense of the basic needs of the majority. This process not only constitutes structural genocide perpetrated by the haves against the have-nots today, it also represents structural genocide against future generations who will not be able to meet their basic needs.
>
> The unequal distribution of the planet's natural resources and the unequal consequences of climate change resulting from capitalism are not only problems for the have-nots in today's society; they will also negatively impact billions of people in the future.
>
> (2012: 7, 92–93)

What we wish to suggest, then, is that the 'life stage dissolution' and resulting 'generational mulch' that Hayward describes impede efforts towards environmental protection that might take into account future generations – that the bi-directional processes of 'adultification'' and 'infantilisation' inhibit and frustrate any attempt to ensure intergenerational equity.[1] We make two arguments in support of this proposition.

First, we suggest that the increased marketing of 'childish pleasures' (Hayward, 2012: 216) to and for adults fosters a 'forever young' philosophy (Danesi, 2003: ix) and a growth in – and desire for – instantly obsolete objects (see Brisman and South, 2013b; Ferrell, 2013; Hayward, 2012). As Hayward, evoking Leech, explains, marketers and merchandisers are consciously and deliberately

> hoping to rekindle in grown-ups the tastes and habits of children so that they can sell globally the . . . consumer goods for which there is no discernible 'need market' other than the one created by capitalism's own frantic imperative to sell.
>
> (2012: 216, quoting Barber, 2007: 7)

Or, as Piper (2008: 19) puts it, we seem to be experiencing a trend of 'the growing importance of the child in late modernity as a symbol of nostalgia, the child envisioned as "a longing for times past, not 'futurity'" (quoting Jenks, 1996: 106–107). This process or trend, we submit, redirects or re-emphasises adult attention inward (or shortens their gaze, if you will), making them *less* future-oriented, *less* willing to contemplate their intergenerational responsibilities at precisely the time when this is needed.

On this point, consider Giddens (1999), who uses the term *risk society*, drawing upon Beck's (1992) examination of the manufacture of risk as a product of late modernity, and who describes society as organised in response to risk. According to Giddens,

> the idea of 'risk society' might suggest a world which has become more hazardous, but this is not necessarily so. Rather, it is a society increasingly preoccupied with the future (and also with safety), which generates the notion of risk.
>
> (1999: 3)

At first glance, Giddens's argument might seem to be at odds with our proposition about the linkage between 'infantilisation' and intergenerational *ir*responsibility: where we identify a *lack* of focus on the future, Giddens asserts that this is a growing concern. As Grossberg (2001) points out, however, 'increasingly, the future is defined as either indistinguishable from the present (and therefore as the servant of the present rather than vice versa), or apocalyptically (as radically other than the present, without any continuity)' (133). With this notion of 'future' in mind, Giddens's point really becomes one about uncertainty, anxiety, insecurity and fear – not 'parallel fear', which is seen as, or attached to, specific events, issues

1 To be clear, we are not claiming that we are the first to connect future orientation and environmental protection. Recently, Carmi and Arnon (2014) found that in a representative sample ($n$ = 1216) of the Israeli population, individuals with developed future orientation demonstrated more pro-environmental tendencies and that on a cross-cultural level, in countries that, in general, conduct future-oriented practices, the environment benefits because their citizens tend to behave in more pro-environmental ways. Their study confirms other studies (e.g. Arnocky et al., 2014; Milfont et al., 2012; Rabinovich et al., 2010) that have concluded that future orientation drives pro-environmental behavior motivation – that pro-environmental attitudes and engagement in environmental protection and sustainable behaviors require a focus on future outcomes at the expense of immediate benefits. Rather, we are attempting to highlight some of the reasons why there might be a *lack* of future orientation and what this might mean for environmental protection.

or threats (Altheide, 2002: 59; Critcher, 2011: 263), but 'nonparallel fear', which is general, pervasive and unfocused (Altheide, 2002: 59; Critcher, 2011: 263). As Critcher explains, dangers today seem both 'unprecedented and boundless . . . a quite different type of fear from that experienced by those who lived through the Second World War or the Cold War which followed it' (2011: 269, citing Bourke [2006]).

So, with a generalised, pervasive, unfocused fear about a 'future' that is either 'indistinguishable from the present' or 'radically other than the present' (or as divorced from the present – without any continuity), we can start to see how Giddens's ideas actually support the idea that 'infantilisation' might be contributing to a neglect of ***intergenerational responsibility***, exacerbating ***intergenerational injustice***. Indeed, even markers of 'adulthood,' such as having children and family obligations, do not necessarily inspire greater ecologically directed intergenerational responsibility but instead prompt demands for immediate security – support for low taxation, anti-welfare fiscal policies and lack of voter support for green political parties – contributing further to intergenerational injustice.

This leaves us, then, with Giddens's notion of 'risk'. Would not a society organised in response to risk seem like one that might be cautious about acts or omissions in the present that might jeopardise future environmental quality? The answer might appear to be yes, but as Hulme (2009: 196) explains, there is a difference between 'situated' and 'un-situated' risks. The source of a 'situated risk', Hulme (2009) explains, 'is local and tangible . . . and this makes it easier to believe – rightly or wrongly – that [a] local population ha[s] a degree of control over the risk or the possibility of addressing it' (196). In contrast, the source of an 'un-situated risk' is 'distant and intangible . . . and the causes of the risk are diffuse and hard to situate' (Hulme, 2009: 196) – a conceptualisation that resonates with Beck's (2002: 41) idea of 'de-bounded risks', which are those that are not linked to specific geographic locations or national boundaries and which have unlimited temporal dimensions. Thus, even in a society organised in response to risk, the perception that a given risk or category of risks is 'un-situated' or 'de-bounded' – as is often the case with environmental risks and especially the case with the risks posed by climate change (see Aas, 2013; Hulme, 2009; McNall, 2011; see generally Snider, 2000: 187 and accompanying notes) – will militate against preventive action or steps to ensure intergenerational equity. Moreover, as Wells explains, while a *risk society* is one in which risk is 'a justifiable basis for policymaking', which would seem to imply a greater likelihood of ***support*** for measures that would help fulfil our obligation of intergenerational justice, the '"demonopolization of scientific knowledge claims" . . . means that a variety of competing and conflicting interpretations of the processes whereby risk is caused are able to coexist in what is, effectively, an expert marketplace' (2011: 227, quoting Beck, 1992: 29). This 'demonopolisation', coupled with the 'democratisation' of expertise – the 'increasing "equalization" of experts and non-experts' (Wells, 2011: 228), further reduces the likelihood of adequate response to environmental risks with policies reflecting any commitment to social justice (Aas, 2013: 25, 126) or any sense of intergenerational responsibility.

In other words, we argue that the 'infantilisation' that Hayward describes makes us (adults) far more present oriented – far less willing to address what we perceive to be 'un-situated' (environmental) risks – and far more inclined to engage in some but not all areas of risk ***taking*** (Barrett, 2013: 163). This is happening at a time in which societies and economies are ***manufacturing risks***, to borrow from Giddens (1999: 4), and creating new (environmental) hazards. Simultaneously, our growing preference for 'infantilised soft news' (Hayward, 2012: 224) makes us dismissive of science and scientific experts (see, for example, Gad, 2013).

'Risk is never socially neutral', White (2008: 59) reminds us. Or, as Mythen and Walklate (2006) point out, 'people are by no means equally affected by various risks' (388). While our first argument is that processes of 'infantilisation' increase the risks and threats for future generations and jeopardise the existence and quality of life of future generations, our second contention is that processes of 'adultification' erode (actual) adult feelings of intergenerational responsibility and undercut efforts to bring about intergenerational equity.

Consider, for example, *What's the Big Idea?*, the seventh book in the *Ivy and Bean* children's book series written by Annie Barrows, illustrated by Sophie Blackall and published by Chronicle Books. In this particular story, Ivy and Bean, two seven-year-old schoolchildren, learn about global warming in a class presentation by a group of ten-year-olds. More specifically, they see a picture of a worried-looking polar bear, learn that everywhere in the world 'is going to look like [the Gobi Desert] because of global warming' and that 'global warming is a total disaster and it's all our fault' (2010: 21). The next scene, which is worth quoting in full, unfolds as follows:

> When school was over, Ivy and Bean slumped like two sacks of potatoes on the bench outside their classroom.
>
> 'Watcha doing?' asked Leo.
> Ivy and Bean looked up. 'We're worrying about the polar bears,' said Ivy glumly.
> 'What polar bears?' asked Leo. Leo was in a different class.
> 'There's not enough ice for them to live on,' said Ivy.
> 'They're going to die out, like the dinosaurs,' said Bean.
> 'The heat's going to get them,' said Ivy.
> Leo kicked the bench. 'You guys want to play stomp tag?'
> Ivy and Bean stared at him. 'It's the pollution,' said Bean.
> 'From cars,' said Ivy.
> 'And cow poop,' Bean reminded her.
> Leo made a snorty sound. He thought cow poop was funny. Ivy and Bean frowned at him. 'I'll be it,' he said.
> 'What?' said Bean.
> 'I'll be it. You can even stomp me for free if you want,' said Leo. He stuck his foot out. 'Go ahead.'
> Bean shook her head. 'We're busy,' she said.
> Leo looked up and down the breezeway. It was empty. 'What are you busy doing?'
> 'We're busy worrying,' said Bean.
> After a while, Leo found some other kids who wanted to play stomp tag, and Ivy and Bean got up and began to worry their way home.
> 'Poor trees,' said Ivy, patting one.
> 'Yeah,' said Bean. She kicked a car parked at the curb. 'Take that!' she yelled and felt a little better.
>
> (Barrows, 2010: 22–23)

It turns out that Ivy and Bean are not the only seven-year-olds worried about global warming; the rest of their class is also troubled. Their teacher, however, tells them that science is 'the solution' to stopping global warming and suggests that they come up with ideas to 'fight global warming' to present at their school's science fair. In the ensuing chapters of the book, Ivy and Bean continue to exhibit adult-like consternation about global warming and experiment with different ways to address it. Although some of their ideas and those of their classmates are fantastical, as would befit seven-year-olds, others (such as using mirrors to reflect incoming solar radiation) are being considered by proponents of geoengineering (see Hulme, 2014: 8). Meanwhile, the adults are depicted as buffoons or impatient troglodytes. In the end, Ivy and Bean decide that if they '[taught] grown-ups to be happy in nature,' they (the adults) would love nature and care about it and global warming and 'wouldn't drive stinky cars'. Ivy and Bean's final project involves leading their parents and other adults outside the building where the science fair is being held into the cool night air – being careful, all the while, not to scare the adults because, as Ivy reminds Bean, 'they [grown-ups] don't like surprises' – where they encourage the adults to lie down quietly on the grass and look up at the stars. Initially, the adults express some reluctance and annoyance but ultimately wind up enjoying the experience. Ivy and Bean commend themselves for teaching their parents and other adults to care about global warming but still rue the fact that they did not find 'the one big solution' (Barrows, 2010: 120).

While there is something slightly endearing about Ivy and Bean's earnestness, in light of our previous discussion about 'life stage dissolution,' Barrows's child-adult role reversal is not nearly as outlandish as the author may have intended. Indeed, *What's the Big Idea?* is not particularly unusual in and across various media for its infantilising and adultifying tropes and for its emphasis on the role of young people in environmental protection (see Brisman, 2013). In fact, the book falls right in line with a disturbing pattern in children's literature of individualising environmental degradation (e.g. attributing global warming only to personal transportation choices) and excluding any reference to the role of corporate entities or the state – a practice that rehearses the neo-liberal logic that it is the duty, responsibility and province of ***individuals*** (if there is a duty or responsibility at all) to protect and preserve nature – the natural environment – our planet and its ecosystems (Brisman, 2013: 276; see also Carlson, 2012: 1118–1119; see generally Giroux, 2004: 52, 59–60, 85, 117).[2]

Admittedly, it is important to (continue to) empower children and teach them how to be engaged citizens so that they will be able to participate in environmentally beneficial decision-making processes and act in ecologically responsible ways. But the 'adultification' of Ivy and Bean and similar characters comes perversely close to placing the onus on youth and absolving adults of responsibility for the future of the biosphere – of asking the next generation to instruct the present generation about how to consider and act in the interest of future generations. Such processes of 'adultification' discharge adults of their

2 Broome (2012) offers a refreshing argument that emphasises the role of governments in reducing the threat of climate change and safeguarding our future. According to Broome:

> Governments are strongly mandated to promote the flourishing of their people. It is their serious duty to make life good, or at least to provide people with conditions that allow them to make life good for themselves."
>
> Significant progress can be achieved only by governments, because only governments have the power to get all their people to change their behavior. Governments have the moral duty to respond to climate change, and you as a citizen have a duty to do what you can through political action to get your government to fulfil them.
>
> (2012: 65, 73–74)

Unfortunately, much of children's literature emphasises citizens' duties with scant reference to governments and political processes.

intergenerational responsibility while working in tandem with processes of infantilisation and self-absorption to augment the risks and threats that jeopardise the existence and quality of life for future generations.

## Conclusion

Modern consumerism feeds narcissism, self-absorption and infantilised short-term horizons. As Bernardini puts it:

> The actor-consumer of this system tends to childishness without pleasure, to indolence without innocence, dresses without formality, has sex without reproducing, works without discipline, plays without spontaneity, buys without a purpose, and lives without responsibility, wisdom or humility. . . . The postmodern infantilization coincides with a kind of collective regression, largely as a result of stringent market logic.
>
> (2014: 41)

Lasch (1979; see also Giroux, 2004: 59–60) saw such trends as emergent in a culture of narcissism in which individuals take centre stage to pursue experience and consumption for the purpose of self- and ego satisfaction but are then left regressing into infantilisation and emptiness. Lasch's analysis was a critique of the 'personal growth' industries of the 'therapeutic state' (see also Cohen, 1985), but his overall intellectual and political message is often missed, and this was a critique of obsession with economic growth. According to Kramer (2013), Lasch felt that 'one of the major tasks confronting the left . . . is to show how the urban crisis and the more general "environmental crisis" originate in capitalist production' and the strategic shift needed is to move debates concerning 'ecological catastrophe away from the sphere of consumption, in which by buying "greener" we might save ourselves and the world, and back to the processes of production, where the exploitation and expropriation actually occurs' (see also Stretesky et al., 2013). Drawing on Lasch, Kramer summarises by considering whether 'the perpetual demand for "growth" comes with its own costs – to our environment, our traditions, and even our psychological well-being'. The answer would seem to be 'yes', and there is evidence to support this. But unwelcome evidence has no purchasing power, and as analysts of our powers of denial have told us, when cognitive systems are threatened, structural amnesia and strategic ignorance forcefully come into play (Cohen, 2001; Douglas, 1986; McGoey, 2012). This helps explain why 'we take things for granted' as 'common sense' and turn away from challenges about which we feel we can do little. A major enabling script that we rely on in doing so is to express the 'hope' or 'expectation' that 'others' – such as the next generation – will act in a more responsive and responsible way. This, however, returns us to the significance of Hayward's argument. For if it is the case that 'life stages' are being ineluctably and acquiescently eroded to be replaced by 'generational mulch', then it becomes even more unclear where any responsibility to secure intergenerational equity and environmental sustainability might lie. As a result, all generations – now and in the future – may suffer. Indeed, current generations may feel that they cannot afford to do too much, too quickly, to protect the planet – because a slowdown in economic growth will mean a retreat from progress and that will threaten civilisation (or, at least, civilisation as we know it) – while future generations may learn to live with the idea that it is, by then, too late to do anything at all.

## References


Aas, K. (2013) *Globalization and Crime*, 2nd edition, London: Sage.

Altheide, D. (2002) *Creating Fear: News and the Construction of Crisis*, New York: Aldine de Gruyter.

Arnett, J. (2000) 'Emerging adulthood: A theory of development from the late teens through the twenties', *American Psychologist*, **55**(5): 469–480.

Arnett, J. (2004) *Emerging Adulthood*, Oxford: Oxford University Press.

Arnett, J., Kloep, M., Hendry, L. and Tanner, J. (2010) *Debating Emerging Adulthood*, New York: Oxford University Press.

Arnett, J. and Tanner, J. (2006) *Emerging Adults in America*, Washington, DC: American Psychological Association.

Arnocky, S., Milfont, T. and Nicol, J. (2014) 'Time perspective and sustainable behavior: Evidence for the distinction between consideration of immediate and future consequences', *Environment and Behavior*, **46**(5): 556–582.

Barber, B. (2007) *Consumed: How Markets Corrupt Children, Infantilize Adults and Swallow Citizens Whole*, London: Norton.

Barnett, H. (1999) 'The land ethic and environmental crime', *Criminal Justice Policy Review*, **10**(2): 161–191.

Barrett, C. (2013) *Courting Kids: Inside an Experimental Youth Court*, New York: New York University Press.

Barrows, A. (2010) *Ivy + Bean: What's the Big Idea?* San Francisco: Chronicle Books.

Beck, U. (1992) *Risk Society: Toward a New Modernity*, London: Sage.

Beck, U. (2002) 'The terrorist threat: World risk society revisited', *Theory, Culture & Society*, **19**(4): 39–55.

Bernardini, J. (2014) 'The infantilization of the postmodern adult and the figure of kidult', *Postmodern Openings*, **5**(2): 39–55.

Bourke, J. (2006) *Fear: A Cultural History*, London: Virago.

Brisman, A. (2011a) 'Rio declaration'. In D. Chatterjee (ed.) *Encyclopedia of Global Justice*, Vol. 2, Heidelberg: Springer, pp. 960–966.

Brisman, A. (2011b) 'Stockholm Conference, 1972'. In D. Chatterjee (ed.) *Encyclopedia of Global Justice*, Vol. 2, Heidelberg: Springer, pp. 1039–1040.

Brisman, A. (2013) 'Not a bedtime story: Climate change, neoliberalism, and the future of the Arctic', *Michigan State International Law Review*, **22**(1): 241–289.

Brisman, A. (2015) 'Environment and conflict: A typology of representations'. In A. Brisman, N. South and R. White (eds.) *Environmental Crime and Social Conflict: Contemporary and Emerging Issues*, Farnham, England: Ashgate, pp. 285–311.

Brisman, A., McClanahan, B. and South, N. (2014). 'Toward a green-cultural criminology of "the rural"', *Critical Criminology*, **22**(4): 479–494.

Brisman, A. and South, N. (2013a) 'A green-cultural criminology: An exploratory outline', *Crime Media Culture*, **9**(2): 115–135.

Brisman, A. and South, N. (2013b) 'Conclusion: The planned obsolescence of planet earth? How green criminology can help us learn from experience and contribute to our future'. In N. South and A. Brisman (eds.) *Routledge International Handbook of Green Criminology*, London: Routledge, pp. 409–417.

Brisman, A. and South, N. (2014) *Green Cultural Criminology: Constructions of Environmental Harm, Consumerism and Resistance to Ecocide*, London: Routledge.

Brisman, A. and South, N. (2015) '"Life-stage dissolution", infantilization and antisocial consumption implications for de-responsibilization, denial and environmental harm', *Young*, **23**(3): 209–221.

Broome, J. (2012) *Climate Matters: Ethics in a Warming World*, New York: W. W. Norton.

Bruni, F. (2014) 'Dear millennials, we're sorry', *The New York Times*, 8 June.

Carey, B. (2010) 'A snapshot of a generation may come out blurry', *The New York Times*, 3 August.

Carlson, J. (2012) '"I don't dial 911': American gun politics and the problem of policing', *British Journal of Criminology*, **52**(6): 1113–1132.

Carmi, N. and Arnon, S. (2014) 'The role of future orientation in environmental behavior: Analyzing the relationship on the individual and cultural levels', *Society and Natural Resources*, **27**(12): 1304–1320.

Cohen, S. (1985) *Visions of Social Control*, Cambridge: Polity.

Cohen, S. (2001) *States of Denial*, Cambridge: Polity.

Critcher, C. (2011) 'For a political economy of moral panics', *Crime Media Culture*, 7(3): 259–275.

Danesi, M. (2003) *Forever Young: The "Teen-Aging" of Modern Culture*, Toronto: Toronto University Press.

Douglas, M. (1986) *How Institutions Think*, Syracuse, NY: Syracuse University Press.

Ferrell, J. (2013) 'Tangled up in green: Cultural criminology and green criminology'. In N. South and A. Brisman (eds.) *Routledge International Handbook of Green Criminology*, London: Routledge, pp. 349–364.

Gad, J. (2013) 'With social media, who needs "experts"?' *USA Today*, 31 May.

Giddens, A. (1999) 'Risk and responsibility', *The Modern Law Review*, **62**(1): 1–10.

Giroux, H. (2004) *The Terror of Neoliberalism: Authoritarianism and the Eclipse of Democracy*, Boulder, CO: Paradigm.

Grossberg, L. (2001) 'Why does neo-liberalism hate kids? The war on youth and the culture of politics', *The Review of Education/Pedagogy/Cultural Studies*, **23**(2): 111–136.

Hall, M. (2013) *Victims of Environmental Harm: Rights, Recognition and Redress under National and International Law*, London: Routledge.

Hall, M. (2015) *Exploring Green Crime: Introducing the Legal, Social and Criminological Contexts of Environmental Harm*, Basingstoke, England: Palgrave Macmillan.

Hayward, K. (2012) 'Pantomime justice: A cultural criminological analysis of "life stage dissolution"', *Crime Media Culture*, **8**(2): 213–229.

Hayward, K. (2013) '"Life stage dissolution" in Anglo-American advertising and popular culture: Kidults, Lil' Britneys and middle youths', *The Sociological Review*, **61**(3): 525–548.

Heckenberg, D. (2009) 'Studying environmental crime: Key words, acronyms and sources of information'. In R. White (ed.) *Environmental Crime: A Reader*, Cullompton, England: Willan, pp. 9–24.

Hiskes, R. (2008) *The Human Right to a Green Future: Environmental Rights and Intergenerational Justice*, Cambridge: Cambridge University Press.

Hiskes, R. (2014) 'Environmental human rights'. In T. Cushman (ed.) *Handbook of Human Rights*, London: Routledge, pp. 399–409.

Hulme, M. (2009) *Why We Disagree about Climate Change: Understanding Controversy, Inaction and Opportunity*, Cambridge: Cambridge University Press.

Hulme, M. (2014) *Can Science Fix Climate Change?* Cambridge: Polity Press.

Jenks, C. (1996) *Childhood*, London: Routledge.

Kofele-Kale, N. (2006) *The International Law of Responsibility for Economic Crimes*, Aldershot, England: Ashgate.

Kramer, M. (2013) 'Christopher Lasch and the role of the social critic', *The Point*, 7: 1–12.

Lasch, C. (1979) *The Culture of Narcissism: American Life in an Age of Diminishing Expectations*, New York: W.W. Norton.

Leech, G. (2012) *Capitalism: A Structural Genocide*, London: Zed Books.

McClanahan, B. (2014) 'Green and grey: Water justice, criminalization, and resistance', *Critical Criminology*, **22**: 403–418.

McGoey, L. (2012) 'The logic of strategic ignorance', *British Journal of Sociology*, **63**(3): 553–576.

McNall, S. (2011) *Rapid Climate Change: Causes, Consequences, and Solutions*, New York: Routledge.
Milfont, T., Wilson, J. and Diniz, P. (2012) 'Time perspective and environmental engagement: A meta-analysis', *International Journal of Psychology*, **47**(5): 325–334.
Mythen, G. and Walklate, S. (2006) 'Communicating the terrorist risk: Harnessing a culture of fear', *Crime Media Culture*, **2**(2): 123–142.
Piper, C. (2008) *Investing in Children: Policy, Law and Practice in Context*, Cullompton, England: Willan.
Preston, B. (2011) 'The use of restorative justice for environmental crime', *Criminal Law Journal*, **35**(3): 136–145.
Rabinovich, A., Morton, T. and Postmes, T. (2010) 'Time perspective and attitude-behaviour consistency in future-oriented behaviours', *British Journal of Social Psychology*, **49**(1): 69–89.
Ruggiero, V. and South, N. (2010) 'Green criminology and dirty collar crime', *Critical Criminology*, **18**(4): 251–262.
Schally, J. (2014) *Agent of Harm and Good Corporate Citizen? The Case of Tyson Foods*, Department of Sociology, University of Tennessee, Ph.D. Dissertation.
Schneeberger, K. (2011) 'Intergenerational equity: Implementing the principle in mainstream decision-making', *Environmental Law & Management*, **23**(1): 20–29.
Shiva, V. (2008) *Soil Not Oil: Environmental Justice in a Time of Climate Crisis*, Cambridge, MA: South End Press.
Snider, L. (2000) 'The sociology of corporate crime: An obituary: (Or: whose knowledge claims have legs?)', *Theoretical Criminology*, **4**(2): 169–206.
South, N. (2010) 'The ecocidal tendencies of late modernity: Trans-national crime, social exclusion, victims and rights'. In R. White (ed.) *Global Environmental Harm: Criminological Perspectives*, Cullompton, England: Willan, pp. 228–247.
Stretesky, P., Long, M. and Lynch, M. (2013) *The Treadmill of Crime: Political Economy and Green Criminology*, London: Routledge.
Takemura, N. (2010) 'The criticality of global environmental crime and the response of chaos criminology'. In R. White (ed.) *Global Environmental Harm: Criminological Perspectives*, Cullompton, England: Willan, pp. 210–227.
Thornton, J. and Tromans, S. (1999) 'Human rights and environmental wrongs: Incorporating the European Convention on Human Rights: Some thoughts on the consequences for UK environmental law', *Journal of Environmental Law*, **11**(1): 35–57.
Weiss, E. (2008) 'Climate change, intergenerational equity, and international law', *Vermont Journal of Environmental Law*, **9**(3): 615–627.
Wells, H. (2011) 'Risk and expertise in the speed limit enforcement debate: Challenges, adaptations and responses', *Criminology and Criminal Justice*, **11**(3): 225–241.
White, R. (2008) *Crimes against Nature: Environmental Criminology and Ecological Justice*, Cullompton, England: Willan.
White, R. (2011) *Transnational Environmental Crime: Toward an Eco-Global Criminology*, London: Routledge.
White, R. (2012) 'The foundations of eco-global criminology'. In R. Ellefsen, R. Sollund and G. Larsen (eds.) *Eco-Global Crimes: Contemporary Problems and Future Challenges*, Farnham, England: Ashgate, pp. 15–31.
White, R. (2013) *Environmental Harm: An Eco-Justice Perspective*, Bristol, England: Polity Press.
White, R. and Heckenberg, D. (2014) *Green Criminology: An Introduction to the Study of Environmental Harm*, London: Routledge.
Wyatt, T. (2013) *Wildlife Trafficking: A Deconstruction of the Crime, the Victims, and the Offenders*, Basingstoke, England: Palgrave.

# Index

For Product Safety Concerns and Information please contact our EU
representative GPSR@taylorandfrancis.com
Taylor & Francis Verlag GmbH, Kaufingerstraße 24, 80331 München, Germany

www.ingramcontent.com/pod-product-compliance
Ingram Content Group UK Ltd.
Pitfield, Milton Keynes, MK11 3LW, UK
UKHW052055230926
475702UK00031B/2831

*9780367024055*